PAUL
HASLUCK

Geoffrey Bolton, Emeritus Professor and former Chancellor of Murdoch University, is a historian whose publications include *Edmund Barton: the one man for the job* (2000), winner of the New South Wales Premier's History Award in 2001, and *Land of Vision and Mirage: Western Australia since 1826* (2006). He was ABC Boyer lecturer in 1992 and is an Officer of the Order of Australia.

PAUL HASLUCK

A life

GEOFFREY BOLTON

UWA PUBLISHING

First published in 2014 by
UWA Publishing
Crawley, Western Australia 6009
www.uwap.uwa.edu.au

THE UNIVERSITY OF
WESTERN AUSTRALIA

UWAP is an imprint of UWA Publishing
A division of The University of Western Australia

National Library of Australia Cataloguing-in-Publication entry:

Author: Bolton, G. C. (Geoffrey Curgenven), 1931– author.
Title: Paul Hasluck : a life / Geoffrey Bolton.
ISBN: 9781742586588 (paperback), 9781742586816 (hardback).
Subjects: Hasluck, Paul, 1905-1993.
    Politicians—Australia—Biography.
    Statesmen—Australia—Biography.
    Governors general—Australia—Biography.
    Australia—History—20th century.
    Australia—Politics and government—20th century.
Dewey Number: 994.04092

Typeset by J&M typesetting
Printed by McPherson's Printing Group

The author and UWA publishing gratefully acknowledge that
publication of this book was assisted by a grant from
the Western Australian History Foundation.

Contents

Part I

Years of aspiration, 1905–51

Chapter 1

Beginnings

The memorial service was conducted late on a midsummer afternoon in 1993 by the dean of Windsor at St George's Chapel in Windsor Castle, home of England's senior order of knighthood, the Order of the Garter. As custom dictated, the dean received the banner, which had hung for fourteen years over the stall of the deceased knight, and laid it on the altar 'with a prayer to revere the name of the departed Knight and those Companions of the most noble Order "who have left to us the fair pattern of valiant and true chivalry"'.[1] There had been fewer than 700 knights of the Garter since the order was founded by Edward III in 1348, its numbers limited to twenty-four distinguished members chosen by the monarch. Before the twentieth century the knights were selected almost exclusively from royalty and the British aristocracy, but as the century progressed there was change. During the twentieth century a few notable statesmen, such as Sir Winston Churchill in 1953, became knights. These were followed by figures distinguished in the armed services, law and medicine, and by a few from those parts of the British Commonwealth where Elizabeth II is still head of state. Those chosen from Australia have all been former governors-general: at first the Englishmen Slim and De L'Isle, both eminent soldiers; and later three Australian-born – Casey, Hasluck and Stephen.[2]

This service honoured one of those three Australians, Sir Paul Meernaa Caedwalla Hasluck, Knight of the Garter, Knight Grand Cross of the Order of St Michael and St George, Knight Grand Cross of the Royal Victorian Order, and a privy councillor. Two years later the banner was entrusted to St George's Cathedral in his home town of Perth, where it has since hung above the door leading out of the south transept. At St George's Chapel in Windsor, Sir Paul is commemorated by a candle on a handsome oak stand, lit during Easter ceremonies as a symbol of the risen Christ. When the adjacent St George's Hall was restored in 1997 after the destruction of its ceiling by fire, miniatures of the coats of arms of all the departed knights of the Garter were displayed in its alcoves and window bays. The Hasluck coat of arms shares a window bay with Anne, Princess Royal; Viscount De L'Isle; the Emperor Haile Selassie of Ethiopia; and Albert I, King of the Belgians, in whose support Britain went to war with Germany in 1914.

All this might suggest that Hasluck's was a personality and a career steeped in some of the most ancient and conservative of British traditions, but a closer look at the coat of arms, which he designed himself, would reveal complexities. The shield itself bears the symbol of three Catherine wheels, apparently the device of a sixteenth-century kinsman who lived during the reign of Elizabeth I. But the supporters are a pelican and a cormorant, two of the most common birds on the Swan River, close to the home where Hasluck lived most of his life.[3] The crest includes the seven-pointed star of the Australian Commonwealth and a representation of the xanthorrhoea, an ancient Australian plant. Puns are frequent in the art of heraldry, and it may be no coincidence that among the old colonists the xanthorrhoea was known as the 'blackboy' because of a fancied resemblance to an Aboriginal boy holding a spear; Aboriginal policy was one of the major themes of Hasluck's public career. These features offer a more than sufficient hint that, although Hasluck's historical consciousness led him to respect and value the continuities of English tradition, his ultimate loyalties were profoundly Australian. 'My own deeper love and knowledge of Australia is refined by a shared love of England', he wrote.[4]

Hasluck's sympathies went beyond family piety to a deep appreciation of the shaping influence on Australian society of the culture received from Britain and its European neighbours. These insights coexisted with an intense responsiveness to the Australian environment of his youth and upbringing, and a staunch belief in the creative potential of the arts in Australia. He also believed that the institutions of government inherited from Britain were trusty instruments for good governance and social change, and could be adapted constructively for use in new societies. In one sense his life can be seen as a continuing effort to bridge two loyalties: a deeply ingrained love of country; and commitment to a life of the intellect that of its nature transcended a narrow nationalism. His perspective was shared by many of his own and the following generation, coming naturally to Australians of the early twentieth century whose parents and grandparents had retained contact with what was known as 'the Old Country'. He lived into the last decade of that century when the ties seemed to be loosening, and perhaps in his old age came to insist more sharply that to be a good Australian it was not necessary to deny the nourishing influences of the past.

His Western Australian origins were not privileged. He was born at Fremantle on 1 April 1905, the second son of Salvation

Army officers Ethel Meernaa Caedwalla Hasluck and his wife Patience (née Wooler). Perhaps inured to an unusual name, Ethel registered the child as Paul Meernaa Caedwalla Hasluck. Paul was a family name; 'Meernaa' was a South Australian Aboriginal word said to mean 'joyful spring of fresh water', from a spot in the Flinders Ranges. In later life Paul Hasluck's father preferred to be known by that name rather than 'Ethel'. 'Caedwalla' was also a family name of Anglo-Saxon origin, but in later years it misled a British civil servant into conjecturing that Paul Hasluck had Welsh forebears. In fact, he described himself as coming from 'an English line, with no trace of Scots, Welsh or Irish'.[5]

Meernaa Hasluck arrived in Western Australia as a child of not quite four on the *Lady Louisa* on 19 December 1875, accompanied by his younger brother Oswald, 51-year-old father Lewis Hasluck and 25-year-old mother Rosa Jane (née Croker). Lewis was putting a history of business and family troubles behind him. He was the fifth son of Samuel Hasluck, who early in the nineteenth century moved from Birmingham to London and established himself as a goldsmith and jeweller in Hatton Garden. Samuel prospered and acquired a gentleman's residence in West Ham. Several of his sons followed him in the trade, among them Lewis. In November 1847, at the fashionable church of St George's, Hanover Square, Lewis married a young woman named Fanny Newby. The marriage did not last long. Divorce was difficult and expensive, and Fanny survived until 1894, leaving Lewis to enter into the two long-term relationships of his later life without a marriage ceremony. In 1849 he emigrated as a young man to South Australia after family disagreements, returned to England in 1851, spent time in Gibraltar in 1852, returned to Australia in 1853, took part in the Ovens River goldrush in Victoria, and around 1855 went back to England partnered by a widow, Isabella Hussey.

By 1861 Lewis was a farmer employing three men and two boys on a 90-acre (36.4-hectare) property at Ringwood in the New Forest region of Hampshire. The decades following the repeal of the Corn Laws were not prosperous for English farming, and probably after his father's death in 1863 he returned to London as a watchmaker and jeweller with Isabella, two stepsons and three sons to maintain. His luck was poor: the business was hit by a destructive fire and two burglaries. (Long afterwards, in Western Australia he was to meet members of the gang who had committed one of the robberies only to have been betrayed to the authorities and transported as convicts.)[6] In 1871 he eloped with Rosa Jane Croker and the next year she gave birth to a son, who was registered as Ethel Meernaa Caedwalla. Apparently Lewis, who already had five sons and stepsons, was determined that the next child would be named 'Ethel' irrespective of gender. 'Meernaa' was a memento of his Australian travels, but 'Caedwalla', an obscure Anglo-Saxon king from the late seventh century, remains a mystery.[7] After moving with Rosa to France, Brighton and Hammersmith, and fathering a second son – Oswald – in 1874, Lewis and Rosa decided to emigrate in 1875.

Lewis never saw his older children again, though they stayed in contact. They remained in England with their mother and found their way into the professions. The eldest son, Paul, after whom his nephew was named, became a prolific author and editor of technological publications. In Western Australia Rosa passed as 'Mrs Hasluck', but it was only in July 1896, after

7

receiving news of Fanny's death, that Lewis was free to marry her in a private ceremony. Nine days later he died of pneumonia. Isabella died in 1899, three years after Lewis.[8]

Lewis Hasluck could hardly have selected a more obscure destination than Western Australia. It was the most isolated and struggling of the Australian colonies, still tainted by its role as a penitentiary for nearly 10,000 convicts transported between 1850 and 1868, and as yet showing hardly a trace of the mineral riches that had transformed the rest of Australia. In Perth, Lewis Hasluck tried his hand at many trades, among them fruitmonger, commission agent and miscellaneous craftsman, his commissions including a hardwood coat of arms for the Supreme Court.[9] Later he moved to Fremantle as a municipal supervisor, but lost the job because he would not condone petty malpractices by some members of the council. He was promised a land grant of 100 acres (40.5 hectares) at Torbay, west of Albany, but it was unworkable, swampy country. While at Albany in 1887 he took up the cudgels on behalf of a party of migrants who had been abandoned by the land company that brought them to Western Australia and were being unfairly treated by local officials. The officials were reprimanded, but the episode did nothing to improve Lewis Hasluck's fortunes.[10]

Returning to Perth he supported himself and his family as a watchmaker, jeweller and pawnbroker with a shop in Perth's Wellington Street, then the unfashionable end of the small town, although the precinct improved somewhat after the opening of the central railway station in 1881. Almost immediately, although more than sixty years old, he took part in one of the first expeditions to the Yilgarn goldfield in 1887, and called on his experience as jeweller and sometime prospector to praise the quality of the gold found near the future Southern Cross – but he did not profit from the great goldrushes that followed. He was regarded as the colony's chief expert on works of art, and was art master at the Perth High School for a time.[11] He occasionally wrote for Perth's *Morning Herald* and took an active but contentious role as a critic of the Perth City Council and member of the Mechanics' Institute. To keep his French from becoming rusty he would travel to Swanbourne to converse with Louis Langoulant, a settler of Channel Islands origin. His son recalled that 'He had a poor opinion of some of the prominent citizens, chiefly because they were not so well educated as he was'.[12] He left few of the world's goods when he died in July 1896. He seems to have been regarded as a quirky character but respectable. Thirty years after Lewis's death, when the newly formed Western Australian Historical Society was assessing Paul Hasluck's suitability to serve as assistant secretary, it counted in his favour that old colonists of standing remembered his grandfather.

Lewis's widow did not remain long in Perth. Accompanied by her colonial-born daughter Neenaa she paid a visit to England in 1900, returning there permanently about the time of Paul's birth in 1905, but retaining occasional contact for the rest of their lives through letters and rare visits. Meernaa Hasluck, however, seems to have adapted easily to colonial life. In later years his son encouraged him to write down his recollections of growing up in Perth.[13] He sketched a homely but vivid account of a small town whose sandy streets bore evocative names such as Fenians' Row, and were lit by guttering streetlights fuelled by whale oil. At Perth Boys' School the younger boys regarded Meernaa as a hero, because when the teacher tried to cane him he took the cane away and broke it across his knee.[14] Later he attended a private night school, Letch's Academy, qualifying in February 1890 for a vacancy in the Colonial Post Office at £80 a year.[15] When the Coolgardie goldrush of 1892 brought migrants and investment surging into Western Australia, the twenty-year-old clerk was thrust into responsibilities that marked him for rapid advancement. He was promoted to take charge of the travelling postal service on the railway between Perth and Albany.

Then in 1893 he became interested in the Salvation Army. It was only three years since the army's first members had arrived in Western Australia, and their exuberant evangelising did not appeal to all tastes. Meernaa attended several meetings, but still considered himself taken up with worldly pursuits. (His dissipations were extremely mild, consisting mostly of a fondness for the theatre, an occasional cigarette, and an even more occasional flutter on the office sweepstakes.) Transferred to Coolgardie, he advanced rapidly in the postal service and by late 1895 was drawing a salary of £200 a year. But in September of that year he underwent a profound mystical experience at a Salvation Army meeting and found himself called to become an officer. His mother encouraged his decision; we do not know what old Lewis Hasluck thought.[16] He was young, single and energetic, and the Salvation Army worked him hard. After three months of training in Melbourne, he was sent during the next eight years to appointments with fifteen different corps, mostly on the goldfields.[17] Set apart from most young people of his time by his distinctive uniform and religious convictions, he gained respect because of his even temper and sincerity. Like his father before him he lived a little apart from the mainstream, not least because he did not share the eager interest in getting and spending evident in a suddenly rich Western Australia.

Meernaa married another Salvation Army officer, Patience Wooler, who was three years his senior. She had emigrated from England to Western Australia in 1892 and was employed as 'companion' to Margaret Hare, wife of the Resident Magistrate of York. It was a role similar to that of a modern au pair, where she 'lived as a member of the family, looked after the young children, did some sewing and helped run the household'. A member of the Brockman family before her marriage, Margaret Hare was only seven years older than Patience, whose memories of York in later life were 'of colonial gentility, quietness and happiness'.[18] She absorbed the values of her employers, but was drawn to another calling. Moved by concern for the unfortunate, she joined the Salvation Army and was sent to 'rescue work' among unmarried mothers and what were known as 'fallen women'. While stationed in Perth she met Meernaa Hasluck and they corresponded for four and a half years while she was working in Victoria and South Australia. Meernaa proposed by mail and was accepted, and she returned to Western Australia only ten days before their marriage at Northam on 22 January 1901, the day of Queen Victoria's death.

Her marriage to Meernaa Hasluck brought together two people who did not conform to the stereotype of the Salvation Army as a mostly working-class movement. Both Meernaa, through his education and civil service career, and Patience, through her experience with the Hare family, would have fitted easily into the professional middle class. Instead, they belonged to that significant minority of Salvation Army officers whose background and abilities led them more into the caring management of welfare than the evangelical aspects of the army's work. Perhaps Meernaa was also aware that if Lewis Hasluck had not acknowledged him and emigrated to Australia, he himself might have become a fatherless waif on the London streets. Neither he nor Patience wanted to imitate his mother and sister in returning to England. Patience made one visit in 1903, probably to show her family her first son, but the experience 'left her intensely Australian for the rest of her life and with no wish ever to travel to England again'.[19] But Meernaa's membership of the Salvation Army placed a strain on the family dynamics, as his mother Rosa and his brother Oswald joined the Seventh Day Adventists, whom Meernaa regarded as 'spreaders of false doctrines'.

The Haslucks had six children: Lewis Norman, who was born in December 1901; Paul in April 1905; Harry in 1907; Rosa Hope in 1912; and two others who died young. Shortly before Paul's birth, a persistent throat complaint obliged Meernaa Hasluck to retire from active service with the Salvation Army. He changed his uniform to support the family as a tram conductor in Perth.[20] This meant they enjoyed a steady, if modest income in a weatherboard cottage in Beaufort Street, Highgate Hill, about 3 kilometres from the centre of Perth and not far from the affluent new suburban development at Mount Lawley. On his fourth birthday Paul was sent to the nearest state school, Norwood, but stayed only a few months. Late in 1909 his parents resolved to 'go back into the work' of the Salvation Army. They were posted to North Fremantle, now a trendy address but in 1910 little better than a slum. After a few months they were transferred to York for a year. There were weeks when the family had no money, and it was a great day when Meernaa, digging in the garden, turned up a shilling.[21] Yet they were happy. York was an easygoing farming community, and the Haslucks were kept well provided with food and necessities.

Young Paul revelled in his first long experience of country life. 'Because of one year of happiness at the age of six and seven', he wrote as an old man, 'I have deep sentimental roots in York'.[22] The idyll did not last. The Haslucks were transferred to Kalgoorlie, which was then slowly declining as its gold became harder to win. Here Paul found himself confronted with the aggressively fundamentalist side of Salvation Army practice:

> How I hated the long, hot and oppressive atmosphere of the meetings. The noise tormented me. I disliked people who shouted. My head ached at the banging of the drum. I could understand about heaven to which good people went but was repulsed by rough-voiced men who pointed fingers at you and roared about hell and damnation.[23]

Fortunately, the posting at Kalgoorlie lasted less than a year. Late in 1912 the Haslucks finally found stability when they were placed in charge of a boys' home at Collie, 200 kilometres south of Perth. Here they stayed for what Meernaa Hasluck described as 'four very happy years'. Paul considered them 'the happiest and most influential years of my boyhood'.[24]

The goldrush decade of the 1890s had brought prosperity and population to Western Australia, but it also brought social problems. One was the care of orphans and children whose parents lacked the means or the capacity to look after them. Several churches established homes for destitute children, and in 1899 Sir John Forrest's government granted the Salvation Army 20,000 acres (8,100 hectares) north-east of Collie. On this site the army built a girls' home and two boys' homes intended to provide the children with a healthy environment in which they would learn useful bush skills fitting them for farm life. In 1908 the homes had figured in a newspaper article headlined 'Orphans worked like horses, fed like dogs'.[25] The Salvation Army refuted the charges, but its staff knew that henceforward their performance must be above criticism.

The Haslucks were put in charge of Number 2 Boys' Home. Its dormitories accommodated between fifty and sixty of the younger lads, who worked in the orchards and vegetable gardens of the self-sufficient community, attended the one-teacher school, and in their spare time fished and swam in the Bingham River. As Meernaa Hasluck recalled: 'We fought bush fires more than once, and caught many perch and brim [sic], which the boys appreciated. We were a happy family'.[26] On Sundays there were religious services in the morning and, unless the weather was foul, long walks in the bush in the afternoon. The manager's family lived in a cottage with a fenced garden separated from the main establishment, but Paul and his brothers attended the same school as the other boys, and took part in their games and work. It was, Paul remembered, a mixture of a somewhat exclusive family life and institutional life.[27]

In *Mucking About* Paul Hasluck says little about his primary schooling except that it was 'homely rather than academic', though in his unpublished writings he describes how a teacher unmercifully caned his brother Lewis for disagreeing about the correct spelling of a word.[28] Paul seems to have avoided such epic chastisement. It cannot have been easy for the academically bright son of the management to hold his own among fifty parentally disadvantaged schoolmates, but Paul Hasluck remembered his years in Collie as idyllic. He developed a number of skills he retained as an adult, including an aptitude for carpentry and a love of horses. He also discovered a profound sense of emotional identification with the Australian bush – it is not too much to term it spiritual or mystical – that remained with him for the rest of his life. And he came to know and admire several Aboriginal children of his own age. They were, he later wrote, 'on a pinnacle and were given the reputation of all sorts of superior qualities'. 'Black Paddy' Kumunkus, a Nyungar handyman at the homes, who was a great tracker and useful with horses, was something of a local hero.[29]

The homes seem to have been rather insulated from the Collie community. Western Australia's only coalmining centre, Collie was peopled mostly by staunch Labor voters, many of them Methodist. The *Collie Mail* seldom carried news items about the Salvation Army homes, and major local events such as the coalminers' strike of 1913 seem to have made little impact on these homes. Contact with the outside world was maintained by the delivery each evening of copies of the *West Australian* a day and a half old. For the Haslucks and their staff, visits to Collie for provisions and library books were not a light undertaking, involving a round trip of more than 30 kilometres by horse and sulky. Fortunately, young Paul was not solely dependent on the resources of the Collie library for reading matter, as the family owned a five-volume encyclopedia and a good selection of suitable novels – Dickens, Thackeray, Scott, Kingsley – which he absorbed voraciously. Friends noted his taste for reading and gave him books. 'When not working or playing games or mucking about with animals, there was nothing else to distract me from reading', he recalled, 'and at the time I had no hobbies'.[30]

In 1914, when Paul was nine, the Salvation Army convened a world congress in London following the death of its founder,

General William Booth. Meernaa Hasluck was sent as one of the Australian delegates. He could take one family member with him, and Paul was chosen. His mother was needed at the Boys' Home, and his elder brother Lewis had visited England as an infant, so it happened that an intensely receptive Paul spent two summer months in and around London on the eve of the First World War. The journey began on an adventurous note, for when their liner, the *Medic*, left Albany on 20 April, police with loaded revolvers removed from the ship two men wanted for crimes in Tasmania. Travelling by way of Durban, Capetown and Tenerife, and enjoying the usual shipboard sights of flying fish and the reception of King Neptune at the Equator, Paul and his father reached London at the end of May. They stayed with Paul's grandmother and aunt at Twickenham.

Within their first week they saw what Paul's father described as 'a flying machine – it makes a very peculiar noise in the air'. For him the highlights of the visit were the massed meetings and processions at the Salvation Army congress, but Paul was more impressed by 'the sights – the Tower of London, the Horse Guards, Hampton Court, Tussaud's waxworks, Windsor Castle, Eton, Westminster Abbey, St Paul's and the rest of them'.[31] Five days after they left London on 31 July, war broke out and their ship, the *Otway*, was detained off Gibraltar for several days before proceeding by a hot and circuitous route through the Suez Canal and the Indian Ocean, a journey prolonged by the need to dodge the German raider *Emden*. By coincidence, one of the other passengers on the *Otway* was Paul's future wife, the then six-year-old Alexandra Darker, but they do not seem to have met. The long voyage ended at Fremantle on 5 September, and soon Paul and his father were reunited with their family at the Boys' Home.

For Paul the experience was immensely stimulating. He had seen an aeroplane and visited a cinema to see silent films, neither of them experiences shared by any of his schoolfellows. He had

> ridden on an underground railway, visited a castle, touched a headman's axe and the execution block...and had experience of the sights and sounds of the English countryside and of the red poppies amid the English wheat, or travelled on a bus, or bought picture postcards from a man under the statue of Boadicea on the Embankment.[32]

It all gave a new dimension to his reading, but it also sharpened his sense of being different from his brothers and sister, as well as from the other boys at school who had not shared these experiences.

During the next eighteen months, Paul's parents watched his intellectual development and decided he ought to be encouraged to try for a Perth Modern School scholarship. Recently established by the state government, Perth Modern School recruited an annual intake of forty girls and forty boys by open competition through examinations in English and arithmetic. If a Western Australian child was not destined to leave school at fourteen, and if the child's parents could not afford to send him or her to a private secondary college, 'Mod' offered the state's only 'ladder of opportunity' – as it was so often described.[33] If Paul were to have his chance of scaling the ladder, he should have better teaching than his one-teacher school could provide. In 1916 his parents applied for a posting nearer Perth, although they were happy in their work at Collie and would leave behind the grave of a stillborn son, born earlier that year when his mother was forty-seven years old.[34] They were offered the management of an aged men's retreat at Guildford, east of Perth. There they moved towards the end of 1916, leaving behind a reputation as strict but caring guardians of whom their boys spoke in later life with affection.

Paul's four years at Collie laid the foundations of many of the interests and attitudes of his adult life. From his parents he was already absorbing ideals of responsibility and diligence, with a sense of social conscience. He learned to value the capabilities of Aboriginal Australians, and would never succumb to the demeaning stereotypes that classed them as an unteachable 'dying race'; but his experiences also suggested that life in a well-run institution offered disadvantaged young people more hope and opportunity than their home environments. His interests and perspectives were already beginning to differ from those of his siblings and his schoolmates, and this in time shaped him into a bit of a loner, strongly protective of his private self. Perhaps it was during those years that Paul Hasluck developed the comfort with solitude that remained with him throughout his life, although his wife thought it was a family characteristic.[35] Possibly an unmet need for intellectual companionship sharpened a quick temper he must always try to control. But his intellectual awakening to the riches of British culture was matched by a profound and observant love of the Western Australian bush and its people, and this would remain with him throughout his life.

The shaping influence of this environment can be illustrated by a passage Hasluck wrote in his old age:

My childhood memory is of the jarrah forests of South Western Australia in winter. In those days railway sleepers were hewn in the bush, not sawn at a mill. Sleeper cutters camped in the bush, usually a pair of them sharing a tent and a camp-fire, with a wooden bar on two forked sticks to support the billy and two broad sheets of bark leaning above it to keep the rain off the fire...If they were cutting in new country there would be no road, and, among those steep gravelly hills, covered with dense bush, a track had to be found to take the dray...Axe in hand, on foot, the carter or his mate found a way and marked the trees with a blaze, with a swift downward stroke slicing off the bark to reveal the white gleaming outer surface of the sapwood so that it glistened like a mirror. He made each blaze in the face of a trunk that could be readily seen from the last marked tree. As a small boy I walked with them, took part in the calculated exploration of a way where there was never a way before, the breathless moment of decision, the swish of the blade, the smell of the wounded tree, the puckered eyes looking ahead to find where the tracks should go next, the sense of bushmanship and the checking with the sun that made one aware of where the final destination was in spite of all the windings around the hills...'They blazed a track' is a simple phrase but a rich one. The words hold the Australian experience in a small compass.[36]

Hardly a trace is left of that shaping bush environment. Three or four years later, the Salvation Army decided to close the homes at Collie. The move was justified on the grounds that there was less need for orphanages than there had been twenty years before, but maybe – especially during the war, when many Salvation Army officers were ministering to the armed forces –

it was hard to find staff who would serve the orphanages with the same devotion as the Haslucks. The estate was sold to a timber company and the proceeds invested in building a home for alcoholics near Kelmscott. Having cleared the land, the timber company sold on to farmers. In 1993 Korean investors acquired much of this land for plantation timber. Where the Haslucks' cottage stood is now a substation for Western Power, surrounded by pylons.

Chapter 2

Apprenticeship

Young Paul Hasluck felt comfortable with the move to Guildford. One of Governor Stirling's original town sites of 1829, and situated 13 kilometres east of Perth's central business district, Guildford had a mellow rural environment that often led Western Australians to compare it to an English village. Many relics of the colonial past stirred the twelve-year-old Paul's imagination.

> In a more intimate way than I had found in reading history
> I began to be aware of a life and activity that had been going
> on in my own country before I was born.[1]

He listened to the inmates of the Aged Men's Retreat yarning about their past: one had been transported as a convict in the 1860s, another had been a circus clown, a third a magistrate in India. The time spent in their company had its sequel. Ten years later Paul would be an oral historian systematically recording the recollections of old Western Australians. The old kitchen-man found him one evening reading Thackeray's *The History of Henry Esmond*, and recommended going on to *Vanity Fair* and Reade's *The Cloister and the Hearth*.[2] At the Guildford state school he found acceptance in the playground. 'It was the first nearly normal life I had known', he recalled. 'Friends of those days have lasted.'[3] His headmaster, Francis O'Leary, recognised his ability and groomed him for the scholarship examination to Perth Modern School. He was successful, so that the next five years of Paul's life, from 1918 to 1922, would be spent scaling the ladder of opportunity at Mod.

'I am myself unsure whether it was a good school for me', he wrote in later life.[4] He considered that the school failed to give him guidance, so that apart from English, history and a manual arts training that improved his woodwork, 'I think I was badly taught, wasted a lot of time, and was always being interrupted or turned away from subjects in which I was interested'.[5] In his first two years he was seen as 'an average student in most subjects', who did not seem to be holding his own as the work grew harder, and failed several subjects; but he improved in time to pass the Junior Certificate examination at the end of his third year.[6] His slow start meant he was not identified as one of the 'high flyers' who should be groomed for university study, and this probably reinforced a characteristic reluctance to push himself forward. Meanwhile, he had the run of a well-stocked library, and made some good friends. 'I was popular and had some trivial fame for a ready tongue, good swimming and rough football and some skill at bowling, handicapped by total failure as a batsman.'[7]

Partly in order to live closer to Modern School his parents went back to short-term work in Perth's western suburbs. Instead of the rural stability of life at Collie or Guildford, the adolescent Paul found himself thrust back into the fervid atmosphere of hot-gospelling that had repelled him as a child in Kalgoorlie. Increasingly, he felt himself to be out of step with the rest of his family. While troubled at his inability to share their beliefs, he continued to admire his parents as models of self-denial.

When Western Australia was ravaged by an epidemic of pneumonic influenza in 1919 and staff could not be found to wash the bloodstained sheets from the army's institutions, it was the 50-year-old Patience Hasluck who took on the task; when verminous and filthy old vagrants entered the Aged Men's Retreat, it was Meernaa who cleaned them up.[8] It did not help that his parents were very poorly paid and apt to be shunted from one posting to another at short notice by a Salvation Army bureaucracy that in Paul's eyes exploited his parents' selfless dedication.

With his elder brother Lewis, a level-headed and self-reliant youth, Paul remained on good terms, although Lewis did not share Paul's intellectual leanings. Like many Western Australians of his generation, his ambition was to have a piece of land of his own. He left school at fifteen, and gained his wish after an unsatisfactory period with a Perth furniture manufacturer. Years earlier, Meernaa Hasluck had invested in a 20-acre (8.1-hectare) block of land at Herne Hill in the foothills of the Darling Range to the east of the Swan valley. The vicinity was largely undeveloped bush with a few market gardens and small vineyards. The family scraped together a little capital to set Lewis up on the property, and he settled there contentedly, clearing and cultivating his block.[9] Paul had less in common with his younger brother and sister, who seemed to have no trouble conforming to the Salvation Army ethos. For the time being, Paul evidently suppressed his doubts, even serving in the Subiaco citadel junior band. He was not a teenage rebel. Instead, his headmaster, Joseph Parsons, described him as a 'singularly tractable boy'.[10]

He took refuge in solitude. The large country town that was Perth in the 1920s was nowhere far from undeveloped bush, and he walked and cycled long distances exploring it. On wet weekends he found his way to the State Library and Museum, trying out subjects such as geology and anthropology that were not covered in the Modern School curriculum. Both at school and at weekends he was voraciously reading his way into English literature, finding a special pleasure in the contemplative seventeenth-century poet George Herbert and in Wordsworth, with his feel for landscape that matched Paul's empathy for the Australian bush. In his notebooks in which he recorded his literary voyages of discovery he pondered the relationship between humans and their landscape. 'Back to nature', he wrote, was all right for those who lived among pleasant scenes such as Wordsworth's Lake District or Thoreau's North American forests, 'but what of the waste places of the earth, the terror of it, the despair?' The conquest of the land was an age-old struggle and, an environmentalist before his time, he explored the concept that farmers must learn to 'humour' the land.[11]

These were not tastes shared by many of his sporting school-mates, and reinforced 'a growing shyness and withdrawal into myself',[12] though to outward appearances he was a good mixer and sufficiently popular. He was a corporal in the cadet corps and chairman of the debating society. Placed in what was termed the commercial stream, he was getting better results in his last two years at school, strong in English literature and history, though still struggling with his French. No doubt he also felt pressure from his mother's hope that he might become a medical missionary, though the process was lengthy and expensive, and he had no vocation for it.

Paul claimed that until his final year he had no inkling that school might be followed by a university education, and this may not have been surprising. The infant University of

Western Australia offered courses such as agricultural science and geology that attracted students strong on the science side, but the prospects were less obvious for those inclined towards the humanities. Most, like Paul's slightly younger schoolfellow Herbert Coombs (already known as 'Nugget'),[13] would go after leaving school to the Teachers' Training College in Claremont, there to satisfy an apparently unending demand for state primary school teachers. This did not appeal to Paul. Law attracted him more, but as yet it was not taught at the university, and to become an articled clerk involved expense far beyond the Hasluck family's means. Then, during his final year, a friend put it into his head that someone with his flair for writing might be suited to journalism. In July he prepared for the workforce by seeking testimonials from his teachers and other respected citizens. All gave him an excellent character for intelligence and integrity. 'He is a thoroughly reliable lad in every way', wrote his English master, Charles Sharp, 'honourable, and amiable, and not without a certain sense of humour that ought to stand him in good stead in the kind of work he wishes to take up'.[14]

His ambition became reality through one of those chance encounters that used to be quite common in the tight-knit Perth community. Paul's father met in the street Horace Stirling, whose family had owned newspapers in Perth since well back in the nineteenth century, and had published contributions by old Lewis Hasluck. When it emerged that Paul wanted to be a journalist, Horace Stirling undertook to mention him to his nephew Jack, who was a subeditor on the *West Australian*. In September 1922 the seventeen-year-old Paul Hasluck was offered a job working in the newspaper's office six nights a week between 6.00 pm and 11.00 pm, for a pound a week. The duties 'meant writing sundry little paragraphs, sub-editing the weather reports, making a digest of advertisements and running a lot of messages'. The vacancy had arisen because his predecessor 'had gone off his head and been put into the lunatic asylum'.[15] The chance was too good to refuse, but it interfered with his preparations for the Leaving examinations. Paul took his Leaving Certificate with distinctions in English and Industrial History and a pass in Commercial Methods and Bookkeeping, but failed in French.[16] (This did nothing to quench his interest in French literature, and he subsequently worked to achieve reasonable conversational fluency and an excellent reading knowledge.) He made a good impression at the newspaper office, and in January 1923 he was taken on as a cadet journalist to serve at that level for three years on a commencing salary of 30 shillings a week.

The *West Australian*, Perth's only morning newspaper, was a dignified broadsheet modelling itself, if not on the London *Times*, then on substantial English provincial dailies such as the *Manchester Guardian* and the *Yorkshire Post*. Such newspapers were conscious of their responsibility for providing thorough and accurate reporting of significant events to a readership including the community's decision-makers. It was assumed that this readership was capable of absorbing paragraphs of more than two sentences and words of more than two syllables. Under a dominant editor–proprietor, Sir Winthrop Hackett,[17] the *West Australian* was soberly conservative in its politics, though it liked to regard itself as a somewhat headmasterly critic, offering balanced judgements on Labor and non-Labor governments alike. After Hackett's death in 1916, his editor and successor, Alfred Langler,[18] kept up this tradition. The '*West*' also kept its readers abreast of cultural developments, especially in the

26

United Kingdom, though sport, popular entertainment and ladies' fashions were not neglected.[19]

Experience in such a newspaper office gave young Hasluck a first-class training in committing his ideas quickly to paper, and expressing those ideas in clear, readable prose. His editor, Dudley Braham,[20] an Oxford graduate with international experience, and his subeditors – one was known as 'The Butcher' – insisted that his English be grammatical and well crafted, so that in later life Hasluck was apt to deplore what he saw as the falling-off of journalistic literary standards, as well as a diminished regard for accuracy. Throughout the English-speaking world young journalists who shared this training knew that some among them would find their way to recognition not merely as reporters but as men of letters. London's Fleet Street had provided a launching pad from which ambitious youngsters from the provinces, such as H. G. Wells, Arnold Bennett and John Buchan, won their way to international fame as writers. After the First World War, newcomers such as J. B. Priestley were joining their ranks. Even in Western Australia, the novice journalist Paul Hasluck could aspire to literary creativity, though whether as poet, novelist or dramatist it was as yet too soon to decide. He claimed in his autobiography that he cherished no aim further than writing book reviews and essays for the Saturday literary pages, but it would not be long before wider ambitions stirred.[21]

He soon found that his job brought him into contact with a rich cross-section of humanity for an observant young man to write about. He relished 'the chance to see events and people and to study facets of life I had never seen before':

Without being personally involved in crime, politics, the practice of the law, the running of public institutions, municipal affairs, learned societies or trade unions, or street accidents, fires, sporting events and various forms of business activity, farming or buying and selling, I had experience of all of them. I was eager for experience and curious about phases of life hitherto closed to me.[22]

He had to be versatile, as his duties ranged from covering Australian Rules football matches on Saturday afternoons to the trade-union round. One evening might find him taking copy of the next morning's editorial to Langler at his West Perth house, there to sit on the verandah and listen to the city's eminent citizens laying down the law about books and politics. Another night he might be accompanying the police around the slums of what is now known as Northbridge, checking out the illegal brothels and Chinese opium dens that were quietly tolerated provided they gave no trouble. Fifty years later Hasluck was to set down a vivid reconstruction of the community that was Perth in the 1920s. For the present he was coming to sense that this community might provide as much stimulus to the literary imagination as the Potteries of Arnold Bennett or J. B. Priestley's Yorkshire.

With the stirrings of artistic imagination came an increasing sense of tension between the simple certainties of his home environment and the challenges of a wider world. He described this tension in a largely autobiographical novel drafted about ten years later:

I was brought up in a humble home where not only the precepts but the daily practice of my parents taught me meekness. One should never push oneself forward. One should consider others and defer to others. It was rude to assert one's own view or to insist on one's own rights. It was more blessed to give than to receive. One should not boast about one's own achievements. One should not advance one's own interests but seek the common good. Sacrifice was all...So was I crouched between this burden of my virtue and the attractions of the world. My innocence was sure to be assaulted. My ambitions could never be enjoyed. I could never be as virtuous as I was taught to be but I could never be as glorious an adventurer as I had power to be.[23]

Paul Hasluck never learned how to be a rebel. Too early in life he developed a knack of suppressing his own opinions and doubts in the interests of loyalty to his seniors. This dutiful silencing of his private judgement sometimes fed resentment and a loss of temper that was all the sharper for having been bottled up. In later life he retained from his upbringing other characteristics that would not be to his worldly advantage. It took him many years to realise 'that the sense of duty installed by my parents was undiscriminating'.[24] He had no talent for self-promotion, trusting that hard work and consistent competence would eventually be rewarded by recognition. This naïve faith was to seem largely justified during the next twenty years of his career, leaving him in this respect ill equipped for the political arena when he entered it in middle life.

His immediate problems were simplified but not resolved after the Salvation Army transferred his parents to South

Australia in 1925, and the younger children went with them. (It has been pointed out that, whereas many young people assert themselves by going to live somewhere else to escape parental influence, in Paul's case it was the parents who left and gave him space, but in so doing deprived him of an opportunity for self-assertion.)[25] Paul had left home when he started work, renting a sitting room and sleep-out in a private house. He still went regularly to church on Sundays, admittedly in the often justified hope that somebody would invite him home for a meal afterwards.[26]

After a while he set himself a regime of lengthy bush-walking in the Darling Range on Sundays as a substitute for churchgoing. 'Wordsworth', he wrote, 'gave me more than the Pauline epistles'.[27] Because his newspaperman's routine made him unavailable for team games at weekends, he valued his bushwalking and swimming as means of keeping fit. Often alone, he was sometimes joined by one of his friends from Perth Modern School days: Leslie Rees,[28] who later made a name writing children's stories set in the Australian bush; or Dom Serventy,[29] already a skilled naturalist.

He spent some of his time with his elder brother Lewis, who had also parted company with the Salvation Army and was concentrating on his vineyard. Paul helped him sink a well, build a house, and set up a wireless aerial on the roof – from which on a good day it was possible to pick up the sounds of a concert broadcast in Perth 40 kilometres away.[30] It pleased Paul that through working with his practical, good-humoured elder brother he was making himself into a proficient carpenter as well as rediscovering a love of farming. At intervals during the rest of his life he was given to wishing he had become a farmer.[31] Yet it cannot have escaped him that Lewis was finding it hard to make ends meet, so that when he married in 1927 he was obliged to take work at the government railway workshops at Midland Junction, with only weekends to devote to his property.[32]

Journalism paid better. At the end of 1925, when he finished his three years of cadetship, Paul was earning £3 10s a week, enough to afford a motorbike for his weekend travels. After graduating to adult rates of pay in 1926 he bought a small car, a baby Austin, later replaced by a six-cylinder Chevrolet. He schooled himself to be a careful financial manager, but led a lively social life. He was much in demand at 'smoke socials' because of his skill in stringing together topical rhymes for sing-songs around a piano. Between 1923 and 1926 he trained with the Citizen Military Forces as a sergeant in the 44th Battalion, enjoying the camaraderie though intellectually no believer in war.[33] He was encouraged to undertake officer training, and if he had done so he might have entered the Second World War in command of a company or a battalion and followed a very different career path later in life. But as he turned twenty-one in 1926, other intellectual interests were competing for his time.

During these years he was reading voraciously over a wide range. Among the authors he discovered were John Ruskin, William Morris, John Middleton Murry, John Galsworthy, Richard Aldington, Arthur Quiller-Couch, Maurice Hewlett, William James, Christopher Morley, Walter de la Mare and, by way of light relief, A. A. Milne, Kenneth Grahame and J. M. Barrie. Perhaps unusually for a young Australian at this time, he was also reading the Indian writers Rabindranath Tagore and Dhan Ghopal Mukerjee.[34] These names support his recollection that his main interests at this period were religion and poetry.

Among the poets, some of his favourites were the seventeenth-century mystics Thomas Traherne, Henry Vaughan and George Herbert, who were not much in literary fashion. He copied Vaughan's poem 'My soul, there is a country' in its entirety, as well as a favourite quotation from Traherne: 'You never enjoy the world aright, until the sea floweth in your veins, till you are clothed with the heavens and crowned with the stars'.[35] It may be that his emotional response to their poems came from that same part of his being that responded to the solitude of the Australian bush. He was also reading a good deal of Australian verse, though at that time he would have encountered little of the same emotional depth.

Then he discovered the author whose thought probably influenced him more than any other. This was the sixteenth-century French essayist Michel Eyquem de Montaigne. Living at a time when France was rent by civil war between Catholics and Protestant Huguenots, Montaigne, a landowner in the Bordeaux district, managed to play a useful diplomatic role in the public life of his time while at the same time perfecting the essay as a form of self-expression and self-exploration. What he meant to Hasluck must be quoted at some length:

> Montaigne is neither systematic nor committed. His quality is in the mood, the temper, the spirit with which he considers any and every subject rather than in the strength of his convictions on a chosen theme. He excludes nothing. He entertains ideas about all sorts of subjects…He does not think that he himself is important or that he can decide what will happen and make it happen. He has some notion of eternity; his curiosity is universal; he muses on the vanity of human wishes and the

32

transience of fame. He has a limited and benign ambition and has no illusions of power or grandeur. He sees personality in its diversity and frailty, including himself, and not as an heroic stance that can be fixed in a single image to command the world's favour. He finds solace in thought, not in public praise. He hopes that any argument can be conducted reasonably and temperately and end with a concession to reason and not in the maintenance of a dogma. He is a questioner rather than one who trumpets his own opinions in a loud blast. He is altogether unfitted to be a political candidate in Australia and he would be wholly incapable of using the services of a public relations consultant.[36]

Paul Hasluck could have been describing his own outlook on life.

In old age Paul Hasluck remembered those years as a very happy period in his life.[37] He was a compactly built young man, intelligent and well mannered, perhaps already unusually hardworking, an average performer in sports but good with his hands. Surprisingly for one who had matriculated with two distinctions, he did not consider himself clever enough to think of university – early evidence of the self-critical streak that made his judgements on himself at least as hard as those on other people. He had no trouble in conforming to the neat and formal dress standards expected of professional men of his day. In *Mucking About* Hasluck described his younger self as 'a rather eager and puppyish fellow, making friends with anyone'.[38] In reality, many seem to have found him a quick-witted and good-humoured companion with a conversational ease that might have surprised those who knew only the reserved and at times censorious cabinet minister of later years. He retained friends from Perth Modern School and made more as he settled into his job. Several of his colleagues were a few years older than he, and as the law forbade persons under twenty-one to enter premises licensed to sell alcohol, it may be that the product of a teetotal Salvation Army household was inhibited for a while in joining them at the Palace Hotel 'dive', for several decades the watering hole for Perth newspapermen.

Among the younger journalists the colleague who most shared his interest in the writing of Western Australian history was Malcolm Uren,[39] but he and Paul Hasluck seem never to have been close. Hasluck formed a much stronger friendship with Walter James, usually known as 'Bob' to distinguish him from his father, the prominent barrister and ex-Premier Sir Walter James.[40] Beneath a hedonistic façade and sometimes bawdy wit, Bob James shared Paul's growing interest in literature. In November 1925, with a few friends, they decided to form an Arts Club at which a membership restricted to young men would read and discuss papers on cultural subjects.[41] With the earnestness of youth they drew up an elaborate constitution and hired a room in McNeil's Chambers for Saturday-night meetings. Paul Hasluck was foundation chairman and Bob James secretary.

The first meeting began inauspiciously: 'In the absence of Mr Nevile, who was to have lectured on "Mirabeau and the French Revolution", Mr V. Rodda lectured on "Sex"'. Later presentations were more uplifting. There was a debate on a motion: 'That Australia has developed a national literature', won by the affirmative side, and on 22 March 1926 'Mr Hasluck delivered an interesting and instructive lecture on "Some tendencies in modern Australian poetry" which was well received'. In June it was resolved to form a 'first night' theatre party, whose members would adopt a distinctive dress of bowler hats and sticks, but at the next meeting a proposal to rescind this motion led to a lengthy debate until 'The Chairman, who was trying to look wise although bewildered by the arguments regarding procedure', suspended standing orders in order to arrive at a compromise. By now the club was financially troubled, with debts for rent and cleaning, and many overdue subscriptions. At what turned out to be its final meeting, a strong motion of censure was passed on a speaker who failed to turn up. 'After much worthless and purposeless lucubration the meeting closed.' In its playful way the Arts Club provided Paul Hasluck with his first apprenticeship in the conduct of meetings and the management of wayward colleagues.

Having published a few articles on local history in the *West Australian*, he was the obvious choice to report on a meeting on a winter night in 1926 when 'a dozen or so ladies and gentlemen of social distinction' met at The University of Western Australia with Professor Edward Shann in the chair to found the [Royal] Historical Society of Western Australia.[42] By the end of the evening Paul Hasluck had been drafted as the new society's honorary research secretary. He was left a free hand in defining the duties of this position. Most of the members of the society came from colonial families whose roots in Western Australia reached far back into the nineteenth century. 'Our monthly meetings', he found:

were occasions not only for hearing someone read a paper or give extracts from some family diary or family letters, but also for a social get-together over a pleasant supper where much of the conversation was really a process of identifying each other and recalling how your cousin and my aunt used to do this or that, and his grandfather was the first person to take cattle from here to there, and someone else's uncle was standing on the beach when somebody's grandfather did something rather important. We were as happy as a tree crowded with parrots and out of the social chatter a good deal of historical seed was scattered.[43]

Hasluck came to realise that there was more to Western Australia's history than the written record. At that time there were old men and women surviving whose memories went back before the goldrushes of the 1890s and even beyond the coming of convict transportation in 1850. Their knowledge would be lost unless he recorded their recollections. It was an era before tape recorders, but Hasluck was a proficient Pitman's shorthand writer who could take 130 words a minute. Before the year was out he had conducted his first interview, with an old identity he knew from his boyhood in Guildford, William Traylen, a retired Methodist minister and politician known as a vigorous campaigner for improving Perth's water supply.[44] Unfortunately, Traylen's memory was failing and he died a few months later, but the experience encouraged Hasluck to continue.

In 1927 he struck gold in interviewing James Kennedy, who had not only accompanied John Forrest's transcontinental exploring party in 1874 but could also provide from memory a map of Perth's main streets in 1860, identifying nearly all the residences and businesses. Others followed: a woman who prided herself on having introduced arum lilies to the Busselton region despite the objections of her neighbours, a man who had taken supplies to the first pastoral parties in the Pilbara in 1864, and another who remembered the Balladong Aboriginal people of York dying by the wayside during the measles epidemic of 1860. Until his marriage in 1932, Hasluck drove himself to all parts of the South West, yarning with old-timers and recording their stories. Ironically, in later years he was given to disparaging oral history as unreliable, but in his own contribution he created a uniquely valuable resource for colonial history while deepening his own already strong identification with Western Australian country.[45]

Among the members of the old colonial families, Hasluck discerned a strong group loyalty, and a reticence 'to go around opening cupboards where other people kept their skeletons'.[46] This, he conjectured, was not surprising in a society where there had been probably fewer than 4,000 family units before the goldrushes of the 1890s. He saw something of the same clannishness as surviving into the 1920s. Shared experience and family connections loomed larger than distinctions based on class. His own career fortified his view that a sense of common local identity was a stronger cement for society than class divisions, which seemed surmountable in the Western Australia of his day. The Western Australian elite distinguished themselves by manners as much as by wealth. His background in a Salvation Army family of slender means did not preclude the intelligent and respectably behaved young Hasluck from acceptance in the affluent homes of Sir Walter James and Sir Alfred Langler.

Younger historians, writing from the perspective of the late-twentieth and early twenty-first centuries, have questioned Hasluck's indifference to class as a divisive factor in Western

Australian society.[47] They argue that the perspectives of a scholar-ship boy who made good were not shared by his contemporaries in the urban working class, and offer a partial and misleading picture of Western Australian society. The conflicting points of view can possibly be reconciled. The attitudes Hasluck described as characteristic – the clannishness, the unwillingness to enter into contentious and divisive issues or to rattle the skeletons in other people's cupboards, the hope of social mobility for young men of ability – took root in the isolated Western Australia of the nineteenth century. They survived in the South West and the older suburbs of Perth for some decades afterwards. Later comers who arrived during the goldrush of the 1890s and afterwards, and sections of the urban working class in particular, may not have been so ready to accept these attitudes, though some did. This does not mean that Hasluck's experience of them lacked validity or that their influence immediately vanished, only that historians must learn to take a more pluralistic view of Western Australia in the first half of the twentieth century.

Hasluck's view of the past stressed the capacity of the Western Australian community to assimilate each wave of newcomers:

There had been successive adjustments of the colonial circle. In the very early years there had been distinctions between gentry and working classes, but, with the inauguration of the transportation of convicts in 1849, the circle gathered in all those who were truly among the early settlers. After the cessation of transportation the presence of expirees led to a distinction between the bond and the free. The gold rush of the eighteen-nineties made the distinction between the true Sandgropers and 't'othersiders'.[48]

That distinction was eroding by the 1920s; when the Western Australian secession movement arose in the early 1930s, some of its keenest advocates would be 't'othersiders' who had arrived with the goldrush. One group remained outside this benign process of assimilation and acceptance. The oldest Western Australians of all, the descendants of the Aboriginal people who were in possession before 1829, were socially and politically excluded. Many saw them as 'a dying race'. To an intelligent young observer of social conscience, it would seem only just that steps should be taken to gather them into the same circle as other Western Australians. During the next few years, amid other journeys of intellectual discovery, this realisation would come to the forefront of Paul Hasluck's concerns.

Chapter 3

'Skipping up the stairs of culture'[1]

Events were conspiring to overcome Paul Hasluck's diffidence about undertaking university study. In 1926 the ownership of the *West Australian* and its associated newspapers passed from Sir Winthrop Hackett's estate to a Melbourne-based company, though editorial policy and control remained in Perth. Under the terms of Hackett's will a large share of the proceeds went to The University of Western Australia, so that it could plan to move from its makeshift quarters at Irwin Street in the centre of Perth to a set of magnificent buildings at Crawley, 4 kilometres to the west. It happened that since 1924 Hasluck had been a member of the committee of the Western Australian branch of the Australian Journalists' Association; he held this office until 1940 and in later years would cite it as proof of good trade-union credentials.[2] The president of the association, John Curtin, was keen to improve the educational standards of its members, and supported the university in offering extension courses for journalists. Hasluck's friend Leslie Rees, who was about to graduate from the university, persuaded the authorities that it was time a Diploma of Journalism was established, and was given the job of putting the case to a meeting of the Australian Journalists' Association. Rees was dismayed to find that several of the hardened old newspapermen present saw no need for involving their profession with university education:

> And I was absolutely aghast, and suddenly somebody came to my rescue, and it was Paul Hasluck. He was just a very young chap, you know…And he made a diplomatic speech of a kind that he's probably been making all his life since. And he said: 'I'm one of those who appreciate the efforts of our journalists here and their tradition, but I think we could improve things and I think it's a good idea'.[3]

The four-year diploma was duly established, although the content of the course was more practically oriented than Leslie Rees or some of the academic staff hoped. As its advocate, Paul Hasluck felt honour bound to enrol, gaining distinctions in his first two years and receiving the Lovekin Prize for the most distinguished journalistic work. In 1928 he and his contemporary Griff Richards were the Australian Journalists' Association representatives on the university's Board of Journalistic Studies.

Attendance at the Irwin Street campus during 1927 and 1928 drew Hasluck more and more into the social life of the university. At the same time he was also involving himself in Perth's leading amateur dramatic society, the Repertory Club. He says: 'I did so because I wanted to see plays, not because I wanted to act or do any other form of stagework',[4] but it was not long before he was in demand as a useful stagehand, and so graduated to acting in minor roles. 'I was never much good but they used to keep on asking me to do small parts for lack of anyone else of the right size and shape.'[5] It was thus not surprising that he was drawn into the University Dramatic Society and became its vice-president in 1929. The society's repertoire at that time consisted largely of readings of drawing-room comedies and a few safe classics. In 1929 Hasluck wrote to the *Black Swan*, the university's literary journal, urging the society to extend its range. He suggested that in addition to contemporary British or Australian drama it would be worth attempting 'a miracle or mystery play'.[6]

The idea took, and later that year the society decided to perform *Everyman*. In this morality play from the early sixteenth century, Death summons Everyman, who in the last hour of his life discovers that his friends – Fellowship, Kindred, Cousin and Goods – will not go with him. He is dependent on the support of Knowledge and Good Deeds, whom in the past he has neglected.[7] It was, Leslie Rees thought, a courageous decision: 'The play needed entirely different treatment from any other play presented in Perth for years'.[8] The producer was a third-year student, Alexandra Darker, whom Paul had met a few times at play readings. Paul was drafted to play the leading character, Everyman. A note from Alix Darker survives:[9]

> Dear Paul Hasluck, I have managed to secure God for Thursday, 5 to ¼ to 6; Death also. Could you come? Not only because you can stand any amount of rehearsal of that early part, but – I should like your valuable opinion of God's lines.[10]

The play attracted a small but appreciative audience, though the production was perhaps a little low-key. Leslie Rees in his critique wrote: 'Mr Hasluck, for instance, whose fault I think is usually to underact, rather than the contrary, might have shown his annoyance at the arrival of Death a little more strikingly than he did', but added that he 'got into his grave neatly and without allowing his knees to creak at all audibly'.[11] Alix Darker must have approved of her leading man, as the production was to lead to courtship and marriage, but for the present their friendship developed at an unhurried tempo, enlivened by bouts of quick-witted verbal sparring.

Until that time Paul Hasluck's life seems to have been without serious romantic interest. In that era young men with professional ambitions were advised not to take on the responsibilities of marriage until they had established themselves and could support a suitably middle-class lifestyle. Both Paul's brothers, who were not ambitious, married young and became family men. Paul remembered his social milieu in his early twenties as

> very much a man's world. Girls were not much of an attraction when there were so many interesting things to do without them…Girls did not enter much into the planning of our recreation and amusement and we seldom met them in other than a social setting.[12]

This was not quite the whole story. A young woman meeting him for the first time declared to her friends that she was fascinated by his conversation, and he knew the importance of a well-chosen bouquet of flowers.[13] And in *Mucking About* he relates how as a reporter in the Arbitration Court he was impressed enough with 'a saucy young woman witness' named Kathleen to make her acquaintance after the court rose and to spend several evenings with her family – but he writes of them as Dickensian characters who interested the novelist in him.

And Kathleen had a boyfriend, but she eventually dropped him and went off to work in a pub in Northam, and she passed out of Paul's life.[14]

Alix Darker was a different matter entirely. She had style, intelligence and wit. She came from a Queensland family who, after emigrating from England, had prospered more than the Haslucks. Richard Thomas Darker (known as Tom), a locomotive foreman at Ipswich who rose to senior administrative rank, and his wife Wilhelmina had a numerous family, of whom one son became a colliery proprietor and several others entered the professions.[15] One son, John Darker, went to Western Australia for employment in the railways under C. Y. O'Connor, later serving as an engineer in the Public Works Department. He married a schoolteacher, Evelyn Hill, who was one of the first woman graduates at the University of Sydney. They were in their late thirties in 1908 when they had their only child, Alexandra Margaret Martin Darker, the name 'Martin' commemorating an Anglo-Irish ancestor who served for many years in parliament and was credited with founding the Royal Society for the Prevention of Cruelty to Animals.[16] After John Darker died in 1925, his widow sent her daughter to The University of Western Australia, where she graduated as a Bachelor of Arts in 1929. During 1930 and 1931 she was a housemistress and taught French at Miss Parnell's School for Girls, which was in the process of transforming itself into St Hilda's College Mosman Park.

Paul Hasluck occupied an increasing amount of her time and thoughts. They shared an enjoyment of theatre, books and dancing, and Paul was an entertaining companion. 'I do love your letters', she told him.

When you are famous and dead, people will read them and write books on them and you (for I shall be dead, too). And they will say, 'Ah, such letters are never written now. It is a lost art'.[17]

She bought him a wristwatch with a loving inscription, and in August he bought her a ring. By the end of the year they were an engaged couple. Having lost her father as a teenager, Alix was attracted by Paul's ability to combine responsibility and stability with a talent to amuse. Her mother approved of him too, though in her one surviving letter to Paul she commented:

You start well with youth, health and education on your sides. I can't help having one tilt tho' at your sex. I mean the average man who in countless ways in a home lets the wife know she is inferior in her judgments. It is a male heritage and it will take centuries to rid many homes of that feeling.[18]

Paul came to live at her house in Mount Lawley, an arrangement not uncommon for engaged couples in those innocent days, when a potential son-in-law could make a useful contribution to the household and its income.

Meernaa and Patience Hasluck were also pleased with their prospective daughter-in-law. They were now back in Perth in charge of the People's Palace, a Salvation Army hostel providing the travelling public with cheap, clean and alcohol-free accommodation. Both parents were proud of Paul and his growing reputation, and his visits were especially welcome to them, as Lewis was busy with his Herne Hill property and the younger

45

brother and sister had remained in the Eastern States, where both had become Salvation Army officers.

Meanwhile, Paul Hasluck and Leslie Rees were forming great hopes for the University Dramatic Society. They wanted to develop it as showcase for locally written plays. When the *Black Swan* offered a prize of two guineas for the best poem submitted, Hasluck won with the only entry. He used to say it was the only money he ever earned from poetry.[19] He tried his hand at writing fairy stories for children, and planned a novel entitled 'The scoundrel with clean hands' about a bad man who never the opportunity to be bad.[20]

In October 1929 Hasluck sought advice from two veteran journalists who had been trying for years to promote Australian writing and drama, Edward Vidler in Melbourne and William Moore in Sydney.[21] Moore's reply was prompt:

> I don't see any chance for its development in Perth till there is some movement started to produce Australian plays. If the University Dramatic Society won't do it, then an outside society. Possibly the University will do it if a strong bid can be arranged.[22]

In Melbourne, he wrote, he had found it hard to start such a movement until he discovered a promising dramatist in Louis Esson, but in Perth 'perhaps you won't be able to depend on local writers entirely until a movement becomes established'. He suggested that Perth's young writers should form a dining club to discuss their work: 'The *Black Swan* has a distinctive literary style, and we in the East would like to raise our hats to you'.[23] Vidler sent Hasluck a number of books, but was less encouraging: 'With regard to Australian plays there have been very few published and those possibly not the best'.[24] If young Western Australians wanted the advancement of literature and drama in their community, they would have to do it themselves.

As it happened, several of Hasluck's closest allies – Leslie Rees, Dom Serventy, Bob James – left for Europe during the summer of 1929–30, either to study at Oxford or Cambridge, or, in James's case, simply to enjoy a year of wandering the Continent. Then, as it would be until well after the Second World War, young Western Australians wanting experience of an intellectually and culturally wider world looked more often to London and Paris than Sydney and Melbourne. Paul himself had thought of accompanying Bob James, but perhaps because the onset of the Great Depression made the future somewhat unpredictable, or perhaps because of his courtship with Alix Darker, he did not do so. This meant that he was left to carry the responsibility for many of the initiatives he and his friends had discussed. During 1930 and 1931 he was not only networking enterprisingly, but he also emerged as an acute and influential drama critic as well as improving his own skills as a creative writer. He came to feel that in recent years he had concentrated too much on writing and editing historical articles. With the encouraging influence of his fiancée, he began to experiment with new forms of literary expression.

From England, Leslie Rees continued to offer encouragement and advice. He urged Paul to edit an anthology of verse to celebrate the university's move to the new campus at Crawley: 'I know of nobody else (among students) who can bring a sufficient knowledge of verse values and at the same time a journalistic technique to the task'. He fretted about the pressures to turn the *Black Swan* into a newspaper and, unsuccessfully, urged Paul to become editor.[25] Paul declined, but the *Black Swan* remained a literary journal, with the establishment in May 1930 of the *Pelican* as a fortnightly student newspaper. Hasluck became its drama critic. In this role he showed something of the same trenchant and even brutal candour he in later life brought to his political reminiscences. He concluded his first review, of a play entitled *The Arabian Nights*: 'Finally we must commend the producer for having produced it, the audience for having heard it, and the last 40 years for having forgotten the rotten play'.[26] When the University Dramatic Society staged a reading of *The Importance of Being Ernest*, he commented, 'one does expect the performers to glance through their parts beforehand [and] to refrain from kittenish giggling during the reading', and of the leading man who played Algernon Moncrieff: 'Of course he took the main part...but he might have killed it a little less ostentatiously'.[27] He was at his most savage when reviewing an evening of locally written one-act plays:

If there had been a spark of entertainment in Sol Sainken's 'Beware of Bears' it would have been exhausted by Mr McClintock's first clumsy breath. An absurdity of the slapstick vaudeville type, it is a rotten play, and was rottenly performed. It is a pity that something more worthy of Western Australia has not been found.[28]

Hasluck wrote such verdicts from the stance that in his role as critic he must not pull his punches, but that this should have no bearing on his personal relationships outside the professional role. It worked with Sainken, who remained on good terms with him in the future, but it could not be taken for granted that everyone shared this capacity to separate the personal from the professional. Subsequently, in public life, Hasluck found that those he had occasion to castigate often carried the bruises outside office hours. They did not share his sense that public and private roles could be separated. He resigned from the *Pelican* at the end of 1930, perhaps sharing Rees's disdain of its 'buffoonery'.[29] His reviews impressed the *West Australian* sufficiently to lead to his appointment as drama critic. He held this position for ten years, writing under the pen-name 'Polygon' to show that there were many sides to every question. (He shared the initials 'P. H.' with another young writer of the time, Peter Hopegood, and wanted to avoid confusion.)

It was not enough to be a critic. Several of Paul's friends were trying their hands at writing plays for performance. Coralie Clarke, for instance, who was soon to marry Leslie Rees, wrote a one-act play, *Shielded Eyes*, that was produced by the University Dramatic Society in 1930 with Paul Hasluck in the lead role.[30] During 1931 Paul put together his own one-act play, *A Game of Billiards*.[31] It takes place in the saloon bar of a country pub and consists of a series of yarning dialogues shaped with a good ear for the rhythms of the vernacular. At the end an inconspicuous stranger is found to be Death, who comes for the local entrepreneur; maybe the idea was suggested by Paul's role in *Everyman*. The play was published in *Black Swan*, and in November 1931 William Moore asked for a copy, noting as he did that nothing had been done by the University Dramatic Society or the Perth Repertory Club to stage Australian plays: 'Now that Hobart has made a definite start, Perth seems to be the last to come in'.[32]

Alexandra Darker was also trying her hand as a playwright. In 1931 the *Black Swan* published her one-act sketch entitled *Discretion or Valour?*[33] A young engaged couple sit in the waiting room of the fortune teller Madame Cassandra, and watch as other clients consult the clairvoyant and emerge troubled by even the most apparently favourable predictions. Eventually the young woman persuades her fiancé to leave without consulting Madame Cassandra, saying, 'I will not learn the future. The future is only the present of every moment and every moment I love you'. It would be tempting to read an autobiographical element into the play, and in the light of later events to admire the young woman's confidence. Paul was also allowing an autobiographical undercurrent in his poetry. It was surely not a coincidence that a couple of love lyrics were addressed to someone called 'Melisande', a name (in poetry at least) with the same syllabic metre as 'Alexandra'. But he was also writing verse about the quirks and idiosyncrasies of those he met in daily life, and one such poem, 'A drunken man on Highgate Hill', found its way into several anthologies.

Along the dark wet lanes of golden light
A midnight tippler lurches towards the night,
Bold on earth's edge, against the city's glow, he stands
And signals silence.
　　　　Universes cease
Their clamorous gyrations. All is peace.

Then, with wide-sweeping hands,
He wakes to crashing concord the massed bands
Of all creation; till, reverberate,

Tremble both earth and superstructed dome.
Leading some mad gay march, with pride elate,
Man, drunk with heady power, goes singing home.

Lord of all harmony, he grunts his raucous bars
Where street lamps blaze far brighter than the stars.[34]

Around this time, too, Paul and Alexandra collaborated on a novel, 'Murder Farm'. It is set in rural Western Australia in a landscape that may owe something to the Peel estuary where Alix spent holidays, and might be described as 'Australian Gothic', attempting with mixed success to blend the natural and the supernatural. The supernatural and perhaps the less convincing elements draw on European folklore and literature, but there is no trace of an Aboriginal presence. After their marriage Paul made one or two attempts to find a publisher but without success.[35]

Meanwhile, William Moore's reaction to *A Game of Billiards* was heartening. It was, he wrote, 'the first play to come out of West Australia with a local atmosphere and a subtlety worthy of the name of drama'.[36] He forwarded it to Carrie Tennant[37] as an entry in Sydney's Community Playhouse tournament scheduled for April 1932. The play was accepted and staged on 13 April 1932. Moore wrote: 'While the company acted their parts very well I felt that the producer hadn't caught the subtlety of the play as I hoped'. He added that he still had the utmost confidence in the play, though the opening dialogue might be pruned a little.[38] Moore's wife enlarged on the theme:

You see, a thing that is all on the surface will go down with an average audience so long as there are pretty dresses and a laugh now and then – but a play which, like Louis Esson's, or your own, goes deeper and is not external, demands the most careful representation.[39]

This advice came too late. The promotion of Australian drama, and even the fate of his own play, can no longer have been at the forefront of Paul Hasluck's thoughts. He can seldom have been busier than in the first fortnight of April 1932, preparing for his marriage to Alexandra Darker and their immediate departure for an extended trip to Britain and Europe. There were written introductions to useful contacts in England to collect, among them a characteristic testimonial from the Premier, Sir James Mitchell, to the Australian High Commissioner in London:

> Mr Hasluck is a very able young fellow and I am sure he has
> a career before him. He is keenly interested in this country
> and in all our work, and, as he now proposes to take a trip to
> the Old Land, I am anxious that he should be brought into
> contact with people who can feel assured that his character and
> reputation are entirely beyond question.[40]

On 13 April, the same evening that *A Game of Billiards* was produced, there was a graduation ceremony at The University of Western Australia's new Winthrop Hall, at which Paul was awarded one of the first Diplomas of Journalism, but he received the degree in absentia. He was preparing for another and more important ceremony.

On 14 April Paul Hasluck and Alexandra Darker were married at St Andrew's Presbyterian Church in Perth. Unusually for the time, the bride forwent the traditional symbols of womanly submissiveness: she wore no veil and was given away by her mother. That evening the couple sailed for London on the P&O liner *Balranald*. As was customary, their relatives came to Fremantle's Victoria Quay to see them off, but when it was revealed that the ship's departure was delayed until midnight the families reluctantly left. Then the young couple skipped down the gangplank to enjoy the first meal of their married life together in a Fremantle restaurant.[41] The early days on board were less than romantic, as Paul suffered from seasickness, but before long they were enjoying the voyage, with the customary stops at Colombo, Aden, Port Said and Malta. They stayed in London for three weeks before purchasing a baby Austin and touring England. Here Alix discovered she had less enthusiasm for visiting cathedrals than Paul, that English beaches were cold, stony and weed–infested, and that nightingales were 'much over-rated birds'.[42]

They spent time with Western Australian friends. Dom Serventy took them around Cambridge. In London they went dancing with another newly married couple, Nugget Coombs and his wife, Lallie, with the young women in long evening gowns, Paul in a dinner suit and Nugget resplendent in white tie and tails – for in those days the young, even if relatively impecunious, enjoyed dressing formally.[43] Nugget was undertaking a doctorate at the London School of Economics, and he and Paul sparred amicably. According to Paul in later life, Nugget's conversation was elevated with the incense of Keynesian economics and the tinkling bells of Laski, while the choir chanted of economic and social factors and the swinging censers of modern thought drove off the evil spirits of banking. Salvation lay in a managed economy, and social justice would end all disparity.[44]

Paul's temperament was sceptical and empirical, and he was never at home with theory unless it was backed by plentiful factual evidence. When Coombs called him 'one of those nineteenth-century liberals' he took it as a compliment.[45]

Paul and Alexandra obtained tickets for the British Library, then housed in the famous Round Room of the British Museum. He undertook research on the nineteenth century in Western Australia, including a good deal of material on settler–Aboriginal relations. Some of this material would later find its way into *Black Australians*, his first major publication on the history of Aboriginal policy. Alix was contemplating a novel set in Tudor England and read widely in sixteenth-century sources.[46] In the evenings they went to the theatre or attended lectures by eminent personalities who in Australia were only names. They listened to the elderly anthropologist Sir James Frazer, author of *The Golden Bough*, and heard a debate between G. K. Chesterton – 'a huge tubby man' – and H. G. Wells. They were taking on intellectual cargo that would stand them in good stead in the future.

In August and September they travelled in continental Europe. Paul, wishing to improve his knowledge of international affairs, enrolled for two summer schools at Geneva organised by the International Federation of League of Nations Societies.[47] He was one of 122 participants, about a third of them from the United Kingdom (among whom he was numbered). In an anticipation of his stance in later life, he found himself more cautious than many of his fellow students about the prospects for permanent peace and disarmament. He was considerably involved in discussions with Canadians and South Africans about the economic and international future for the self-governing members of the British Commonwealth, and was enlightened by encounters with Indian students, whose views on the future of their country ranged widely but mostly showed a strong urge for self-determination. The summer schools would prove a useful foundation for a future diplomat and foreign minister. In these weeks Paul and Alexandra also travelled in France and Germany. Although the Nazis were on the ascent in Germany they were not yet in office, and Paul learned that many still considered a second world war unthinkable. 'The year 1932', he wrote, 'was possibly the last year in Western Europe when life was light-hearted'.[48]

This comment referred to the international situation, but it has since been criticised as underestimating the impact of the Depression.[49] Paul was by no means insensitive to poverty. Back in London he was appalled at the 'abject poverty, personal hardship and hopeless inactivity in Britain', and spent ten weeks as a volunteer worker with two missions to the slums, one Anglican and the other Salvation Army. He sent the *West Australian* some graphic accounts of existence among the aged and unemployed, whose lot was cast in a more disheartening social and physical setting than anything known in Australia.[50] The experience did nothing to radicalise his political views, but left him with a strengthened social conscience.

In January 1933 Paul and Alix overlanded to Naples, where they joined the *Orsova* for the return trip to Australia. Alix remembered the voyage as much more agreeable than the journey over. The lecturer in charge of history at The University of Western Australia, Fred Alexander,[51] who had been a delegate to the League of Nations during his sabbatical year, and his wife, Grethe, were also on board. During the voyage Alexander persuaded Paul to enrol for the degree of Bachelor of Arts at the university as a part-time student. Alix always claimed that Paul made up his mind after encouragement from her mother and herself, but if Alexander did not provoke the moment of decision he at least ensured that Paul was able to make a late enrolment after the academic year had started.[52]

Their tickets enabled them to go on to Sydney without extra cost, but Alix preferred to disembark at Fremantle to spend time with her mother and friends. Paul went for his first visit to the Eastern States. In Sydney he visited William Moore and his wife, and spent an evening with the engineer who designed the recently opened Sydney Harbour Bridge, Dr Job Bradfield, an old friend of Alix's father. He also saw Canberra and Melbourne for the first time, and visited Vance and Nettie Palmer, at that time two of the most influential and persevering advocates for Australian literature. Passing through Adelaide he called on his parents, who had recently been transferred back there. Before leaving Perth they helped Lewis Hasluck to buy another 20 acres (8.1 hectares) to add to his smallholding, stipulating as good Salvation Army folk that the land should be used for growing only currant vines, not wine varieties.[53]

Back in Perth in late March, Paul found the *West Australian* housed in handsome new custom-built premises, though his colleagues complained that the new building had not coped well with Perth's worst heatwave in years. The political scene was dominated by a campaign for Western Australia's secession from the Commonwealth. With his strong sense of Australian nationalism Paul, albeit a third-generation Western Australian, was opposed to secession. Alix, whose sympathies were more local and personal, favoured it despite her family background in Queensland and New South Wales. Many voters of t'othersider origins supported secession; it was a striking proof of Paul's ideas about the assimilative quality of Western Australian society. As they walked away from casting their votes at the referendum on the issue in April 1933 and found that they had cancelled each other out, they agreed: 'Well that was a waste of time'.[54] Neither of them at that time placed politics at the forefront of their lives, although even then Alix's opinions tended to be more conservative than Paul's.

It might have seemed that, after attending to the normal priorities of the newly married, such as providing themselves with a house and furniture, they would resume the cultural activities that had engrossed them during their courtship: creative writing, theatre, renewed work with the Historical Society. They would indeed contribute to all these activities during the 1930s, but Paul's energies were about to be absorbed by a cause that would be one of the major challenges of his life. This was the condition of Western Australia's Aboriginal people.

Chapter 4

Encountering Black Australians

With all his excursions into drama and publishing as well as his responsibilities as a senior journalist, the issue that during the 1930s came to have the most significance for Hasluck's future was a growing interest in Western Australia's Aboriginal minority. In the Kimberley district and the inland of the state, a few Indigenous groups still pursued the hunter-gatherer life of their predecessors. Many more camped as workers and dependants on pastoral stations, where they could maintain links with their country and traditions. Change came more radically for the Nyungar, Wongi and Yamatji peoples of the South West. In the 1850s and 1860s the British Government in its wisdom sent to Western Australia nearly 10,000 male convicts with no women. Many fathered children on Aboriginal women, and these families survived as a useful if casual workforce in country districts; some became smallholders. Convict ancestry and Aboriginal ancestry were not social advantages in colonial Western Australia, but, with their reluctance to probe the skeletons in other people's cupboards, the colonists of that generation often resorted to a policy of 'Don't ask, don't tell'.

In 1905, the year of Hasluck's birth, a well-intentioned royal commission resulted in legislation placing all Aboriginal people and many of part-Aboriginal descent under the control of a 'Chief Protector of Aborigines'. At the same time the state government promoted the rapid expansion of the wheat belt into the lands east of the Avon River, which had previously been covered by pastoral leases for light winter grazing, where the Nyungar could travel and camp unmolested. Many were now obliged to live in insanitary and under-resourced camps outside the small country towns of the South West. There they were gradually debarred from schools and other facilities in response to local prejudice rationalised as a concern for hygiene. In the eyes of at least one Nyungar spokesman, the responsibility lay with the newcomers among the wheat-belt farming families, many of whom came from outside Western Australia, 'as the "old-timers" generally treated the Aborigines well'.[1] This process was not systematic and took some years, so that Hasluck's memory was accurate when he remembered the Collie and Guildford of his youth as taking Aboriginal people for granted as part of the general community. As he recalled:

They troubled nobody, and nobody troubled them in the easy rent-free part-nomadic life they preferred…The general opinion in the nineteen-twenties in the South-West, as I remember it, was that they were decent well-behaved people, who might be a bit different from the rest of us but who were entitled to live in the way they chose.[2]

During the late 1920s, Hasluck showed a developing awareness and interest in Aboriginal culture, an interest stimulated by his work in oral history and curiosity about the Aboriginal origins of placenames.[3] He picked up a number of stories from the Minang region of the Nyungar (in the hinterland of Albany), and pieced them together in an article in the *Black Swan*.[4] At an adult education class in 1929, Hasluck won the approval of Katharine Susannah Prichard and dismayed a university academic by arguing that Australian history began many centuries before the Dutch navigators of the seventeenth century. This was not the perspective of many historians at that time, and showed a quickening recognition that the Aboriginal people were the first Australians.

During 1930 and 1931 he made friends with Jesse Hammond, an energetic and lively minded old colonist with considerable knowledge of the Nyungar people of earlier generations.[5] Hasluck encouraged him to write it all down, and in July 1932 while in England, he received a letter from Hammond reporting that he had completed the manuscript 'History of the Natives of the South-West' and had shown it to several authorities such as Dr Battye, the State Librarian, and Mr Neville, the Chief Protector.[6] 'I am hoping to see it after it has passed through your hands', Hammond wrote. '[Y]ou will quite understand that I give you a free hand just how, and where you like with the history, feeling that you will do me justice in all cases'.[7] After returning to Perth in 1933, Hasluck gave the manuscript careful editorial attention, and it was published under the title *Winjan's People*.

In the introduction Hasluck wrote:

Mr Hammond's story stands as he told it – a piece of evidence which anthropologists will be able to evaluate as they deem fit, and which the ordinary reader will find all the more interesting because it is plainly and honestly told...He hopes there is something of value in it, and that those who read may have their interest aroused in the human people whose land we have taken and whose lives we have blighted.[8]

As this passage shows, from history Hasluck was moving to a growing concern with the problems of the present. Political consciousness was also beginning to stir among families of Nyungar descent. In 1925 the state parliament contemptuously threw out a proposal to allow 'half-castes'[9] qualified to vote at Commonwealth elections to enter their names on the state electoral roll. This provoked a number of South West families who fell into this category to demand the full rights of citizenship. In March 1928, seven of their spokesmen went to the Premier, Philip Collier, with their grievances. The *West Australian* reported the meeting sympathetically, and if Hasluck was not the journalist who covered it, he certainly knew the men concerned. He sympathised with their wish for acceptance into a mainstream community that rejected their right of choosing assimilation. Collier, prompted by Neville at his most supercilious, did nothing.

Conditions worsened for the Aboriginal people of the South West during the Depression of the early 1930s. Even Neville admitted in 1932

that never before have the natives sunk to such a condition of penury…Eking out an existence on Government rations alone, they are undoubtedly deteriorating, particularly the children… Deaths due to influenza and pulmonary causes are steadily on the increase.[10]

It was not just that it was much more difficult to find even casual jobs in the face of competition from the hundreds of white unemployed who were taking to the bush in search of work. The authorities classified as many people as possible as 'Aborigines' because the sustenance rates for which they were eligible were much lower than for non-Aboriginal unemployed. Hasluck knew of one case where two ex-servicemen of part-Aboriginal descent were working on the roads with other unemployed

> but, on their ancestry being discovered, they were denied
> sustenance and required to live on a native camping reserve
> and subsist on native rations. Thus men who had been living
> a normal life were forced back to the economic level of
> detribalised aborigines.[11]

Urged by local residents, the Aborigines Department took to rounding up the part-Aboriginal people in country towns and dumping them in the thoroughly unsatisfactory government settlement at Moore River, 120 kilometres north of Perth. The Guildford fringe dwellers were among the first to be compulsorily resettled in 1931. In January 1933, while the Haslucks were abroad, more than eighty Aboriginal people were rounded up from the Northam camp and forced into the overcrowded Moore River on spurious grounds of hygiene.[12]

Returning from his work in the London slums with 'a livened concern for the underprivileged and with a clearer resolve that in working to make a better Australia we all had to work for social justice as well as for cultural advancements',[13] Hasluck found that during his absence an Australian Aborigines Amelioration Association had been set up by a number of organisations led by the Women's Service Guild. A fellow journalist, Walter Chinnery, persuaded him to join, although, as he later wrote, 'my only personal experience with Aborigines had not disclosed any contemporary social problem':

At that time those of us who were reformers, did not think of race conflict or occupy our minds with racial issues. Hence we had no predisposition to regard all aborigines as being the same and as being necessarily a separate race requiring separate development. Rather we saw a small underprivileged minority of Australians at all stages of transition to civilized habit... We thought then that they would eventually merge into the Australian community and assumed that this was the best thing that could happen to them. Hence those who were already living close to the whites should be given further opportunities of 'advancing', and additional measures should be taken in health, hygiene, education and employment to encourage others to move closer to whites. There should be no discrimination against them but encouragement to 'improve' – a word which really meant becoming more like white people...We should not hope for 'sudden salvation' or try to hustle people into a new way of life but work steadily for a gradual move upwards generation by generation.[14]

In 1933 he found a kindred spirit in Sister Kate Clutterbuck, an energetic seventy-year-old who after thirty years of service in an Anglican orphanage wanted to set up a home for part-Aboriginal children in need of care. With boyhood recollections of his parents' work at Collie to convince him of the value of such institutions, Hasluck helped and encouraged her. In little more than a year Sister Kate succeeded in establishing a cottage home at Queen's Park, in what was then a semi-rural environment about 10 kilometres south-east of Perth's central business district. At first the site was 'just a sandpatch with a three-strand wire fence in a state of dilapidation', but the buildings were clean and well run, and improvements followed. Although Sister Kate accepted state government support through the Chief Protector of Aborigines, A. O. Neville, she rejected his suggestion that the children should be taught in a segregated schoolroom. She insisted that they go to the local state school, and Hasluck supported her. There would be no segregation. 'Her purpose was that they were young Australians who had the same opportunities. She had great compassion and she loved', wrote Hasluck.[15] Some contend that standards fell away after Sister Kate's death in 1951, but her regime was one to foster Hasluck's confidence in the benefits of institutionalised care.

Consciences were stirring during 1933. A recent arrival in Perth, a Queensland pastoralist's daughter, Mary Montgomerie Bennett, used her influential contacts in London to publicise Aboriginal disadvantages.[16] In his later years Hasluck considered that her confrontational style led only to 'the customary unintelligent debate in which some people were only finding fault and other people only offering excuses',[17] but she got results. The ensuing controversy prodded the state government into appointing the first royal commission for thirty years to investigate the legal, social and economic position of Aboriginal people in Western Australia. The Royal Commissioner, Henry Moseley,[18] had no specialised knowledge of Aboriginal affairs, but was a seasoned magistrate often used by state governments when an inquiry requiring the application of common sense was necessary. Hoping the investigation might 'not be just a shallow report about present-day wrongs and the answers to recent complaints', Hasluck wrote a series of articles for the *West Australian* in March 1934, tracing the development of Aboriginal policy during the last century and calling for 'a calm examination of facts and…steady and unsentimental but boldly idealistic thinking about the facts'.[19]

This call for calm and rational thought may have been designed to appeal to the hard heads in government, but the articles were infused with moral passion. Foreshadowing many of the themes he would develop in his first major publication, *Black Australians*, he argued that there had been no planning for the future of Aboriginal Western Australians in the direction of either assimilation or separate development because of the widespread but false belief that they were doomed to extinction. He sardonically predicted a report of the future: 'This day the black population passed away peacefully after a long and painful illness during which it received the solicitude of its friends'. 'We have pauperized them', Hasluck wrote, claiming that 'Generally speaking, throughout the century, our intentions towards the aborigines have been entirely honourable. In the sum of effects our performance has been villainous'. The time was overdue for shaping policies based on a far wider knowledge of Aboriginal society and a clear commitment to spending money on these policies. Hasluck's articles marked a shift in policy at the *West Australian*. As recently as 1932, during his absence overseas, the newspaper had seriously conjectured that two German aviators forced down in a remote part of the Kimberley district might have been eaten by Aboriginal people.[20] In fact, they were eventually rescued by Aboriginal people. It was high time to break from these demeaning stereotypes.

As a result of his newspaper articles it was arranged that Hasluck would accompany Moseley on the royal commission's fieldwork. He arranged leave of absence for three months from the *West Australian* and his university studies, and handed over to his wife his duties as honorary secretary of the Historical Society. In this role Alexandra had to fend off a certain amount of patronisation from the older ladies in the society, but she held her own in a fierce debate about a cache of a convict's letters recently discovered at Toodyay. Several of the older members wanted the letters destroyed or suppressed, arguing that 'the State had been founded as a free colony by gentlefolk; the convicts came later and unwanted, and should not be associated with it'.[21] The letters survived, and Alexandra Hasluck later used them as the basis of one of the first serious works on Western Australia's convict past. The episode illustrated that many Western Australians disliked raking over the more disturbing aspects of their history.

During April and May, Moseley, sometimes accompanied by Hasluck, inspected the Aboriginal reserves in the South West, finding little good to say about the conditions there, especially at Moore River. At the end of May the royal commission – Moseley; its secretary, David Hayles; Paul Hasluck; and a driver – moved on to the Kimberley district. It was fifty years since this northern province of Western Australia had been occupied by a pincer movement of overlanding cattlemen from Queensland and New South Wales, and Western Australians arriving mainly by sea. In many places, after initial years of mortal conflict, Aboriginal inhabitants and pastoralists arrived at a regime where the former provided an unpaid labour force for the cattle stations and in return were given rations and allowed to remain camped on their own country with time out during the wet season for traditional hunting and rituals. Poor beef prices in the 1920s meant that many cattlemen depended for survival on an Aboriginal workforce. But even in the 1920s there had been incidents of frontier violence, while in areas too remote for profitable pastoral activity a considerable number of traditional hunter-gatherers remained, some of them in occasional contact with Christian missions.

The inquiry began at the port of Wyndham, a single street squeezed between a barren hill and the sluggish waters of Cambridge Gulf, with the district's only meatworks at its northern end. Hasluck was already struck by the contrast between the ancient landscape and Aboriginal culture, and the ephemeral structures marking fifty years of modern settlement, putting his thoughts into poetry:

> *The muddy tide streams up the gulf*
> *Behind the iron-roof town;*
> *Mangroves, hot marsh, gaunt jetty piles*
> *Are slowly sinking down,*
>
> *Twice daily, under sun or moon*
> *Tide masks with watery change*
> *The red threat of eternity*
> *Bared on the stony range…*
>
> *Men in frail chronometric faith*
> *Tick-tocking hours ordain —*
> *Little split pieces of their life*
> *Cut up and grouped again.*

Wrist watch of clerk or magistrate
The painfully turning wheels
Dragged by the drooping donkey team;
The hotel bell for meals;

The sunburnt winchman's clattering speed;
Slow pendulum of bales
The tally clerk's completed sheet;
The closing time for mails;...

While the grey sandplain spreads beyond
The compass of their stride
And the wide plateau stretches north
Where stockmen never ride...

Come tide or ebb, the glistening shores
The tide of doom yet hear
Where an old tribesman drones his chant
And flakes his crystal spear.

The ancient voice is heard again
Of men who knew of timeless things
And yearly found beyond the range
The constant, life-renewing springs.[22]

During June the party travelled in a Dodge utility along the unmade roads between Wyndham and Broome, encountering a world far different from the rural South West. As Anna Haebich has commented:

Hasluck seems to have been overwhelmed by his first glimpses of the Kimberley landscape and described flying over 'a land which seems not to belong to mankind, but to the sun, a land which is so vast and whose meaning is so hard to grasp, that any idea of a Providence who made the earth as a garden for the chosen beings to inhabit must be lost.'[23]

But, as she also noted, although he was impressed with the contribution of Aboriginal workers to the pastoral industry:

he was concerned by the pastoralists' attitudes as expressed in such comments as 'the black should never leave the wood heap' and the 'less a boy knows about things the better'. He concluded that the pastoralists' 'humaneness' was 'of the type which the Royal Society for the Prevention of Cruelty to Animals lives to foster.'[24]

At Argyle station homestead, later the site of the Ord River dam, Moseley interviewed the pastoralist M. P. Durack while Hasluck and the younger members of the party climbed a nearby hill in company with Durack's daughters, Mary and Elizabeth, later notable as writer and artist.[25] The doyen of Kimberley cattlemen, M. P. Durack spoke with the authority of nearly fifty years' experience when he made Hasluck aware of his views on the proper relationship between the races in northern Australia. 'We are, in a negative way, attached to them and they to us', claimed Durack:

Perhaps you of the South will ask why, after all these years, there is no deeper feeling than a 'negative attachment'...The

69

fact as we see it is this – the man in the country who goes in for talking to the black, exchanging ideas with him, asking him if he is satisfied with his lot and treating him literally as his 'black brother', receives no respect from the native in exchange...[26]

The pastoralists, said Durack, tried to be kind and just but lacked the time or training to do more than that:

We of the North, in our philosophy (a lackadaisical one if you like) believe the blacks have, in their present state the most enviable of attributes, contentment. By raising their standard of living and education you may take it from them. Is there some method by which you can give them more than you take away?[27]

However understandable these attitudes may have been in the Kimberley context, they raised issues far removed from the grievances of the Nyungar people of the South West. Nor was Durack's advice about keeping an appropriate distance from the Aboriginal people compatible with some of Hasluck's own experiences. At the government station at Moola Bulla, near Halls Creek, Hasluck went riding with some of the Aboriginal station workers, developing 'a feeling of companionship' for them.[28] He also continued to respond to the environment:

This is not a young land. This rocky world is very old and tired. It is because we are not old in wisdom, as the Hebrews and Chinese are, that we blunder in its wastes and find no meaning in its wilderness except thirst. We are too young in mind to read its secrets.[29]

At Wallal, between Broome and Port Hedland, he wrote that 'Watching the tide on a bare shore, one senses, in the crowded, stunning impact of a single second of revelation, the meaning of timelessness and eternity'.[30] Early in July the party enjoyed a spell in the relative amenity of Broome, then a pearling port past its best days, and Alix took the opportunity for a few days' holiday with her husband. After this interlude the royal commission went by sea to visit the missions on the west Kimberley coast. A memorable day for Hasluck was spent at the Munja mission at Port George IV, travelling in the mission ketch with its Aboriginal skipper, Stephen Booramoolpul:

> Two Australians sat on the tilted deck of the ketch, listening
> to the cluck of waters and the music of wind, and plumbed
> the depths of patriotism, absorbing the goodness of the land,
> watching the outlines of the rock cape against the pale grey
> sky. 'Him proper good place.'[31]

'Patriotism' was not quite the right word in the context of Aboriginal society, but Hasluck was trying to communicate to his readers a sense of profoundly felt identity with country on which he and Stephen Booramoolpul could find common ground, just as the Aboriginal people of Moola Bulla would have responded to his love of horses.[32] It was rare for a writer at that time to try to express emotional empathy with Aboriginal Australians and to acknowledge that Aboriginal capacity, when given a chance to express itself, was not inherently inferior to that of other Australians. It was challenging to reconcile such insights with the social and political questions of the place of Aboriginal Australians in the contemporary community.

Hasluck also condemned the government's neglect of Aboriginal health, epitomised for him by an encounter with sixty lepers camped without shelter in the Derby police paddock awaiting shipment to Darwin.[33] He demanded the appointment of a travelling medical officer, and establishment of a clinic for the treatment of leprosy and venereal diseases, with regular regional medical surveys. He urged that white Australians develop a concept of trusteeship towards the Aboriginal population, actively working to improve their future.[34] He had encountered the concept of trusteeship at the League of Nations and in his university studies; now his visit to the Kimberley district showed an opening for its practical application in Australia.

By this time Moseley was bored with travelling and impatient to return to Perth. According to Hasluck, he 'spent most of his time reading novels in the cabin or sitting looking dignified in khaki shorts on the deck...That man's barren intellect shows up very shabbily outside polite society'.[35] The royal commission had still to visit the Pilbara district, but spent little time there, and its work was superficial. Hasluck reported from Port Hedland: 'This morning we spent ten minutes in the Court while Harry bullied some halfcastes'.[36] In later life his assessment of Moseley was kinder. Hasluck wrote of 'enjoying his confidence and repaying it with discretion', and acknowledged that Moseley allowed him, separately from the work of the royal commission, to send reports to Perth on the problems of disease among the Aboriginal population.[37]

Moseley's report, submitted early in 1935, proved to be unadventurous and bland, strongest on legal and administrative matters. He candidly admitted that in drawing his conclusions he preferred to rely on his own common sense rather than trying to reconcile the contradictory opinions submitted to him in evidence. He identified the 'half-caste' as 'the great problem confronting the community today' because of their increasing numbers and the poor condition of most of the town camps, and recommended the establishment of special community settlements for part-Aboriginal families.[38] Hasluck shared this concern; possibly he had some influence in generating it. It was probably at this time that he 'knew the disheartening experience...of failing to find a single member of Parliament who would make a speech on the subject'.[39]

He was dissatisfied when legislation prepared in 1936 as a result of the Moseley commission went no further than extending the control of the Chief Protector of Aborigines (now to be renamed the Commissioner for Native Affairs with enlarged powers) over a wider range of people defined as Aboriginal. Once again he used his access to the media to press his arguments. Thinly disguised as 'Our special correspondent', Hasluck published four articles in the *West Australian* asking whether these people were always to remain a separate caste or whether they would be assimilated into the rest of the population. '*If there are any feelings of humanity in the community the present order will not be allowed to continue*', he wrote.[40] Many led lives without hope or dignity. Instead of keeping them in a segregated category they should be assisted into the mainstream community. Farm schools should bring education to the children, and settlements be provided for the aged and infirm.[41] Still wedded to the frugality taught by the Depression, the state government took no notice of these suggestions beyond constructing a single village with several huts and a kindergarten.[42] Meanwhile state parliament passed the 1936 legislation with little change.

Commissioner Neville envisaged such developments as leading to the eventual absorption of the Aboriginal minority into the mainstream population. In April 1937 he persuaded the first conference of Commonwealth and state Aboriginal authorities to resolve that 'the destiny of the natives of Aboriginal origin, but not of the full blood, lies in their ultimate absorption by the people of the Commonwealth'.[43] Hasluck's position at this time was more nuanced. Assimilation, he thought, did not require the abandonment of all Aboriginality. It called for:

> conformity to the minimum standard that the community set for people to live alongside each other and to share the same opportunities, privileges and responsibilities. At that time, while recognizing that social acceptability also required that the Aborigines should wish to be accepted, I did not pause over that question as long as I would do now [1988] for, in those days, all the signs we saw were that aboriginal society was breaking down, tradition and tribal discipline were weakening, and Aborigines themselves were being attracted more and more towards the ways of the white man and the benefits that came from conformity.[44]

Assimilated Aboriginal people might still cherish their ethnic traditions, just as Australians of Scottish descent took pride in their clans. What mattered for Hasluck was acceptance of a common citizenship, and the opportunities and responsibilities that went with it.

Judith Brett has commented that Hasluck showed compassion and a deep interest in the fate of the Aboriginal Australians, a belief in their capacity, intelligence and moral sensitivity in an era when few gave them a second thought. But, she added, he lacked empathy for Aboriginal attachment to their culture:

> So he sees traditional Aboriginal society as a bit like a trap for people. And if only they could escape from that like he escaped from his Salvation Army childhood then they can make of themselves what they like and become members of mainstream Australian society.[45]

This judgement tends to overlook Hasluck's responsiveness to Aboriginal feeling for country, and it is worth noting that as Minister for Territories he is known to have acquired a substantial collection of Aboriginal artefacts and artworks.[46] Hasluck's observations during the 1930s suggested that many younger Aboriginal Australians were choosing to leave traditional society, only to find no acceptance in the outside world. The issue was how they could live 'not alongside us, but with us'. He was not urging that Aboriginal people should make themselves into imitation white Australians, but that they should have access to the same opportunities and rights of citizenship.

Hasluck's travels with the Moseley commission sharpened his awareness of the variety and complexity of Western Australia's Aboriginal population, but the Nyungar preoccupied him most. Though he might urge the acceptance of mixedblood Nyungar as fellow citizens, he was beginning to sense that it was already too late. The 1930s Depression took away their chances of remaining in the workforce. Through legislation and prejudice the Western Australian majority were coercing the Nyungar into regarding themselves as a people apart who must find their sense of identity in their Aboriginal ancestry. Banished to the under-resourced and ghetto-like camps and reserves of the South West as a social problem, the Nyungar were coming to regard themselves as a 'separated caste'.[47] 'I myself did not concentrate as much as I might have done on this question', Hasluck later reflected. 'The situation needed a single-minded fanatic.'[48] In the rather torpid state politics of the 1930s it was difficult to see how even a single-minded fanatic could have made much impact after parliament had diluted the already sanitised recommendations of the Moseley commission. During the next few years Hasluck found a different way of contributing to an understanding of Aboriginal policy. He would become a historian.

He was now qualified to enrol as a postgraduate at The University of Western Australia after receiving his Bachelor of Arts degree at a ceremony on 2 March 1937. His tertiary studies had not been entirely smooth sailing. In 1933 he was given credit for two units undertaken as part of his Diploma of Journalism, and passed two more subjects with distinction. He was enrolled for two subjects in 1934, but his absence with the Moseley commission meant that he missed the whole of the second term and had to work hard to catch up after his return. In order to attend daytime lectures he arranged with the *West Australian* to take the shift as night subeditor, working from 5.00 pm to around 2.00 am, and returning home to sleep until midmorning. Alix agreed to this regime, but she recalled that 'for several days we would communicate with each other only by means of notes'.[49]

His schedule was disrupted in November 1934 by an urgent call to visit his father who was seriously ill in Adelaide, so he had to sit the examinations in that city. He still managed to secure a distinction in economics and to pass with credit in Fred Alexander's class, 'Modern Political Institutions', which he remembered as 'a tough course but a good one'. Based on constitutional history and some study of the machinery of government in English-speaking democracies, the unit included the stages by which members of the British Commonwealth evolved towards self-government, with a hint that the Asian and African members of the Commonwealth might at some future time evolve towards autonomy on similar lines. Hasluck considered that the course 'had a strong influence on shaping my views on politics, public administration, and the teaching of political science', and this would be of consequence in his future career.[50]

He experienced an unexpected setback at the university examinations in 1935. Although he gained 'A' grades (distinctions) in English and French he failed in 'Modern European History'. Fred Alexander, who taught the subject, used to say that Hasluck spent too much time on his extracurricular activities; even so, the verdict may have been a little harsh.[51] It may be that the young man found more attraction in European literature than in the politics of Bismarck's Germany and the French Third Republic. He repeated the unit in 1936 and passed it, together with a unit in economics, with a 'B' grade (credit). Altogether his record was good enough to allow him to proceed to postgraduate research. At that time this was a decision taken by few. Australian universities offered only the Master of Arts as a research degree, as the PhD was not to arrive until after the Second World War. Western Australia's own history provided a focus for Hasluck's research interests. The state's history to 1900 had recently been covered by Dr James Sykes Battye in a magisterial volume,[52] and there was little point, so soon after its publication, in attempting to go over the same ground. There was an obvious need for a biography of Western Australia's local hero, the explorer–politician Sir John Forrest, who died in 1918. The subject attracted Hasluck sufficiently for him to conduct a number of interviews with old colonists who had known Forrest when young, and he wrote a well-constructed first chapter for a potential biography.[53] But the theme that increasingly claimed his attention was the relationship between Aboriginal people and settlers in Western Australia during the first decades of contact after the colony was founded in 1829.

As early as 1932, during his visit to London, he had taken notes on the subject at the British Library. Since that time his involvement in questions of Aboriginal welfare kept driving him back to question how it was, despite many stated good intentions by government officials, that the plight of Aboriginal people in Western Australia had turned out so wretchedly. In November 1937 he enrolled for the degree of Master of Arts, working on the topic 'Official policy and public opinion towards the Aborigines of Western Australia from 1829 to 1897'.[54] In later life he sometimes wondered if he 'might have done better by campaigning than by academic study during 1937 and 1938',[55] but the political climate in Western Australia was discouraging. His research must have been a lonely enterprise, since his supervisor Fred Alexander claimed no more than a layman's knowledge of Aboriginal policy, and there was probably only one other postgraduate in Australia working in the field.[56]

Despite a life busy with many other activities he completed the thesis for submission in January 1940. The two examiners were warm in their praise. The internal examiner, the Warden of St George's College, 'Josh' Reynolds, admitted to disagreement with some of Hasluck's conclusions, 'but the only other general criticism which I would like to offer is like that of a man who, having drunk one goblet of elixir, asks for more'.[57] The influential professor of anthropology at The University of Sydney, A. P. Elkin, considered the thesis 'a first class piece of historical research'. He admired its analytical quality, requested a copy for the Fisher Library, and recommended publication.[58] It was not long before Melbourne University Press accepted the manuscript, but *Black Australians* did not appear until 1942, by which time the debate on Aboriginal policy was at a hiatus while Australia confronted the most critical stage of the Pacific War. Only 500 copies were produced, and Hasluck felt that 'its publication attracted little notice'.[59]

In academic circles at least *Black Australians* was enthusiastically reviewed, and established Hasluck's credentials as a scholar. Maintaining his enthusiasm, Elkin wrote that in its combination of academic quality and first-hand experience, balancing official policy with public opinion, 'Mr Hasluck's book is an outstanding contribution to Australian historical research'. He added 'he has set the standard for similar research into native problems elsewhere in Australia'.[60] Another Sydney anthropologist, Ian Hogbin, while suggesting that Hasluck might have made more of land as a factor in explaining conflict between Aboriginal people and pastoralists, given both economies required extensive tracts of country, pronounced the book 'from every point of view a notable contribution to Australian history'.[61] A respected academic turned member of the House of Representatives, Grenfell Price, wanted to discuss Hasluck's views on the federal policies that should be adopted in the light of Western Australian experience.[62] Altogether, *Black Australians* made more impact than Hasluck allowed himself to imagine.

The relevance of his historical approach lay in his insistence that official policy towards Aboriginal people had gone astray from the good intentions of the early nineteenth century. A hundred years later, policymakers needed to recover an ethical perspective, beginning with recognition that the citizen rights of the original occupants of Australia were absolutely equal to those of other Australians. Hasluck argued that when Western Australia was first colonised in the 1830s and 1840s, the British Government expected that Aboriginal Australians would be protected while they were drawn towards Christianity and 'civilised' practices. He quoted Governor John Hutt as asking in 1839:

> Are they to be swept off by aggression and disease...or, if they survive, will it be to sink into a state little better than the slave, or gradually to be absorbed into and become one people with their intruders?

Hutt could not find in traditional Aboriginal society the codes of moral obligations, religion and governance that would enable them to develop a social system as a separate community: 'If the aborigines and colonists are destined to occupy this land in common as British subjects they ought to be encouraged to mingle together as one people'.[63] However paternalistic, such a view at least acknowledged the common humanity of Aboriginal people and settlers.

Later in the nineteenth century it became increasingly common for the settlers to see the Aboriginal people as subhuman. By the time the British Government handed over responsibility for Aboriginal policy to the Western Australian authorities in 1897, Hasluck wrote:

> With nearly seventy years of practical experience to give
> them the advantage of information and the disadvantage of
> preconceived opinions, with the settled ideas that the natives
> were dying out and were of inferior class, and without a single
> shred of idealism, the people of Western Australia received
> into their care the sacred charge of several thousands of human
> beings. The Imperial Government ended its rule of uncertainty,
> inconsistency, and neglect and handed on a charge that was
> ill-kept, contaminated, hopeless and despised.[64]

What should be done in the mid-twentieth century? Some recommended the segregation of Aboriginal people in inviolable reserves[65] but Hasluck rejected this expedient. 'There is an air of unreality about such a policy, as it can only be applied to-day in the unwanted parts of the continent', he wrote, 'but its acceptance is further proof of the continued rejection of such a policy as that proposed in Western Australia in the eighteen-thirties and 'forties'.[66] That policy, of regarding Aboriginal Australians 'as a British subject and as a fit candidate for civilization', should, he thought, be revived, though it might be necessary to impose protective restrictions. The starting point, wrote Hasluck,

> is that the native and half-caste are British subjects to whom
> special conditions are being applied temporarily, not that they
> are primitive savages who may become British subjects if they
> can fight their way out of their natural disadvantages.[67]

In 1940 this was radical thinking, but it would be more than ten years before Hasluck had an opportunity of translating his ideas into policy, and during that time the world would have undergone momentous changes.

Chapter 5

'We had to do it ourselves'

While Paul Hasluck was travelling with the Moseley commission, Alexandra had discovered the site of their future home, a block of land in Claremont with views of the Swan River that could never be built out. There they built the house, 2 Adams Road, that would be the family home for the rest of their lives. They moved there late in 1935. Paul remembered: 'There was still a certain formality: when we moved into our own house in Adams Road four or five ladies from neighbouring houses left visiting cards'.[1] They had a number of academic neighbours, among them Fred and Grethe Alexander and Walter Murdoch's daughter Catherine with her husband, the gentle, scholarly young Englishman Alec King. Claremont, midway between Fremantle and Perth, was an old suburb retaining something of a village character, with tradesmen, grocers and butchers who made household deliveries and knew their customers. The river was in constant use for fishing and boating. The neighbourhood was still rural enough for Paul to hire a horse regularly and enjoy riding in the bush.

Once established, the Haslucks hoped for a family, but for some years children were slow in coming. The conventions of the time meant that Alexandra did not hold a job of her own. In her autobiography she recalled a routine of morning teas and lunches with her friends, with occasional evenings enlivened by 'Mah Jong parties, usually all female, when we talked and laughed, with cries of "Pung" when the game demanded it, and swopped [sic] some dirty jokes our husbands had gathered'.[2] Privately she honed her literary skills by writing historical articles for the *West Australian*, and worked for some years on an historical novel entitled *Tudor Blood*. Unfortunately, London publishers rejected it because, while the research and writing were good, the characterisation was not.[3]

Paul's literary ambitions were less clear. Journalism, as he recalled later, 'was ceasing to engage the whole of my curiosity, enthusiasm or energy'.[4] He had no ambition to become a managing editor, and friends noticed that he did not push himself forward.[5] A perceptive colleague thought that after returning from the Moseley commission

> he was very dissatisfied, he didn't mix with other people except one or two he was friendly with. Didn't care much for the people above him and became somewhat alienated away from the job.[6]

In new premises and under new ownership, the *West Australian* office struck him as changing 'from a club into a factory', where commercial pressures led to declining standards, although a twenty-first century reader of the *West* in the 1930s might find that deterioration hard to detect. At the same time he was questioning his future as a creative writer. He had plenty of ideas for novels, most of them in the 'family saga' format employed by contemporary writers such as Georges Duhamel, Hugh Walpole and the somewhat older John Galsworthy. Brian Penton's novels,

Landtakers and *Inheritors*, tracing the impact of the Australian environment on a settler family, stimulated Paul to contemplate a novel set in Western Australia's South West, to be entitled *Into the Forest*. When he reviewed *Inheritors*, Penton wrote to him:

> To read some criticism which shows that the author of it has read one's book and weighed its words and his own before putting his opinion forth is a rare and delightful experience.[7]

But Hasluck wrote no fiction.

In later years Paul Hasluck saw 1935 as a turning point. He concluded:

> the chief reason I never became a creative writer was that I was too considerate of others. If I had kicked over the traces, been utterly selfish, deserted my wife and given pain to my parents, my own life story might have been different...A better artist than I would have been a bigger cad.[8]

These are understandable thoughts in a man who in tractable youth and diligent young manhood never enjoyed the experience, as his friend Bob James did, of wandering footloose overseas or of taking an unpaid year off to test his vocation as a writer. Possibly these thoughts were stimulated by three months away from the routines of domesticity while he travelled with the Moseley commission. This was not the whole story. As critical of his own work as he was of other people's, he may have sensed that the qualities that made him a careful and readable historian with a shrewd sense of human motivation did not provide the spark of free-ranging imagination animating the greatest authors of fiction. Measured against them, he may have lacked confidence that he possessed that spark. Some years later, commenting on a novel (*The Little Company*) by Eleanor Dark, he wrote:

> While her method leaves an impression of great sincerity and of sensitiveness, it does not reach the standard of the greatest novelists, who give me a sense of their mastery over their creation, of their understanding of life, of their superiority over their puppets and the creatures they have animated.[9]

He applied the same standards to himself.

So, as Hasluck put it: 'I persisted in being dutiful and responsible and considerate and behaved as I was expected to behave and became a model prisoner'.[10] He never spelt out what he meant by 'a model prisoner'. It went deeper than appearances, though he was already presenting himself as a personality who was seldom seen in public without a suit and tie, and who about this time grew the neat moustache that would later become a cartoonists' trademark for him.[11] The 'model prisoner' was one who conformed to the standards expected of him by family and society, suppressing anarchic or Bohemian impulses, and with them perhaps suppressing the seeds of creativity. As a recompense for this conformity he might be enabled to serve more effectively as a citizen, and he soon schooled himself to plan his time efficiently over a remarkable range of activities. The creativity no longer directed towards writing novels found its outlet in a series of brilliant cultural initiatives. During the next five years, often in tandem with Alexandra, Paul Hasluck made an innovative and lasting impact on nearly every aspect of the intellectual life of Western Australia.

For the immediate future he resolved to confine himself to writing poetry. At that time, as literary scholar Bruce Bennett argued, Hasluck was one of the younger Australian poets reaching for a romantic nationalism that went deeper than that of the *Bulletin* bards of the 1890s. 'He contrasts the deadness of the suburbs with the mystical possibilities of the outback, the open bush. He's a bit earlier into this than some literary historians have noticed…'[12] Hasluck was scornful of:

> *The proud invocations of inbred Aussidolators*
> *Searching Lawson and Furphy for something to quote,*
> *Spinning high romance in the shoddy brutalities of Kelly,*
> *And making each speech one long peroration*
> *Hung round with the smell of stale eucalyptus.*[13]

His own feelings for country found expression in a long poem, 'Songs of Australia':

> *We have no songs ready written and set to music.*
> *Life is a song and we feel it – the swinging axe, the long clean curve*
> *   of the furrow;*
> *The buzz of the gear, click of blades and the grey fleece falling off like a*
> *   jacket, billowing white on the floor, soft to touch, wool for spinners.*
> *There's a song.*
> *And the lies told at smoke-oh – dogs we had, snakes we killed, sheep*
> *   we shore, mates we knew – all a lifetime singing again as we perch*
> *   on the woolsacks.*
> *We wrung out sweat and ate dust for the idlers, whore-keepers,*
> *   war-makers, and fat politicians.*
> *That is small; they are nothing.*[14]

A reader encountering the poem for the first time might suspect the influence of Walt Whitman or one of the later American poets who followed him, such as Carl Sandburg, but Hasluck disclaimed Whitman as a model. With his taste for French literature, he preferred to see Paul Claudel as an exemplar, and the conservative Catholic Claudel took his models from the Vulgate translation of the Old Testament psalms.[15]

What Hasluck made his own was his admiration for the rural workers he had observed in Western Australia since his boyhood, as well as an agrarian radicalism widespread in the aftermath of the 1930s Depression but now largely forgotten. In other poems he denounced:

> The whinging [sic] loungers in the city pub; the cheapjack hustler in
> the train; the politician with his jowls of lard; the shrewd accountant
> with his knowing mask and fifty bankrupt farmers in the bag; the
> golf-course pirate and the Bondi shark; and civil servants hand in
> glove with god trotting to hidden ends down devious ways.[16]

Many years later the recollection of such lines led Ric Throssell (whose own diplomatic career was considerably damaged by his left-wing sympathies) to wonder how the writer of such brave verses could transform himself into a cautious Liberal politician.[17] But Hasluck was never a socialist. Hasluck's sympathies throughout his life lay with communities of independent small farmers supporting their families on the produce of the soil. He was, after all, Lewis Hasluck's brother, and he grew up in a Western Australian generation dominated by a yeoman myth of rural productivity; but he knew that market forces often treated the smallholder unkindly and that small country towns

88

might decay even while agrarian capitalism flourished. These ideals would remain with him when in later life he came to make policy for Papua New Guinea.[18]

If his dreams of becoming a creative writer were at a standstill, he could at least do good service in promoting cultural interests in his community. During the mid-1930s discussion groups and book clubs were springing into life around Perth, and Hasluck found himself in demand as a speaker. The local office of the Australian Broadcasting Commission, under the management of Basil Kirke, was actively promoting radio talks on a wide variety of subjects. Hasluck's manner went well on radio. Between 1935 and 1937 he spoke on authors as diverse as eighteenth-century English farmer and pamphleteer William Cobbett and contemporary Australian poet Shaw Neilson, and gave numerous book reviews before drawing back to concentrate on his postgraduate research.[19] In one broadcast he used the opportunity to proclaim some challenging opinions:

The reason why a number of Australian poets and artists
have not dealt with suburban life but have scooted outback
has been that in the bush a recognisable native quality of the
place has not been obliterated. I do not advocate that the
whole land should be left in a primitive state, with white men
timorously begging pardon of the blowflies and mosquitoes for
ever intruding there at all. My point simply is that we should
work with the country to reveal the qualities that belong to its
place...I also doubt whether, so long as our physical and hence
cultural environment is covered up with so many shams and
imitations, we can hope that the environment will call forth
from us any real emotional response...

The exaggerated praise of Adam Lindsay Gordon and
of Kendall in Australian literary history is partly due to the
readiness to recognise something that resembled Swinburne,
and today the exaggerated praise given to some of the younger
poets is partly due to the resemblance between what they do
and what some other fashionable contemporary in Britain and
America is doing.

Poetry in this country is not a new art, nor was it brought
into the country by European settlers. For centuries before
ever a white man came to this country, human beings were
moved by Australian experience to deep emotion and mystical
revelation. They felt elation and also sadness from the events
of their lives – their hunting, mating, birth and death and
their fear of darkness and the unknown. They gave heightened
utterance of their experience by the rhythmic and emphatic use
of words. Corroboree songs were made by individuals. They
were learnt and passed on from group to group. Some of them
became famous among the tribes. It is not this land that is
hostile to poetry. Poetry is native to our soil.[20]

This emphasis on continuities with Aboriginal culture
matches the message that was being developed at the same
time by Rex Ingamells and the Jindyworobak movement in
South Australia.[21] But although Hasluck was in touch with
a number of poets and novelists in eastern Australia, such as
R. D. Fitzgerald, Brian Penton and Kenneth Slessor, there is
nothing in his papers to show any contact with Ingamells until
1941, when Ingamells approached him with a request to include
his poetry in a Jindyworobak anthology.[22] Hasluck did not
follow the Jindyworobak practice of trying to graft Aboriginal

language and concepts into Anglo-Australian verse. He decried a nationalism that rejected 'foreign influences', and described the Australian poet's task as 'to rediscover humility, survive the heat of a determined egalitarianism, seek again his privacy and his identity, and trace the more deeply-flowing streams of consciousness'.[23]

Probably he played his most influential part as 'Polygon', the *West Australian*'s drama critic.[24] Together with Albert Kornweibel, who as 'Fidelio' served as the newspaper's music critic, he was to have a profound impact on Perth's cultural standards during the 1930s. It was a time of great activity in the world of amateur theatre. 'There was a new play almost every week of the year, most of them competently done, and a steady audience of about a thousand for each season', Hasluck was to recall.[25] Paul and Alix attended each opening night, formally dressed like most of the audience in black tie and long frock. Afterwards they would go to Newspaper House, where she watched 'Polygon' type out his review for the following morning before finishing the evening with a late supper.[26]

'Polygon', it has been said,

> wrote with a clarity and depth of dramatic criticism unmatched
> before or since. His reviews, or perhaps more appropriately
> his essays of Shavian proportion, revealed a highly intellectual
> mind and thorough understanding of the arts.[27]

His was probably the greatest single influence in moving Perth's audiences and performers away from a diet of accepted classics and English drawing-room comedies and towards a more venturesome and international repertoire. Keen to promote

Australian drama, he gave plays by Western Australian writers his most exacting judgement. His style was still capable of
its old asperity, but he deployed it with greater subtlety. Of
the Shakespeare Club's *Romeo and Juliet* he simply commented:
'Unfortunately the prompter had also to take a leading part in
the performance'.[28] Of a comedy, he wrote: 'The cast might
have played their parts more vigorously...But, of course, one
cannot fling oneself too recklessly into the business of being
funny if one is a bit uncertain about the lines'. When the Perth
Repertory Club took over the old *West Australian* newspaper
building, Albert Kornweibel wrote a one-act play for the occasion, reviewed by 'Polygon':

And I've ever since admired enormously his skill, his discretion,

his tact and his kindness, because he didn't want to say

anything unkind about my work, but he plainly saw what

I can see now as plain as a pikestaff where it lacked, and he sort

of obliquely indicated that. But at the same time he went out of

his way to say one or two pleasant things. And that's the man

who later became Governor-General, and that's why I feel

very boastful.[29]

As a critic, Hasluck was constantly encouraging theatre
groups in Perth to venture more boldly in new directions.
When the radical-minded Workers' Art Guild was formed early
in 1936, Hasluck became an associate member, though he was
unable to share the left-wing politics of many of its leading
members.[30] He wrote enthusiastically about the guild's opening
production, Clifford Odets' *Till the Day I Die*: 'One came away
from the theatre with the excitement of a prize fight in the air',

though he added that comment on its partisan ideology would be out of place in an assessment of its public performance.[31] Hasluck commended a program combining *Waiting for Lefty* and *Where's the Bomb?* as 'meritorious dramatic propaganda', adding: 'Probably a young man would not want to take his maiden aunt to it, but his "young lady" will probably want to take him'. Although some readers of the *West Australian* denounced the guild's productions as 'coarse and vulgar pieces of Socialist propaganda', Hasluck approved of their role in stirring up 'stuffy Perth audiences' who were 'politically brassbound and flabbily cosmopolitan'.[32]

Late in 1936 the opportunity arose for him to demonstrate his ideas practically. In the previous year T. S. Eliot's *Murder in the Cathedral*, based on the life and martyrdom of St Thomas Becket was premiered in Canterbury Cathedral, the first time for centuries that a church had been used as a venue for drama. Hasluck and his friend Alec King, lecturer in English at The University of Western Australia, decided to produce the play in the open air in the quadrangle of St George's College, despite the venue's many problems of lighting and movement. 'It was a success', he remembered, 'one of the few things that have turned out better than I hoped'.[33] It played to a full house every night, and was probably the first performance of the play after the original production at Canterbury, and certainly one of the most innovative initiatives in Australian drama in the 1930s. It was followed in December 1938 with a second open-air production in the same venue, *Zeal of Thy House* by Dorothy Sayers, about the building of a medieval cathedral. Some notable names can be found on the programs of these plays. Alix Hasluck designed the costumes, and the actors included Harry Giese, later to be

Hasluck's colleague in the Northern Territory; Gordon Freeth who was to sit with him in the federal cabinet; and 'Red' Burt, who as Sir Francis Burt would be a distinguished Chief Justice of Western Australia.

'If at that time there had been any possibility of a career in the theatre, I might have chosen that direction', Hasluck was to recall.[34] As it was, from 1937 to 1939 he was to be a profoundly energising influence on drama in Western Australia. Early in May 1937 he called a meeting where he successfully promoted a plan for holding a drama festival involving as many as possible of the amateur groups springing up in both urban and rural Western Australia. The idea was widely supported. Energetic organisation ensured that the festival ran from 2 to 9 October, attracting 1,200 patrons on the first night and 6,000 over the whole week. Perhaps this reflected a recovering state economy, but it also helped that prices were kept to a maximum of 3 shillings, with many seats available at 1 shilling. Hasluck persuaded the *West Australian* to donate a prize of £75 for the best original play. It was awarded to 'The Golden Journey' by a writer concealed under the pen-name 'Jaxartes', and the action took place at the Mullewa railway station. Hasluck in his role of critic considered it 'the only play…that expresses something of the life that belongs peculiarly to Western Australia'.[35]

In 1938 and 1939 successful drama festivals were staged, providing a model without parallel elsewhere in Australia. At his own expense Hasluck travelled around Western Australia adjudicating plays presented by country drama clubs in their local halls. 'This experience', he wrote, strengthened my faith that the little theatre movement was one activity which could come close to the whole community and that in the long run there would be a better outcome from helping to improve the dispersed effort of the little theatres all over Australia than in establishing big centralized companies to play to privileged audiences in a few big cities.[36]

Problems of infrastructure had to be met. Few Western Australian towns, even Perth, possessed venues suitably designed for the performance of drama. Mostly buildings designed for other purposes, such as shire halls and church annexes, had to do duty. In 1938 Hasluck convened a working party to draw up a memorandum setting out the facilities required for good theatrical performances, including the minimum-standard requirements for stages, in the hope that local authorities and others planning the construction or renovation of public buildings could be guided by a set of workable criteria. The annual drama festivals were seen as a means of encouraging improvements and publicising information.[37] But the 1939 festival was overshadowed by the outbreak of war between Britain and her allies and Nazi Germany, and this was to put a stop to these hopeful initiatives. The next year, when Paul departed for Canberra, A. J. Bishop wrote offering him 'the somewhat empty honour' of being vice-patron of the Drama Festival, commenting:

Although your drama criticisms have been themselves the subject of very serious criticism from time to time, there is no doubt that your work in that direction is going to be sadly missed.[38]

With the same spirit of practicality that marked his promotion of drama in Western Australia, Hasluck turned to publishing. At that time Western Australia had neither a university press nor serious commercial publishers. With an enthusiastic Alix fully involved, he planned the Freshwater Bay Press, drawing on models such as the Golden Cockerel and Fanfrolico presses, which produced limited editions whose content was enhanced by good design. Eventually the Haslucks envisaged a Colonial Texts Society of perhaps 1,000 subscribers that would print the journals of early explorers and other documents from colonial history.[39] Energetically researching editing and book production, they decided to establish the venture by publishing an anthology of Paul's own verse under the title *Into the Desert*. This appeared in June 1939, and was reviewed by almost every major newspaper in Australia, something that would not be expected in the early twenty-first century. Respected critics took note of the collection. Nettie Palmer praised it, but made some informed suggestions about the improvement of internal rhythms; H. M. Green chose one or two poems for a national anthology.[40]

Most of the critics of *Into the Desert* concentrated on the verse rather than the format. To a Melbourne friend who considered they still had a lot to learn about typesetting and page management, Hasluck responded:

> I trust you may like the next one better. Both the printer
> and I and his employees will know more about things, and a
> good deal of that old prejudice against doing things in
> anything but their own accustomed way which cramps the
> average wage-earner and average employer may have been
> broken down.[41]

'The next one' was to be a translation of Bishop Salvado's memoirs on the founding of the Benedictine community at New Norcia. In June 1939 Hasluck wrote to members of the Commonwealth Literary Fund seeking support for the project, and received an encouraging response from John Curtin, who was one of its trustees.[42] But it emerged that, as Hasluck put it, 'the Micks are talking about bringing out an edition and there is no call for two'.[43]

The next publication by the Freshwater Bay Press, in March 1940, was of a different nature: *Venite Apotemus* (*Come Let Us Drink*) by 'Tom Turnspit'. The pen-name concealed the identity of Bob James, who was developing into a serious writer on food and wine, and whose learned commentary provided 'the perfect text for tackling the problems of footnotes'.[44] Walter Murdoch wrote that he was 'much amused by its contents', but thought the use of colour 'a trifle disturbing'. This criticism was endorsed by authorities Hasluck respected – John Gartner of the Hawthorn Press and typesetter Benjamin Fryer – who also offered useful comments on layout and choice of typefaces. Fryer was nevertheless encouraging:

> There are small towns all over the United States with presses
> run by university students, learning printing as they go, they
> do work far better than the average printer ever dreams of. And
> they earn a living at it![45]

By this time Australia was six months into the Second World War, and the future improvement of the Freshwater Bay Press had to be put on hold. The Haslucks were never to have the opportunity of reviving its operations. Like the Drama

Festival, the Freshwater Bay Press was another product of the vigorous cultural life of Perth in the late 1930s cut short by the war, and revived only many years later by Hasluck's son and daughter-in-law.

The war brought an end to yet another 'might-have-been' in Hasluck's career. In the early years of their marriage, the young couple seldom travelled far from Perth. Alix was shy in strange company and did not much enjoy roughing it in bush pubs.[46] They made a major excursion in 1938, when Paul decided they should use a windfall of £300 to join a cruise going by way of the north-west ports to Java, Sumatra, Singapore, Bangkok and Saigon, stopping for a few days in each place. Paul felt a need to extend his knowledge of South-East Asia, and Alix was keen to visit antiquities such as Borobudur and the ruins of Angkor.[47]

The journey was in itself sufficient evidence of a shared intellectual curiosity quick to reach out beyond the conventional thinking of their time, but it led in an unexpected direction. At Batavia (now Jakarta) they stayed comfortably with a Dutch official whose responsibilities included the massive archives of the Netherlands East India Company that had governed much of Indonesia in the seventeenth and eighteenth centuries. They had never been closely examined and might contain records of early voyages to the Australian coast. Paul's imaginative ambition at once went to work. He would teach himself to read seventeenth-century Dutch so that he could research, translate and publish these records at some future date, perhaps through the Freshwater Bay Press. He set about learning the language, but then came the war, and with it before long the Japanese occupation of Java followed by the war of independence that created modern Indonesia. Seventy years after Paul

Hasluck's inspiration, those archives have yet to be edited for scholarly publication.

The rest of the journey took them to a conventional tourist destination in Singapore ('definitely a place of joy for the privileged few and an ill-managed ramshackle slum for the rest', Paul thought) and to country less often travelled, as they went by train through up-country Thailand and thence by mail-bus into French Indochina (now Cambodia and Vietnam). Having experienced the splendour of Angkor Wat, they finished at Saigon (now Ho Chi Minh City), observing again the contrast between the comfortable circumstances of Europeans and a professionally educated minority of Vietnamese, and 'the poverty-stricken shambles in which the rest of the population lived'.[48] If Paul Hasluck was to play a contentious role during the Vietnam War of the 1960s, he could at least claim to be one of the few Western statesmen of his time who had actually set eyes on that distressful country. He himself believed the entire voyage was a memorable and formative experience, allowing him some inkling of historic cultures of great depth and complexity.

With all his excursions into drama and publishing as well as his responsibilities as a senior journalist, Hasluck was not neglecting his academic activities. Besides pressing ahead with his postgraduate thesis, Hasluck ran tutorials in history at the university for Fred Alexander. (His students included the young trainee teacher Kim Beazley senior, who later served opposite him for many years in the Commonwealth parliament.) Hasluck showed an aptitude for the work, and it was arranged that he would be seconded from the *West Australian* as a full-time temporary lecturer at The University of Western Australia for twelve months during 1940 while Alexander went on study leave to the United States. The prospect of an academic career was opening before the young man who had once doubted his fitness for university study. It came at a happy time in his personal life. After years of waiting, and following appropriate medical advice, Alix Hasluck was at last pregnant, with a child due at the beginning of 1941.

His year of lecturing at the university offered a rewarding change from journalism. He found that he was a successful teacher. The Vice-Chancellor, George Currie,[49] wrote praising

> the able and generous way in which you interpreted your duties
> to the University in your term of office. The freshness and
> originality of your outlook made a contribution to the studies
> of many students which they appreciate…[50]

But there were no suitable vacancies at the university, and meanwhile other choices confronted him. The war effort called for recruitment of fit and able men. Hasluck's family background was one of sturdy patriotism; in the First World War, although a family man, a Salvation Army officer and more than forty-five years old, Meernaa Hasluck more than once tried unsuccessfully to enlist. His spirit was undimmed in the Second World War: 'We British Australians love liberty and justice and equality and will not stand by and see ourselves robbed of our birthright', he told his daughter.[51] In August 1940 Lewis Hasluck, although a family man of nearly forty and a probable case for exemption as a skilled tradesman, signed on as a private with the 8th Division. While Lewis was away on active service, old Meernaa Hasluck, who had retired from full-time duties with the Salvation Army in 1937 but was still busy helping out at the central Salvation

Army Fortress, spent many hours assisting his daughter-in-law and two young granddaughters on their vineyard. Shortly afterwards, Paul's sister Rosa applied to enlist as an army nurse; she served in Palestine, Egypt and New Guinea. In December 1940 Paul, at the age of thirty-five and with his first child as yet unborn, had to decide where his duty lay.

Then he succumbed to appendicitis. During his recovery, the long-awaited first child arrived, a son, born on 15 January 1941. He was named Rollo John, Rollo after a medieval Norman ancestor his mother's family claimed, and John after Alexandra's father. Soon afterwards a convalescent Paul was on his way to Newspaper House to discuss his future with his employers when he bumped into John Curtin, a friend of long standing from the Australian Journalists' Association. He asked the older man's advice. Curtin, now a Labor member of federal parliament and leader of the opposition with only the slimmest of margins behind Robert Menzies' Coalition government, had an idea. The recently expanded Department of External Affairs was looking for qualified graduate staff to assist in the creation of Australian foreign policy; Paul Hasluck was just the sort of man who would interest them.[52] Hasluck later found out that when Curtin returned to a meeting of the Advisory War Council in Canberra he 'butted into some conversation about the need for different people in Canberra and mentioned my name'.[53]

Unaware of this intervention, Paul wrote to the department, and while he was awaiting a reply, Curtin's advice was reinforced. Fred Alexander, while on study leave in the United States in 1940, was commissioned by the newly appointed Australian Minister to Washington, Richard Casey, to take soundings of American public opinion. Casey was sufficiently impressed with

Alexander's performance to recommend he be offered a job with External Affairs. For family reasons Alexander was unable to accept, and the permanent head of the department, the irascible Colonel Hodgson, responded: 'Well, if you won't stay yourself, at least you'd better find someone for us'.[54] Alexander thought of Paul Hasluck, who within a short space of time received an official invitation to join the department.

Paul Hasluck may not have realised how much he was leaving a familiar and supportive environment in which his abilities were recognised and valued. Old Sir James Mitchell, now a long-time incumbent at Government House, whom Paul occasionally visited for yarns about the colonial past and had once described as a mentor, wrote to him:

> You will be greatly missed in Perth and I believe you will
> greatly miss Perth, anyway beautiful as Canberra is, it is not
> Perth...I shall miss you the more because there is no one to
> take your place.[55]

In Canberra he would be an unknown who had to prove himself.

In the past eight years he had come a long way. With zest and energy he was simultaneously pursuing a range of cultural activities, but even if he might once have lumped them together as no more than 'mucking about', he had developed a driving concern to improve standards in Western Australia and strong practical skills in effecting change. In drama, in literary standards, in the quality of book production, he believed the provincial need not be second-rate. The remedy lay neither in theory nor in slavishly copying models from elsewhere, but in the practice and maintenance of high critical standards. In the same way his sympathies in understanding Aboriginal problems had deepened, making him an inspired advocate for change and reform. His strengths were practical, lying in the identification of cultural or social problems and the energetic application of measures to remedy them. If his own artistic creativity fell short of his hopes, he might yet hope to serve as a constructive influence in the promotion of an Australian culture, and a university post might well have provided a base for exercising this influence. But the times were out of joint, and the war was sweeping him into new directions nobody could have predicted.

Chapter 6

Canberra in wartime

Paul Hasluck arrived in Canberra in March 1941. Housing was scarce in the raw bush capital, but he managed to rent a house near the Manuka shopping centre, where he was joined by Alix and the baby Rollo.[1] The house was large and cold, Rollo was a difficult baby, and Alix was unwell and often unhappy. 'My idea of Hell has always been of a freezing region', she wrote to a friend in Perth, 'and here I am for my sins. I would go back West like a shot if it rested with me'.[2] Nobody advised her that newly arrived young wives were expected to pay calls on the wives of senior officials in the department and the legations, and this caused difficulties for her socially, although there were friends to visit on winter evenings, many of them also newcomers. Canberra, with its two cinemas, was culturally and socially much less stimulating than Perth. Alexandra wrote satirically about the standard of conversation:

> No woman here ever converses. A couple of sentences on any one subject is all they can manage, even the ones with Oxford & Cambridge degrees. But if you bring up the subject of the kitchen stove, or the best way to make quince jelly, they can go on for hours…[A friend] gave a teaparty that was a great social

success because all the ladies got on to the subject of toothpaste & thrashed it out for half an hour.[3]

There were consolations: the surrounding countryside was beautiful, and there were outings across the New South Wales border to Queanbeyan. 'It is just an Australian country town but it is real and vulgar and vital and has some sound reason for its existence.'

At first Paul found satisfaction in his work, but his reactions to the Commonwealth public service were negative:

There are no Australians in this hole – no one who is proudly and vehemently Australian and keenly aware of Australia and interested in every part of it. The people are clever enough at their jobs, I suppose, but as a people they are denatured. This place annoys me. The best that can be said for it is that it is a completely sterile and safe cage in which public servants can work clearly without any major excitements to disturb their routine. One misses the intellectual movement that there was in Perth...[4]

The public servants, he added, were

really worse than any one could have imagined them to be. Lovable and engaging and even capable in some instances, but so very small and tidy and wrapped up in regulations. In a newspaper office the only questioning arises when it is being decided whether a certain objective is really wanted. That point settled, we go ahead and get it. In the service they never seem to make up their minds what they want and that state of affairs causes them scarcely any worry. I am sure that if a public servant got into Heaven by the wrong ladder he would nurse a grievance against the archangels instead of joining in tennis matches or poker schools or whatever it is that archangels do up above on sunny days.[5]

Ironically, Hasluck as a minister was famed for his insistence on proper public service procedures.

Unfortunately, he was ceasing to enjoy his work. In his first months he had few defined duties beyond preparing 'material for publication, broadcasting or parliamentary purposes', including newsletters on current events to be sent to Australian representatives overseas.[6] A leisurely pace of work had survived in the department from pre-war days, and the administrative machinery was rudimentary. Hasluck chafed at the inactivity. He had not passed up the option of enlisting in order to become an underemployed Canberra bureaucrat. He wanted an opportunity that would prove his worth in External Affairs, but did not know where to look for supportive leadership. The Minister for External Affairs, Sir Frederick Stewart, was only a recent appointee. A Sydney businessman with a good record in social policy, his other portfolios of Health and Social Services kept him too busy to do much more than deplore the rise of Japanese militarism. His one intervention in Hasluck's work was to insist on the removal from one of his newsletters of an accurate forecast that Menzies and his ministry might soon fall.

The permanent head of the department, Colonel Roy Hodgson, came to External Affairs from a background in military intelligence and retained much of the style of the plain, blunt soldier; he seemed happier in the execution of policy than as a taker of initiatives. Hasluck respected him but considered him a better manager than diplomat.[7] He did not manage to get on good terms with Hodgson's deputy, John Hood, a former Tasmanian Rhodes scholar about his own age. Alix Hasluck described him as 'a tall melancholic man of saturnine appearance, with a problem'. Paul thought him a 'dead hand' who would not talk or make decisions and took no interest in forward planning.[8] Hood, who had taken first-class honours at Oxford and served as a subeditor on the London *Times*, had apparently been against recruiting Hasluck, a subeditor on a provincial Australian daily, having candidates of his own whom Hodgson refused to favour. Throughout the war, Hood's attitude towards Hasluck resembled that of a prefect at an elite boys' school towards the diligent outsider who manages to carry away too many prizes. Hood's wife, the daughter of a titled Englishman, was coldly unhelpful towards Alexandra Hasluck; perhaps she too found Canberra difficult.[9]

William Forsyth, who worked with both men in External Affairs, put it thus:

John [Hood] came to have less tolerance for Hasluck and at length perhaps none at all; his patrician temperament was bound in any case to lack empathy with the hyper-industrious, tidy-minded, energetic and able but always prickly, sometimes fuming, and occasionally explosive product of a less urbane cultivation.

Unfortunately, their areas of responsibility overlapped, and this caused friction:

Paul seemed to resent John's taciturn but impregnable insistence on the primacy of the political function at the level of action, perhaps resenting more the aloofness of John's armour than the firmness of his stance...I do not recollect any man other than Hasluck who put Hood into a bad temper.[10]

A man of different temperament from Hood's might have welcomed the newcomer, perhaps even mentored him in the ways of the public service. As it was, Hasluck was reinforced in traits that some colleagues found difficult throughout his public life: reliance on his own efforts, a reluctance to place trust in others, and a passionate concern about accuracy in detail that sometimes led to uninhibited eruptions of temper at what he perceived as other people's shortcomings. He was on better terms with other colleagues, but believed himself to be the first 'outsider' to be brought into the conduct of foreign affairs.[11] Perhaps an understandable though unjustified resentment was caused among his colleagues by the informality of his recruitment to the department in 'a position that two years later 1500 applicants for the cadet scheme coveted'.[12]

Stuart Macintyre has pointed out that graduate recruits to the Department of External Affairs were chosen by examination and interview from a large field of applicants. These newcomers formed a sort of freemasonry against the resentment of some of the older and less formally qualified departmental officers, but Hasluck fitted into neither group. He had not committed himself to a career in the public service but was on secondment, and was closer in age to some of the slightly older graduates with whom he would mix from the Department of Post-War Reconstruction.[13] Having spent many years in Western Australia, he had enjoyed limited opportunities for networking nationally or internationally, though his knowledge of international affairs was probably greater than that of most of his recently recruited departmental colleagues.

In October 1941 the Coalition lost office to Labor under John Curtin. Hasluck and his colleagues allowed themselves a momentary hope with the appointment of a new Minister for External Affairs, the Attorney-General, Dr H. V. Evatt. A former justice of the High Court, Evatt was known to be an intellectual with broad cultural sympathies, but disappointment came soon. 'He has not come near us yet', Hasluck confided to his diary a fortnight after Evatt's appointment, 'has upset the Department on several matters and generally shows a disposition to try and find something to reform or "squash" rather than to understand'.[14] Irked at what he saw as the continuing lethargy of the department, Hasluck in November complained to Hodgson that he was often set trivial tasks and wanted a better way to serve the war effort, otherwise he might return to an academic career in Perth.[15] His seniors at the *West Australian* were also keen for him to return to the newspaper as a leader writer, and Paul Hasluck had his moments of nostalgia, although as his friend Griff Richards warned him: 'Perth, of course, is charming, but the office would make you a raging lion after your first hour back in it'.[16]

Hodgson gave him no explicit guidance but sent him to an interdepartmental committee convened by the Department of Labour and National Service on the subject of 'reconstruction of external relations'. This committee met on 4 December 1941. With Hodgson's support, Hasluck prepared a statement arguing that Australia's postwar reconstruction would involve the interplay of home and foreign policy in such issues as trade and immigration.

> Therefore it would be unsound to base Australian post-war
> reconstruction projects on any assumption that post-war
> conditions would be roughly similar to those in the pre-war
> world and that Australia would be able to shape its policy
> in isolation.[17]

He found the participants at the meeting extremely vague about its purpose. The committee never met again, but this was apparently enough to establish him as the Department of External Affairs' specialist on postwar reconstruction. From this time on he argued that External Affairs should set up a separate division to define Australia's position in matters of postwar planning.

All changed a few days later, when Japan entered the war with the attack on Pearl Harbor. Japanese forces thrust rapidly southward. Singapore fell on 15 February 1942 with the surrender of 15,000 members of the 8th Division, among them Lewis Hasluck. Two days later came the first bombing of Darwin. It was Paul's duty to stay at his post. Apart from Hodgson and Hood, only one other officer besides Hasluck was retained in the department at this moment of crisis, all the others being deployed elsewhere. This led, he recalled, to 'a somewhat frantic sharing of duties' at a time when many feared Japanese invasion, or at least the bombing of Canberra by hostile aircraft.[18] There were preparations for the evacuation of Canberra. Hasluck contemplated the possibility that he might have to lead a guerrilla existence as a mounted scout in the hills behind Canberra.[19] Amid the turmoil, his appointment with the department was renewed and in April 1942 he was appointed officer in charge of a new section of the department on postwar policy, with one graduate assistant as staff. He told his parents that, although he was offered appointments in two other departments, including one in Melbourne with a larger salary, he chose to stay with External Affairs as 'more useful and interesting'.[20]

Meanwhile, Paul and Alix had moved to another house, also close to the Manuka shopping centre, where they remained for the rest of the war. It was not large, but had a long backyard with peach trees and a strawberry patch, with room for growing vegetables. Here Paul used a pick to dig an air-raid shelter out of the tough Canberra clay.[21] The increased pressures of family life were not easy for Alix. Rollo and his parents suffered frequently from colds and other ailments. Despite the help of a cheerful and robust young nursemaid and home help, Alix found Canberra uncomfortable, with its wartime shortages, high cost of living and poor heating. She was also pregnant again. 'It takes me untold ages to do one', she wrote to Henrietta Drake-Brockman, 'and now I suppose I'll be like a rabbit if I'm not careful'.[22] Because of wartime rationing, pretty maternity clothes were unavailable, and for most of her pregnancy she wore an unbecoming khaki flannel. After the birth of their second son, Nicholas Paul, on 17 October 1942, the maternity garments were 'ceremoniously and with heartfelt rejoicing burnt in the backyard'.[23]

Alix was not pleased when Paul decided to solve the challenge of petrol rationing by buying a ten-year-old bay mare from a young man who had been called up for military service. He named her Edythe and, contrary to Canberra regulations, kept her in an enclosure in their backyard.[24] Each morning he rode her to West Block, where the Department of External

Affairs was housed, and tethered her to graze on a nearby hill-side. At weekends, and once or twice in the dead of night, the mare Edythe sometimes did duty between the shafts of a sulky sent to Queanbeyan to get beer for the teetotal community of Canberra. But she liked to bite, and Alix had no time for her.[25]

Gradually the sense of imminent crisis lifted from the war. In May, 'tense and quite unspeakable to',[26] Paul hovered over a radio in a corner by the fireplace while news trickled through of the naval battle in the Coral Sea that forced back a Japanese fleet. By September the tide of battle in Papua New Guinea had turned. Prime Minister Curtin's sense of history seems to have been stimulated by these critical events, as in June 1942 he convened a committee under the chairmanship of the historian of Anzac, Dr Charles Bean, to draw up plans for the creation of a repository of national archives. Hasluck was appointed to this committee and played a leading role in drafting its recommendations.[27] The work came readily to an experienced journalist and skilled wordsmith. During 1942 Evatt came to value Hasluck as a draftsman who could be called on at short notice to reduce large and complex documentation to a presentable speech or position paper.

Meanwhile, postwar reconstruction was assuming greater prominence in official thinking. In October 1942 Evatt convened a weekend meeting of officials, lawyers and public servants in Melbourne, with Hodgson and Hasluck representing the Department of External Affairs. The conference led to the rapid production of a publication urging the empowerment of the Commonwealth Government for the purposes of postwar reconstruction. Hasluck believed Evatt foresaw that social reform in Australia might be facilitated if supported by international agreements enabling the Commonwealth Government to use its constitutional external affairs power.[28] As one of the main authors of the publication, Hasluck was kept busy networking with colleagues in other departments as they consulted on Australia's external economic interests in a postwar world. He formed a close working relationship with Fin Crisp, who was seconded to a new Department of Post-War Reconstruction created in December 1942 with Chifley as minister. Others included Coombs, now director of rationing, and the economists Roland Wilson and L. F. Giblin.

Hasluck was at last working at a satisfactory pitch, although the ill-defined relationship between his postwar reconstruction unit and the department's political section under Hood remained a source of contention, especially after the recruitment of W. D. Forsyth as research officer. Forsyth had just published a provocative study of immigration policy, in which he argued that British migration would be insufficient to meet Australia's postwar needs.[29] He was also to develop an interest in issues of colonial policy and trusteeship. Although he and Hasluck were never the closest of colleagues, their skills complemented each other constructively.

At the end of November, Hasluck was sent to his first overseas conference. This was convened by a then prominent think tank, the Institute of Pacific Relations, a body founded in 1925 to promote research and discussion on the Pacific area at a time when official diplomatic contacts were few. Its conferences brought together a mixture of officials and prominent citizens, and were credited with a significant influence over thinking on foreign policy among its member nations, especially the United States. The 1942 conference was scheduled for twelve days in December at Mont Tremblant, an isolated ski resort about 200 kilometres north of Montreal.[30] The leader of the Australian delegation, Richard Boyer, was a Queensland pastoralist of social conscience, once a Methodist clergyman, now a commissioner and later chairman of the Australian Broadcasting Commission. The other delegates were Lloyd Ross, trade unionist and historian; Eleanor Hinder, a social worker with fifteen years' experience in China; and Paul Hasluck.

The theme of the conference was to consider how the United Nations (already in theory the postwar successor of the failed League of Nations) could best establish practical conditions of racial, political and economic justice and welfare. The conference was divided into four study groups that would report to a plenary session with ideas for further research leading to national and international action. Twelve months earlier, British Prime Minister Winston Churchill and United States President Franklin Roosevelt had put their signatures to a document known as the Atlantic Charter, pledging support for basic freedoms ('the four freedoms') that must be upheld by the world community after the war, and much of the debate at Mont Tremblant hinged on the implications of that charter. Was it 'a real commitment on the part of the British and American Governments or an unattainable ideal issued for propaganda purposes'?[31] In later life, Hasluck commented that, as a newcomer to international conferences, he found the atmosphere at Mont Tremblant 'more emotional than I had expected of a body organized into "round tables" and "study groups"'. It soon emerged, to the alarm and pessimism of the Australian delegation, that Britain and the United States were at odds. The Americans pushed the idea that the Atlantic Charter gave a guarantee of independence to Asian countries such as the Philippines, India, Thailand and Korea, in contrast to Churchill's recent assertion that he had not become the King's First Minister in order to preside over the liquidation of the British Empire. The British retorted that the United States Congress had not yet endorsed the Atlantic Charter and might lapse into isolationism as had happened after the First World War.

Some members of the British Commonwealth – Canada, Australia and New Zealand – found themselves playing an unexpectedly prominent role as mediators, challenging both Churchill's Empire Toryism and an American tendency to evade postwar commitments except in the Pacific where they would be the major power. As Hasluck reported: 'Whereas the Americans were diverse, the United Kingdom delegation was English of the English, and as unanimous as a herd of cattle with their horns lowered facing a strange dog'.[32] British thought on East Asia lacked dynamism: 'The Americans and Canadians who were attacking British colonial rule...wanted to hear blunt answers and categorical assurances rather than patient explanations from wiser and sadder men'.[33] As for the Americans: 'The possession of superior power inevitably has led to the assumption of superior wisdom'.

Hasluck came away from Mont Tremblant with an increased conviction that Australia must not only identify its own national interests, but could play a distinctive role together with the other self-governing members of the British Commonwealth. They supported 'a global welfare policy covering both collective military security and equality of economic opportunity aimed at progressive rising living standards in all countries'. This experience of cooperation prompted Boyer to urge the Department of External Affairs to take the initiative in arranging further conferences between Canada, New Zealand and Australia in preparation for the United Nations organisation of the future. For Hasluck it was a stimulating learning experience, his first exposure to international debate and the practicalities of maintaining the Anglo-American alliance. He made a good impression and was not displeased when Lloyd Ross told him he was something of a revolutionary; Nugget Coombs, said Ross, had told him that Hasluck was a nineteenth-century liberal, but 'you are more up-to-date than he is'.[34]

Hasluck returned to Canberra to find that in his absence Hood had tried to dismantle the postwar section of the department by moving its staff to other duties. Paul soon put a stop to this, but the departmental infighting dismayed him. He wrote to Coombs:

> This interdepartmental and even intradepartmental pother
> is bloody awful. I often envy the front line soldier for the
> comparatively clear picture he must have of who and what
> he is fighting.[35]

Yet there must have been moments of cooperation. In May 1943 Forsyth reported that Hood and Hasluck were trying to set up a committee to deal with 'the political and strategic aspects of reconstruction', only to be told by Evatt to take no action until he returned from a visit to Washington.[36]

On this visit, Evatt took neither Hood nor Hasluck with him, instead borrowing Coombs from the Department of Labour and National Service and taking his private secretary, a new junior recruit to External Affairs, Dr John Burton. Hasluck was unworried by these arrangements. To Alan Watt at the Washington Embassy he wrote an introduction for Coombs:

> I have known him since school days and have a very high appreciation of his fundamental decency and idealism. He is an able man with a strong sense of reality which keeps him keenly aware of the limitations which political conditions, personalities, and established forms of interest place in the way of change, but at the same time he is a most determined worker for, and hence we can assume a firm believer in, progress towards better conditions of life. He has a much wider breadth of interest and appreciation than most professional economists whom I have met and is one of the few men in administrative circles in Canberra who has a comprehensive outlook.[37]

Coombs distinguished himself by his advocacy of full employment as a postwar objective at the Food and Agriculture Conference at Hot Springs, Virginia, in the face of American scepticism. This goal was to become identified as one of Australia's distinctive contributions to the debate on shaping the postwar world, with Coombs and Burton as its most persistent champions. Hasluck, although sympathetic, was less certain of its feasibility, not least because powerful sectors of opinion in the United States feared that full employment could be secured only through government intervention with the workings of the market. He also considered

> that unemployment was basically a consequence and not a cause of economic ills and that the proposal for an international

agreement on full employment was a proposal to collaborate in treating the symptoms rather than to combat the disease.[38]

He preferred an emphasis on the development of resources and the reduction of tariff barriers.

This mission saw the first rise to prominence of John Burton. Ten years younger than Hasluck, Burton was the son of a prominent Methodist clergyman. 'To many, the son appeared to have inherited his father's missionary zeal in a secular form and to have become a crusader for his ideals in the world.'[39] With Hasluck, like himself an appointee from outside the departmental cadre, he was at first on friendly terms. They shared little jokes about Evatt. 'I find the Minister rarely has much idea of the line he wants to follow', Burton wrote,

> and he will accept a draft quite easily. I have not had so many ideas put over for a long time! The boss has behaved quite well and everyone is commenting that he is much less difficult this time than last.[40]

He soon formed a warm personal relationship with Evatt, who, Burton told Hasluck, wanted him to report to him personally; 'in other words, he refuses to allow me to be an officer of the Department'.[41] Burton was soon colluding with Evatt's tendency to work outside official channels of communication and keep his permanent officials in the dark. This became a source of friction.

Nevertheless, Evatt was also making use of competent officers such as Hasluck and Alan Watt who were not his pets. Peter Edwards put it cogently:

These men were simply too able and hard-working to be ignored; they could prepare speeches that said what he wanted to say and could carry out his instructions efficiently, regardless of their *arrière-pensées*.[42]

Hasluck at the time saw the federal cabinet as 'going through a stage of puzzlement and worry' about postwar prospects, unsure whether they offered a great industrial future or a renewal of the 1930s Depression:

> As we wrestle with the problems of young nationhood, one set of urgers says, 'Better go back to mother'; another says 'Suspect everyone'. The situation is psychological as well as economic... But of course, in all these things my attitude, like Furphy's, is offensively Australian.[43]

During 1943 the responsibilities of Hasluck's postwar section continued to grow, not least because Hood, having failed to dismantle the section, was in the habit of referring to it every piece of business that could not be defined narrowly as 'political'. Also, as the Allies painfully pushed the Japanese out of Papua New Guinea and the Solomons, debate arose about the future of the south-west Pacific region. It was essential that External Affairs take an active part, and Hasluck chaired a departmental committee on reconstruction in Australia's external territories. He looked with a baleful eye at the competing initiatives of the army's Department of Research and Civil Affairs, which, under the unorthodox Lieutenant Colonel 'Alf' Conlon, was apt to poke its nose into the problems of administration of territories recovered from the Japanese. Hasluck claimed that Conlon's unit was 'a barrel of ratbags' who did little but create bad relations between Australian and Allied military authorities, and he was pleased at its exclusion from influencing External Affairs. To the end of his life, he could never be persuaded otherwise, although the unit included men of high intellectual calibre, including some of his future friends.[44]

Hasluck shared Evatt's growing mistrust of American ambitions in the postwar world, especially the possibility that the United States might expand its hegemony in the South Pacific region. The Americans could deploy large resources for economic warfare, but Hasluck wondered if they were 'directed towards defeating the enemy or pinching the pre-war trade of their Allies'.[45] As Hasluck told Watt, there seemed to be too little interest in the United Kingdom in the future of the South Pacific territories, 'and rather too lively an American interest on the other hand', and it was important that Australian interests should not be prejudiced. Watt replied discouragingly:

> Here in Washington post-war plans are kept in the hands of a very few people and are jealously guarded...The United States is not very interested in what Australia wants or thinks, and is disinclined to give us vital information.[46]

During the rest of 1943, Hasluck continued to gnaw at this problem, regaling his colleagues with a clerihew:

> *Americans saved us from the Japs –*
> *Perhaps,*
> *But now we are too Yankfull*
> *To be truly thankful.*[47]

120

In November 1943 he represented the department at a conference on civil aviation when Hood refused to go, reporting
that a potential shortage of civil aircraft might leave Australia
unable to expand or even to service its pre-war routes, creating
a vacuum to be filled by ambitious American airlines.[48]

Hasluck was not uncomfortable with Evatt's growing conviction that the smaller nations of the world, with Australia well
to the fore, should mobilise to form a countervailing influence
to the great powers. A spur to action was provided later in
November, when Churchill, Roosevelt and the Chinese leader
Chiang Kai-shek met at Cairo and decided that Japan should be
dispossessed of its island colonies in the Pacific. Manchuria and
Taiwan, both under Japanese occupation, should be restored to
China, and Korea should become independent. There was no
consultation with Australia or any of the smaller Pacific powers.
This fostered fears that the smaller powers would be left out
of arrangements for postwar settlements.[49] Evatt and his senior
advisers saw that they must become more proactive in protecting
Australia's regional interests in Papua New Guinea and the south-
west Pacific. The obvious ally was New Zealand, where the war
had brought forward a small but eminent diplomatic service. At
Evatt's initiative, a conference between the two governments
was planned for Canberra on 21 January 1944. Hasluck was put
in charge of the arrangements and appointed secretary to the
conference. It was his first great opportunity to play a distinctive
role in shaping Australia's nascent foreign policy.

Chapter 7

Towards San Francisco

The Paul Hasluck who addressed himself to the groundwork for the Australia–New Zealand conference in January 1944 was not the hopeful idealist who had arrived in Canberra nearly three years before. As a Western Australian lacking much experience outside his own state he felt himself under pressure to measure up to his more travelled colleagues, but his working environment was less supportive than it had been in Perth. Evatt, with the barrister's knack of demanding advice and input at a moment's notice, was temperamentally incapable of imposing orderly procedures on the staff of External Affairs.[1] Neither the gruff Hodgson, himself struggling to keep abreast of the rapidly expanding responsibilities of the department, nor the laconic and unfriendly Hood, had provided sympathetic mentoring, so that Hasluck continued to feel himself an outsider, unsure of his colleagues' acceptance and uncertain of giving his trust. It did not help that the department's lines of authority were never clearly defined.

Hasluck became increasingly confirmed in a habit of relying on his own judgement, backed by hard work and mastery of all the documentation. He was less open to the shaping of ideas in the cut and thrust of argument with colleagues. He drove himself hard, and this sometimes led to outbursts of bad temper when others failed to keep up. Young diplomatic cadets found him a demanding supervisor who taught them the meaning of accuracy: 'every source must be scrupulously detailed, checked and rechecked, every submission concise and comprehensive'.[2] Off duty he could be as genial and convivial as ever, but he was seldom relaxed during long working hours. Nevertheless, it was acknowledged that no more efficient, reliable and intelligent departmental officer could be entrusted with the preparations for the conference. And at this stage of their association he could work constructively with Evatt. Both were highly intelligent, well read and capable of working under great pressure. If Evatt was the quicker to seize and absorb new ideas, Hasluck's mastery of detail provided the essential ballast in translating those ideas into practicality.

At the outset of the conference, Evatt disconcerted the New Zealanders by proposing that their agreement be embodied in a formal treaty. Independent action of this kind by self-governing members of the British Commonwealth, while not quite unprecedented, had never been taken in wartime.[3] Some in the Australian Department of External Affairs, such as Alan Watt, thought it would have been sufficient for Australia and New Zealand to confine themselves to a statement of postwar aims. The New Zealanders reasonably feared that Britain and the United States would be displeased. They were won around, but insisted that some of Evatt's more provocative ideas be dropped from the text of the pact, among them the notion that Australia should take over control of the Solomons and the New Hebrides (now Vanuatu).[4]

Hasluck became the principal draftsman of the treaty. He liked working with the New Zealanders, and showed tact and skill in reconciling the different viewpoints. Drafting the agreement tested his capacity for hard work, including an all-night session, but it was a valuable introduction to the detailed conduct of diplomacy. Hasluck later wrote:

> This was my first experience of participating in the drafting of a text of this kind, and in the three or four hours we worked together I conceived a very high respect for Dr Evatt in this form of draftsmanship. As a person who had tried to write verse, I had often previously given a good deal of attention to the finer shades of meaning of English words when used in an evocative and literary way, but my eyes were now opened to the even finer shades of gradation of meaning, from all to nothing, that can be given to English words when they are used carefully in a legal and political way.[5]

His own skill at draftsmanship was to be one of his strongest assets as an officer of the Department of External Affairs, and his role was recognised. From Wellington his colleague Patrick Shaw wrote: 'Everyone attributes a large part of the speedy agreement to the preparatory work and that means you and your section'.[6]

Under the terms of the agreement, Australia and New Zealand were to consult regularly about defence, commerce, regional foreign policy, and the fostering of full employment. They claimed a place at any peacemaking conference, and insisted that they have a voice in deciding the sovereignty of not only the former Japanese territories, but any of the Pacific islands. The doctrine of trusteeship would apply to these territories, committing to social and economic policies that would advance the indigenous peoples towards self-determination. Agreed policies would be overseen by a regional commission; this was the genesis of the South Pacific Commission set up in 1947. Australia and New Zealand would also insist on control of their own immigration policies, and would urge the creation of an international authority to control aviation routes, or in default a British Commonwealth instrumentality. The British could probably have stomached most of this except for the strong emphasis on colonial trusteeship, but the United States was reactive to two further clauses. One insisted that 'a regional zone of defence comprising the Southwest and South Pacific Areas shall be established', and the other spelt out – in a way the Americans could not help sensing applied pointedly to them – that wartime defence installations would not constitute any basis for territorial claims or rights after the end of hostilities.[7]

Although Hasluck later wrote that the calling of the conference reflected Evatt's 'almost psychological antipathy to any power that was greater than Australia',[8] his differences with Evatt at that time were over matters of tone rather than substance. He fully shared Evatt's view that Australia should shape its own foreign policy in accordance with its own regional interests, and that the United States should not be encouraged to seek hegemony in the South Pacific, but he saw no need to ruffle the feathers of the great powers unnecessarily. Unlike Evatt he was already moving towards a recognition that, in an international community shaped first and foremost by power relationships, Australia must use judgement in achieving effect while working within its limitations.

Despite his good performance at the Australia–New Zealand conference, Hasluck found life no easier in the department.

Having taken a well-earned beach holiday with Alexandra and the children, he returned to find that Hood was once again interfering with the postwar section. Hasluck complained to Hodgson: 'If I am not to be allowed to resign from the department, I regard it as essential to the efficient performance of my duties that those duties be clearly defined'.[9] A few weeks later the post-hostilities planning section of the department was upgraded to the status of a division, with Hasluck at its head, but this did little to improve his relations with Hood. John Burton was made responsible for the economic side of the new division, but this caused further ructions, as it was never made clear whether Burton was subordinate to Hasluck. Before long they were at loggerheads. Ric Throssell, who came to External Affairs as a diplomatic cadet in 1944, recalled:

> you had this ludicrous situation going on, with Hasluck writing on cables, 'Dr Burton, please advise', and Burton would screw 'em up and throw 'em into the waste paper basket and then go down and get another clean copy for himself – a clean copy. There was a huge rivalry between them.[10]

The rift arose after an International Labour Conference at Philadelphia in April 1944, when Burton was seconded to the Australian delegation led by the Minister for Supply and Shipping, John Beasley.[11] Encouraged by Burton, Beasley spoke strongly on the necessity of high and stable employment levels to stimulate trade and consumption, thus entrenching Australia's reputation as a rather lonely champion of postwar full employment. Burton wrote the report of the conference, which was published as a white paper. Presumably, considering he wrote in his role as adviser to Beasley, he consulted nobody in External Affairs. Hasluck, who was less convinced of the feasibility of securing international recognition for the full-employment goal, complained that the report 'had gross inaccuracies as a record and faults of grammar', but to no avail.[12] Later he reflected:

> I might mark that row as the dawning of the realization that
> I was working with false men, but I think it was still the
> grammar rather than the politics that irritated me most.[13]

A scholar in politics, Hasluck was to draw criticism later in his career for devoting too much attention to the style and grammar of draft documents.

Peter Edwards has pointed out that Hasluck and Burton supplied different needs for Evatt, who 'probably saw value in having two able exponents of opposing viewpoints as advisers, the one relatively orthodox, the other more idealistic and adventurous'.[14] In old age, Burton asserted that Hasluck had no philosophy of foreign affairs.[15] More than any ideological difference, the great irritant between Hasluck and Burton was in their approach to bureaucratic conventions. Hasluck brought from his time with the *West Australian* – which, with the passage of years, he may have idealised somewhat – a belief in clearly delineated chains of authority and allocation of responsibilities. Burton, with no such experience behind him, was prepared to play along with Evatt's often chaotic working methods, his habit of concentrating single-mindedly on one issue to the exclusion of all else, his readiness to ignore proper channels of communication, to cut corners and to withhold information from officials who might consider themselves entitled to it. He was not content to echo Evatt's opinions obsequiously; rather, he used his access to the minister to try to shape and influence policy, perhaps realising that it was no use going through orthodox channels in a department headed by Hodgson and Hood. Yet despite the huge rivalry between Hasluck and Burton, they would find themselves during the next twelve months working together strenuously and efficiently in the common cause of Australia's international standing.

Tension was toxic in the Department of External Affairs. In September 1944, Hood told a new arrival, Paul McGuire, that Hasluck was 'Hodgson's Yes-man'. A Catholic intellectual who might have been expected to share some of Hasluck's interests, McGuire instead was given the impression that he had 'all the appearances of a self-centred, boorish, ambitious careerist'.[16] A careerist Hasluck was not; a week or two earlier, vexed by constant wrangles with Hood and Burton, he submitted his resignation from the department. He was corresponding with the managing editor of the *West Australian*, C. P. Smith, who offered him reinstatement as a leader writer with facilities for resuming work on his biography of Forrest.[17] Apparently Evatt requested Hasluck to stay, and he withdrew his resignation.[18]

Soon afterwards a new prospect opened. Hasluck's participation in the 1942 conference planning the histories of the Second World War was bearing fruit. In 1943 the general editor appointed for the Official War History, Gavin Long,[19] asked Hasluck informally whether he would be prepared to undertake the volume about the home front, and Hasluck accepted.[20] Cabinet confirmed his appointment in November 1944, subject to his being no longer a member of the Commonwealth public service. Hasluck was energised by the prospect. In conversation with 'Syd' Butlin, the University of Sydney professor responsible for the economic volumes of the Official War History, they agreed that 'It looks as if we will be writing the social, political, and economic history of a revolutionary decade, not merely of some brief war years'.[21] It was anticipated that he would work on the project from 1947 to 1951, though from what institutional basis was still up in the air. He now felt obliged to write to C. P. Smith, advising him there was virtually no chance of his return to the staff of the *West Australian*. Smith replied that he could give no guarantee of a vacancy three or four years hence, but added: 'With your prestige and ability there should not be much doubt about you finding a suitable job'.[22]

Would he have been happier? A few months later Alexandra Hasluck was in Perth with the children while Paul was overseas, and she expressed some firm opinions. Western Australia, she wrote, was a lotus land:

> you will sink down into a timeless ooze and see things go past vaguely like looking up through water...The first week I came back, I wondered how I could stand the place, so far away, so don't care for anything that is happening in the world, or in Australia, so completely wrapped up in itself.[23]

Her attitude had changed since her first reluctant year in Canberra, for she was thinking partly in terms of her husband's reputation. If he came back, she wrote, he would be discredited:

> Everyone here thinks you have gone so far ('How he has got on' in grudging or admiring terms) that if you come back to something they will think less of you.[24]

Even without this wifely reinforcement, Paul Hasluck's sense of patriotic duty no less than his engagement with the intellectual challenges thrown up by his work made it unlikely he could have returned contentedly to his old niche at the *West Australian*.

Yet his position in the Department of External Affairs was insecure. Evatt had been chafing at Hodgson's management of the department for some time, and in October 1944 sent him off to Canada on a couple of stopgap diplomatic missions before securing his appointment as Ambassador to France in March 1945. No formal appointment was made of an acting secretary of the department to serve in Hodgson's absence. Hood was the senior officer, but it was generally understood that Evatt did not intend to nominate him for the permanent headship of the department. This must have been a comfort to Hasluck, though he continued to complain about Hood's interference whenever he was overseas. Although he was in Evatt's good books for the present, Hasluck was still only a temporary appointee to the department, lacking the protection the Public Service Board extended to permanent officers. His acceptance of the Official War History commission suggested he was not interested in making a lifetime career in diplomacy:

I expected to remain at Canberra in the Department of
External Affairs until the end of the war and perhaps for a
brief period thereafter, during which my preparatory work on
armistice terms and post-hostilities planning would still be
needed. Then I would be free to leave the department and
start working on the war history while looking for an
academic appointment.[25]

Events turned out otherwise. Planning for the postwar world was gaining in impetus as the fortunes of war shifted in favour of the Allies, and Hasluck's Post-Hostilities Planning Division was coming to play a pivotal role at Canberra. In August 1944 the United States hosted a conference at Dumbarton Oaks attended by representatives of the United Kingdom and the Soviet Union. During seven weeks they thrashed out a plan for a new international body, the United Nations, which might be more effective than the old League of Nations in maintaining peace and security. The British kept the Australians informed about the progress of the talks, and accepted comments from the Department of External Affairs. As Hasluck recalled, Evatt concerned himself mainly with broad principles, and most of the detailed submissions were drafted by Hasluck at External Affairs and his ally Kenneth Bailey at the Attorney-General's Department.[26]

In this process of planning, Hasluck came into his own. His colleague Forsyth, often a critic, paid unstinting tribute to 'the magnitude and importance of the preparatory groundwork carried out in External Affairs under the direction of Hasluck':

He brought ability, knowledge of affairs, vigour and a liberal outlook as well as standards of scholarship, a commendable self-respect – and, it must be added, some degree of self-righteousness – to his tasks. Paul was a dynamo of energy, and his thoroughness and orderliness were building up an invaluable instrument for advice and policy making in all foreseeable fields in which the Australian government would be faced with the making of decisions in external matters. He assiduously assessed and directed the budget of papers coming to us from [overseas] and other sources.

Hasluck's indefatigable minuting of this ever-moving stream of documentation, precise, clear, and comprehensive was an achievement and a contribution possibly unequalled in any foreign office of his day.[27]

This work of preparation provided the foundation for Australia's future diplomacy, and was an essential basis for Evatt's performance in the early years of the United Nations.

After Dumbarton Oaks it was desirable for Australia and New Zealand to update their postwar policies, and a meeting was convened in Wellington for November 1944. Prime Minister Curtin was unhappy with Evatt's tendency to antagonise allies and subordinates, and insisted that the Deputy Prime Minister, Francis Forde,[28] accompany Evatt. Neither minister made much of a contribution to the talks at Wellington, as Evatt was ill and Forde more interested in public relations. This left Evatt's departmental officers, Hasluck, Burton and Forsyth, to exercise their own discretion, and in Hasluck's view made for greater precision in the conference's statements about international organisation, trusteeship and colonialism.[29] His imprint may be discerned in the clarity with which the Wellington conference framed its findings.

The conference arrived at twelve resolutions later endorsed by the governments of Australia and New Zealand. They included commitment to the Atlantic Charter, and agreement that the territorial integrity of members must not be changed by the use or threat of force. Powers responsible for dependent territories (as Australia expected to be for New Guinea, and New

Zealand for various Pacific islands) should accept the principles of trusteeship for the advancement and welfare of indigenous peoples, and should be obliged to report regularly to the United Nations. Australia and New Zealand, having participated in the war from the outset, were entitled to a voice in the drafting of armistices and peace treaties at the end of hostilities. They might have to accept exclusion from the arrangements in Europe concerning Germany and Italy, but they would insist on their right to take part when it came to Japan, and the future of East Asia and the Pacific.[30]

None of this was incompatible with the Dumbarton Oaks recommendations, but it all depended on the cooperation of the three great powers. In February 1945 the Allied leaders, Churchill, Roosevelt and Stalin, met at Yalta and endorsed the principles outlined at Dumbarton Oaks. The United Nations would have as its central decision-making body a General Assembly to which all member nations would belong. A good deal of authority would be delegated from the General Assembly to a Security Council including at least eight members other than the great powers, whose membership was taken for granted. In the event, France and China managed to get themselves recognised as great powers alongside the United States, the Soviet Union and Britain, but Australia could cherish a hope of taking its turn on the Security Council and arguing its own distinctive concerns. In Hasluck's words: 'We also thought that more attention should be given by the world organisation to social, economic and humanitarian problems...Power was to be restrained by principle'.[31]

An international conference to plan the future United Nations organisation was to take place in April 1945 at San

Francisco. There would be a preliminary conference in London to coordinate the approaches of members of the British Commonwealth. Curtin, who could not go himself as his health was failing, decided to repeat the experiment of sending Forde and Evatt together as the appropriate senior politicians.[32] He never spelt out whether Forde as the senior cabinet minister or Evatt as Minister of External Affairs was to lead the delegation. It was, to use Hasluck's term, 'a calf with two heads'.[33] With both men out of the way in the early months of 1945, Curtin could give the Treasurer, Ben Chifley, a clear run to establish his credentials as acting Prime Minister and likely successor.

Evatt responded by mobilising the strongest possible support team to accompany him. Hasluck would be included in the delegation, along with Burton and Forsyth from External Affairs, reinforced by Alan Watt and the economist J. B. Brigden from the Washington Embassy. Evatt recruited Kenneth Bailey, the very able professor of law from the University of Melbourne, who was on secondment to the Attorney-General's Department and with whom Hasluck had built a close working relationship. Evatt's team was reinforced by two outsiders, Macmahon Ball, a senior political scientist from Melbourne who had edited a volume of Evatt's speeches, and Sam Atyeo, a remarkable character who occupied an ill-defined position on Evatt's staff. A Melbourne-trained artist living in France before the war, Atyeo was rescued from a prison in Martinique at Evatt's intervention and attached himself to the minister. Amusing, irreverent and bawdy, Atyeo and his wife, Moya Dyring, introduced an incongruously Bohemian element to the straitlaced delegation. Their presence was a further breach of sound bureaucratic principle, and as such Hasluck found it hard to approve of them, but Atyeo proved a good-natured colleague. Although he teased Hasluck as 'Pompous Paul', he never used his role as Evatt's 'court jester' to damage Hasluck's interests, and more than once helped to defuse sticky situations.[34]

Perhaps in an attempt to restrain Evatt, Curtin added a number of consultants to the delegation. Only one came from External Affairs: Sir Frederic Eggleston, the Minister to Washington who had previously served in China. He was experienced and sagacious, but immobilised by arthritis. Among officers from other departments, the ablest were Roland Wilson, the secretary of the Department of Labour, and Fin Crisp from Post-War Reconstruction. Defence was strongly represented by a senior public servant, Percy Coleman, and three senior servicemen as advisers. In addition, a considerable number of politicians, trade unionists, representatives of women's interests (as they were termed) and other observers made up a supernumerary cast whose role was never well defined and who had little influence on the progress of negotiations.

During Hasluck's absence the Post-Hostilities Planning desk in Canberra would be occupied by a newcomer to the section, Ian Milner,[35] who had been acting head of the Department of Political Science at the University of Melbourne. He was appointed to a newly created position as special investigation officer in External Affairs in November 1944. Milner came with strong testimonials from respected professors Max Crawford and Boyce Gibson, and from his Vice-Chancellor, Sir John Medley. Hasluck had first met him at an Australian Institute of Political Science summer school the previous summer, and Milner's biographer conjectures that Hasluck suggested he should apply. He comments: 'Milner and Hasluck's politics would not have been in sympathy, but they had distinctly similar personalities: a certain initial diffidence, masking firmness, even steeliness of resolve'.[36]

Hasluck was aware of Milner's left-wing sympathies, but his previous experience in Perth with communist acquaintances such as Katharine Susannah Prichard (who was Ric Throssell's mother) and the landscape architect John Oldham suggested that, although they held opinions far removed from his own, they were essentially decent people who could be trusted as colleagues. He could not have perceived the potential for security risk in the way Milner followed the line of Stalinist Russia without deviation.[37] In 1944 Hasluck had negotiated with the British authorities for access to their documents on postwar security, including a good deal of confidential material. Milner came to Canberra in February 1945 and took charge of the Post-Hostilities Planning Division in March. There he seemed a competent and efficient colleague, although in time he was to be strongly suspected of passing information to the Soviet bloc.

Hasluck had other preoccupations as he prepared to leave Australia in mid-March. It was at this point that, having arranged for Alexandra and the children to vacate their house in Canberra and return to Perth, he received word of the death of his elder brother Lewis as a prisoner of war of the Japanese. Lewis had succumbed to illness and privation on 6 April 1944. Paul sent a telegram to his parents: 'Don't lose heart. We shall teach our children to be proud of him'.[38] An intensely private man, he kept his grief to himself. In handwriting much smaller than his usual neat calligraphy he wrote a note of Lewis's wretched end, with his mates too feeble to give him a decent burial. Probably at the same time he started on a memoir of Lewis, but after a while

136

it deviated into fiction and was left unfinished.[39] Lewis found a place a few years later in one of his most substantial poems, 'In time of drought':

> *Humble before the heroes, I realize*
> *The inadequacy of courage and of strength;*
> *And death is failure without birth.*
> *My brother's courage gave to earth*
> *A mound of his own length. He paid out courage in one lot,*
> *But faithfulness in plodding days*
> *And the wise husbandry of vines*
> *He set in trellised lines*
> *Shall keep perpetual praise.*[40]

When Paul Hasluck died many years later, his family found in the wallet that he always carried a photograph of Lewis in his army uniform.

It cannot have escaped Paul that Lewis – good-natured, earthy, quintessentially Australian – had sacrificed his life for his country while his brother served in the safety of the home front. According to his friend Peter Ryan, it was a sensitive point with Paul Hasluck that he never heard a shot fired in anger.[41] It can hardly be doubted that Hasluck's already sturdy sense of patriotic duty to Australia was strengthened just at the time when he was setting out to serve his country in what could be seen as the most important diplomatic negotiation of its history. He was not immune to the hope that at San Francisco the nations might agree to a sounder and safer world order than in the past, and that Australia might play a constructive part in reaching this outcome. But disillusionment would follow.

Chapter 8

At the workshop of security

On 15 March 1945 Hasluck left Canberra. Evatt had phoned from Los Angeles in a good humour, expressing eagerness to see Hasluck and his colleague W. D. Forsyth as soon as possible, but the journey began badly. Paul was suffering an extremely severe reaction to a vaccination, and his hotel room in Sydney was dirty and stuffy, 'the sort of room that suggests chamber pots and blowsy extra-marital caresses'.[1] For the long flight to the United States he took a characteristically broad range of reading: two nineteenth-century works, Disraeli's *Sybil* and Kingsley's *Yeast*; a modern political novel, Harold Nicolson's *Public Faces*; a thriller; two books on current affairs; and the maverick politician J. T. Lang's *Communism in Australia*.[2] Arriving at Los Angeles, he and Forsyth found that although their accommodation at the Biltmore was a great improvement on Sydney, they had to deal with Burton, 'who seems mainly concerned to assure us that the Minister does not want to see us and we need not get in touch with him'.[3] These games of office politics sorted themselves out during the next fortnight, so that by the time the delegation departed for London in early April, Hasluck was prepared to concede that 'Burton is now quite agreeable though of course unchanged by nature', whereas he was growing tired of 'Forsyth's sulks and resentments'.[4]

The London conference went from 4 to 13 April. The British meant it to be

> a rather mild family talk, at which the United Kingdom, as one
> of the big three and one of the sponsoring powers, would give
> information and explanations to the Dominions and answer
> their questions in order to assist their preparations for the San
> Francisco conference.[5]

Evatt changed that. Comprehensively briefed by Hasluck and Bailey, and working with furious concentration, he soon made it clear that Australia would take its own line at San Francisco. Hasluck and Bailey suggested that the roles of the Security Council and the International Court of Justice required more explicit definition. Evatt developed these issues into a demand that the 'middle powers', among them Australia, should have a stronger voice in the security system. He also argued for greater emphasis on economic and social questions and – to Britain's vexation – decolonisation.

To define the questions of agreement and disagreement among the members of the British Commonwealth, the conference appointed a committee of advisers. Hasluck and Bailey served on it under Evatt's close supervision. Hasluck's contribution lay in his increasingly adept skills as a draftsman, complemented by Kenneth Bailey's mastery of legal technicalities. Together they were able to have some input into the shaping of Australian policy. Clarity was achieved, but it was becoming obvious that Australia would not necessarily comply with the United Kingdom and that Evatt controlled Australia's policy. The patriot in Hasluck was not unhappy about this outcome, although privately he disagreed with some aspects of Evatt's thought, particularly on colonial issues, where he tended to ignore his specialist adviser, Forsyth. To his wife Hasluck wrote: 'Australia took quite a prominent part…and in this case I think it can fairly be stated that Australia was Evatt, Bailey and myself'.[6]

It was Hasluck's first visit to London since his honeymoon with Alexandra nearly thirteen years before. Official duties meant he saw little of the war-damaged city, though he managed to take in an Emlyn Williams play. He met many of the great, including at a sherry party at Buckingham Palace where there were, as he put it, 'enough striped pants and morning suits, worn with graceful dignity, to reassure everyone that all was right with the world'.[7] The royal family made a pleasant impression. Winston Churchill was not as physically big as he expected, but his eyes were exceptionally clear and bright, and his features not coarse and pudgy but soft and pinkish like a baby's bottom. Anthony Eden looked like a modish used-car salesman. Lord Cranborne, the Secretary of State for the Dominions, was an 'Osbert Lancaster Englishman'.[8] Hasluck had a good Australian irreverence for the British aristocracy. When, en route to the United States, the delegation touched down at Bermuda and was entertained by the Governor, Lord Burghley, Hasluck described him as 'a bloke who used to run around at the Olympic Games jumping over hurdles'.[9]

At San Francisco the Australian delegation's accommodation reflected its divided character. Evatt and the officers of External Affairs, together with Kenneth Bailey and Sam Atyeo, occupied quarters on the seventeenth floor of the Sir Francis Drake Hotel. Forde, Roland Wilson, Fin Crisp and the Defence personnel had offices and bedrooms on the eleventh floor. Keith Waller, the External Affairs officer who acted as secretary to the delegation, had an office on the eleventh floor and a bedroom on the seventeenth. Evatt instructed the Department of External Affairs team to have no dealings with the other parts of the Australian delegation, but in practice the public servants made sure there was enough effective communication to avert any outward show of disunity. 'There was no real conflict on policy', in Hasluck's recollection, 'simply because only Evatt made the decisions on policy without using anyone except the officials'.[10]

Evatt and his team, with Hasluck prominent among them, would be the powerhouse of the Australian delegation. The bland and amiable Forde was content to bathe in the limelight of the international stage without taking initiatives in policy. It sufficed him to make genial public appearances, to speak convincingly from the conference papers placed in front of him, and to figure in the media. In Hasluck's view:

> He just has not got the mental equipment to understand what
> the conference is about. He is the type who makes speeches full
> of platitudes, but he does not even know they are platitudes.
> He says something that was a platitude 25 years ago, and is not
> even applicable as a platitude to the current situation, and trots
> it out in the belief that he is really master of the subject.[11]

Later in the conference Hasluck's exasperation grew. To his wife he described Forde as an 'unutterable fool' who whenever possible had to be restrained from public speaking.[12]

The conference began on 25 April and was scheduled to close at the end of May, but got off to a slow start. Fifty-five nations were represented, including all the Allies and many of the neutrals, but of course excluding Germany (which surrendered on 8 May) and Japan. In the opening days of the conference, wrote Hasluck,

> there was a good deal of fuss and flummery and everyone scurrying about. Self-importance was in its best clothes. Our own delegation needed a good deal of patience and acceptance of futile enterprises.[13]

In the early days there were even a few opportunities for relaxation. Fin Crisp's diary records an evening out with Hasluck at which dinner was followed by a visit to a burlesque show.[14] Before long the pressure of work would be too great for such agreeable interludes.

Very quickly, Evatt and the officials from External Affairs, augmented by Bailey, established themselves as the makers of Australian policy at San Francisco. The work of the conference was divided among four commissions. Evatt ensured that one of his officers was appointed secretary and executive officer of each of the Australian delegations to these commissions. Two central bodies, an executive committee and a steering committee, coordinated the work of the four commissions. Evatt, with Hasluck as his lieutenant, secured membership of both committees, as well as the right to attend any of the four commissions. When the work of the commissions was subdivided into twelve committees, at least one of the Evatt team was present on each committee.[15] Forsyth credited Hasluck with effecting these arrangements, 'fortunately for Evatt who seemed incapable of bureaucratic mechanics or incurably allergic to them'.[16] Although Hasluck was not formally Evatt's chief of staff, his duties included the daily coordination of committee meetings and the briefing of Australia's representatives. This was often complicated by Evatt's habit of departing from the schedule to drop in on committee meetings and take over from the regular spokesman. His ubiquity astonished, though it did not always impress, the delegates from other nations.

So it was that Evatt, with Hasluck at his side, was able to keep abreast of developments at each level of debate and to coordinate all this input into effective policies. In the eyes of an observer who saw much of the action at this time:

> Hasluck, I think, more than anybody, was responsible for framing the policies that Evatt followed in the post-war world. From the time in 1943 when Evatt fastened his attention to what the post-war world would be like – what Australia's role should be in it – Hasluck was the principal guide that fed the ideas into him. There were others such as Bill Forsyth, Ken Bailey, etc. etc. but Hasluck was the main one, the main architect of policies. And he worked like a Trojan for Evatt...[17]

Under the intense pressure of working towards a common goal, the Australian delegates mostly suspended their office jealousies. Hasluck found himself praising Evatt's tremendous capacity for work, forming close alliances with Kenneth Bailey and Alan Watt, and even writing in complimentary terms about Burton.[18]

He found that at the meetings of the executive and steering committees, while the representatives of the major powers – Britain, the United States, the Soviet Union and China – sat at the top table, Australia, because of its alphabetical priority, was placed close by. Thus he had a first-class opportunity of observing

143

the world's leaders and commenting on them. Anthony Eden, he decided, came out fairly well:

> But he illustrates the defects of treating foreign affairs as an elaborate science with rules of its own, instead of a matter of facts and human relations. One suspects that he is constantly stopped in his thinking by his ideas, 'But you couldn't possibly do that.'

The United States Secretary of State, Edward Stettinius, was

> a terrible flop…who still seems to think that a big toothpaste smile and the businessman's ringing sincerity after the style of a Rotary Club, a handshake and a pat on the back are a substitute for cold hard arguments. He is a most incompetent chairman.[19]

Unexpectedly, his greatest admiration was for the Soviet Union's Foreign Minister, Viacheslav Molotov:

> He is easily the outstanding person of the conference, in fact the most impressive figure I have met – Churchill or the King or anyone else included…He has a wise passivity and of course complete command of himself, which I should say is derived from a consciousness of strength of his own country and of himself…He does not seem elated over his successes for he expected them; he does not show any chagrin over his reverses because he probably expected them…He clearly looks upon foreign politics as a skilled and continuing adjustment of forces.[20]

The Soviet Union, Hasluck perceived,

> was engaged realistically in the business of protecting the
> security of the Soviet Union and serving their own national
> interests...There were no illusions nor any profession about an
> ideal of internationalism but a plain recognition of the plain
> facts of power.[21]

Increasingly, Hasluck was coming to see the successful diplomat as a practitioner of intellectual skills pragmatically applied to specific problems rather than an advocate of any ideology. This placed him at variance with Evatt, for whom the United Nations still seemed to promise 'a new province for law and order' in which the nations would sink their own self-interest in the pursuit of goals such as colonial trusteeship, full employment and the peaceful resolution of territorial disputes. Both were working in what has been described as a new environment of multilateral diplomacy, which called on skills in communication and negotiation at a higher level than much conventional diplomacy. Neither Evatt nor Hasluck had previous experience of conventional diplomacy, and they and their Australian colleagues were on a steep learning curve.[22] Hasluck, for his part, was experiencing huge disenchantment with the practice of international diplomacy. He had arrived at San Francisco believing himself to be a member of 'the worst diplomatic service in the world',[23] a verdict probably coloured by his experience of bureaucratic infighting at External Affairs. He soon found that the representatives of other nations were far from statesmanlike, and while they gave lip service to high ideals, their practice was marked by duplicity and self-interest.

He told his wife: 'I become more and more cynical watching this crowd at work and less certain that truth is ever to be found from the lips of man or that man can ever be of great stature', identifying himself with the mood of Old Testament texts denouncing the depravity of humanity, such as Jeremiah and Ecclesiastes.[24] Alexandra Hasluck briskly and promptly replied that 'such prating' made her mad.

> I hate those whining old prophets, and if people are going to be idealists, they should stop being pessimists, because the two cancel each other out. You always expect perfection, it's not fair.[25]

But Paul Hasluck continued pessimistic.

> And don't you ever believe what you read in the papers about high-minded statesmen laying the foundations of peace. They are a collection of monomaniacs all trying to put something across their neighbours.[26]

Paul Hasluck was now forty years old, a rather mature age to be undergoing such radical disillusionment with the processes of international politics. For the first thirty-six of those years he had lived and worked in a Western Australia, remote from first-hand experience of these processes. Although his last four years in Canberra had given him plenty of lessons in the art of policymaking, it would have been easy to convince himself that Australia's infant diplomatic service was lacking in values internalised in the older, established foreign services of other nations. He came to San Francisco with his patriotic ideals strengthened by the wish for a postwar world worthy of the sacrifices of Australians such as his brother Lewis. His 'childhood faith that unless the foundations are true and honest and based on an ideal, the final outcome cannot be sound' could not long survive in an environment where 'Everyone here thinks everyone else is unworthy of trust, and I fancy everyone is pretty nearly right'.[27] Little could be expected from a United Nations organisation whose structure would be largely determined by deals cut among the great powers.

From this abyss of pessimism he soon raised himself by a growing realisation that all the desperately hard work by Evatt and his team was producing positive results. In the same letter that described the San Francisco delegates as a collection of monomaniacs, he also wrote:

> the Australian delegation is going pretty well and is getting a great number of the things it wants, so although the spiritual climate is not very exhilarating there is a certain amount of good humour around the place.[28]

Evatt was leading a tenacious, but eventually unsuccessful fight to limit the capacity of the Great Powers to impose a veto on Security Council measures for the pacific settlement of disputes. 'I have never known Dr Evatt more persuasive or more masterly in the handling of a subject', Hasluck recalled later.[29] The decision to allow the United States, the Soviet Union, Britain, China and France an unrestricted power of veto was one of the agreements reached between Stalin, Churchill and Roosevelt at the Yalta conference in February 1945, and the Russians were determined to keep to it. As Hasluck later observed: 'The consistent pursuit of national advantage by one member has naturally provoked a response from others and has led to a general deterioration of international relations all round'.[30]

Australia's motion to restrict the veto was lost by ten votes to twenty with fifteen abstentions, but although unsuccessful the fight had the result of knitting the members of the Australian delegation together. When the time came to set up a fourteen-nation coordination committee to integrate the findings of the other committees and working parties, and incorporate them into the text of the charter of the United Nations, Hasluck and Bailey were nominated to membership. Pleased at their capacity to stand up to Great Britain and the United States, Evatt was prepared to tell them: 'Go ahead and use your own judgment'.[31]

After more days of intense pressure, the Charter of the United Nations was ready to submit to the participating governments for adoption. Hasluck's mood was one of relief and elation. For Evatt he had come to entertain great respect, and if subsequently he was to express criticisms about his minister's achievements at San Francisco, they were not apparent in mid-June 1945. Evatt, he wrote, 'has certainly made his mark in this conference and established Australia as, next to the Great Powers, one of the most important and influential delegations at the conference'.[32] Despite his directness, Evatt had made a wonderful impression and was very popular. 'Many praise the contribution of the Australian delegation, especially to the improvement of the Charter. Certainly Evatt, Bailey, Burton, Watt and I have worked like the devil'.[33]

The effort has been worth it…Australia's name stands higher in world affairs, and we have won a great deal of respect and many friends…[Evatt] has made me proud to be an Australian and particularly to be one of the same team…He really has fought magnificently and with great judgment in very difficult circumstances.[34]

In later years Hasluck was to comment less enthusiastically about Evatt's performance at San Francisco:

he was working for a success at San Francisco rather than addressing himself to the continuing tasks of good international relations. He was eager to play a leading role in making the Charter and of being the champion of small powers. His ambition was clearer than his policy.[35]

This was a verdict reached after personal ill usage by Evatt and disillusionment with his subsequent performances on the international stage. In the euphoria of June 1945 there was no room for such reservations. Hasluck could afford himself some of the credit. He had shown a capacity for unremitting hard work, which his colleagues admired.[36] He had honed some of his personal skills, discovering a talent and a taste for public speaking among some exacting audiences, and greatly improving his hard-won mastery of spoken French. He found pleasure in the informal side of diplomatic exchanges, such as a serious conversation with a Russian colleague about the possibility of bringing the Moscow Ballet to Australia. But his idealism was giving way to a cold-eyed pragmatism. A few months later he was to write:

though diplomats may be liars and dissemblers when dealing with matters of national policy they can get down and talk some clear sense from each other when given a practical problem. I used to put my faith in ideals almost wholly and I still think they must underlie any worthwhile work, but as to method in building the future, more useful progress can be made at times by ceasing to look for basic principles and confining attention narrowly to a particular task in hand.[37]

He was still uncertain about his future. Despite Alexandra's warnings about the parochialism of Western Australia, parts of him still hankered for Perth, and he hoped to keep open his lines of communication with the *West Australian* and The University of Western Australia. He did not want to return to Canberra, where Hood, as usual during his absences, had been intervening in the Post-Hostilities Planning Division and was still the senior man in the Department of External Affairs. There was still no permanent head of the department, a muddled scene that needed sorting out: 'I wish to God I had never been mixed up with the bloody show'.[38] Alexandra, though she did not wish for a lifetime as a diplomat's wife, thought he should remain for the time being with the department, and he considered it possible that he might secure a secondment to the infant United Nations or one of the embassies, Washington or London. He talked to Evatt:

I am afraid I am still too proud to ask for any particular post or to push my claims to any favour, but I told him first that I had three years to fill in before starting the history. I wanted to fill it in a place where I would do effective work and in a capacity that would count as some qualification when I started to look for another job when the history was finished.[39]

Evatt made no immediate rejoinder, but both men must have realised that the San Francisco conference was only the beginning of the process of creating a new world order. If Australia used its newfound standing to continue taking part in international diplomacy, there would be plenty of work for Hasluck.

For the immediate future Evatt had an unexpected proposal. Instead of returning at once to Australia they should take a break after the fatigues of the San Francisco conference. First the Evatts, together with Hasluck, Burton and the Atyeos, should spend a few days recuperating at the Yosemite National Park, and then they should come home by way of a trans-Pacific sea voyage, during which they would write an account of Australia's role at San Francisco. Unlike Evatt, who hated and feared air travel, Hasluck would have preferred not to go by sea, being a poor sailor. He had also complained frequently during the San Francisco conference about separation from his wife and family. Alexandra missed him too. She was back in Perth with their two small children, living in uncomfortable domesticity with her rather demanding mother. It did not help that the mails were irregular and it was one of Perth's wettest winters.[40]

Hasluck nevertheless agreed to Evatt's idea. Perhaps he worried that Burton, left alone with Evatt, would not only consolidate his position as Evatt's adviser, but would also shape the historical record of the San Francisco conference. Perhaps the historian in him relished the opportunity of helping to write that record. Almost certainly he recoiled from the thought of returning to Canberra. Hasluck was becoming obsessive about Hood; he said he had 'never known a man with such depths of malevolence and deceit', and would assert that

The whole of the work I have done there in the last three years has been pulled down, my position has been destroyed and my usefulness is gone and I just cannot face the prospect of living in the midst of the departmental intrigues.[41]

Understandably, he preferred to stay with Evatt. He may not have known that Hood had some justification for keeping an eye on the Post-Hostilities Planning Division, since Hasluck's stand-in, Ian Milner, was in the habit of taking home sensitive documents from the files without authority. It was not then known that he probably copied them for transmission to the Soviet Union.

Between the hectic pressures of the San Francisco conference and the no less intense months that lay ahead, the weeks of time out in July 1945 form a curious interlude. The few days at Yosemite were almost halcyon. Evatt was in a sunny mood, and Hasluck and Burton, both keen horsemen, went for long rides together through the valleys and ridges of the national park.[42] The voyage across the Pacific seemed equally removed from the world of diplomacy and politics. The scheme of writing a history of the San Francisco conference was soon quietly abandoned, and the travellers settled down to a peaceful existence of relaxation and reading, the greatest antagonisms arising from disputes about that most competitive of shipboard games, deck quoits. Hasluck and Sam Atyeo, never previously close, discovered a common enthusiasm for jazz. Evatt was 'boyish in a pair of shorts'.[43] Even the arrival of news that Curtin had died, and that the Labor caucus had elected Chifley as leader by a substantial margin over Forde, did not long disturb the tranquillity of the voyage. If nothing of note was achieved, the journey at least provided a period of recuperation for Evatt, Hasluck and Burton after they had been stretched to the limit.[44]

Hasluck was not destined to spend long in the uncongenial environment of Canberra. It was decided that after arriving home he should proceed almost immediately to London to represent Australia at the executive committee of the Preparatory Commission, which would precede the convening of the first session of the United Nations. There was just time to visit Alexandra and the children for a few days of reunion in Perth before he was once more travelling by a slow and tedious air journey to London. He arrived in London a few days before 15 August 1945, when Japan's capitulation brought an end to the war. He thought the London celebrations lacked animation: 'They mostly trudge around waiting for someone else to do something extraordinary', he reported.[45] The verdict does not match other accounts of enthusiastic crowds who had turned out for the opening of parliament and wanted to cheer the royal family as they drove through Westminster, and reflects a sombreness in Hasluck's own mood. He wished he could have celebrated the coming of peace among his own people in Australia. After six years of war and sustained aerial bombing, London was drab, rationing was tight, and he found that, unlike in San Francisco, 'the physical conditions of life are not very convenient here'.[46]

He felt lonely and hungered for intelligent conversation. One of the new intake of diplomatic cadets, Alan Renouf, was already in London to serve as Hasluck's offsider. He was diligent and efficient, though he soon found that his 'capacity for work was exceeded by that of Hasluck'.[47] Hasluck's first impressions of Renouf were mixed: 'He is excellent while we are at work but I

become most painfully conscious of the differences in our age…
He is just a healthy young barbarian'.[48] Worse, he 'had scarcely
read a book, is not interested much in ideas, has no social interests
apart from sport and is completely insensitive and without any
finer shades of perceptiveness'.[49] But there was good human
material in the young man, and Hasluck was soon mentoring
Renouf inside and outside the office, with both enjoying the
experience. 'I never knew any young Australian in our foreign
service who developed more quickly both insight and skill in
conference work', wrote Hasluck. As Renouf recalled:

> To me, he was an excellent teacher whose teaching extended
> beyond work. I had never been to the theatre. Hasluck
> introduced me to it, and what an introduction it was: Laurence
> Olivier and Ralph Richardson in 'Henry V' at the Old Vic. He
> also introduced me to foreign cuisine, a marked contrast to the
> fare of Canberra hostels in wartime.[50]

Hasluck's debut at the Preparatory Commission was fraught
with problems. The other delegations were all headed by
ambassadors or ministers senior in status to Hasluck. For the
Australian delegation the obvious appointee at that rank was
Stanley Bruce, a former Prime Minister who for thirteen years
had served as the immensely experienced and capable Australian
High Commissioner in London. But Evatt was not on good
terms with Bruce, and rebuffed his protests at being superseded
by Hasluck. Instead, he instructed Hasluck to have nothing to
do with the High Commissioner. While Hasluck felt that his
effectiveness would not be diminished by his lack of diplomatic
rank, he was concerned at 'the direct and open snub' to Bruce

and 'the failure to use his exceptional qualifications in this field'.[51] Defying instructions, he sought an interview with Bruce and told him that, although he would take his instructions from Evatt, he would send all outward communications to Canberra through Australia House so that they could be seen by Bruce. Bruce candidly told Hasluck his side of the story, but with gracious professionalism said that he accepted the decision and would work to facilitate Hasluck's role in London.[52]

The delegation was small and given insufficient guidance and support from Canberra. Hasluck estimated that in two and a half months to the end of October 1945 he sent more than 100 cabled messages to Canberra and received only three replies.[53] With some difficulty Hasluck secured permission to recruit an addition to the secretariat staff, Terry Glasheen, and the economic side was strengthened by the arrival of Arthur Tange as an adviser, but there were other colleagues he found less agreeable. Where the frenetic pressures of San Francisco had created camaraderie among the Australian delegates, old habits were starting to crop up in London, and he was finding Burton 'a rather unpleasant young man'.[54] It was some consolation that the long interregnum at the head of the Department of External Affairs was at last drawing to an end. None of Hasluck's colleagues in the department was acceptable to Evatt. The new man would be William Dunk, a career public servant with a Treasury background. In his memoirs Dunk confessed, 'I never had tickets on myself as a budding diplomat',[55] but he had a talent for administrative efficiency and could be expected to impose order on External Affairs. 'He is not what we would call an educated man or a man of very great intellectual gifts', Hasluck told his wife, but he is experienced in administration, firm, pretty easy to get on with, and will do the department a lot of good by putting it in order and stopping most of the monkey business.[56]

The negotiations in London continued at a strenuous pace. Hasluck calculated that in the ten weeks from mid-August he attended 160 different meetings and was losing weight at about the rate of a kilogram a month. This demanding routine did nothing to dispel the feelings of loneliness that had dogged him ever since his arrival in London. He was, he wrote, 'a pessimistic man in the midst of a hopeless world'.[57] Now, undistracted by the pressure of nonstop committees, he succumbed to a deep and bleak interval of depression. The term 'midlife crisis' had not yet been coined to describe the sense of melancholy and futility that sometimes overtakes outwardly successful men around the age of forty, but Paul Hasluck's letters to his wife in the early days of November 1945 read like a classic case of the syndrome. He felt a failure in every respect: as a husband, as a friend, as a creative artist, as the shaper of a successful career.[58] For a man who strove to keep his emotions well under control it was a terrible experience, though it should not have been wholly surprising. The year had begun with news of his brother's death and had involved almost total separation from his wife and children. He had spent a year of punishingly hard work during which his professional life had found no reliable sense of support or reinforcement and his ideals had taken a considerable battering. He was at the end of his tether.

Gradually he emerged from the pit. He took himself to a doctor, who told him that his condition resembled that of a man who had been on prolonged active service, and that what he required was an immediate month's holiday. This was impossible, but Paul Hasluck managed to spend three days in the countryside near Gloucester, where he slept long hours and explored churches and cathedrals. Alexandra wrote supportively, although even using airmail there was often the lapse of at least ten days between the dispatch of a letter and the receipt of a reply; perhaps there were phone calls, but they could only have been brief and few. One of the most telling aspects of Paul's depression was his belief that he could not make and keep friends, with the possible exception of Bob James, who was now married and back in Perth, working for the *West Australian* and counting the days until he could afford to quit and look after a vineyard at Glen Forrest, in the hills behind Perth. The young Paul Hasluck of Perth, the journalist who was into every aspect of cultural life, seemed to possess an easy aptitude for friendship, with mates as diverse as the music critic Albert Kornweibel, the scholar Alec King and the naturalist Dom Serventy. The forty-year-old diplomat was more reserved. Observant young Alan Renouf, reflecting many years later, saw him as a loner: 'He didn't want to get on very well with people usually'.[59] Somehow he had begun to assume a protective shell of formality that over the years would become increasingly second nature to him.

Later in November, Dunk as the new head of the department wrote to Hasluck inquiring about his future plans.[60] Hasluck replied at some length in a personal and confidential letter. He wrote that although he was deeply interested in his work and had some confidence in his ability to do it well, he was not attracted to the department as a career, partly because 'few of us had confidence that certain of our colleagues would act in a conventional or fair-minded way or follow normal public service methods in doing public business'.[61] (He meant Burton.) After the Preparatory Commission conference was over, he understood that the services of temporary wartime employees were to be terminated, and that he would have no place in the department. Still, he would welcome the opportunity to do useful work. By the same mail he was enclosing an official memorandum on future Australian participation in the work of the United Nations.

> I would ask you to consider it apart from anything I have said in this letter and as an impersonal and objective statement on a question which I am handling officially.[62]

The memorandum was an able and considered analysis of the tasks that would confront the first General Assembly in 1946. It argued that Australia would require both delegations and permanent representatives of high calibre at the General Assembly, the Security Council, the Economic and Social Council (ECOSOC) and other specialist bodies.[63] In addition, arrangements would have to be made about security agreements and the trusteeship of colonial territories. It cannot have escaped Dunk – and maybe Hasluck did not intend it to escape him – that Australia would be well served if its representatives included an officer with the experience and reputation Hasluck had accumulated. Within days he was told that he would be counsellor in charge of the Australian mission to the United Nations and acting representative on the Atomic Energy Commission.

While Hasluck was making arrangements for his future, he was also taken up with the meetings of the Preparatory Commission between 23 November and 23 December. There was much jockeying among the delegates as they sought to enhance their prospects of winning membership of the Security Council or otherwise taking prominent positions at the first meeting of the United Nations General Assembly. Hodgson, who had come over from Paris for the occasion, and Hasluck were the chief negotiators for Australia. They shepherded Evatt's interests devotedly. At one point there seemed a possibility that the United States, the Russian bloc and most of the Latin American nations would be prepared to support Evatt as President of the General Assembly. Hasluck sent Evatt a personal and urgent message, 'that our proposed delegation is not as strong in personalities as occasion warrants or as our ambitions require'.[64] This seemed a pretty direct hint that Evatt should come to London himself, but he had been away too much from Canberra and was detained there. In the event, the short list for the presidency consisted of Paul-Henri Spaak (Belgium) and Wellington Koo (China), with the former eventually chosen. Hasluck thought that British disapproval might have prejudiced Australia's chances.[65]

The Australians were no more successful in the debate over the future site of the United Nations headquarters. Evatt was eager for San Francisco, a venue he thought would ensure attention to the Pacific region. The Western Australian Hasluck, with an Indian Ocean perspective, would have preferred Vienna or Athens, and kept this in mind as a second preference while loyally arguing for San Francisco. The great powers, the Europeans and the Latin Americans all preferred a site on the Atlantic Ocean side of the world in the north-east of the United States, and railroaded the Preparatory Commission into acceptance. Hasluck found himself in a minority of one. He was later appointed to the commission to recommend a headquarters site, but relinquished the task to a junior colleague.[66]

At the end of 1945, while Hasluck disagreed with some aspects of Evatt's approach to international diplomacy, the differences were not so great as to make it impossible to work with him. As a critic of the American potential for hegemony in the South Pacific and as an architect of the Australia–New Zealand agreement of 1944, Hasluck shared Evatt's zeal for ensuring that the Great Powers pay due attention to their smaller colleagues such as Australia. He had no problem with Evatt's concept that Australia and New Zealand should shoulder regional responsibilities in the South Pacific and embrace the concept of colonial trusteeship. He was not unhappy with Evatt's dexterous attempts to define the concept of 'domestic jurisdiction' so that other nations would have no pretext for interfering with Australia's immigration and population policies. But although Evatt's courtroom aggressiveness made him a formidable presence in debate, Hasluck doubted his skill as a tactician. Evatt spent much time and energy trying in vain to limit the capacity of the Great Powers to exercise a veto on the proceedings of the Security Council; Hasluck and Watt considered that if peace and security depended on the unanimity of the Great Powers, it was unwise to dig away at this foundation.[67] Evatt, supported by Burton, placed much importance on the inclusion of full employment as one of the aims of the United Nations Charter; Hasluck was less convinced of its practicality.

Evatt took pride in the quantitative aspects of Australia's contribution at San Francisco, boasting that 'Of the 38 amendments of substance which Australia proposed no less than 26 were either adopted without material change or adopted in principle';[68] Hasluck, however, felt that 'we have sometimes butted unnecessarily into other people's arguments without waiting to consider whether the argument was getting on all right without us'.[69] It could not be denied that during the creation of the United Nations Organisation, Evatt's performance had established Australia's credentials as a nation possessing a voice of its own in international affairs. In pressing Evatt's claims to be considered for the presidency of the General Assembly, Hasluck may have hoped his energies would be absorbed more constructively in the challenges of the role. Unfortunately, the events of 1946 would show that Evatt was incapable of modifying his style and methods. As Watt put it, 'He did not understand the value of occasional diplomatic silence, or the need to balance present successes against possible long-term losses'.[70] And he would show a distinct lack of appreciation for a colleague such as Hasluck, who sought to enhance Australia's standing by methods less grandiose and ambitious than his own.

Chapter 9

Resignation

Hasluck's new responsibilities meant he would remain in London over the winter, moving to New York in March 1946. While in London he attended a preliminary meeting of the General Assembly from 10 January to early February, as well the Security Council entrusted with carrying out the agenda devised by the Preparatory Commission. Membership of the Security Council would ensure an effective voice in policymaking. The United States, the United Kingdom, the Soviet Union and China were to occupy permanent seats on the Security Council, together with a number of elected members. Canada and Australia both had a chance of election. Canada was seen as the senior member of the British Commonwealth next to Britain, and had been involved in atomic energy planning, but Australia had established itself at San Francisco as the more independent voice. Voting was close until the Canadians gracefully withdrew in favour of Australia. This recognised the need for representation of the south-west Pacific region, but it could also be seen as a tribute to the standing of the Australian delegation.[1]

The Security Council met at Church House in London 'in a room rather too small for efficiency and without a faith big enough for its mission'.[2] Its chairmanship was to rotate through the various delegations in alphabetical order, beginning with

Australia. In Evatt's absence, leadership of the Australian delegation was assumed by Norman Makin, the recently appointed Australian Ambassador to Washington, assisted by Jack Beasley, who had just arrived as Australia's Resident Minister and High Commissioner in London. Both had been members of the federal cabinet and had served for short periods as acting Minister for External Affairs, but in the event Beasley seldom attended, leaving most of the role to Makin.[3] As Renouf described his performance:

> Makin thanked the Council effusively for being first chairman. While Hasluck's face preserved an oriental calm, Watt's constantly moving with nervous coughs, was the reverse, and Bailey's showed absolute disbelief, while there was raucous comment and guffaws of laughter from the irrepressible Sam Atyeo.[4]

But Makin was prepared to take advice and show appreciation.

The work of the Security Council proceeded smoothly, and despite periods of illness, the Australian delegation, as Hasluck put it, 'finished in a canter'.[5] At the end Hasluck won praise from respected senior diplomats. America's Adlai Stevenson wrote that he had enjoyed their contact, and only wished it had been more frequent. Sir Gladwyn Jebb, the British acting Secretary-General of the United Nations, wrote:

> I hope and believe that you yourself will go from strength to strength in the Australian Foreign Service since it strikes me that the British Commonwealth will want many officials as tough and intelligent as you in the next few years, and there aren't that number available.[6]

The Makin episode nevertheless left Hasluck somewhat sensitive to points of protocol. Whereas nearly all the other delegates to the Security Council had ambassador status, Hasluck was only a counsellor because Evatt reserved the ambassadorial role for himself. Hasluck accordingly made a point of always representing Australia at the Security Council himself, never sending any other member of the delegation except Renouf as his designated understudy.

Hasluck arrived in New York late in March 1946 to face predictably chaotic problems of settling in. The temporary quarters of the United Nations were at Hunter College, in the Bronx district of New York. It seemed a daunting task to find office accommodation with rooms for the minister, six departmental officers, a technical adviser from the Atomic Energy Commission, four secretary–stenographers, two messengers and three security men. Through a fortunate chance meeting, Renouf alerted Hasluck to a tenancy at a low rent on the forty-fifth floor of the Empire State Building, then still the world's tallest skyscraper. It was, Hasluck wrote, 'admirable for our present purposes', but there were moments of disadvantage. One day Renouf found that the elevator men were on strike. Hasluck's reply was 'So what? We will walk up and down' – all forty-five storeys.[7]

Communications were at first difficult. The delegation had to borrow its first typewriter from the Australian consulate, and had no Typex machine for direct communication with Canberra. For some months Hasluck had difficulty acquiring a car. It also soon became apparent that Australian diplomatic allowances based on public-service principles in Canberra would not go far enough to meet the cost of living in New York. Money problems, Hasluck wrote in June, were 'perpetually a migraine. We just cannot live in New York on present pay and allowances without becoming shabby'.[8] It had been decided that Alexandra and the children would join him in the United States in early May, and this was possible only because Alexandra used the dividends from a shareholding inherited from her father's family. In preparation, Paul was able to rent a colonial house in Bronxville, an hour's drive from the office, in a congenial neighbourhood. The upheaval for the family was nevertheless considerable.

In Alexandra's words, she

> stepped right from a 4½ day train journey that was a nightmare of discomfort right into the midst of the most fantastic existence, dining nightly with millionaires and the great of the earth.[9]

Although she was pleased with the Bronxville house, there was much domestic management to see to: finding the right clothes, looking after the children, and employing 'a coloured maid, who doesn't understand me, nor I her, but we are slowly getting to like each other'.[10] Although barely recovered from a painful reaction to a vaccination, she found herself in a hectic round of social engagements: 'dinners with millionaires like the Nelson Rockefellers and with people like Sir Alexander Cadogan…I hardly even now have a word with Paul'.[11] She was less happy about the Americans: 'It frays my whole being to have to tell them the whole time how wonderful they are, which they expect and wh. it is my job to do'.[12] 'I am so homesick I would come home like a shot', she wrote a fortnight later, adding, 'When I see how worried and over-worked Paul is, I think it wld. be best if we returned to a quiet job in W.A. His headaches are getting so awful'.[13]

Paul was tense and edgy because he was about to make a major speech at the United Nations. Colonel Hodgson, who had been sent to head the Australian delegation until Evatt could take over, had gone back to Paris because of his wife's serious illness, leaving Hasluck in charge. The question under debate concerned Iran. During the war, Britain and the Soviet Union had sent troops there to ensure their lines of communication and supply, but when hostilities ceased the Russians stirred up separatist movements in the border provinces of Azerbaijan and Kurdistan. The Kingdom of Iran complained to the Security Council, and in May 1946 the Red Army began to withdraw from Iranian territory, but at the same time the Soviet delegation temporarily boycotted the Security Council, leaving no opportunity for debating the turn of events. Hasluck prepared a speech attacking the Soviet Union for its disrespect for the processes of consultation essential for the effective working of the United Nations. Evatt gave him no instructions, and he was relying entirely on his own judgement.

The speech made headlines. Alexandra reported that the evening papers in New York had photographs of him with glowing references to him as a young diplomat.[14] Australian newspapers such as the *Sydney Morning Herald* and the *West Australian* reported that the speech had made a profound impression. For the rest of May the media paid attention to Hasluck, as the Australians were serving on two important and contentious committees, one examining the Iranian issue and the other reporting on the fitness of Spain, then under the Franco dictatorship, for admission to the United Nations. 'Evatt was not pleased', Hasluck remembered.[15] He was doing his work too well. Renouf remembered an occasion when Evatt asked him to furnish a weekly report on 'what Hasluck was up to', adding, 'I think he's building himself up, not me'. When Renouf refused, Evatt said, 'I'll fix you'.[16]

Evatt arrived in New York at the end of May, concentrating his attention on the Spanish issue and the Atomic Energy Commission. Both activities kept Hasluck extremely hard at work as Evatt's draftsman, sometimes in all-night sessions. On one occasion he had to sleep overnight on the job, borrowing a pair of Evatt's pyjamas. Alexandra Hasluck commented that the pressure was still giving her husband bad migraines.[17] The committee on Spain submitted what Hasluck described as a report 'remarkable for its clever drafting and political cunning'[18] but the Soviet Union imposed a veto, and the issue was shelved. Hasluck was less impressed with Evatt's performance as temporary chairman of the Atomic Energy Commission, with responsibility for drafting a treaty creating an international atomic energy authority and a system of control. Evatt, although underprepared, seemed hell bent on securing a treaty during his month in office without trying to build up understanding between the United States and the Soviet Union. He departed at the end of June, leaving Hasluck, with the assistance of Ralph Harry and two distinguished scientists, Mark Oliphant and George Briggs, to spend the rest of the year working on many technical problems while the central issue remained unresolved.[19]

Without consulting Hasluck, Evatt took Renouf with him to the peace conference in Paris, and from there Renouf retailed office gossip to Hasluck in New York. He reported:

Evatt is annoyed with you about ticking off Gromyko when
he left the Council. He maintains that this was a breach of
instructions and Molotov was very incensed with it. I think
the real reason, however, is the publicity you received for
your work.[20]

Without the in-depth support that had been available to him in
San Francisco, Evatt lost some of his international standing at
the Paris peace conference by intervening too often in matters
that were not obviously relevant to Australia's interests. It cannot
have pleased him to see Hasluck consolidating his reputation
at the United Nations. 'Burton does not help your cause at all',
Renouf warned Hasluck. Burton was hoping to supplant Dunk
as secretary of the Department of External Affairs. In October
1946, while Dunk was overseas, Evatt appointed Burton acting
secretary, instead of the more senior and experienced deputy
secretary, Alan Watt, who was sent away to the United Nations
mission.[21]

Watt was a welcome reinforcement, as for several months
the Australian delegation had been short-staffed. Arthur Tange
was a strong right-hand man in economic and social affairs, and
two junior officers, John Moore and 'Alf' Body, shouldered
their responsibilities effectively, but instructions from Canberra
were spasmodic and infrequent, seemingly dependent on Evatt's
personal attention.[22] Hasluck's colleagues found that he was
already developing a punctiliousness – some thought an excessive punctiliousness – in the conduct of office routine. When
Tange wrote a letter directly to the United Nations Secretary-
General instead of sending the letter through Hasluck as head of
mission, Hasluck wrote him a formal letter of rebuke instead of

simply dealing with the matter by a quiet word. The incident appears to have rankled with Tange, and yet Hasluck had a high regard for him.[23] It may not be fanciful to suggest that his years as a drama critic had left him with a readiness, not always understood by others, to differentiate his behaviour as a private individual from the conduct imposed on him by a role. He could be cold, meticulous, and sparing of praise towards colleagues and subordinates during office hours, but entirely different after hours.

At the time, Hasluck's style of conducting business was of little concern to the Department of External Affairs, but his popularity with the media was a source of hazard. As he later wrote:

> At this period my difficulties increased because I was very much in the news. The American newspapers…had my picture and pronouncements on the front page. In spite of my sedulous repetition of Dr Evatt's name he did not get a mention. I could not avoid this. Perhaps the peak of my fame in the world was when youngsters recognized me in the street and asked me for my autograph.[24]

Socially the Haslucks were much in demand. Alexandra Hasluck described New York as 'a series of taxi-rushes to famous or sumptuous hotels'. Protocol decreed that the United Nations ranked ahead of all other diplomatic organisations, and as precedence was alphabetical, the wife of the Australian delegation went into functions first ahead of all the others. 'Imagine how nerve wracking', she told her mother. 'To know when to get up, when to leave a party – no one else can till I do & I haven't a watch.'[25] She found she could cope well. A good-looking and intelligent woman not yet forty, she attracted the heavy courtly gallantries of eminent statesmen such as Trygve Lie and Herschel Johnson and, more agreeably, Field Marshal Jan Smuts. She found him a 'dear old man' who asked her to amuse him, 'but he kept veering off into Biblical conversation'.[26] The pace was hectic but stimulating, even if at times 'I hardly ever see Paul except over the top of a newspaper for a few minutes at a hurried breakfast at about 7.20 a.m.'[27]

Alexandra Hasluck missed the reopening of the United Nations General Assembly on 23 October 1946, but attended President Truman's reception at the Waldorf Astoria. 'I met a lot of people who said nice things about Paul & about me. Champagne flowed again & there was a marvellous buffet.' She enjoyed giving dinner parties, 'with French Counts & Barons, Ambassadors & what not. (You ought to see my social manner now)', she told her mother.[28] Her reputation as a hostess was boosted when she served lamb as a main course, unremarkable in Australia but relished by Americans, who were largely unused to it, and Europeans, who had endured years of short rations. She also enjoyed talking with the ambassadors' wives, among them Madame Gromyko from the Soviet Union. It was all a huge contrast to Canberra or Perth, even if the social life had to be balanced against the demands of domesticity and the frequent illnesses of the children in the North American winter. But it would not last.

The first few weeks of the General Assembly produced few surprises. The main business concerning Australia was the negotiation of the trusteeship agreement under which Australia would administer Papua New Guinea, and the main burden fell on the skilled legal authority, Kenneth Bailey.[29] Makin, the Ambassador to Washington, was to head the delegation, but Hasluck continued to represent Australia at the Security Council. Watt, although senior to Hasluck, left him in that position because he did not wish to diminish Hasluck's prestige or interrupt the continuity of his work.[30] Evatt was less considerate. In December it was again Australia's turn to chair the Security Council. Evatt sent word that Makin, and not Hasluck, would fill the chair, provoking an angry cablegram from Hasluck. Makin's nomination undermined his standing and suggested that he lacked the government's confidence. 'If it signifies my replacement I would appreciate plain advice to that effect so that I may make arrangements accordingly.'[31]

Evatt replied that Hasluck's replacement had never entered into the department's consideration, and there was no undermining of his status. Makin had chaired the initial meeting of the Security Council, and the cycle would now be rounded off.[32] Hasluck replied that the mission to the United Nations was totally separate from the Embassy at Washington, and was not subsidiary to it. As he was associated both on the Security Council and the Atomic Energy Commission with policies that had come under criticism from the Soviet Union, might it be preferable for him to take a month's much needed leave during January, leaving the way open for Makin's appointment as acting representative?[33] But Evatt and Dunk refused, saying that it was imperative that Hasluck be on hand to assist Makin during his period of chairmanship.[34]

At the same time as Hasluck was fighting for his status as head of mission, he was complaining about his pay. 'Financially my situation is hopeless', he wrote. His salary reflected neither his past service nor present duties. While most of his colleagues and some of his juniors had been promoted during the previous two years, he remained in a highly responsible position with the modest rank of counsellor. In an exchange that dragged on into the new year, Dunk explained that allowances were determined by a committee of Treasury, External Affairs, and the Public Service Board. The Public Service Board had knocked back the upgrading of Hasluck's position to the rank of senior counsellor.[35] Hasluck's reply was unexpected. Trygve Lie, the Secretary-General of the United Nations, was offering him a position in charge of the United Nations European office based in London. With a tax-free salary of US$10,000 a year and a staff of eighty working for him, it was a tempting offer. Hasluck cabled Canberra:

> Salary, standing and prospects are much better than anything Department can offer and reflect higher estimation of my capacity than the Department has ever shown. My preference would be to continue in Australian service if possible but Secretariat offer is most attractive and my experience of Australian service during the past two years has been extremely discouraging. I do not intend to play off one position against another and eventually will make my own decision on all the facts.[36]

Evatt and Dunk were astonished. Hasluck, they thought, should be grateful for his opportunities to represent Australia. 'We cannot see why you should be discouraged by your constant assignment to important and interesting work in which you have chosen to specialise.'[37] Hasluck replied that his assignments 'were highly valued as opportunities to serve and have been paid with service to the best of my ability', but 'needless acts of disparagement' and lack of trust fed his sense of discouragement.[38] 'I fully understand your position and will do everything to meet it', replied Dunk. 'On your side, however, you must realise my own administrative problems.' Staffing was frustrated by a lack of experienced people; perhaps Hasluck should consider joining the permanent staff of External Affairs, as it would be easier for him to conform to standard public-service practice. Meanwhile, he would recommend Hasluck for a special salary allowance.[39]

Matters subsided for the next few weeks, though tensions still simmered. Alexandra Hasluck told her mother:

> Everyone here cld. see thro it all. Sir Alex Cadogan said to
> Paul that Evatt was jealous of him. All the pressmen were
> furious & the Australian pressmen told me how wild they were.[40]

Hasluck refused Trygve Lie's offer of the London post, although it was repeated more than once. He said he wanted his children to grow up in Australia. Also, as Alexandra Hasluck told her mother, 'we wld have been stuck there. There wldn't have been a job in Australia big enough for him to come back to'.[41] Meanwhile, Hasluck dutifully shepherded Makin through the Security Council, a task eased by Makin's kindly and appreciative temperament.

Makin returned to Washington at the end of his month as President of the Security Council, and during February Hasluck spoke for Australia. When the Security Council unanimously (with the Soviet Union abstaining) voted to set up a commission on disarmament, progress was delayed while the Americans and the Russians wrangled about the potential overlap between the new body and the existing Atomic Energy Commission:

> Mr Hasluck gave a frank expression of Australia's discouragement at the evident lack of confidence in one another's intentions which had led to such a stubborn fight between the Soviet Union and the United States over the function of the commissions whose members would be, as he pointed out, identical. No two Powers, however great, could allow themselves the luxury of deadlocking, over a question of method, the fifty-five nations who had demanded disarmament.[42]

Evatt himself could not have put the case for the smaller powers more effectively, and the United States delegate, Warren Austin, was reported as responding 'with some asperity'. Undeterred, Hasluck persisted in trying to bring order and rationality to the proceedings of the Security Council, despite the posturing of the Great Powers. Later in February the United Kingdom complained to the Security Council about an incident when two ships of the Royal Navy were blown up by mines while proceeding through the Corfu Channel not far from the Albanian coast. Gromyko, on behalf of Albania's patron, the Soviet Union, scornfully refuted the British complaint. It was left to Hasluck's voice of reason to suggest that the Security Council should set up a small committee to elucidate the available evidence.[43] But this was to be his last initiative in that forum.

On 25 February news arrived that Dunk would be moving on to the chairmanship of the Public Service Board, for which he was admirably suited. He had succeeded in his task of introducing sound administrative structures into the Department of

External Affairs, and was happy to move away from working with Evatt. Cabinet approved Burton as the new secretary of the Department of External Affairs; during the previous twelve months he had been a major source of foreign policy advice for Dunk and served as acting secretary when Dunk was overseas. That finished it for Hasluck. Though he had not aspired to the position himself, he saw Burton's appointment as cabinet endorsement of Evatt's methods. He would continue to run the department as his personal fiefdom rather than through public-service practice. In his next phone conversation with Evatt, he told the minister he wished to retire, not only because of Burton's appointment but because he would like to return home and take up his commitment to the Official War History. He would stay on in New York if required until the end of 1947.[44]

For a few days Hasluck heard nothing. Then friendly journalists told him Evatt was spreading the story that he was being dismissed for disobeying instructions.[45] On 4 March Hasluck walked into the office of Ralph Harry, the junior diplomat who had succeeded Renouf as his aide, and said quietly: 'Evatt has appointed Burton as secretary of the Department. I have resigned. You are in charge'.[46] He cabled Evatt:

Owing to my lack of confidence in future administration of the Department I hereby tender my resignation and ask that arrangement be made to enable me to return to Australia as early as possible.

Evatt replied asking him to stay in his post until they could speak by phone. But when more than a week elapsed without any word from Canberra, Hasluck told Evatt he intended to hand over to a successor on 25 April, take accumulated leave in the United States, and return to Australia by sea, with his resignation becoming effective upon completion of his leave.[47]

This drew a testy rebuke from Dunk:

It is felt that these constantly recurring threats of resignation have produced a most unsatisfactory situation and indicate that your efforts are no longer directed to carrying out the Department's policy with the intensity which the position requires…Minister has been sympathetic to your difficulties and has tried to meet them. You have appeared at times to lack understanding of our responsibility to this organisation as a whole and the difficulties in allocating staff and quickly adjusting allowances to meet local conditions.[48]

And, seasoned public servant that he was, Dunk asked, did Hasluck want his work recognised by an honour? Dunk had not had the opportunity of much first-hand contact with Hasluck, and his annoyance rankled several weeks after the showdown. 'Personally I always found him a difficult man to deal with', he wrote to the Consul-General in New York. 'He was a good technician on U.N. affairs but a poor administrator, and I always thought rather weak on policy.'[49] This ungenerous assessment probably reflected the influence of Burton.

Hasluck replied immediately. Except for his discussion in September 1944 with Evatt he had never threatened resignation, but had rejected persuasions to leave the Australian service. He was not resigning because of salary and conditions, nor because of the lack of promotion, nor because of the strain on his health, nor because of anything Dunk had done: 'I have always been willing to believe that you did what you thought possible to help although your efforts yielded nothing'. But:

> I have lost confidence in the Administration itself when by
> Burton's appointment Cabinet set its approval on a whole
> system of petty intrigue, talebearing, favouritism and personal
> attachment to the Minister which as an Australian citizen
> I consider contrary to public service principles.[50]

Two days later he wrote to Evatt in milder language. He did not wish to belong to a department conducted by methods he regarded as contrary to the best principles and traditions of the Australian public service.

> The above views are directed against a system and a principle
> and are not intended to express any opinion regarding the
> capacity of the new Secretary himself. The criticism amounts
> to criticism of the Cabinet, and when a representative abroad
> has reached that point he has no alternative but to resign.[51]

It looked otherwise to Evatt. He replied that he had treated Hasluck with the utmost patience 'but unfortunately now you have allowed personal feelings to affect your judgment'.[52] Makin and Hodgson would take over his duties. At this point Makin intervened, telephoning Evatt to inform him that he was treating Hasluck unfairly.

> He has done nothing wrong in wishing to retire and you are
> bringing all the trouble on your own head by the way you

are handling the affair. Hasluck has been loyal to you and you should stop trying to discredit him.[53]

This had the effect of lowering the temperature. Within his own family circle, Evatt permitted himself no stronger criticism than that Hasluck had been 'pernickety'.[54] Burton's influence on events is obscure. Hasluck thought him responsible for the department's graceless media release announcing Hasluck's resignation and describing him as a 'temporary clerk'. On the other hand, Burton also wrote to Hodgson saying that when Hasluck returned to Canberra he would like to arrange a small party of friends and colleagues for him. Did he realise how little that would appeal to Hasluck in his current frame of mind?

In reporting his resignation, the London *Times* wrote: 'Delegates of the Security Council have lost one of their most competent colleagues'.[55] Many of Hasluck's United Nations colleagues sent supportive messages. Herbert Bayard Swope from the United States told him: 'The entire United Nations Organisation is the loser by your resignation'. A French delegate, François de Rose, wrote:

It is one of the greatest losses that the Security Council could
suffer and I am sure that it will pay for it…Allow me to state
very plainly that you have set very high in my mind
Australia's competence, sincerity, fairness, rectitude of
judgment and thought.[56]

Trygve Lie renewed his offer of the London job. Hasluck at first wished to hold the opportunity open 'in the event that Evatt, who has become a little vindictive, should make it impossible for us to carry out our plan to return to Australia'.[57] Soon, when it became clear that this fear was groundless, he made a final refusal. He was unwilling to weaken his ties with Australia by becoming an international public servant, and gave no encouragement to a suggestion that he should become Governor of Trieste, a port at the head of the Adriatic disputed by Italy and Yugoslavia and temporarily under United Nations administration.[58] Alfred Stirling at the Washington Embassy was not surprised, but blamed Hasluck's resignation on Canberra's changed policy on trusteeship, although none of Hasluck's private or public statements supported this interpretation.[59]

A journalist who observed Evatt closely remarked that he

had a rough, sometimes precise insight into those who worked for him. He seemed to know their weaknesses and fears and knew the exact tactic or word likely to reduce them to size.[60]

When he told Hasluck that his judgement was affected by personal feelings there was just enough plausibility in the suggestion to make it rankle. Hasluck would have been less than human if he had been able to ignore the apparent lack of appreciation by his seniors, though as Dunk pointed out, by declining to join the permanent staff of the Department of External Affairs and by committing himself to start work on the Official History late in 1947, Hasluck had placed himself in an anomalous position in the public-service hierarchy.

Hasluck never expressed a wish for a permanent senior post in the department, and would have accepted the appointment of a senior officer such as Alan Watt as secretary. But he took offence at Burton's appointment not merely because of his youth or opinions, but because it broke down the boundaries that should exist between the public service and personal relationships. Burton had become 'like one of the family' to the Evatts.[61] Within the office, in the recollection of one who was a junior diplomat at that time, 'the Department acted more as a secretariat for Evatt with Dr J. W. Burton as his chef de cabinet"'.[62] Even the cautious Alan Watt commented that

> there can be few precedents for appointment to the most senior post in even a recently established foreign service of a man aged thirty-two who had not served in a diplomatic post overseas.[63]

By endorsing Burton as secretary of the department, the Chifley government had in Hasluck's eyes given its approval to Evatt's habit of by-passing normal channels of communication in the public service, and listening to and rewarding his personal favourites. Whether or not this had anything to do with the appointment, Hasluck now regarded the Labor government as conniving at improper practice. From his previous stance as a middle-of-the-road agnostic in politics, he was now nudged towards support of the Liberal Party, which since 1945, under the leadership of Robert Menzies, had been working to rejuvenate the parliamentary opposition.

His wife helped this process. A dismayed spectator of her husband's treatment, Alexandra Hasluck thought of an elegant rejoinder. Even before the final breach with Evatt she had a plan in mind:

> if I can get Paul into Parliament, the Evatt can beware because Paul wld make a much better foreign minister than he & will

have all this experience. He is fed up with the diplomatic life
as run by the Dept of Ex Affairs, but I think he would like
the running of foreign policy. I don't plug the idea much yet,
but try & understand how it is. What can he come back to
that won't seem tame & backwash after this. I think my idea
is the only possible one. In the next 3 years he can write his
War History wh. won't be much trouble to him, & he can be
getting known again in the West & then at the next elections –
Well, we'll see.[64]

'Be careful what you wish for', says an old proverb, 'as your wish
may be granted'. Two months later she returned to the idea:

And I also have my plan for Paul, wh. he's getting keen on.
So we decided to come home & write the history. The latest
is, that whether Evatt managed to get away from Burton's
influence long enough to come to his senses, or whether he
began to wonder how he would appear in Paul's History, he has
been putting out feelers thro Col. Hodgson to find out whether
Paul will be appeased if Evatt makes a statement in the House
praising Paul's work & hoping that they can call on him in
future as an adviser in Foreign Affairs. He knows perfectly well
that the moment our boat docks in Sydney the reporters will
be after Paul, & if Paul gives the real reason for his resignation,
a charge of nepotism wld be brought against Evatt & the
Government & there might be an awful fuss.[65]

Although Evatt made no parliamentary statement, speculation continued about Hasluck's potential to make damaging
allegations about him. When eventually Hasluck first sat in

parliament in 1950, he found himself on the government back-benches opposite Evatt in a new role as deputy leader of the opposition. Parliamentary legend has it that whenever Hasluck was scheduled to speak, Evatt's mischievous colleague Eddie Ward would tell him that Hasluck intended to 'spill the bucket' about his past experiences, and Evatt would come bustling into the House of Representatives in a state of perturbation.[66] But there is evidence pointing in another direction. When Paul Hasluck made his maiden speech in parliament, Evatt sent him a congratulatory note. And Clyde Cameron, the veteran politician who became a devoted historian of the federal Labor Party, told a kindly story. Years later, in the 1960s, when Evatt's powerful intellect had been brought low by illness and he was an invalid living in a twilight world, only two members of parliament came to visit him. One was Justin O'Byrne, a notably good-natured Tasmanian senator whose thoughtfulness was characteristic. The other, by now a busy cabinet minister, was Paul Hasluck. Patiently he sat with Evatt yarning about their experiences in San Francisco and trying to rouse him with talk of men they had both known, such as Eden and Stettinius.[67] It was a graceful conclusion to their frequently stormy relationship.

Chapter 10

Academic interlude

Suddenly the pressure was off, and Hasluck had time to spend with his wife and family. Trygve Lie renewed his offer of appointment as the United Nations representative in Europe, and other financially attractive opportunities of overseas work were suggested, but Paul Hasluck had made up his mind to return to Australia and see his children grow up as Australians. The lease on the Bronxville house came to an end, and the family spent some weeks in the late spring as tourists, driving through the eastern and southern United States on a round trip to New Orleans and then returning for a month on Cape Cod while they awaited a passage back to Australia. Although it was nearly two years since the end of the war passenger shipping was not yet back to normal. When official channels moved sluggishly it took a conversation between Alexandra Hasluck and another mother at the children's nursery school, whose husband was in shipping, to secure a passage on the *Port Chalmers* leaving New York on 4 July for Sydney via the Panama Canal. In 1980 Paul Hasluck wrote:

> That period of family travel and the month-long voyage through Panama and across the Pacific were the longest, happiest and most care-free period of leisure I have ever had in my life.[1]

Perth seemed an attractive destination; during the voyage he wrote 'After six years of the most infernal overwork and some rather trying conditions, I am looking forward to being in a civilised place with civilised people again'.[2]

It was not in Paul Hasluck's nature to refrain from intellectual activity even on holidays. He caught up with his reading, and cleaned up odd jobs such as dealing with a request from Dr Battye, the Western Australian State Librarian, for information about whaling records in the United States.[3] More substantially, during these months he drafted an account of the workings of the Security Council, which was to be published in 1948 under the title *Workshop of Security*. Its dedication struck a surprisingly mellow note:

> What made the past three years some of the happiest years in my experience was this continuing argument on something worth arguing about with people who knew their subject and cared for a good result...I have found that what comes uppermost in my mind is a memory of readiness in discussion, sincere purpose, ease of friendliness and the intellectual morality of most of the debates.[4]

Immediately on resigning, Hasluck had written to Fred Alexander at The University of Western Australia advising that he was returning to Perth to work on the Official History and inquiring about the prospects for academic employment. He thought of offering a special course on the United Nations. Alexander replied that he could arrange for Hasluck to give an adult education course. There might be opportunities in syndicated journalism, and he would also speak to Richard Boyer,

Hasluck's colleague at Mont Tremblant, who was now chairman of the Australian Broadcasting Commission.[5] In the event Alexander found something more attractive. He approached the head of the Commonwealth Office of Education, Professor R. C. Mills, an acquaintance of many years, and asked him for a modest sum to support Hasluck while he worked on the Official History. Mills replied: '"Oh nonsense. Why don't you go out and appoint him a Research Fellow?" Since that meant that he would foot the bill, that happened very readily'.[6] The grant was enough for a readership, a research post next in status to a pro-fessorial chair. So it was that Hasluck's future was secured by the time he and his family returned to Perth and in October 1947 recovered possession of the Adams Road home from its tenants.

After all their travelling it was a pleasure for the Haslucks to resume normal home life. Paul renewed his skills as a home handyman. He and his family visited his parents in their modestly comfortable retirement in a neat brick-and-tile house only 2 kilometres from their original cottage in Highgate. He encour-aged his father to write down his reminiscences of growing up in Perth in the tranquil years before the goldrush of the 1890s, and Meernaa responded happily to the task.[7] He took his sons camping in the bush at Lake Leschenaultia in the Darling Range, and played with the idea of acquiring a piece of land. The opportunity was to arise in 1950, shortly after he became a member of parliament. One of his constituents came for advice about his financial problems. It turned out that the man owned 60 acres (24.3 hectares) of bush in the Darling Range at Paulls Valley, north of Kalamunda in the hills inland from Perth. It had been taken up by a timberman in the 1930s and was almost totally undeveloped. Hasluck immediately bought the block for

£250, sight unseen. For the rest of his life this land would serve him as a refuge, where he could indulge his love of classical music and jazz, often played fortissimo.[8]

Hasluck looked forward to 'the pleasant associations and stimuli of university life' in the serene environment of The University of Western Australia, with academic responsibilities that, although 'bothersome', were few.[9] It was still a small university with fewer than 2,000 students. His colleagues in the Department of History numbered three: Fred Alexander and Josh Reynolds from the pre-war staff, and the young John Legge, who had served in Alf Conlon's unit during the war and was lecturer in charge of Asian and Pacific history. Legge said of Hasluck:

> I liked him but felt that he had some odd limitations. He had a
> streak of arrogance and considerable intellectual stubbornness.
> His considerable intellectual powers were not always matched
> by a receptivity to alternative ideas. He was apt to be overly
> convinced of the rightness of his own opinions.[10]

The years working for Evatt in External Affairs had toughened Hasluck. He retained the scepticism Montaigne had taught him, but had lost a little of Montaigne's receptiveness to new and unfamiliar ideas.

At the practical level it was hard to reconcile Paul Hasluck's long-term career prospects with residence in Western Australia after his research fellowship came to an end. He had severed his links with journalism. The University of Western Australia had neither the plans nor the funds to create a senior academic position appropriate to his abilities. Elsewhere in Australia possibilities showed up from time to time. A new Australian National University at Canberra was in the planning stage, and before long research chairs would be created in such appropriate disciplines as international relations, politics and history. Paul Hasluck would have made a most appropriate professor either there or at the Canberra University College where undergraduates were taught.[11]

Despite misgivings about living in Canberra, Hasluck was sufficiently interested to accept when the historian Keith Hancock, whom he had met in London in 1945, invited him to a conference in Canberra in April 1948 planning the future shape of the social sciences, Pacific studies and humanities that would be taught at the Australian National University. With admirable confidence, Hasluck proclaimed that 'The finest and wisest results of advanced research are in history and philosophy'.[12] In 1948 he was also invited to join the Social Sciences Research Council (the ancestor of the present Academy of the Social Sciences in Australia) and played an active part, retaining his membership after his election to parliament.[13] Resuming an interest developed during his early years in the Canberra public service, he also attended a conference planning Australia's national archives. Here he read a paper combining his experience as historian and public servant. It was to have a seminal influence on future policy.

He began by asserting that government archives were first and foremost

> made and shaped to serve the needs of administration. They only serve those needs if they are complete and accurate in the

meaning given to those terms by the administrative officer on the actual day on which the record was made.[14]

Archives should not be created or retained with the needs of future historians in mind, as officials and librarians would be tempted to take decisions about which files needed to be retained as potentially 'historical', and thus either unconsciously or deliberately distort the record. It was not satisfactory to tack the archival sections on to the existing national and state libraries, as several empire-building librarians suggested; it must be acknowledged from the outset that archives served a separate and distinct purpose. As he put it many years later:

If this primary administrative purpose in the creation
of archives is not maintained at all times the value and
dependability of the record for all...other purposes will be
damaged. Documents are not the only repository of truth;
documents may sometimes mislead; documents have to
be interpreted as well as quoted. But for those who make
documents and those who have custody of them the old
ideal still stands: 'Keep the record straight.'[15]

The Australian national archives system would not be complete until the Commonwealth and each of the six state governments accepted responsibility for the preservation and proper handling of official records. This did not require centralisation, but common standard practices were essential. Documents were not to be destroyed without the permission of an archival authority, and agreed codes of description and identification must be adopted, and suitable access provided. At the time Hasluck spoke only a minority of states had made a start with developing government archives, and there seemed no sense of urgency among the remainder; Queensland, for instance, would not begin until 1959. Even with all the states participating, the Commonwealth would have to commit itself to funding an Australia-wide survey of archives and a generous contribution towards the training of archivists and common services such as publication. It was a big agenda, and it would take many years to fulfil. Hasluck's memorandum may be credited with bringing clarity and definition to the task.

The Official History presented a formidable challenge. Hasluck had very few models of Australian contemporary history to guide him. For the *History of Australia in the War of 1914–18*, Professor Ernest Scott of the University of Melbourne produced a single volume in 1936 nearly twenty years after the events it described.[16] By the time of its publication most of the main decision-makers of that period, with the exception of 'Billy' Hughes, had retired from politics, so that Scott could pass dispassionate, though in practice very mild, comment on their activities. The Second World War covered a longer period and left a much bigger archival record. Apart from Curtin, most of its major figures – Chifley, Menzies, Fadden, Evatt – were still vigorous participants in public life. The writing of its history would demand rare qualities of diligence and objectivity in its author. Hasluck's experience at External Affairs of working under extreme pressure to tight deadlines, building on his years as a journalist, showed that he possessed great reserves of stamina and discipline, but even the logistics of obtaining access to his sources presented problems. Holding the view that political history concerned itself with the shaping of government policy, he approached his sources with clear objectives:

> I did not attempt to consume and digest yards and yards of departmental papers and then write a summary of what I had found, but went to the filing cabinets or the shelves with definite questions in mind, and looked diligently for the answers.[17]

The archives from which the raw material of his history would be drawn were in Melbourne and Canberra, a long distance for an author working in Perth. Fortunately, the editorial staff of the Official History included an excellent research assistant, Nancy Penman, who had been compiling materials for Hasluck's volume since 1945, and who now found herself spending much of her time on it. 'The material you are sending me is admirable', Hasluck told her after they had been at work for two weeks.

> I hope you don't mind my shooting these further peremptory requests at you from time to time, but I find the easiest method is to jot down my needs as soon as I become conscious of them and put them in an envelope addressed to you.[18]

During 1948 he was able to undertake two trips to Melbourne and Canberra to consult the archives at first hand, but he would have been the first to acknowledge his dependence on Nancy Penman's professionalism.

He gave a first priority to understanding the changing administrative structures of government before and during the war, since they were the essential underpinning of policy as it evolved. Several times he was able to give Nancy Penman guidance based on his own experience. She should maintain a 'stubborn inquisitiveness' and be cautious in accepting evidence from the Public Service Board, as its officers subedited the material sent to them by the various departments, 'and this may lead to the production of a complete story which is much neater than the facts were'.[19] In asking for the records of the Inter-Departmental Committee on Economic Research,

> I should give you a hint that there may be a slight difficulty as the Committee was eventually prevented from functioning in order to meet the wishes of Dr Evatt who was unwilling to share any phase of foreign policy with other departments, and preferred that interdepartmental negotiations should be conducted, when they were unavoidable, in such a way as to ensure the adoption of his own views rather than to elicit the advice of the departmental experts.[20]

Not surprisingly, he had most trouble with the records of the Department of External Affairs. Burton tried to block his access to them, and the general editor of the series, Gavin Long, had to ask Chifley to intervene. Hasluck found that many documents had vanished from the files and those that remained were especially chaotic and fragmentary, reflecting the haphazard structure of the department. In its early years filing was sometimes entrusted to untrained part-time staff, so that 'Trouble in Syria' was filed under 'T' because the temporary clerk 'did not know if Syria was an Australian state or a North American town'.[21] Minutes of phone calls or conversations were not kept.

Often it was necessary to work with the duplicate records in other government departments.[22]

In old age Hasluck was wont to disparage the value of oral testimony as a historical source, but when he embarked on the Official History he showed a prompt and proper readiness to draw on the recollections of the colleagues with whom he had worked and who had taken part in decision-making. 'I know you must be terribly snowed under with trade talks as well as the cares of your own department', he told Nugget Coombs 'and it is a bit hard to ask a man to dig up the materials of history while he is still making it'.[23] He interviewed Robert Menzies twice in 1948. The second time he wanted to check the background to Menzies' speech given as Prime Minister at the outbreak of war in 1939, writing that he hesitated

> to impose further upon your generosity, but I think you will realise that this, too, is one of the unrecorded pages of history that could only be written down from the memory of those who took part.[24]

As the project progressed and he moved beyond politics and administration to the social history of the wartime era, his range of correspondents broadened. He questioned Sydney's Cardinal Gilroy about his view of social conditions.[25] At one stage he thought of exploring popular culture, including the songs the soldiers sang. 'Perhaps you might go, notebook at the ready and spy-glass in hand, backstage at the Sydney Tivoli', he wrote to Nancy Penman, but the history as published is sadly silent on popular culture.[26] Not unsympathetic critics have since commented that the completed volume did not contain enough social history, and it is clear that Hasluck wrestled with this problem. He feared there might not be enough verifiable evidence; he felt incompetent to explore sociological questions; not enough primary research had been undertaken. The latter he saw as a matter of 'finding the right people, talking to them, and taking down their stories from their lips'.[27] Evidently his later disenchantment with oral history had not yet hardened.

Sometimes he bounced ideas off his correspondents. Admitting to Roland Wilson that 'one of the greatest difficulties is to keep a perspective view of the whole field', he mused:

From the administrative side the War was a prolonged exercise in planning and control...Perhaps we advanced so far that instead of having planning without controls we eventually reached the stage where we were applying controls without planning. I do not know. At any rate as the War progressed planning seemed to be less and less a matter of the preparatory examination of problems and the consequent devising of plans, and more and more a matter of finding the resources to give effect to policies which had been imposed on the country out of the necessity of waging war.[28]

To explain the condition of Australia when war broke out in September 1939 he was increasingly drawn into surveying the history of the period between the two world wars. His correspondence reveals a tension between exploration of these shaping factors and the need to avoid verbosity. He raised questions that were to occupy Australian historians during the next two generations. How was it that at the end of the First World War, after a few proactive years of involvement in foreign affairs under Billy Hughes, 'there was a gradual but very marked abandonment of interest in them during the next ten to twelve years'?[29] What forces shaped the development of John Curtin's ideas on foreign policy from pacific internationalism to a departure from isolationism?

And how should he integrate the varying assessments of Robert Menzies as Prime Minister from 1939 to 1941? The veteran Labor frontbencher Edward Holloway thought Menzies lacked the experience needed in a prime minister, because as Attorney-General he had comparatively little hands-on administrative training. 'He was an unusual man with ordinary, not to say conventional ideas.' He added that Hasluck had been 'bloody kind' towards the Labor Party.[30] From the Liberal side of politics, old Sir Frederic Eggleston considered Menzies 'too detached':

> He is insensitive both to ideas and to human factors. With all his techniques he is living in the 19th century so far as ideas go, and he can offend his best friends without being aware of it. The fact is that he succeeded too early and thus never felt the need of self-criticism or self-discipline.[31]

These judgements were made of the Menzies who had not been tempered by years of political adversity, but they must have given Hasluck cause for reflection. Menzies was now leading the resurgent Liberal Party, which had emerged from the ashes of the old non-Labor parties in 1945, and this had an immediate bearing on Hasluck's future. It happened that in 1948 the Commonwealth parliament approved a major enlargement of its numbers, which resulted in the number of House of Representatives seats in Western Australia increasing from five to eight. One of the new seats thus created was named Curtin in honour of the recently deceased Prime Minister. Despite its name, it was carved out of a sweep of Perth's western suburbs extending from Claremont to Leederville that might be expected to lean towards the Liberal Party. In March 1949 Hasluck was adopted as its candidate in Curtin.

Hasluck always insisted that he had not sought the preselection, and this may be believed, but Alexandra Hasluck was not the sort to let go of an idea once she had formed it, and although it was not her style to go lobbying, Western Australia was still a tight-knit community. It would not have been surprising if some of her acquaintances came to share her view that Paul would make a good member of parliament. With his earlier record of constructive involvement in Western Australian public affairs, he was a strong candidate. Seeking a successor to John Curtin in the Fremantle constituency in 1945, the Australian Labor Party endorsed the young Kim Beazley senior, whom Hasluck had known and tutored at The University of Western Australia. The Liberals would now have an intellectual no less scholarly and with a wealth of public experience. Clive Palmer,[32] then the state general secretary of the party, put the proposition to Hasluck. He spent a few days in research, liked the idea, and accepted. 'I was asked to do it, and complied.'[33]

Perhaps Palmer was only just in time. Hasluck had not lost all interest in an academic appointment, and although he let pass soundings-out about chairs of history in Queensland and Adelaide, he was more responsive to an informal approach from Professor Wolfgang Friedmann, a German refugee academic who held the chair of jurisprudence at the University of Melbourne. Friedman was on a selection committee looking for

195

someone to fill a new chair of political science. At a meeting of the Australian Council of Social Sciences, Hasluck had argued

> that a school of political science should concentrate on the
> study of political institutions, both national and international,
> leaving the school of philosophy, the school of law and the
> school of history to handle within their disciplines, in close
> co-operation with the new school, such subjects as political
> philosophy, international law, constitutional law, and
> political history.[34]

Although Friedmann assured him of strong support, the competition was strong, and Hasluck had not made a formal application before he was offered the Curtin preselection: 'I let them all down and went into politics'.[35] The chair went to Macmahon Ball, another academic with diplomatic experience who was also disappointed with Evatt.[36]

Paul Hasluck entered politics as a matter of public duty. As he wrote at the time:

> Coming back as an ordinary citizen, I found that the ordinary
> citizen had lost the enjoyment of many of the best features
> of life in Australia...Class war was being actively preached. I
> always have believed that the foundation of good government
> in Australia, and the sharing of the benefits of life in Australia,
> rest on the maintenance of family life and of faith in the
> decency of common man. Because I believe in parliamentary
> democracy, Parliament appears to be a way in which one can
> best serve, to try to maintain what he regards as the Australian
> way of life.[37]

Hasluck's roots were among those whom Menzies had described as 'the forgotten people', neither affluent business people nor trade unionists.[38] Throughout his years in politics he believed that

> the Liberal Party has made its ground and holds its ground
> because it appeals to the wage-earner, the small man, the
> housewife – the so-called 'ordinary folk' who believe in the
> individual.[39]

Such people, including his own parents, were dismayed at the Chifley government's forays into the unfamiliar, especially the proposal to nationalise the banks. They were inconvenienced by the disruption to transport and power services caused through militant industrial action. Hence they felt an unease Hasluck interpreted as concern for the future of their familiar way of life. The senior Haslucks were not radically minded; at the height of the 1930s Depression when the unemployed were protesting in the streets of Perth, Patience Hasluck had observed that there was 'always a certain section who are not satisfied and try to stir up strife',[40] and in the 1940s, according to his daughter-in-law, Meernaa Hasluck was almost 'frothing at the mouth' at the iniquities of the Chifley government.[41]

No doubt in Paul Hasluck's case it made a difference that Labor was led by Chifley and Evatt, whom (especially Evatt) he saw as condoning deteriorating standards in the conduct of the public service, as distinct from an old friend and mentor in John Curtin. Yet he was not quite convinced that his vocation lay in politics. On a research trip to Canberra in March 1949, he encountered old associates at the Department of External

Affairs, most of whom were pleased he would soon be part of Canberra life. But he wrote to Alexandra that he was 'inclined to wish that he had not got the endorsement for Curtin because he hated Canberra so much and his sights of political life there'. She scribbled across the top of his letter: 'This sort of letter makes me mad!'[42] Yet no study of Paul Hasluck's two decades in federal politics should ignore an underlying ambiguity in his attitude. His sense of duty impelled him to take part in public life, and he enjoyed the exercise of authority and the intellectual challenges of policymaking; but in the world of politics he was working against the grain of the creative and imaginative parts of his being, the aspects he had decided to subordinate in order to become 'a model prisoner'.

Hasluck's venture into the political arena placed him under two constraints. Federal elections were due at the end of 1949, and by that time he needed to have as much as possible of his history of the Second World War complete and ready for publication. It was also important that the candid objectivity of the historian should not be compromised by the allegiance of the Liberal parliamentary candidate. In November 1948 Hasluck submitted a partial draft to Gavin Long, a skilled and sensitive editor who challenged some of Hasluck's criticisms of Labor and its attitudes: 'I think that, having regard to your present affiliation and position, you lay yourself too widely open to a charge of baiting, provoking and blackguarding', he wrote,

I therefore suggest (a) the most judicious revision of adjectives and adverbs, (b) a slightly less superior-sounding tone at some points, (c) a little fuller and more respectful treatment of Curtin's views on defence, and (d) (above all) a considerable shortening of those long passages that by their very length and repetitiousness suggest to the Labor reader a deliberate harping on Labor's admitted shortcomings which are OK in a political piece but in questionable taste in an official history.[43]

 At a later point Long wrote:

You will understand my special concern about this section. The whole history will be judged by it more than any other part. If the political and literary leaders on the Left consider it less than scrupulously judicial their judgment is likely to be sweepingly applied not only to the remainder of your work but to all the rest of the history.[44]

He was appealing to values of intellectual honesty that Hasluck shared, and the author took note of Long's comments. Perhaps he realised that the trenchant style of judgement of 'Polygon' the drama critic was not appropriate in Hasluck the official historian. In the event, any perception of conflict of inter-est was dealt with by a suitable modification of his contract, approved by the Labor minister responsible for the Official History, Victor Johnson, a fellow Western Australian.[45] It was as well that Long and Hasluck dealt thoroughly with the issue, as shortly before the 1949 elections Long had a confrontation with Evatt. Himself a biographer who often wrote like a defence counsel, Evatt refused to credit that Hasluck could write impar-tially, and Long had to insist several times that Hasluck was 'a detached historian'.[46]

Detachment came at a cost. Three years later, before the volume appeared, Hasluck complained to his wife:

In any case it lies heavy on my conscience as a dishonest piece of work. For the sake of the series and fearing the charge of political bias I have suppressed several conclusions, unfriendly to Labour, which, I know, were fully justified by the evidence. In this excess of discretion…I suppose I have turned out a very bad historian. When Holloway, the Labour minister, was reading the manuscript – and he was a member of the Labour Executive, and the wartime Labour Cabinet – I asked him the direct question, whether he thought it had been fair to Labour. He answered: 'In many places, more than fair.'[47]

During the first half of 1949, Hasluck forged ahead with drafting and revision, paying heed to Long's admonitions.[48] A revised draft went to Long in July, who assured him that 'Even in its present diffuse state it makes good reading'.[49] Thus encouraged, Hasluck, who knew that fluent writing sometimes made for prolixity, happily discarded large quantities of detail about administrative routine.[50] The completed manuscript, running to more than 200,000 words, was submitted in 1950. Long considered that it was surely the most substantial work of Australian history that had yet been written, and would be likely to remain so for a considerable time into the future.[51]

The book was scheduled for publication in mid-1952, but to Hasluck's growing impatience its appearance was delayed until more than a year later. It troubled him that, instead of ensuring it was issued at a time of comparative political calm, the book was launched in the early weeks of a federal Senate election, but in the event this hardly mattered.[52] Most of the reviewers were enthusiastic. Academic historian Laurie Fitzhardinge thought it was 'fair and accurate, and stands as a very impressive achievement',[53] but missed any reference to what he called 'the "worm's-eye-view" of the man in the street'. Writer and critic Inglis Moore offered a similar criticism in an otherwise favourable review.[54] But the history and its companion volume have worn well. For poet and publisher Max Harris 'that vast volume of the official history of the government and the people...was really a deadly exposure of war and greed'.[55] Sixty years after its appearance it is still an essential source for the history of the Second World War:

> Hasluck's volumes have stood well the test of time because his patient and adroit scholarship produced the solid foundation on which all subsequent studies of...Australia's political and social developments during the second world war have built.[56]

By the time the volume was published, Hasluck was deeply entrenched in politics. In mid-1949 the Chifley government confronted a major coal strike with a firmness that surprised friends and enemies alike. Eventually the government prevailed, but the public at large were aware of inconveniences: 'We have gas at breakfast time and for two hours in the evening', Hasluck reported,

> Lack of refrigeration seems to have made us very short of meat, and for a reason which I cannot fathom, to have increased the age of the beasts slaughtered by many many years.[57]

In such an environment, opinion began to shift towards the Liberal–Country Party Coalition led by Menzies. As reported, Hasluck's electioneering speeches stuck mainly to a contrast between the increasing government intervention that could be expected if Labor remained in power and the greater scope for private enterprise that a Coalition government would foster. His own touch might be seen in the comment that 'The character of the people was far more important than the strength of government or the plans of political theorists'.[58]

Hasluck did not take victory for granted and campaigned energetically. His only opponent in Curtin was the endorsed Labor candidate, William Lonnie, whose qualifications included membership of the state executive of the Returned Servicemen's League and a well-informed interest in health and education issues. By a coincidence he was, like Hasluck, the son of Salvation Army officers.

Paul and Alexandra Hasluck both found that they enjoyed campaigning. 'Paul turned out to be very good at this', Alexandra remembered,

> He really enjoyed making contact with strangers and yarning
> with them, and in certain districts found that his name was
> already known by reason of his father's connection with people
> through his religion, or through a historical knowledge of
> families of the early days.[59]

Together they set up new branches of the Liberal Party. She discovered an effective talent for radio broadcasting, improving many of the uninspired scripts turned out by Liberal Party headquarters, and gaining attention with a weekly program of talks on the commercial radio station 6PR.

At the first meeting of his campaign committee in September 1949, Hasluck told his supporters:

in an electorate like Curtin we can go a very great distance
by a word-of-mouth campaign...I am also inclined to place
a high value on personal visits by the candidate to
representative voters.[60]

He believed that six out of ten voters would respond to reasoned
argument, and set out to knock on as many doors as possible.
For each household he sketched a report of its members and
their concerns, compiling hundreds during September and
October. More than sixty years later his pen-portraits provide
lively vignettes of the 'forgotten people' of Perth in the immediate postwar years, surely providing material for some social
historian of the future:

> Saw Mr Iles – elderly working man, very disinclined to talk of
> politics, at a guess because he did not want to have an argument
> – so we had a yarn about football – West Perth barracker.

> Husband strongly Labour and drinks – for sake of peace in
> house please do not trouble them.

> Jewish family – all highly intelligent young men, with a keen
> interest in and grasp of politics – all have previously voted
> Labour [sic] but will respond to sound arguments. Send well
> reasoned printed matter and notice of political meetings.

> Busy self-important little man, moving his big new radio
> set into big polished house – no definite political ideas but
> promised support because he is in favour of vigorous young
> men in big jobs (spoken as a compliment to himself, not to
> candidate).

Mrs Weir (widow), doesn't know which side to vote for...
related to Caporns and other early WA families – values
independence above everything – will probably vote for Paul
Hasluck because of old West Australian interest.

Often he found the voters impatient with the surviving wartime
controls and critical of the federal government's decision to
maintain petrol rationing.

The election on 10 December 1949 was a solid victory for
the Coalition. Menzies would be the next Prime Minister. In
Western Australia Labor retained three of the eight House of
Representatives seats, three were won by the Liberals, and two
by the Country Party. Hasluck won convincingly in Curtin,
with 24,857 votes against 15,781 for Lonnie. He gained a clear
majority in each of Curtin's four subdivisions. It was a striking
affirmation of support. Hasluck was to contest seven more elections, but he was never seriously troubled in holding his seat,
which as a result of redistributions became the safest Liberal
constituency in Western Australia.

Momentarily an even more glittering prospect suggested
itself. There was, Hasluck recalled, 'some expectation that in
forming his first Cabinet [Menzies] would pick at least one
Western Australian member and there was an expectation that
it might be me'.[61] But none of the newly elected Liberals was
chosen. Paul Hasluck would enter the House of Representatives
as one of a large platoon of foot soldiers, none of whom could
have foreseen that their party would retain office for the next
twenty years.

Chapter 11

Political debut

Unlike most of the new backbenchers, Paul Hasluck knew his way around Canberra and was known to many of the senior public servants and politicians on both sides. Shortly after his arrival in Canberra he received consoling evidence that his opinions were valued. He was consulted by the Minister for External Affairs, Percy Spender,[1] about the choice of a new secretary for the Department of External Affairs. Although Burton accompanied Spender to the meeting setting up the Colombo Plan, which he had some share in originating, Hasluck's old adversary was soon shunted sideways. He became High Commissioner to Ceylon (now Sri Lanka), while Spender chose a more congenial head of department from its senior members. Hasluck recommended Alan Watt, but also named Arthur Tange as a rising star with claims for consideration. In the event Watt was chosen, but Tange was to follow him four years later.[2]

In his first year in parliament, Hasluck's speeches were well prepared and not too frequent, and would continue so throughout his parliamentary career. He concentrated on subjects such as foreign policy and Aboriginal affairs on which he felt qualified to speak. During his first parliamentary recess he drafted a motion urging cooperation between the Commonwealth and state governments in measures 'for the social advancement as well as the protection of people of the Aboriginal race'. He sent it for comment to two senior cabinet ministers, Arthur Fadden[3] and Philip McBride, Minister for the Interior with responsibility for the Northern Territory.[4]

Both were sympathetic, but Fadden raised difficulties of financial significance. If the Commonwealth contributed to state government spending on Aboriginal welfare, states such as Queensland and Western Australia with substantial Aboriginal populations would get more than Victoria or Tasmania, where few survived. Moreover, Aboriginal responsibilities were already taken into account in allocating tax reimbursements to the states.[5] They decided to consult Menzies, and meanwhile C. R. Lambert,[6] the officer in charge of the Northern Territory division in McBride's department, came up with another cogent argument. The real case for Commonwealth involvement, he wrote, lay in Australia's international responsibility 'to demonstrate to the world that its provision throughout the Commonwealth for the welfare of the native people was beyond reproach'.[7] He also suggested some strategic amendments to the text of the motion.

Fortified by this advice and by the goodwill of his seniors, Hasluck introduced his motion on 8 June 1950.[8] In a departure from the usual knockabout political practice, he asked Kim Beazley[9] to second the motion; Beazley of course was a Labor man but also a fellow Western Australian of proven sympathy. They wanted to achieve a national and non-partisan approach in arousing awareness of the public's responsibilities towards Aboriginal Australians. With support from both sides of the House the motion passed. Hasluck commented that 'at the time it gave the same encouragement as when a cloudless dawn promises a brighter day to come'.[10] Later in the year, when it was proposed to allocate Commonwealth funding for milk for schoolchildren, he insisted that Aboriginal children, particularly those at the missions, should not be overlooked.[11]

More than once his carefully prepared speeches reflected his experience at the United Nations. His maiden speech was a sobering analysis of the Cold War, stressing the inevitability of power relations as a determinant in foreign policy. In September, following the outbreak of the Korean War, he amplified these views in a speech where he figured as the government's second speaker, immediately following the leader of the opposition, Ben Chifley.[12] He described the North Korean invasion of South Korea as part of a calculated policy on the part of the communist bloc 'designed to keep the western democracies running around the ring, losing their breath, exhausting their strength, and failing to come to grips with the central problem'.[13] He revealed a Western Australian perspective in urging that greater attention be paid to the Indian Ocean, whose gateways – the Suez Canal, the Cape of Good Hope and Singapore – were weakly held by a declining Britain, and might invite Soviet interest. Australia, he argued, should promote harmony with the newly established nations India and Pakistan.

As a backbencher not yet muzzled by a cabinet minister's duty of solidarity with government policy, Hasluck was capable of an independent-minded scepticism. He urged caution in meeting demands for increased defence spending after the outbreak of the Korean War:

Simply to vote a large amount of money…may be likened, to my mind, to a very small man who puts on big clothes, with padded shoulders, and imagines that, thereby, he has increased his strength.[14]

In an unusually bipartisan debate, backbenchers on both sides of the House questioned the value of maintaining an embassy at Moscow when Stalin's regime placed restrictions on the movements and activities of its staff. Hasluck asserted that it was useful to have even restricted diplomatic representation in a totalitarian state, and was immediately supported by none other than Evatt.[15]

He was also dubious about the Department of External Affairs' proposal for a Pacific pact, which eventually resulted in the ANZUS Treaty of 1951 between the United States, New Zealand and Australia. Such a pact, he said in an address at the University of Adelaide, was 'like carrying an umbrella when you have a sound roof over your head'.[16] In the same speech, he complained that the idea of a Pacific pact had 'become almost a proprietary brand, so that one runs the risk of a charge of disloyalty for disparaging it. The fewer contracts there are, the fewer chances of dispute'.[17] He added:

> Surely our diplomatic interest is to keep the situation in
> Asia fluid and not to harden it so that the world will see the
> appearance of Asiatic powers led by Russia versus Pacific
> powers led by the United States.[18]

This advocacy of a flexible approach contrasts piquantly with the stubbornness against China he showed in later years as Minister for External Affairs.

In parliament he urged that the pact be deferred until the peace settlement with Japan was concluded and recognition granted to the government of China; it would be unwise to ignore or to alienate those two nations.[19] As China had recently fallen under Mao Zedong's communist regime, this might seem a surprising view in a Liberal, but Hasluck said: 'I submit that it is a bad principle of democracy to assume on what side in any conflict of interests a nation will be aligned'.[20] This pragmatic approach was noted by the Labor opposition, even while it disagreed with him. Later in the debate Evatt picked up some of the points of Hasluck's argument, and Leslie Haylen[21] commented on 'the sober and humanitarian...spirit in which he tendered his conclusions in relation to foreign affairs'.[22]

Belief in the consistently aggressive thrust of Soviet foreign policy provided the theme for a speech in support of a ban on the Australian Communist Party in which Hasluck's realpolitik could not quite disguise an uneasy tension with his earlier libertarian principles. In earlier years in Perth, Hasluck had looked with amused tolerance at the communist enthusiasts among his acquaintance, such as Katharine Susannah Prichard and John Oldham.[23] Since that time his trust had been betrayed by Ian Milner, whom he had endorsed as his successor in charge of the Post-Hostilities Planning Division during 1945 and 1946 despite Milner's left-wing opinions. As 'Hasluck's man', Milner was regarded with disfavour by Hood and Burton, and at the end of 1946 he was sent off to the United Nations. But he was not simply a victim of office politics. Burton had come to suspect that Milner was abstracting confidential documents from the office and passing them on to the Soviet Union. In 1950, ostensibly for his wife's health, Milner went to live in Czechoslovakia, where the communists had seized power. There he soon acquired a university post and a second wife, and settled permanently. It was not surprising that at that time Hasluck's attitude towards communism and communists hardened perceptibly.

Communists, he believed, should not be admitted to the public service because 'the avowed aims and the well-observed character of the Communist Party' included the subversion of the elected government. 'The matter has ceased to be one of private opinion and become one of a direct threat to security.'[24] Communism was 'an aberration founded in folly'. An idea could not be suppressed, but its adherents must be dealt with if they threatened the stability of the state. 'If [the ban] does impair one small liberty', he argued in parliament, 'it does so in order to ensure that strong defences are erected around greater liberties'.[25] He was immediately followed by Haylen, who congratulated him on taking the House 'slowly and carefully and with a kindly grace down the flower-decked path' that led to the erosion of liberties.[26] Hasluck was absent, though paired with the 'ayes', when the House of Representatives voted in favour of the ban. He seldom gave much credence to the tendency of security authorities to detect conspiracies where none existed.[27]

Hasluck took the parliamentary process more seriously than many of his colleagues. Debate in his view was intended for the serious exchange of ideas about policy, and it vexed him when members indulged in rowdy heckling and point-scoring. To Alexandra he complained about the Labor opposition members whose comments, though audible, were not quite loud enough to catch the Speaker's attention, singling out Eddie Ward, Clyde Cameron and 'that braying onager out of Australia's convict past' Dan Curtin.[28] Even after several years as a minister he was moved to protest against the use of parliamentary privilege to besmirch the reputations of fellow members, and was derided by an opposition veteran for giving 'a Sunday school lecture'.[29]

He made a lonely and unsuccessful protest when the House of Representatives postponed its scheduled time of meeting so that members could listen to the broadcast of the Melbourne Cup. Parliament, he claimed, was demonstrating to the public that work 'was far less important than finding out whether one horse could get its nose in front of another horse in a certain race'.[30] But Menzies, describing himself as 'the most notorious nonracegoer in the House', was 'perfectly certain that none of the 4,000,000 people who listened in to the broadcast of the race this afternoon will have any bitter complaint to make about the fact that honorable members also listened in to it', and the Labor opposition willingly shared the responsibility.[31] Despite this small setback, at the end of his first year in parliament Hasluck could be seen as having made a good start.

He did not know if good performance would result in ministerial office. Two ministers intended to retire from cabinet: Dame Enid Lyons for reasons of health; and Percy Spender, the Minister for External Affairs, to become Ambassador to the United States.[32] Spender also claimed health reasons, but Hasluck thought he had come to realise that he had no hope of ousting Menzies as Prime Minister, 'and, having met people in Washington, found that the diplomatic life is very pleasing to one's self-importance'.[33] Hasluck told his wife there would be scores of claimants for the vacancies and warned her against building her hopes too high: 'I have heard nothing and received no indication of whether or not I am even being considered for any appointment of any kind', but added, 'I know that in qualifications and experience I rank better than any other private member except perhaps Kent Hughes'.[34] If a Western Australian were chosen, it would probably be one of the three Liberals returned to the House of Representatives for the first time in 1949. In that case Hasluck thought his chances best, but Gordon Freeth, 'being more thoroughly and evidently anti-Labor…is looked on more favourably by some sections of the party than I am. I know he has hopes'.[35]

He sketched out the possibilities to Alexandra. He did not consider himself suited for a portfolio such as Army or Navy. Although External Affairs would have to be filled, it would probably go to an existing cabinet minister; a newcomer such as Hasluck would arouse too much jealousy. Perhaps Menzies would take the post himself, appointing an undersecretary. If the External Affairs section covering Papua New Guinea, Nauru and Norfolk Island were detached from External Affairs, it might go to John Howse, a New South Wales Liberal who was undersecretary to Spender.[36] 'Menzies looks at me inscrutably and with no particular fondness', he told Alexandra, adding: 'It is not a matter which works me up very much or stimulates my ambition although naturally it leaves me a little curious and unsettled'. A chance meeting with Chifley at the Hotel Kurrajong brought an unexpected compliment. 'You ought to get in if they do justice', said the leader of the opposition, 'but you won't always find justice in this game'.[37] Soon afterwards the Menzies government, weary of trying to govern with a hostile Labor majority in the Senate and needing a renewed mandate after the High Court threw out the bill banning the Communist Party, obtained a double dissolution of parliament.

At the election on 28 April 1951 the Menzies government lost a few seats in the House of Representatives but gained a majority in the Senate. Although the shortness of the election campaign prevented Hasluck from campaigning on the same scale as in 1949, he retained his seat with a slightly increased majority. For a week he waited for news of Menzies' plans to reshuffle his cabinet, characteristically doing nothing to promote his own claims. Then, concluding he had been passed over again, he took his wife and two young sons for a fishing holiday at Augusta, 350 kilometres south of Perth near Cape Leeuwin. Two days later, as the family returned from a day out, the local postmistress brought news of a phone call from Brisbane. The telephone exchange, which usually closed at 5.00 pm, was kept open into the evening:

> I took the call at a telephone hanging on the wall of a passage-
> way in the Augusta hotel. It was one of those old-fashioned
> instruments with a handle to whirl when you took a call and
> when you ended it. Presently Menzies came on the line. He
> asked me where I was. He asked me if I could get to Canberra.
> He wanted me to do a job for him, but could not say over the
> telephone.[38]

The holiday was cut short, and a protesting family was bundled back to Perth.

Next evening, for the first of many times, Hasluck caught the 'red-eye' overnight flight to Canberra via Adelaide. After his nine-hour journey, a Commonwealth car took him straight to the Prime Minister's office. 'Menzies, pink and immaculate in a morning suit and with the friendliness of a man making a Cabinet',[39] told him he was making a new portfolio of Territories to administer the Northern Territory, Papua New

Guinea, Nauru, Norfolk Island and various minor dependencies. Hasluck accepted, and was whisked off with Menzies to Government House. There, feeling crumpled and travel-worn, he was sworn in with the rest of the cabinet by the Governor-General, William McKell.[40] The swearing-in was followed by a genial dinner, with Menzies at his best as a polished raconteur, from which Hasluck had to depart in mid-evening to attend his first official function, a dinner at Albert Hall in aid of victims of the recent Mount Lamington volcanic eruption. The McKells were there, and Hasluck had a long and instructive talk with the Governor-General who had observantly toured Papua and New Guinea. By the end of the night Paul had spent forty hours on the go.[41]

All the same, it is puzzling that Menzies left it to the last moment to call Hasluck. Like every Eastern States Prime Minister, he tended to disregard the difficulties of colleagues in Western Australia when asked to attend meetings at short notice, but it is hard to imagine that the decision was taken on the spur of the moment. In later life Hasluck claimed to have been far from elated at achieving ministerial status after less than a year and a half in parliament:

> Instead of feeling that my merit had been recognized or that
> I had received the confidence of the Prime Minister I had the
> feeling that I had been brought in reluctantly at the last
> moment as a tail-ender.

Perhaps these reactions were understandable in a man whose previous experience in Canberra had taught him to 'put not his trust in princes'. He could hardly have expected to go to

External Affairs when there was a much more senior colleague, Richard Casey, to fill the place.[42] At the time Hasluck acknowledged that Menzies had probably intended to bring him and Athol Townley from Tasmania into the ministry, but then also had to revise his plans in order to make room for his old rival, Kent Hughes. Hasluck also gave credit to Menzies for 'wanting a certain maturity and experience in a Minister'.[43]

Although he wondered if the Territories portfolio had been cobbled together only when it was necessary to find something appropriate for a Western Australian, it was in fact an elegant solution to the problems of divided control between the departments of the Interior and External Affairs.[44] Hasluck, with his abiding interest in Aboriginal policy and a record of involvement with problems of colonial trusteeship in the United Nations, was well qualified to take it. It would have been hard to find any other member of parliament with superior claims. Hasluck proved to be the only minister capable of overseeing the Northern Territory on the one hand and the overseas territories such as Papua New Guinea on the other. Under his successor the Northern Territory was handed back to the Department of the Interior.

His misgivings should have been solaced by numerous messages of congratulation, including one from a British cabinet minister, Philip Noel-Baker, and another from the Western Australian Premier, Ross McLarty.[45] His old headmaster, Joseph Parsons, thought Hasluck was the first Perth Modern School graduate to become a cabinet minister.[46] The Catholic Archbishop of Perth, Dr Redmond Prendiville, praised his 'advocacy of the cause of our neglected natives'.[47] The biographer Percival Serle wrote: 'I am afraid you will have to grow a hide; it is not really a desirable place for a man of any sensitiveness'.[48] Miles Franklin, who had visited the Haslucks in Perth the previous year, wrote:

> May I congratulate you and say how inspiring it is to have a real writer, above all a poet, as a Cabinet Minister. Our first? – unless we have to accept Sir Henry Parkes. In any case some day we may have a Minister of Fine Arts, and a wool man over it could be inadequate.[49]

Several of his old colleagues from External Affairs wrote supportively. From the Tokyo Embassy Hodgson relayed gossip that Burton was seeking readmission to the public service: 'Surely they would not grant that after all his attacks on government policy'.[50] Alan Watt was one of several who commented on Hasluck's achievement of ministerial office after barely a year in politics, adding that it helped 'restore one's faith in the democratic process'.[51] Perhaps most surprising of all, his old bête noire John Hood, now Ambassador to Indonesia, wrote:

> I was most pleased to hear of the appointment – it would be hard to think of a better one. Also, it seems quite natural to envisage you on the Government bench![52]

Fortified by these messages and by a further conversation with Menzies, Hasluck proceeded to address the problems and opportunities of the new Department of Territories. 'I have inherited a rather neglected field of administration, tangled with nettles', he told his wife, 'and one of the biggest difficulties will be to find really competent men for the job that needs to be done'. And he added: 'I need your backing and confidence in this'.[53] But his appointment as a cabinet minister brought his wife less satisfaction than might have been expected. Alexandra Hasluck flew to Canberra for the celebrations of the fiftieth anniversary of the Australian Commonwealth. There were several parties, including a buffet dinner at the Netherlands Embassy where the Haslucks were the guests of honour. At the grand ball at Parliament House on 13 June 1951, the Haslucks planned to make up a Western Australian party with Nugget Coombs, Gordon Freeth, Ted Dunphy[54] and their wives, but foul weather at Canberra airport meant that Lallie Coombs and Peggy Dunphy could not join the party. Then, after only a few dances, the ball was terminated when news arrived of the sudden death of the leader of the opposition, Ben Chifley. 'Just another piece of his awkwardness dying when he did', Alexandra Hasluck grumbled.[55]

That was not all. The Haslucks played host to the administrators of Papua New Guinea and the Northern Territory, who, she reported, 'were all very keen for me to visit their countries and talk to the women', but Paul was not so eager:

> It is hard to ask Paul things at present. I have been very sad a
> lot of the time here, and won't bore you with it, but it is quite
> obvious that Paul feels no need of me here, and I myself think
> he doesn't like his limelight shared. He does not like sharing his
> life or anything.[56]

Nearly eighteen years were to follow in which she was to experience the stress of marriage to a man who believed in the rigorous separation of public life from private life, and whose concept of duty led him to give priority to the ever-increasing demands of public life.

Until that time Alexandra Hasluck had shared most of Paul's activities, especially in promoting the cultural life of Western Australia. They had many intellectual interests in common, and they enjoyed good conversation. During his years at External Affairs the pressures of work had produced many stormy moments of tension and irascibility, but their letters show a loving relationship. Paul opened his moods to Alexandra, and she offered support and encouragement. She threw herself into campaigning for him when he contested the seat of Curtin, but possibly she did not understand the depth of Paul's ambivalence about entering politics. In old age he wrote that he was still unsure whether he should have chosen politics or an academic career, often feeling that he 'was the wrong driver in the wrong truck'.[57] It was significant that when he visited Canberra early in 1949, he felt repelled by the political environment but Alexandra was impatient with his doubts.

It was probably also significant that, while most men would have been delighted to gain cabinet office after little more than a year in parliament, he disparaged the way the offer came. A biographer is tempted to remember Paul Hasluck's description of himself as a 'model prisoner', suppressing the creative and Bohemian sides of his character in the interests of duty and conformity to the expectations of others. Perhaps at levels he hardly admitted to himself, he resented that decision and his wife's part in the taking of that decision. For the next eighteen years, during which he served constantly as a cabinet minister, he had hardly any time to follow his vocations as poet and historian, but it was his home life that took the greatest strain.

Neither Paul nor Alexandra Hasluck can have realised that he was embarking on one of the longest unbroken terms of ministerial office in Australian political history. Nobody foresaw the longevity of the Menzies government and its successors, who would not be confronted by a successful challenge from the Labor opposition until 1972. Paul Hasluck would be Minister for Territories from May 1951 to December 1963, then after four months as Minister for Defence would serve from April 1964 to February 1969 as Minister for External Affairs, a total of nearly eighteen years followed by another five years as Governor-General. Among his colleagues, only William McMahon and John McEwen would hold ministerial office for longer terms. During twelve and a half years as Minister for Territories, Hasluck was to make a lasting impact on the trust territory of Papua New Guinea, on the Northern Territory, and on national Aboriginal policy. It will be convenient to consider each of these in turn, but first to consider the political and personal contexts in which Hasluck had to operate.

Part II
Years of authority, 1951–93

Chapter 12

Minister for Territories

Neither of Paul Hasluck's predecessors as Minister for External Territories (as it had been) had left a distinctive mark. Eddie Ward, minister under the Labor government between 1943 and 1949, was demoted to the portfolio after stirring an ill-judged controversy over the 'Brisbane line', a supposed plan to abandon northern and western Australia in the event of a Japanese invasion. He was not without ability, and an admirer remembered him as 'approachable, a good listener, humanitarian in outlook and…responsible for the basic policy…that the interests of the native people are paramount'.[1] But that was about the limit of his long-term strategy, and even after the coming of peace he was content to leave the administration of the territories under his regime to the officials in Papua and New Guinea. His Liberal successor, Percy Spender, was a more proactive minister, but in his first six months of office his energies were largely concentrated on foreign policy and the creation of the Colombo Plan. The acting minister from October 1950 to April 1951, the Country Party's Larry Anthony, seems to have made more of a mark in foreshadowing some of the policies Hasluck would later bring forward.

Responding to congratulations from the Chief Justice, Sir John Latham, Hasluck wrote:

I feel that there is a big and urgent job to be done in our territories and, although to date I have been reminded chiefly of the difficulties I hope to be able to keep the opportunities clearly in mind, too. One of the main handicaps will be in building up a strong and competent staff which will have not only capacity but a sense of mission.[2]

As minister in charge of a new department, Hasluck had a little more scope than usual in recruiting his senior staff. From his six years at the Department of External Affairs he brought an intense appreciation of the need for well-defined administrative structures. There would be none of the scope for personal favouritism and faulty communication that had marked Evatt's regime in External Affairs. Hasluck's first concern was to choose a senior public servant as secretary of the new Department of Territories who would be trusted to give advice shaped through established professional channels, leaving the minister with the responsibility of deciding policy informed by that advice, and instructing his public servants about its execution. This was the concept Hasluck was to carry into effect throughout his ministerial career.[3]

'Happy' Reg Halligan was the public servant who had been responsible for the South Pacific section of the old Department of External Territories. Conscientious, experienced, but somewhat unimaginative, he valued bureaucratic conformity above initiative, and the files tended to accumulate on his desk.[4] Hasluck thought him 'a devoted, likable and thoroughly good man' but not a strong enough character. He would be passed over and mollified with appointment as delegate to the South Pacific Commission.[5] Hasluck thought of offering the secretaryship to his former colleague in External Affairs, W. D. Forsyth, who at that time was seconded to the South Pacific Commission and was very knowledgeable about the region. Forsyth replied that he would like the job, but considered himself committed to External Affairs.[6]

Hasluck then offered the post to Cecil ('Eski') Lambert, the officer responsible for Northern Territory matters in the Interior ministry, believing Lambert could contribute qualities he himself lacked. He was aware of Lambert's role in easing the passage of his June 1950 parliamentary resolution, and no doubt that counted. Eski Lambert was a seasoned operator who had risen through the New South Wales public service to a Commonwealth appointment with the rural reconstruction section, then becoming director of regional development in the Department of the Interior. His experience with the economics of rural industry would be of value in both the Northern Territory and Papua New Guinea. Some found him short of charm, and in some circles he and his wife were known as 'Blondie and the Beast', but his professionalism was unquestionable. Joe Cahill, a very experienced New South Wales politician, thought him the best public servant who had come his way.[7] Hasluck wrote appreciatively of his 'keenness and "watch-me-while-I-clean-up-the-mess"' attitude.[8] One colleague remembered: 'If Hasluck expressed even a mild interest in a suggestion from any source, Lambert was likely to make the proposal into a project within twenty-four hours'.[9]

Besides Lambert, Hasluck's right-hand men would be the administrators of the two major territories, Papua New Guinea and the Northern Territory. In Papua New Guinea the administrator since the end of the war in 1945 had been Keith Murray,

225

formerly professor of agriculture at the University of Queensland and first head of the institution that became the Australian School of Pacific Administration.[10] He succeeded in the essential task of restoring confidence in the Australian administration, but was poorly supported from Canberra, so that it was left to Murray to decide policy priorities and, as well as he could from Port Moresby, to cajole the department into action. He made progress in establishing village councils and cooperative societies, but it was a formidable challenge to knit the fragmented clans of Papua and New Guinea into a functional modern state, and much was left to be done. He showed more sympathy with the indigenous people of Papua New Guinea than some white settlers liked; they called him 'Kanaka Jack'. It remained to be seen how Murray would fare under a different regime, even when he was reporting to a minister such as Hasluck who shared most of his goals.

In the Northern Territory, Anthony told Hasluck that 'things were in a mess'. The administrator, A. R. Driver, was coming to the end of a frustrating five-year term in which the problems of reconstruction – restoring infrastructure damaged by war, devising a system of land tenure, restoring morale – were compounded by the difficulty of engaging Canberra's attention. Driver was ready to move to a less onerous post as an immigration official in Italy, which gave Hasluck scope for making a new appointment. His decision struck many as audacious, as he offered the post to Frank Wise, who was at that time Labor leader of the opposition in the Western Australian parliament.[11]

An agricultural scientist who had initiated the banana-growing industry in the Gascoyne region of Western Australia, Wise had a political record that included a major reform of the state bank, and his combination of skills fitted him for Darwin.

It was Wise who had taken the initiative. Having lost two successive elections, he was looking for a change, and it was his life's ambition to play a role of leadership in the development of northern Australia. He made his availability known to Hasluck, and was immediately accepted.[12] The outgoing administrator, Driver, thought the appointment 'perfect'.[13] Hasluck was praised for looking beyond party politics to secure a good appointment; it probably counted as much to him that Wise was a Western Australian.

Possible friction lurked in the fact that Hasluck was a very new minister, whereas Wise had more than a decade of ministerial experience including two years as Premier; but at the age of fifty-four and in full vigour, he was in every important respect an accession of strength. Hasluck and Wise developed an agreed concept of the relationship between minister and administrator that made them a productive working team, though there were occasional bumps. One Darwin official recalled that

> Mr Lambert soon had Mr Hasluck's ear and the Administrator was informed that all matters between the Administrator and the Minister would be via the Secretary. This was a great setback to Mr Wise…it reduced the Administrator to the status of a glorified public servant. This was all gall and wormwood to an experienced politician and ex-Premier.[14]

But a colleague who arrived two years after Wise took office told a different story. Wise, he reported, won the fight with Lambert about direct access to the minister, although there were still times when Wise and Lambert were not talking and a go-between was needed.[15] Wise saw out his five-year term, and even after his return to state politics he could write to Hasluck, 'My great regret is that I was unable to continue to serve you and your Govt. and to see much more done'.[16] Many years later Hasluck wrote of Wise: 'He gave the people of the Territory a better conceit of themselves'.[17]

Government House, Port Moresby, presented Hasluck with harder problems. At first he looked forward to working with Murray, although he knew that Percy Spender, as Minister for the old Department of External Territories, had developed reservations about the administrator. Spender considered the department 'comatose, and the Territory not much better'.[18] Like the frogs in Aesop's fables, Murray should have realised that the King Log personified by the inactive Ward was likely to be followed by a Liberal King Stork. Spender offered Murray an honourable exit by resuming the post of principal of the Australian School of Pacific Administration together with a senior role on the South Pacific Commission, but Murray refused. Instead, he asked for the creation of two posts of deputy administrator. Spender took the proposal to cabinet but could secure approval only for one assistant administrator. After advertisement the appointment went to the fifty-year-old Donald Cleland.

This was contentious. At the time of Murray's appointment in 1945, Cleland was originally the preferred candidate by virtue of a senior position in the Australian New Guinea Administrative Unit during the last three years of the war. But as he had just been the unsuccessful Liberal parliamentary candidate for the Fremantle seat following John Curtin's death, and was about to accept the directorship of the federal secretariat of the Liberal Party, he was passed over as too political, and Murray was appointed instead. In 1951 the appointment of an assistant administrator was handled by an independent public service committee, and Cleland was by far the best qualified in a large field of applicants. The decision was taken before Hasluck became minister, but it was left to him to implement it. Inevitably, the Coalition government and Hasluck were accused of political favouritism, but the process had been entirely above-board. Hasluck cannot have been displeased with the outcome, since he and Cleland already knew and respected each other.

In his early weeks as minister, Hasluck looked for advice from a variety of sources. He consulted Nugget Coombs, who suggested that the Department of Territories could be entirely managed from Canberra:

> the separation of the Department in Canberra and the
> Administration in the Territory is unnecessary and based on
> Colonial office tradition no longer applicable in times when
> modern transport is available…there would need to be a good
> deal of devolution of authority down the line, but great gain
> from the single line of authority.[19]

Hasluck justifiably thought that the strength of local feeling in both communities ruled out any prospect of following this advice.[20]

Hasluck thought it might be useful, following the model of the British colonial service, to create a single Australian Territorial Service whose members might serve in any of the places in the department's responsibility, moving between Papua New Guinea, the Northern Territory and any of the smaller units. He believed such an arrangement would attract ambitious and capable officers, and provide broader experience and better opportunities for promotion. He inquired if the United Kingdom Government could lend Australia an official experienced in colonial administration who could offer advice about Papua New Guinea, but Whitehall had nobody to spare. The proposal was resisted by existing members of the public service, and was vetoed by the chairman of the Public Service Board, William Dunk, who ruled that as a trusteeship territory Papua New Guinea must develop its own public service.[21] Dunk was in the right, but there was already a prickliness between Dunk and Hasluck after the handling of Hasluck's resignation from External Affairs in 1947, and Hasluck found him unhelpful in the early months when he was trying to shape an effective administrative structure for the new Department of Territories.[22]

In practice, the workings of the department were tailored to the needs of each territory. In the Northern Territory much of the administration was carried out from Darwin, with a secondary and at times independent-minded team of officials located at Alice Springs; but ultimate responsibility rested with the minister in Canberra, and while Hasluck was minister Canberra oversaw policy constantly and intervened frequently. Port Moresby was further from Canberra and its administration more complex, but Hasluck's influence was no less pervasive. To some he seemed 'more a super-bureaucrat than a Minister'.[23] Hasluck himself believed that, lacking support from the Public Service Board, he had to fashion the Department of Territories from the staff at his disposal, and this made him a martinet:

In my own case this meant that, not from nature or from theory but out of necessity, I turned from depending on the department to driving it hard, squeezing every bit of effort and thought that it contained. I possibly hurt some people who could not move fast enough…It also meant that, contrary to my earlier practice and experience as a public servant, more of the new ideas had to be given as instructions from above than came up through the roots from below.[24]

Hasluck had a clear view of the relationship between public servant and minister:

It is the responsibility of the public service to examine all administrative matters and to give advice or make recommendations, in good conscience, without trying to anticipate whether a Minister will accept or reject their proposals.[25]

Reg Marsh, who held several senior administrative roles in the department from 1953, gave a graphic description of Hasluck's working methods. He believed Hasluck was in the business of training his public servants. He wanted his advisers to get into the habit of determining 'What is the principle behind this issue?' Experienced public servants would put up a proposal 'to flush the Minister out'. 'Back would come the response from Paul Hasluck: "I am not convinced"…We put up something further, and back would come the response, "Try again"'. Eventually they would arrive at a satisfactory formulation, knowing Hasluck would act on the proposal.[26] Marsh, who had been a school-teacher for several years before entering the public service, could appreciate this approach to working as a learning experience for the civil servant, but others winced at the castigation. According to Dame Rachel Cleland, the wife of Donald Cleland,

If anybody dared to express an opinion contrary to his he could be very rude. So men in the field tended to get wary. After all, no career man wants to make his minister angry.[27]

The Clelands also remembered that it was difficult to get Hasluck to state his criticisms during his visits, but that after his return to Canberra written communications would arrive forcefully setting out what he perceived as shortcomings. She thought he used the prick and the goad too much, and quoted Eski Lambert as commenting: 'The Minister is very brave behind a pen'.[28] With his experience of Evatt's Department of External Affairs behind him, Hasluck knew that the spoken word could often be misremembered, whereas the written word made for precision. A man who found difficulty in curbing his temper was also well advised to avoid provocative conversations. But his memoranda sometimes recalled the trenchant style of 'Polygon' the drama critic.

Another perspective on Hasluck's administrative style was offered by Kim Beazley senior, who sat as a Labor member of the House of Representatives for the neighbouring seat of Fremantle:

I remember one occasion when I asked for certain information from Hasluck's Department. I learned from someone in the Department that a very off-hand reply was prepared for me and was sent to Mr Hasluck to sign. He wrote one of his famous 'rockets' to the Department – 'Mr Beazley is an educated man. He is entitled to the information for which he has asked. I would be ashamed to send a reply like this to him or to any Member of Parliament.' He was a great stickler for correctness.

He was also the only minister I knew who accepted motions from the Opposition. When I got up and moved that there should be an inquiry into the grievances of the Yirrkala Aborigines he accepted it as Minister...straight away.[29]

Hasluck's 'rockets' made lively reading. When the responsibility of removing a hazardous wreck from Darwin Harbour was bandied between two or three government authorities, Hasluck minuted: 'Stop fooling around...It doesn't matter who gives the order as long as it is given'.[30] A report from the Primary Production Board of the Northern Territory was minuted: 'This memorandum is just a page of excuses to cover twelve months of duckshoving'.[31] Occasionally he permitted himself a whimsical note. A stocktaking report from Government House, Nauru, is annotated:

This is admirable. I know of no other institution that has come under my notice in the past ten years where the wastage has been as small as one table fork a year. Most of them seem to lose three or four refrigerators and a few truckloads of furniture.[32]

Within the Canberra office, Hasluck maintained formal and impersonal relations with his staff, who understood this as a reaction against the untidy arrangements and scope for favouritism he had encountered in the Department of External Affairs under Evatt. This tendency grew after 1954, when he acquired as his personal secretary Ellestan Dusting, who was to work with him for fifteen years and became notable in Canberra folklore as the epitome of the protective personal assistant. Member of a public service family that had been in Canberra since its beginnings in 1927, Miss Dusting held firm views about office management. She was surprised to find Paul Hasluck modestly booking his own telephone calls and travel arrangements, and immediately took these matters efficiently in hand. She soon kept masterful control of his appointments diary so that there was no casual dropping in on the minister. Hasluck came to rely on her implicitly.

Some, especially male bureaucrats, found her manner unacceptably brusque. Sir Walter Crocker thought she 'wanted to be noticed, overdid her importance, and threw her weight around'.[33] For Victor Garland, Hasluck's successor as member for Curtin, 'Miss Dusting was a dragon, and a dragon of Paul Hasluck's choosing', though Nicholas Hasluck remembers nothing dragon-like about her manner.[34] Alexandra, however, did not like her. Translating into practice her minister's strong views about the necessity of separating public life from private, Miss Dusting kept his wife at arm's length from the office routine, and Alexandra felt excluded. Canberra being Canberra, there was gossip about the precise nature of the relationship between minister and secretary, but there is no evidence to suggest that the camaraderie of the office led to anything more intimate after hours. Miss Dusting was not exempt from the impersonality of Hasluck's office manner. 'I felt he didn't like me to have any individuality, apart from being his secretary', she remembered, adding that it required anticipation and stamina to work for him, although very occasionally he would unexpectedly propose a picnic for the staff and prepare martinis for them. She recalled that when she took leave to attend an international jamboree of guides and scouts, an important event in her life outside the department, she returned to work to find that Hasluck asked her not one question about her travels, but launched straight into the business of the day.[35]

Those who knew him drew a contrast between his precise official personality and his ease of manner outside office hours. He shared an interest in horses with H. B. ('Jo') Gullett, the government whip, who recalled:

he used to go to the local gymkhana…Introducing him around at Top Naas with a couple of horses, he was very much at home with those horse bushy sort of fellows, and he was looking for a horse to buy.[36]

Ric Throssell, a Western Australian whose career in External Affairs was beset by accusations of Soviet sympathies, but who remained on good terms with Hasluck, said:

I think he's a very nice man. But there was this sort of schizophrenia, this dichotomy in his personality, and his behaviour in the office was quite, quite different from his behaviour outside. In the office he was a cold, dedicated, meticulous, demanding, in some ways diminishing boss, 'cause by the time you'd finished with him you didn't know whether you were right or wrong…But the same day I would go to the Canberra Repertory Society, of which he was president at the time and I was vice-president, and anyway we met at his house at Manuka, and he was a charming, pleasant, unassuming, unpretentious host, and remained that when he was Governor-General.[37]

Throssell's comment invites the speculation that Hasluck, with his background in theatre, saw his ministerial office as a role to be played according to a script of conventions. Paul Hasluck the responsible minister could behave with a toughness and lack of compunction that Paul Hasluck the private man would never have dreamed of claiming for himself.

In his early years in cabinet he made no close friends, but he was soon regarded as a useful member of the team who came to meetings well prepared, and argued his case cogently and at a seemly length. Sometimes, when his argument was knocked back, he sulked, chagrined that his colleagues could not see the merits of his carefully prepared case. Of the senior members of the ministry, he respected the Minister for External Affairs, Casey, but found him underprepared and ineffective in cabinet.[38] The Minister for Supply, Howard Beale,[39] 'shepherded' him when he entered cabinet, but Hasluck wrote of him, 'He had a much loftier disdain for things contemptible than I would ever achieve, and more confidence in himself than I had in myself'.[40] He got on well with plain men of rural background such as the Treasurer, Sir Arthur Fadden, and the Minister for Defence, Sir Philip McBride, but was less at ease with the products of Melbourne and Sydney society. He found Harold Holt uninterested in Papua New Guinea or Aboriginal matters, and William McMahon overly ingratiating. He whiled away the duller stretches of cabinet meetings by sketching very competent pen portraits of them, and at some time in the 1950s developed a habit of writing short essays in which he tried to pin down the essence of their public characters.

Hasluck's relationship with Menzies was complex. At times he found Menzies inscrutable, and was never quite sure of his leader's opinion of him. Perhaps because of his work ethic, he was seldom one of the favoured few who met in the Prime Minister's office after the House of Representatives rose and Menzies relaxed in anecdotal mood while offering his formidable martinis. Another complication could well have been that in writing the history of Australia at war between 1939 and 1941, Hasluck had been critical of some aspects of Menzies' leadership. Although the Menzies of the 1950s had outgrown some of the failings of his first prime ministership, he may still have found it hard to forget that Hasluck the political colleague was also Hasluck the historian. On the other hand, Hasluck was the colleague who most shared Menzies' taste for literature and, in cabinet, Hasluck would sometimes pass little satirical verses about their colleagues on to Menzies, 'who would read them and keep the smile off his face and tuck the little poem away in his pocket'.[41] At the dinner celebrating Menzies' sixtieth birthday in December 1954, Hasluck composed and recited a poem in heroic couplets gently lampooning his colleagues and their foibles.

Observers noted that Hasluck spent more time in Canberra than any other cabinet minister. He was fettered by the tyranny of distance. Ever since Federation, a Western Australian who served for any length of time in a federal cabinet had to resign himself to long and tedious travel. Even after the transcontinental railway was completed in 1917, the journey took three days each way. By the time Hasluck entered politics the advent of air travel shortened the travelling time, but direct flights between Perth and Canberra were still a long way into the future. The journey took at least eight hours including a break at Melbourne, Sydney or Adelaide. Too often Hasluck's schedule meant that he had to travel on the notorious 'red-eye' departing from Perth at midnight and arriving in Canberra as the morning's work was well underway. Hasluck's portfolios, first in Territories and later in External Affairs, also meant that he spent an inordinate part of each year away from home. He developed the knack of sleeping on aircraft, and was known to be irascible if disturbed, but he was also willing to act as a kindly escort to friends' children travelling to school in Melbourne. Unlike most of his Western Australian predecessors, he had children of school age.[42] Although he was an attentive and caring father when at home, the circumstances inevitably threw much of the parental role onto his wife. Over the years this was to become a source of strain in their relationship.

Hasluck could occasionally snatch longer periods in Perth during the parliamentary recesses, especially in the summer. Even during holidays such as Christmas, his work ethic kept breaking in. He often used his leisure time to reflect and compose memoranda on major policy issues for which the pressures of day-to-day administration had left little opportunity. Sometimes it was necessary to fit in a visit to the Northern Territory or Papua New Guinea. 'I don't know whether if I had realised what home life would be like...I would have been so keen for him to stand for election', Alexandra Hasluck later wrote. 'Wives had to get used to running their homes and families alone.'[43] Her responsibilities included the older members of the family. Her own mother was in her eighties and failing. Paul's mother, Patience, died at the age of eighty-five in 1954, but Meernaa lived on into his vigorous nineties, cared for by his daughter Rosa. Paul kept in touch with them as best he could, but there were never enough opportunities.

The bush block at Paulls Valley became a continuing source of solace. He took his sons camping there, and they gradually cut a rough gravel track towards the site of a future shack. Gradually he acquired some of the adjacent land until the holding totalled 140 acres (56.7 hectares). There was a moment of crisis when, in his absence and without his knowledge, the Metropolitan Regional Planning Board compulsorily resumed the block, but he fought the case and was eventually allowed to retain 80 acres (32.4 hectares). To improve his security of tenure he then built a one-room shed and spent weekends there. Such intervals fed his love of solitude and his self-sufficiency while allowing welcome intervals for reading and listening to classical music or jazz.

Meanwhile, the second volume of his War History sat reproachfully in his in-tray, seldom finding enough attention but a constant reminder of the scholarly skills he was forgoing. After the Christmas holidays in 1960–61 he wrote to his wife: 'I've had a rather dull and disappointing time on the War History, and cannot see much prospect of finishing it under present circumstances...What is the use of struggling?'[44] It took him up to twelve months to find time to respond to queries from his editor, Gavin Long. By 1961 the manuscript was in a sufficiently complete shape for Long to write:

It gives the 4430 readers of the first volume what they have been waiting for so long. I'd be happy if the author were to write a few pages of peroration and leave the rest to us.[45]

In practice the manuscript still needed tidying up and reduction, as well as curbing Hasluck's increasing penchant for passing moral judgements on his story. It was nearly a decade before the second volume appeared.

In his early years as a minister, Paul Hasluck compensated for his absences by writing letters to Alexandra vividly describing his travels: 'I am preparing the ground for you to come here with me next time', he wrote on his first major encounter with the dramatic scenery of Papua New Guinea. 'You would love it.'[46] Returning from his first visit to Norfolk Island he wrote a long description of that island community, peopled largely by descendants of the *Bounty* mutineers and administered by Alex Wilson, formerly the rural independent member of parliament whose shift of allegiance in 1941 brought down the Coalition government in favour of Curtin's wartime Labor ministry.[47] In Paul's first year as minister, Alexandra accompanied him to Darwin, Nauru and Papua New Guinea, accustoming herself to the hazards of travel in light aircraft. She found the people of the Northern Territory 'outspoken and a trifle prickly to deal with'. 'I liked them for it', she commented. 'I did not have to deal with them.'[48] She enjoyed Papua New Guinea more, admiring the 'interested and vigorous approach' of its indigenous people in coming to terms with change, and concerning herself especially with the advancement of women. Of all the territories she visited, the scents of historic Norfolk Island remained with her as the most distinctive memory.

But the problems of separation between wife and husband were always lurking in the background as Paul Hasluck pursued his ministerial career. Although Alexandra Hasluck had played the role of an international diplomat's wife ably and not without relish, she was less at home among the politicians' wives. From her earliest years in Canberra she was impatient with small talk.

The shyness of her youth grew into a reserve in middle age that hindered her in networking with new acquaintances. She found few among the wives of her husband's colleagues who shared her intellectual interests, and they in turn found her difficult.[49] In July 1953, Alexandra Hasluck's dissatisfaction reached a point where Paul asked her whether she wanted him to give up the life of politics. 'The family is more important to me than public life', he wrote, 'and if you think that the family is being ruined and that you are getting no "fun" but only worry out of it, then public life had better be ended'. He pointed out that if he did so they might have to leave Perth to follow employment elsewhere.[50] It was decided that he should continue; at the time it was by no means certain that the Menzies government would win the elections due in the next nine months, or that Hasluck would continue as Minister for Territories.

When it became evident that Paul would remain a minister for some time, the Haslucks found new ways of dividing the family responsibilities. Until that time Hasluck lodged during the parliamentary sessions in Canberra with many of his colleagues at the Hotel Kurrajong. When one of the Australian National University's houses became available for a few months in 1953 he rented it, only to be criticised by a member of the Labor opposition hoping to sniff out impropriety. Paul Hasluck explained that he was paying the substantial rent of £8 a week, saying:

I was grateful, personally, to the university authorities for having given me that brief opportunity to get away from the horrors of living, week in and week out, in a hotel bedroom.[51]

Soon afterwards the Haslucks rented 'a very congenial semi-detached house' in Deakin, which Alexandra could visit from time to time. Rollo and Nicholas Hasluck were enrolled as boarders at Canberra Grammar School, enabling them to spend time with their father at weekends. Paul Hasluck recalled:

> I had the most appreciative tasters of my cooking that I have ever had. After a week or two of boarding house tucker the sort of dishes I gave them seemed like haute cuisine, and I must say my casserole of rabbit and my duckling with pickled walnuts were rather good for hungry boys in midwinter. We had happy times.[52]

With her sons at boarding school, her husband often away and an aged mother in care, Alexandra turned to the support of the few women friends who shared her literary and historical interests, notably the kindly patrician Henrietta Drake-Brockman. Born Henrietta Jull, she shared with Alexandra the experience of having been an only child whose father died while she was in her teens. She married an engineer–administrator, Geoffrey Drake-Brockman, and spent five years in Broome in the 1920s. This stimulated her work as novelist and playwright, and led to a friendship with both Haslucks, although it was with Alexandra that she maintained a close lifelong correspondence. A more recent friend was Mollie Lukis, also from an old Western Australian family, the tactful and perceptive founder of Western Australia's archives system and later Alexandra's collaborator on the book *Victorian and Edwardian Perth from Old Photographs*.[53]

Alexandra Hasluck now had time to resume her career as a writer. Discouraged from trying her hand at fiction beyond occasional short stories, she turned her attention to the colonial history of Western Australia. Paul's political activities and his commitment to producing a second volume of *The Government and the People* meant she had the field to herself. With Paul's encouragement and support, she began work on a life of the pioneer botanist Georgiana Molloy, who among the first generation of British settlers in the South West of Western Australia was remarkable for her quick appreciation of the botanical significance of its wealth of wildflowers.[54] Alexandra Hasluck was finding a vocation independent of the life of politics. Paul, meanwhile, was becoming more and more absorbed by that life. Each was becoming habituated to managing alone.

Chapter 13

Aboriginal policy

As Minister for Territories, Hasluck was now on his mettle to devise a national policy for the advancement of Aboriginal Australians. Already he was seen as 'the pre-eminent parliamentary spokesman on Aboriginal affairs', urging that

> the nation must now move to a new era in which the social advancement rather than the crude protection of the natives should be the objective of all that is done in this sphere.[1]

Central to his thinking was the recognition that Aboriginal people should be counted as Australian citizens by right. In Darwin on 25 August 1951 he said that although many Aboriginal people still stood in need of protection or of special legislative arrangements, it was the government's intention that any people of Aboriginal descent capable of looking after themselves should assume full citizenship.

This was a radical break with the past, although Hasluck as the author of *Black Australians* was undoubtedly aware that it heralded a return to the liberalism that marked British colonial policy in the 1830s and 1840s. A hundred years later, Australian legislation at both Commonwealth and state level assumed that Aboriginal people should not be regarded as Australian citizens unless specifically admitted to that status. In Western Australia, for instance, a government of which Frank Wise was a senior member decreed in 1944 that Aboriginal individuals might be admitted to citizenship and voting rights provided they no longer lived in the manner of 'aboriginal natives'. Few took advantage of this concession.

Within three weeks of assuming office, Hasluck made his first submission to cabinet. He sought authority to convene a conference of Commonwealth and state ministers responsible for Aboriginal policy, and this was approved. He also asked for a special financial contribution for measures of Aboriginal advancement. Cabinet rejected the latter request as bringing the Commonwealth into an area of state responsibility. Hasluck knew there was no practical possibility of a Commonwealth takeover of Aboriginal policy. This had been among the fourteen powers sought by the Curtin government in 1944 and rejected by the voters at a referendum at the urging of the non-Labor parties. At that time Hasluck was too preoccupied with his duties in External Affairs to play any part either way in the debate. In the 1950s he had to work in the knowledge that the Menzies government was not keen to enlarge Canberra's powers at the expense of the states, and could not do so without a constitutional referendum such that of 1967, which occurred in an altered climate of opinion.

Hasluck intended the new policies to draw on academic experience. Even before the conference was approved, he wrote to a few leading authorities on Aboriginal affairs – such as Dr Charles Duguid, a Presbyterian doctor with years of experience in Central Australia;[2] and the doyen of Australian anthropology, Professor A. P. Elkin of the University of Sydney – informing them that he would welcome the opportunity of consulting them.[3] Elkin replied that, although the proposed conference was 'logical democracy', ministers came and went while authorities such as he were not consulted. 'However if ministers took the trouble to become really well-informed the proposed federal council might do some good.'[4]

The ministers met in Canberra on 3 and 4 September 1951. All states were represented except Victoria and Tasmania, which at that time were thought to have few, if any, Aboriginal inhabitants. While the conference covered issues ranging from health, education and employment to the entitlement of Aboriginal people to social services and voting rights, its main importance lay in its endorsement of assimilation as the key objective of Aboriginal policy. Official thinking had been moving gradually in that direction since the late 1930s, but it was Hasluck who at this conference secured the acceptance of assimilation as the declared aim of Commonwealth and state governments. In Hasluck's definition, assimilation meant that

all persons of aboriginal blood or mixed-blood in Australia will live in the same way as white Australians do…Full assimilation will mean that the aboriginal shares the hopes, the fears, the ambitions and the loyalties of all other Australians and draws from the Australian community all his social needs, spiritual as well as material.[5]

To meet criticisms that not enough was done to spell out specific measures for the future, the conference agreed to set up a Native Welfare Council composed of Commonwealth and state ministers, and meeting on an annual basis. Hasluck told

Elkin, 'we have rested heavily on the foundations which you laid in past years'.[6] Although Hasluck was consulting him, Elkin seems to have expected to be invited to spend a good deal of time in Canberra helping to shape policy. When weeks and then months went by without any such invitation, he complained, sometimes in letters to comparative strangers:

> I do not think that anybody outside Canberra under the present regime has any influence whatever on aboriginal policy in the Northern Territory. Certainly I have none. It is all planned in Canberra. This seems to satisfy the present Minister.[7]

Although Elkin would have done better to address his criticisms of Hasluck's policies directly to the minister, he was justified in his doubts about the readiness of politicians to grapple with Aboriginal policy. At the Native Welfare Council's first meeting in 1952, only New South Wales, Queensland and South Australia sent representatives. Only one cabinet minister came, and he went home as soon as he found that none of his peers was present. Confronted by such a lack of practical interest, Hasluck abandoned his attempts at securing formal federal–state cooperation for several years. Instead he concentrated on developing the Northern Territory as a showcase for the improvement of Aboriginal wellbeing.

Assimilation was not intended as cultural genocide. Hasluck, in common with most observers at that time, believed that traditional Aboriginal society, a hunter-gatherer regime nomadic within understood boundaries, was in irreversible decline. The younger Aboriginal generation was steadily deserting this way of life in favour of missions, pastoral properties or towns. A report from Alice Springs provided him with a parable of the process, in which empathy and paternalism are oddly mixed:

> When a tribal group starts to disintegrate and the young men are being attracted more and more to white ways, the old men of the group express concern that the 'secrets' are being lost and that there is no-one to whom they can pass on their sacred objects.[8]

They brought their churingas from their hiding places and entrusted them to a government official, who locked them in a safe:

> From time to time the old men come to him and ask if they can see and handle them again. Then he unlocks them and they may either satisfy themselves that they still exist or croon over them a little. Then they go back to the dog-infested ashes of their camps to mourn in loneliness the loss of a culture.[9]

In Hasluck's view the movement 'away from the desert and the bush towards settlement is taking place inevitably'.[10] Assimilation was the consequence and not the cause of these changes. If Aboriginal people no longer wished to live in the manner of their ancestors they should be welcomed into mainstream society instead of being marginalised. Such a formulation overlooked the possibility that Aboriginal groups might still retain a strong spiritual and cultural connection with the country of their origins even though they were no longer supporting themselves there as hunters and gatherers, but this was not well understood in the 1950s. The more pressing problem seemed to be securing social acceptance for both rural and urbanised Aboriginal people, and providing standards of health, education and capacity for employment that would enable them to make choices for their futures. Intellectually, Hasluck accepted that some Aboriginal people capable of entering mainstream society might choose not do so, but his policies were shaped on the assumption that few would refuse the opportunity.

Hasluck took pains to communicate his concept of assimilation to senior officials. In October 1951 he told the House of Representatives:

> Assimilation means not the suppression of Aboriginal culture
> but rather, that for generation after generation, cultural
> adjustment will take place. The native people will grow into a
> society in which by force of history they are bound to live.[11]

He expected it to take many years before all Aboriginal Australians could find 'a fitting place as members of the Australian community'.[12] During his Christmas holidays in Perth he took the opportunity of defining assimilation more precisely:

> The only equality I consider possible, and perhaps the only
> equality that is vital is equality before the law and equality
> in the defined rights of citizenship. Consequential on this
> equality will come a certain measure of equality of opportunity,
> and I think that the extension of the meaning of this 'equal
> opportunity' is the chief practical end of all efforts for social
> justice...Assimilation is the objective of native welfare issues.
> This means that the aborigines and persons of mixed blood are
> expected eventually to attain to the same manner of living and

the same privileges of citizenship as white Australians and to live, if they choose to do so, as members of a single Australian community, observing the same customs and influenced by the same beliefs, hopes and loyalties as other Australians. Their education and training and the provisions in regard to their housing, health and employment will be graduated according to their progress towards this eventual goal.[13]

'If they choose to do so' was the critical phrase. Aboriginal people should not be coerced into change, and no attempt should be made to break up tribal structures or to hasten the process by which Aboriginal people from the bush abandoned their traditional nomadic way of life.

Hasluck was soon confronted with an issue whose repercussions have lasted to the present day. This was the forcible removal of children from their Aboriginal mothers, particularly those with non-Aboriginal fathers. In 1950 a Northern Territory patrol officer reported distressing scenes over the removal of 'half-caste' children from Wave Hill station. Dr Duguid raised concern about the issue, and Hasluck asked Lambert for information.[14] What was the practice in the Northern Territory, who took the decision, and under what power was the decision carried into effect? Were Aboriginal children treated differently from other neglected children? How many children had been removed from their mothers during the past two years, and what had happened to them? Had the parents raised any objections?

In February 1952, Administrator Wise reported to Canberra. Any 'partly coloured' children could be removed if the director of Native Affairs thought it in the child's best interests, but not unless the child was neglected and the mother willingly gave up the child, or 'a painstaking attempt has been made to explain to the mother the advantages to be gained by the removal of the child'.[15] Wise recommended that children under four years of age should not be removed. Hasluck approved the policy, but added a minute: 'No age limit need be stated. The younger the child is at the time of removal the better for the child'. He was reflecting the conventional wisdom of the time, which held that if a mother and child were to be separated, it was least traumatic if the removal was made before strong bonds of love and affection could be formed.[16] Later developments in attachment theory by Bowlby and others have shown that the bonding between mothers and babies begins before birth, and critics from a younger generation, among them former Prime Minister Malcolm Fraser, have seen Hasluck's view as callous.[17] In 1952 it was accepted practice and was seen as the best option.

In recent years the issue has become entangled with the contentious debate over the *Bringing Them Home* report adopted by the Human Rights Commission in 1997.[18] In raising the awareness of contemporary Australians to the distress caused by the forcible removal of children from Aboriginal mothers, the authors of the report highlighted the eugenic motives of the 1930s. At that time children fathered by men of European background were taken from their mothers in the belief that they could be assimilated into the mainstream community and lose most, if not all traces of their Aboriginal inheritance. The *Bringing Them Home* report did not sufficiently indicate that Hasluck's policies in the 1950s were different. They were based not on race, but on the welfare of the child, who should be removed only if obviously neglected, whatever their ethnic background might be. In practice, difficulties still arose sometimes, because some 'half-caste' children were thought to have been rejected by their Aboriginal communities, while others who were accepted would be scheduled to undergo the traditional rites of initiation, and to some patrol officers this was a cause of concern. But it was never intended at any time during Hasluck's years of authority that Aboriginal Australians should be eradicated as the Jewish victims of the Nazi Holocaust had been eliminated. Those who suggest any resemblance are indulging in bad history.[19]

It was central to Hasluck's philosophy that the Northern Territory should get rid of racially based protective legislation. In August 1952 he told the House of Representatives that the Northern Territory Legislative Council would be asked to remove legal discrimination based on race and to provide citizenship for Aboriginal people unless they were considered in need of special care and protection. At the time, the director of Native Affairs in Darwin had power to control the affairs of all adults of Aboriginal descent unless they had been admitted to citizenship by procedures that some found, in Hasluck's words, 'irksome and even offensive'.[20] The new legislation would replace the Native Affairs Branch with a Welfare Branch charged with managing the affairs of all individuals deemed in special need of care or protection, who would be known as 'wards'. In theory they might be drawn from any section of the population, including non-Aboriginal people living in substandard conditions. In practice the new legislation was soon found to confine itself to Aboriginal people.

The Welfare Ordinance as drafted gave the administrator and, through him, the new director of Welfare almost unlimited power to declare people wards. Wards had no citizenship rights until they were released from their status or mounted a successful appeal against their classification. It puzzled Wise and his senior administrators to frame legislation 'without the appearance of any discrimination in favour, or against, Aborigines as a race'.[21] Hasluck was unperturbed. Even if an administrator went mad and started to 'declare' all and sundry, he told Wise, no tribunal would support his decisions if they applied to any persons except Aboriginal people.[22] Elkin told a Northern Territory official that the ordinance

> seems a bit like the same old woman in another hat. After all, what you want really is support from Canberra to get buildings and equipment, where you want them, and as quickly as possible.[23]

When it was introduced into the Northern Territory Legislative Council in January 1953, some of the official members were critical of its wording, but it passed. Porter comments: 'It is surprising, for a man of Hasluck's precision and concern for detail, that the inherent difficulties in the legislation were not resolved'. The practical difficulties included the lack of a systematic register of individuals who had previously been classified as 'Aboriginal', as well as a detailed definition of the criteria by which wards could graduate from that status.[24] But the ordinance was supported by the active lobbying of part-Aboriginal people calling themselves the Northern Territory Australian Half-Caste Progressive Association. They saw the change as an act of emancipation, as it removed all reference to 'half-castes' in the legislation.[25]

Throughout 1953 and 1954, Hasluck bombarded the Northern Territory administration with demands for plans for

Aboriginal welfare policies. 'I do not want a further report of hopes, theories, or principles', he told Lambert. He wanted 'submissions which can be approved, rejected, or attended without delay'.[26] In September a Wards Employment Bill was introduced to the Legislative Council, providing for schemes of job training and apprenticeships for young Aboriginal people. It also obliged employers to pay part of a ward's wages into a trust account, with the intention of fostering habits of saving among Aboriginal people in paid employment. This gave rise to another difference of opinion between Hasluck and the Darwin officials, since they considered it convenient to pay interest already due into consolidated revenue rather than individual bank accounts. Hasluck saw this as 'nothing else but a compulsory diversion of private property to public revenue'. When Wise complained that Hasluck's proposal was 'impracticable', he simply retorted: 'Find a way of putting it into effect'.[27]

Not surprisingly, the Northern Territory officials took their time about implementing the two ordinances. The Welfare Ordinance did not come into effect until 1957, the Wards Employment Ordinance until 1959. The main impediment was the need to conduct a census to determine which members of a population scattered over long distances should be classified as wards. The task was difficult and other priorities competed. Despite sporadic urging from Hasluck it took more than four years to complete the census, even if some officials took the short cut of declaring all Aboriginal people wards regardless of their living standards.[28]

When the figures were published in 1960 it emerged that 15,277 Aboriginal people in the Northern Territory and one other person were classified as wards, while 1,299 Aboriginal inhabitants were exempted. Very few of those defined as wards were released from that classification. Long before this discouraging outcome, Hasluck confessed himself 'a little tired of all the complications raised in the path of a policy of regarding Aborigines as having the legal status and the legal rights of other Australians'.[29] For a supporter of the racially even-handed wards policy, such as Ted Egan, the outcome was disappointing. In general an admirer of Hasluck, Egan's main criticism was that he did not take care to ensure that the legislation operated for non-Aboriginal people.[30]

But there was no slackening of Hasluck's determination that the policy of assimilation should be clearly understood and implemented. In 1956 a new administrator, J. C. ('Cautious Clarrie') Archer, after discussion with senior officials, sent a memorandum to Hasluck setting out his ideas about education policy within the broader context of assimilation. He began:

> In the final analysis, full assimilation will only be achieved through 'economic' assimilation; since no Aborigine can be regarded as having full community rights and responsibilities until he ceases to be a ward of the state, and is able to stand on his own feet. It follows that all our efforts in education (formal and technical) and in the broader sense, our education in cultural and social advancement, have necessarily to be directed to that end.[31]

Hasluck, although he accepted much of the detail in Archer's submission, disagreed profoundly with this statement of first principles. 'Is our doctrine to be "Seek ye first a steady job and all things shall be added unto you?"', he asked:

Does this mean that we can discount the education, discipline, religious teaching, patriotic sentiment, national tradition, moral counsel, social conventions and so on to which our own people are subjected during their formative years and say that all these influences have a lesser effect on making them Australians than their eventual participation in the economic life of the nation?... We want to give the primitive and the under-privileged child something much more than an occupation and a few possessions.[32]

It was a fine ideal to urge that assimilated Aboriginal people should enjoy a shared sense of citizenship with their fellow Australians as well as access to economic opportunity and jobs, but Archer had a point when he stressed the need for vocational education. Apart from the pastoral industry, where Aboriginal stockmen were a vital component of the workforce, opportunities had to be created through the economic development of the Northern Territory. At various times Hasluck hoped that the promotion of agriculture and forestry would create jobs for Aboriginal workers. The mining industry was emerging as another hopeful development. But each of these industries created pressures on the few remnants of Aboriginal land rights.

Hasluck was the first minister, Commonwealth or state, to insist that Aboriginal Australians should share the benefits of mineral development in their country. In 1952 he sponsored federal legislation entitling Aboriginal communities to royalties from mining on their reserves. He also ruled that if mining companies wished to prospect on Aboriginal reserves they would have 'to prove a very strong case and also show that no injury will be suffered by the natives before we allow them to enter on native reserves'.[33] In 1954, when applications for oil exploration began to come forward, Hasluck required that any submission to the minister be accompanied by a precise statement of the effect the granting of a permit would have on the welfare of the Aboriginal people, and a statement of the special conditions proposed to protect their welfare.[34]

Hasluck was vigilant in protecting Aboriginal reserves from encroachment. He rebuffed Frederick Moy, the director of Native Affairs inherited from the previous regime, who assumed that the area set aside for Aboriginal reserves could be reduced in size as assimilation progressed.[35] Moy had recommended that the Wangites reserve, 80 kilometres south-west of Darwin, should be thrown open for pastoral leases, as 'the Reserve is only used by Aboriginals travelling between Delissaville and the Daly River and occasional hunting parties'.[36] Moy and his colleagues seemed to believe 'that employment was the only value that the reserve held for Aboriginal people'.[37] But Hasluck ruled that the reserve should be kept intact if there were no long-term plans for its use. Reserves should not be altered or abolished unless there was a clear benefit for the relevant Aboriginal communities:

These reserves are being held today, not as a refuge to which aborigines can retreat and live in a tribal state, but as reserves of land to meet the future needs of these people...Country with economic potential on reserves for Aboriginal people is to be held until such time as [they] can themselves share in the benefits which arise from its development.[38]

The outcome in this case was somewhat disappointing. Neighbouring pastoralists continued to graze their stock over the reserve, and in 1961 one of them requested that the boundaries of her property be adjusted to take in part of the Wangites reserve. Hasluck consented, but only on condition that the reserve's boundaries be squared off and enlarged to 400 hectares. After Hasluck left the Department of Territories, however, the area was reduced to a fraction of his proposal.

Hasluck's growing exasperation with journalistic standards was fed to a large extent by the often ill-informed coverage in the urban press of stories about Aboriginal people and northern Australia. In 1955 Douglas Lockwood, a journalist with much experience of northern Australia and Aboriginal issues, reported that the secretary of Britain's Anti-Slavery Society, Charles Greenidge, had claimed that a form of slavery existed in the Northern Territory. This brought Hasluck out on the attack:

> The aboriginal in the Northern Territory is certainly not bought and sold as a chattel. He is certainly not bound in serfdom to his employer. He is certainly not subject to corporal punishment. He is certainly not denied the right to bargain for better wages and conditions. He is certainly not denied the right of seeking redress for any injury he may think he suffers. He is certainly not denied the protection of the law. He is certainly not denied a reward for his labour which will rise with his skill and his experience. He is certainly not denied a right to keep his earnings as his own personal property. By all these standards he is not a slave.[39]

It was an eloquent rejoinder, but some of these rights had only recently been attained, in part because of Hasluck's own efforts, and not all of them were upheld in practice.

Assimilation was gradually gaining acceptance in all the Australian states as preferable to the old policies of segregation and neglect, but it seemed that not all Aboriginal people were persuaded of the merits of assimilation. As early as 1955, Hasluck noted uneasily that some urbanised Aboriginal people were continuing to insist on their separate ethnic identity instead of embracing a shared Australian identity. Even with the achievement of the right of citizenship, Aboriginal Australians still found many hurdles on the road to assimilation. The case of the artist Albert Namatjira became a tragic and prominent illustration of these difficulties.[40] Namatjira's landscapes had brought him an income far beyond any of his Arrernte kinsfolk, and the traditions of his people obliged him to share his good fortune with an ever-growing clan of dependants. Before Hasluck became minister in 1951, Namatjira had been disappointed in an attempt to buy a cattle lease on which to maintain his people, and cheated in the purchase of land in Alice Springs. Hasluck offered him land without cost on a reserve outside Alice Springs, but this was not accepted. Namatjira's fame continued to grow during the 1950s and in 1957 he and his wife were granted citizenship, with exemption from prohibitive legislation. This included the right to drink and possess alcohol. The pressure on him to provide some of his friends with liquor was too strong to resist, and in 1958 he was arrested on a charge of supplying a bottle of rum to an Aboriginal and sentenced to six months' imprisonment. Public uproar was immediate. Hasluck intervened and saw to it that the sentence was reduced to three months and served on the Papunya native reserve, and not in prison. His decision was supported by Evatt as leader of the opposition.[41] Yet Hasluck's clemency could not disguise the problematic aspects of assimilation.

In the cities a few voices were raised to argue that assimilation could be achieved only at the cost of the destruction of Indigenous culture and society. Far from accepting Hasluck's view that the younger Aboriginal generations were largely abandoning their traditions, the critics saw assimilation as imposing a stereotypical idea of Australianness on an inherently plural society. European migrants who had fled Nazi Germany's brutal assertion of 'one people, one nation' sensed coercion in policies that encouraged conformity to the norms of a white English-speaking Australia. Such critics were often active in left-wing in politics, and this led Hasluck to suspect that opposition to assimilation was communist-inspired:

> More than any other body in Australia, they try to promote
> resistance to a policy of assimilation and try to maintain the
> racial identity of a separate aboriginal group. There are signs
> that their plausible arguments along these lines are having
> some effect among some soft-minded commentators who are
> certainly not communists themselves.[42]

But the critics grew in number and prominence. At the ANZAAS[43] annual meeting in 1958, one of Australia's most eminent anthropologists, Dr W. E. H. Stanner, put the view that assimilation was a one-sided concept that required all the adaptation to be undertaken by the Aboriginal minority, without any shift in mainstream attitudes. Invited to give the keynote address at the next ANZAAS conference in Perth in August 1959, Hasluck repeated his usual formula: assimilation was intended to ensure that the opportunities for citizenship and the cultural upbringing of Aboriginal Australians should be no different from those of other Australians. Among the audience was Professor Elkin, now retired but still a force in anthropology. He had kept abreast of the intellectual currents in his subject, and relished the opportunity of putting the minister right. He now rose, and in an improvised but forceful argument identified shortcomings in the policy of assimilation.[44]

Elkin preferred a concept of integration. 'I did point out...', he subsequently wrote,

> that what was coming about was the development of the Aborigines as distinct groups with their own values and ambitions, but who yet could live happily in our general Australian system.[45]

This in reality did not contradict the ideal of assimilation, but demanded recognition that it should not be a one-way process requiring all the adaptation to be on the part of Aboriginal Australians. If Hasluck seemed slow to acknowledge this modification, it was because his focus lay in persuading all the state governments to embrace reform. The Commonwealth had no coercive powers, and the work of persuasion took time.

In January 1961, Hasluck at last managed to convene a conference in Canberra at which all the responsible state ministers agreed with the Commonwealth on setting assimilation as their goal, and agreeing on measures of health, education and welfare that should be taken to achieve it. The wording of their agreement was perceptibly Hasluck's:

> The policy of assimilation, in the view of all Australian governments, means that all aborigines and part-aborigines

are expected eventually to attain the same manner of living as other Australians and to live as members of a single Australian community, enjoying the same rights and privileges, accepting the same responsibilities, observing the same customs and influenced by the same beliefs, hopes and loyalties as other Australians.[46]

Much the same criteria were expected of the thousands of European migrants who were entering Australia at that time.

Hasluck reported the conference to the House of Representatives in February in a largely bipartisan debate in which he received several compliments from both sides of politics for his stewardship of Aboriginal policy. Harold Nelson, the member for the Northern Territory, complained about the lack of a permanent and continuous machinery of consultation between the Commonwealth and the states, a point that Hasluck could readily accept.[47] But it was Kim Beazley, usually his strongest ally on the Labor side of the House, who called into question the whole concept of assimilation. It was too imprecise, he contended: 'there are large numbers of persons in the Australian community who believe that the Minister's policy is to breed the Aborigines out by intermarriage into the Australian community'.[48] He thought that 'civilisation' was a better word to define the process. Aboriginal Australians might not have agreed.

Later in the debate, Hasluck drew on his historian's knowledge to illustrate what he understood by assimilation:

The ancient Britons were aborigines. Eventually they were completely assimilated in the successive wave of conquerors and immigrants. Today the ancient Britons live on as a social infusion in the inhabitants of the British Isles with some influence on the language spoken in the British Isles and with a minor influence on the customs of the British Isles.[49]

It was a broad concept, in keeping with Hasluck's ability to take long views. As he told his son Nicholas, he had been impressed by a passage in Alexis de Tocqueville's writings:

I should like to get a clear picture of the movements of peoples spreading over on top of each other and getting continually mixed up, but each still keeping something that it had from the beginning.[50]

In Britain successive waves of invaders – Romans, Saxons, Vikings, Normans – had spread over the original inhabitants, 'transforming them but not obliterating them'.[51] In Australia, and later in Papua New Guinea, Hasluck expected that Indigenous people would be transformed but not obliterated as the result of European contact. For him, assimilation was not the 'cultural genocide' some have called it; it was a historical process that followed prolonged contact between two cultures. Seen in this light, the main problem with assimilation was that it did not take into account the feelings of the families and individuals immediately involved in the process.

Assimilation was even questioned within the department. In September 1961, five Northern Territory cadet patrol officers attended a seminar at Grafton and heard a staff tutor, R. G. Hausfield, suggest ambiguities in the concept of assimilation. He said the term could imply either absorption, 'the eventual swallowing up of the Aborigines by their inclusion in the general community', or else assimilation without loss of racial identity. If the latter, it could be fostered by encouraging and strengthening Aboriginal groups, by providing means of sharing the ownership of land and resources ('This would help economically as well as emotionally'), and by removing discriminatory laws so that Aboriginal people could increase their involvement in the economic and social life of Australia. Hasluck was aware of Hausfield's comments, but left no reactions on paper.[52]

In 1961 the federal parliament set up a select committee on the issue of voting rights for Aboriginal Australians. The committee travelled more than 30,000 kilometres and took evidence from more than 400 witnesses. As a result, in 1962 Hasluck's Western Australian colleague Gordon Freeth, as Minister for the Interior responsible for the Electoral Act, introduced legislation enabling Aboriginal people in the Northern Territory, Queensland and Western Australia to vote in federal elections. Parliament unanimously supported the proposal, which became law. Hasluck spoke in the debate, permitting himself a moment of reminiscence. Twenty-five years earlier, he said, he had not found anyone who agreed with his belief that Aboriginal Australians might be given voting rights, and he envied Freeth the role of piloting the legislation.[53]

There was another unexpected consequence of the parliamentary committee's investigations. Kim Beazley was a member of this committee, and during their travels he met Aboriginal elders at Yirrkala, a Methodist mission in north-eastern Arnhem Land. In February 1962 the Northern Territory administration gave authority to a French company, Pechiney, to mine bauxite there, and an area of 140 square miles (363 square kilometres) was excised from the reserve. The Methodist authorities in Sydney had consented to the deal, but the Yirrkala missionary Edgar Wells and the Aboriginal communities were not consulted, and they invited Beazley and Gordon Bryant, the two Labor frontbenchers on the committee, to visit Yirrkala.

Beazley encouraged the tribal council to send a petition to parliament asserting their right to be consulted. It took the form of a bark painting with text in both Yolngu and English, and because of its unusual format attracted considerable publicity. Beazley presented the petition, arguing that 'The proclamation of large reserves for Aboriginal use means nothing if systematically, when anything of value is discovered in them, areas become excised from Aboriginal reserves'. Then, Beazley recalled, 'To my astonishment Hasluck...rose immediately and said "The Government readily accepts the proposal"'.[54] Promptly he moved for the creation of a select committee in order that doubts and misunderstandings might be cleared up.[55] To Beazley, this response to an opposition proposal was unique in more than thirty years of parliamentary experience. 'Hasluck was that rare politician who can genuinely be called a statesman', he wrote.[56] All was not quite sweetness and light, however, as when the committee was formed Hasluck queried the inclusion of Bryant, who had already lodged objections to the Gove bauxite mine that were still before the warden's court. The Speaker ruled that he could not determine whether Bryant should stand down, and Hasluck said he would not move to unseat Bryant but would leave it to his own judgement whether he should serve.[57] Bryant stayed, and no more was heard of the issue.

Hasluck was not to see the outcome of these investigations, as in December 1963 he was transferred to another portfolio.

Perhaps one index of Paul Hasluck's impact on Aboriginal policy is his appearance in Aboriginal folklore in the Northern Territory. The Yanyuwa people of Borroloola relate that in 1960 the Northern Territory administration, considering their camp insanitary and accessible to white undesirables, removed 133 of their number to a new settlement at Dangara on the Robinson River. The story has it that when Paul Hasluck visited the district in 1960, a senior Yanyuwa told him that his people did not belong in the Robinson River country, and he allowed them to return to Borroloola. Asked about it in 1986, Paul Hasluck had no recollection of the encounter, though he was in the area at the relevant time, but the story shows that he was remembered as a figure of authority who would listen to Aboriginal people.[58] It may be that in time he will join Captain Cook and Ned Kelly in Indigenous folklore.

Aboriginal Australians are not the only ones to have woven a mythology around Paul Hasluck. Academic and political commentators have constructed mythologies about his career to serve the purposes of debate. To conservative author Geoffrey Partington he was the sagacious and far-sighted reformer whose policies could be contrasted to the later impracticable ideals for which Nugget Coombs could be held responsible. To the authors of Bringing Them Home, as for Malcolm Fraser, he stood condemned as the authority who caused babies to be separated from their mothers. Others have used the phrases 'cultural genocide' and 'racism' to condemn the concept of assimilation. In reality the main criticism that might be made of Hasluck's concept of assimilation is that it took too hopeful a view of the capacity of rural industry to provide a path to assimilation for Aboriginal workers.

Within two years of his departure from the Department of Territories, a court determined that Aboriginal pastoral workers should be paid at the same rate as others.[59] This was a logical consequence of Hasluck's concept of equal citizenship, but it bore hard on the workers in question. In the past they had provided the pastoral industry with a labour force that received small wages but whose dependants were maintained by the employers, and whose routine enabled them to maintain traditional connections with country. Unable or unwilling to find the finances to fund equal pay for their Aboriginal workers, many pastoralists decided to do without them. Often the Aboriginal families were ejected to find their way to camps at the various small towns in the Northern Territory and the Kimberley. This change was accelerated – and to some extent would have taken place even without the equal-pay decision – by the advent of new technologies for mustering, such as the use of motorcycles and helicopters. When agriculture was established around the Ord River Scheme and elsewhere, it was found almost impossible to keep Aboriginal workers because the social-services system included the payment of 'sit-down' money, a regular pension that removed the pressure to find paid employment.

Observation had suggested to Hasluck that Aboriginal Australians were abandoning the folkways and culture of a hunter-gatherer society, so that within his own lifetime none would be left following the traditional practices of their ancestors. He expected they would find a way forward within mainstream society, much like migrants whose first language was not English, retaining perhaps some inherited usages but substantially identified with a common Australian culture. He sensed that decades of exclusion might result in the assertion of a distinctive Aboriginality that carried within it the possibility of a divided society, and he strove as an alternative to secure the acceptance of all Australians, regardless of ethnicity, as sharing in a common Australian citizenship.

His achievement may be simply stated. In 1933, when he first began to take a serious interest in Aboriginal issues, every Australian state and territory excluded Aboriginal people from citizenship and placed them under restrictive and frequently degrading regulations. Thirty years later, when he ended his term as federal Minister for Territories, it was uniformly accepted that the first Australians had an inherent right to citizenship, and if some were still subject to restraints and limitations, official policy should work towards eliminating these arrangements as soon as possible. Race should not be the determinant of citizenship.[60] As activist in the 1930s and as legislator in the 1950s and early 1960s, Hasluck was a leading agent of change. The referendum of 1967 that amended the Commonwealth constitution to accommodate this change is remembered as a symbolic moment. It could not have taken place, and would not have secured such widespread public assent, but for the clearing away of much of the old legislation and the attitudes of mind that supported it. In this transition, Paul Hasluck played an important and honourable part.

Chapter 14

The Northern Territory

When Hasluck became minister with responsibility for the Northern Territory nearly six years after the end of the war, the process of postwar reconstruction had not gone far. The war in the Pacific had stirred up a ferment of speculation about the future of Australia's 'empty North', but although there had been a good deal of planning and debate, little had been achieved. The administrator between 1946 and 1951, A. R. Driver, had grappled with many difficulties. He had no previous experience in civil administration, and towards the end of his tenure there were personal problems. Public-service staffing, according to one qualified observer, was 'chaotic', and there was 'ignorance among senior officials about how a government worked'.[1] Driver was unable to establish constructive relations with the Department of Works, whose inadequately staffed Darwin branch had the job of rebuilding a town razed by Japanese bombing in 1942. Militant and obstreperous, the North Australian Workers' Union dominated the waterfront and owned Darwin's only newspaper, the *Northern Standard*, whose views were close to those of the Communist Party of Australia.

In 1947, during Driver's regime, a Legislative Council was set up comprising six elected members and seven of the Northern Territory's officials, with the administrator as president. The elected members, nearly all local businessmen, represented a small electorate, almost entirely non-Aboriginal. The Northern Territory also had a seat in the federal House of Representatives, but the member could speak only by invitation on matters affecting his electorate, and had no right to vote. In 1949 the seat was won by 'Jock' Nelson, a pragmatic Labor man quick to air local grievances.[2] By the time Hasluck became minister, postwar resettlement was bringing newcomers to the Territory, and the North Australian Workers' Union was gradually losing influence. Within a few years the *Northern Standard* was to shut down in the face of competition from the *Northern Territory News*, and Territory politics came to be dominated by local issues and grievances.

On his first ministerial visit to the Northern Territory in June 1951, Hasluck walked around Darwin with Frank Wise. They found a dispiriting sight. The Esplanade was 'a wilderness of high brown grass' with the rubbish of war uncleared. Doctor's Gully was a junkyard, the post office a roofless ruin, and the wreckage of wartime had not been removed from the harbour, its main berth a temporary construction on an upturned hull. Public servants worked in galvanised-iron shacks, poorly ventilated and stiflingly hot for much of the year. Even Government House was 'untidy'. In a small community with several months of unpleasant weather during which disagreements were easily inflamed, it was hard to achieve progress. The non-Aboriginal inhabitants had grown inured to seeing the Northern Territory as a problem area.

Residents in the remote tropical region of the continent thought of themselves, with a sort of inverted vanity, as being different

270

from all other Australians. Some of them had reached a stage where they enjoyed their grievances as much as their blessings.[3]

From the outset Hasluck was determined that the residents of the Northern Territory should enjoy basic services and public utilities equal in quality to those in the rest of Australia. When the discovery of uranium at Rum Jungle called for the creation of the town of Batchelor, he wrote:

> I particularly want to ensure that the town, however large or however small, should be planned and developed in a way which will set a higher standard for the Territory. Here is a chance for us to tackle the social problem of living in the tropics because at last we have what looks like a solid economic foundation as well as a national interest in building good homes and providing good facilities.[4]

Seven years later, approving a town plan for Darwin, he commented:

> It is hard to see where anyone has planted a tree on public property in the past five years…We ought to try to make this the most beautiful tropical town in Australia.[5]

He encouraged local initiatives. When Treasury rejected a subsidy of £1,000 for historical and photographical societies, he took the matter to Fadden:

> I would myself have thought that the claims of the people in the Territory, who are more remote from the major centres of

population and more deficient in opportunities for recreation, would be rated far higher than the claims of the sheltered, pampered and unproductive inhabitants of the national sanatorium that is called the national capital.[6]

Hasluck and Wise built up a team of senior staff in Darwin with quite a strong Western Australian flavour about it. In addition to Wise, Hasluck entrusted a lot of responsibility to Harry Giese, whom he headhunted in 1953 as director of education. They had known each other since The University of Western Australia, where they shared an interest in drama. Their closeness was enough to stimulate around Darwin a persistent but utterly groundless rumour that Giese was Hasluck's brother-in-law. A survivor from the Driver administration, Hugh Barclay, director of lands, was also a Western Australian, but he took longer to warm to Hasluck, and in his reminiscences was frequently critical of the minister. This contrasted with Hasluck's assessment of Barclay:

He had a puritanical stubbornness in arguing the case for change. He spoke quietly but plainly and consistently. At times I may have disappointed him for my lack of enlightenment, but I came to value him highly.[7]

Later Hasluck was to draw senior appointments in the Northern Territory from serving officials who had proved their capacity. When Wise retired as administrator in 1956, he was replaced by a career public servant, Clarrie Archer, who was skilled in civil service management.[8] Reg Marsh became assistant administrator and recalled that once he arrived in Darwin his relationship with Hasluck became perceptibly less impersonal.[9] On Archer's retirement in 1961, Hasluck once again turned to a Labor minister in a state government, appointing Roger Nott, who was Minister for Agriculture in New South Wales.[10] Cynics suggested that the Coalition hoped that when Nott vacated his seat it would fall to the Country Party, as indeed it did. Territory folklore remembered Nott as less effective than his predecessors – 'Wise was wise, but Nott was not', ran a Darwin witticism[11] – but Nott left future historians in his debt by amassing a valuable photographic collection.

During the 1950s the beef cattle industry was the major primary producer in the Northern Territory and the main source of employment for Aboriginal workers. Between the two world wars the industry had existed in a constant state of depression, recovering during the war when a large influx of servicemen created demand, and continuing subsequently as Britain and the nations of Europe climbed out of wartime rationing. A fifteen-year agreement for the export of beef to the United Kingdom meant that for the first time in decades the industry was prospering, and pastoralists could make improvements to their properties after years of enforced neglect. Northern Territory pastoralists held their lands under long-term lease, and complained that their security of tenure was insufficient for them to secure credit from the banks. In January 1953, Hasluck introduced legislation providing for fifty-year leases subject to achieving a satisfactory level of improvements, and introducing a system of homestead leases that required the lessee to live on the property. The Central Australian Cattlemen's Association, representing on the whole middle-sized residential pastoralists, supported the move. Eddie Connellan, whose airline served the region, wrote: 'I and many others deeply appreciate the part you personally played in bringing about the…monumental change on Northern Territory land laws'.[12]

Some of the larger proprietors were less happy. The Northern Territory Pastoralists' Association grizzled about unsympathetic administration and prophesied ruin to the beef industry, only to be told 'the Government must have regard to the public interest, and where there is conflict the latter must prevail'.[13] Absentees, such as the British companies Vesteys and Bovril, resisted longest. The director of lands, Hugh Barclay, proposed that they would have their tenancy renewed if they gave up a portion of their holdings – usually as much as one-third. This would provide scope for smaller resident pastoralists to come in – and perhaps, at some distant date, even Aboriginals. The pastoral companies haggled about compensation. They wanted the book value of resumed leases to be the basis of their payout, whereas Barclay would grant only the value to the incoming lessee. Barclay recalled:

> After a couple of long telephone arguments which got nowhere the Minister took a hand. A general election was due at the end of the following week. And Mr Hasluck told both Vesteys and us that if he could not sign the new leases by the Thursday night before the election the deal was off, as the government might be defeated.[14]

It was known that the Australian Labor Party was hostile towards Vesteys, and had some chance of winning the 1954 election. This concentrated the minds of the negotiators wonderfully. They met in Darwin on the Monday before the election. By

Thursday, Barclay was able to fly to Perth via Adelaide, arriving at the Hasluck residence in Adams Road around 10.30 pm, where the deal was signed.

Hasluck was also responsible for improvements in infrastructure. In 1954 he oversaw legislation providing for stricter quarantine regulations and for the systematic improvement of stock routes. More ambitious plans for transport proved harder to negotiate. Drovers were still sending cattle to market on the hoof in many cases, and there was disagreement about whether this should be replaced by road, rail or air transport. The Queensland Government pressed for the extension of its railway system into the Northern Territory across the Barkly Tableland towards Darwin – at Commonwealth expense, of course. Some stations in the Kimberley district were slaughtering cattle locally and freighting the carcasses by air to the Wyndham meatworks, and the Commonwealth set up an advisory panel to monitor the results, but in an era of cheap petrol the economics of transport pointed to an upgrading of the road system. A committee of inquiry established in September 1954 reported in favour of providing a system of beef roads, and in 1956 Hasluck announced a ten-year plan of road improvements. The program soon proved its worth, and in December 1960 Hasluck ordered Lambert to prepare a submission to cabinet for an extended network of beef roads. Cabinet approved, and the scheme was initiated in 1962.

Hasluck was keen to supplement the pastoral industry with other forms of primary production that would diversify the Northern Territory economy and provide employment opportunities for Aboriginal people. In July 1955 he turned to forestry policy, urging that state forests should be proclaimed, both for the exploitation of existing stands of cypress and for long-term plantations. A start might be made in Aboriginal reserves, where there was insufficient employment for the able-bodied. This, he wrote, would

> build up over the years the basis of a future economic industry
> for the support of the higher social standards which such natives
> will attain in the next generation…The aim which I am setting
> is that in 30 or 40 years time (the period being determined
> by the time it takes to grow a tree) the Territory will be
> able to start to draw a worthwhile proportion of its timber
> requirements of various kinds from Territory.[15]

Unfortunately, it was difficult to secure suitable land for the purpose, and although Hasluck urged that there should be no undue delay, it was 1958 before a program of experimental development in forestry was adopted for the next five years.[16] In 1961 he secured cabinet approval for a pilot forestry operation at Maningrida and other locations. Its two objectives were the provision of timber for the Northern Territory's needs and the training of an Aboriginal workforce in forestry. By the time Hasluck ceased to be minister in 1963, more than 100 Aboriginal men and women were on the project's payroll. The scheme was subsequently mismanaged in several ways, and was largely terminated after a parliamentary inquiry in 1978.[17]

The Territory's rainfall seemed able to support various forms of tropical agriculture, but most experiments earlier in the twentieth century had ended badly. With the agricultural scientist Wise as administrator there was hope of better results in the 1950s. In 1950 CSIRO had established a research station at Katherine that undertook many regional surveys testing agricultural potential, but its findings often met with local apathy. Walter Stern, who was a technical officer at Katherine between 1951 and 1953, recalled how the staff painstakingly collected seed of the fodder crop Townsville stylo from a few neglected patches around Darwin, eventually accumulating sufficient quantities to sow experimental crops. In the second year of planting a magnificent crop was produced. One day, when Stern was alone on the farm, an impressive official car arrived without warning. Its passengers were the federal member for the Northern Territory, Jock Nelson, visiting the farm for the first time in company with the Tasmanian Labor senator Justin O'Byrne. A little later a second car arrived with Paul Hasluck.

The visitors were impressed with the Townsville stylo, and asked whether the pastoralists knew about this development. Stern replied that they were not interested and summoned up the courage to say: 'Last year the government subsidised the purchase of lucerne from the southern states to help them keep their stock alive...do you know what they did with it? They fed their race-horses'. Hasluck left shortly afterwards, but several months later Stern was visited in his office by a station manager who wanted to learn 'about this TS stuff'. 'I smiled', Stern remembered, 'and quietly said to myself "good on you, Hasluck"'.[18] More ambitious projects followed. Research by CSIRO suggested that the flood plains of the Adelaide River might be suited to irrigated rice-growing. An opportunity seemed to arise in 1953 when an Arizona entrepreneur, Allan Chase, proposed to bring his experience of large-scale agriculture in the United States to the Northern Territory. Having requested the Treasurer, Sir Arthur Fadden, to check out Chase's credentials during a visit to the United States, Hasluck approved the project in 1954.[19]

Chase's firm, Territory Rice Limited, secured agricultural leasehold over 303,000 hectares at Humpty Doo on the Adelaide River plains, proposing to irrigate them for rice. During 1955 and 1956 work went ahead and a number of farmers arrived. Unfortunately, Chase's grandiose preparations were not matched by prior research. Humpty Doo proved a disaster. Its planning revealed ignorance of Northern Territory conditions. The soil was saline, and the drainage insufficient. Planting was at first mistimed. When the rice was sown, geese and rats ate the seedlings, and wild buffaloes damaged the fences. The management was out of its depth. By 1959 it was evident the scheme was failing. Four rice farmers remained at Humpty Doo in 1961, and Hasluck authorised an unpublicised overdraft of £63,000 to support them, but in 1962 the land was surrendered back to the Crown.[20] Undiscouraged, Wise, when he returned to Western Australian politics, supported Chase in another problematical venture in the Esperance district. Hasluck, who had not taken much part in the detailed oversight of the scheme, was disappointed, but continued to hope that new industries could be created for Aboriginal employment.

In February 1961 he convened a six-day conference of scientists from CSIRO, the Northern Territory administration, universities, the Bureau of Meteorology and others, to discuss research into minerals, forestry and health. His keynote speech began by reviewing progress made by CSIRO with regional surveys, and advances in research on agriculture and forestry. His tone was bracing:

We don't have to jump on any band waggon. We have been driving the cursed thing and pulling it out of bogs and sand drifts for years past before there was any band riding on the waggon.

Then came the admonition:

There is no reference to fish in your discussions, and there do not appear to be any women scientists present...Please do take an interest in barramundi, oysters, and mangrove crabs and do not shut out women from your discourse.[21]

Early in Hasluck's career as minister he was made aware of the importance of securing the conservation of two of the Northern Territory's most remarkable landmarks, Ayers Rock (Uluru) and the Mount Olga (Kata Tjuta) range. At the time they were part of an Aboriginal reserve, so that permission to enter was required for intending visitors, and it had been suggested that the region might be reserved as part of a National Trust. But, as he explained to Dr Charles Duguid, it was hard to pin down the Aboriginal perspective:

On the one hand there are those who claim that the place is not used by the natives, or is used only occasionally, and on the other hand there are those who regard it as being of vital significance for them...Whether such an excision is made depends solely on the question of what effect it will have on the interests of the aborigines. I feel this is mainly a question of fact.[22]

After a visit to the site, during which Hasluck was advised that there had been little or no Aboriginal occupancy in the area for thirty or forty years, the decision was taken in 1958 to gazette

Uluru and its surroundings as a permanent national park. This was followed in 1959 by the erection of the first permanent buildings near the base of the rock, with a regularly serviced airstrip following two years later.

Olive Pink was a remarkable seventy-year-old who, after losing her job in the drafting division of the New South Wales railways during the 1930s Depression, came to the Northern Territory in the hope of advancing Aboriginal welfare. She had been inspired by visiting Daisy Bates at Ooldea, and, like Bates, wore old-fashioned clothes with a pith helmet. Having studied anthropology with Professor Elkin at the University of Sydney, she worked with the Arrernte and Warlpiri people before embarking on a series of attempts to foster Aboriginal communities, often in the face of opposition. By the early 1950s she was without financial resources and living in a corrugated-iron hut in Alice Springs next to the fire station. It was inevitably a noisy location, and she was soon feuding with the fire brigade. These quarrels and ensuing court cases brought her to the attention of the administration. With Hasluck's encouragement, the assistant secretary, Reg Marsh, visited her, and arranged that her hut should be sold and she should move to a small reserve on the edge of town, on which another hut was erected.

In 1956 Hasluck had the reserve gazetted for the conservation of arid-zone native flora. Olive Pink was appointed curator, with a government honorarium to supplement her pension, but the authorities had not heard the last of her. At first she claimed that her hut was uninhabitable, and lived in a tent until it was repaired to a satisfactory standard. She wrote to Hasluck complaining that Marsh was like Pharaoh because he expected her to make bricks without straw. When he visited the reserve in July 1962, he praised her work as being 'of value and significance', and gave instructions that she should be assisted and encouraged to the fullest extent possible.[23] She formed the habit of naming plants after individuals. Marsh was represented by a cactus, but Hasluck was a flourishing grevillea.[24] After he ceased being Minister for Territories, she wrote to him: 'Your tree will always get my best care. I never forget what you did to help, and especially getting me an aboriginal helper (*on basic wage*)'.[25] This was the genesis of the Olive Pink Botanic Garden, which, more than fifty years later, attracts many visitors to Alice Springs while also constituting a major ecological resource. Olive Pink lived a self-contained existence there until her death, aged ninety-one, in 1975.

Hasluck in his Canberra office may have seemed unapproachable, but he left this impersonality behind when he visited the Northern Territory. One senior public servant remembered:

He used to come up and spend a week at a time – no other minister like it. He'd go out with Lionel Rose [the chief veterinary officer at Alice Springs] on a pastoral property inspection and pick up with a mob of drovers and talk to them. He visited practically every settlement with me and others. And he was therefore much better informed than any of his officers from the Secretary down. So he himself had an intimate knowledge on the ground of what was going on, the people on the ground had his ear, and he listened to superintendents and patrol officers.[26]

Whenever the opportunity offered he went riding. The story was told that on one occasion, visiting a cattle station with

Lionel Rose, he was offered what seemed a suitable mount. 'I wouldn't pick that one if I were you', said Rose. So Hasluck chose another, and was not at all surprised, on his return from an agreeable canter, to learn that he had been offered a horse notorious for its ability to buck any rider.

Oral histories confirm this picture of accessibility. Introducing Hasluck to a Darwin audience in 1991, the administrator declared:

> Never before or since has the Territory had a Minister who took such a deep personal interest in the people and the land, who spent extended periods travelling across the Territory, and really got to the 'grass roots' of the people.[27]

One woman remembered that he visited Tennant Creek several times, asking her about such practical concerns as the price of vegetables and the quality of the water supply from Attack Creek.[28] The citizens of Katherine long cherished memories of the unveiling of a monument celebrating the centenary of John McDouall Stuart's expedition from south to north across Australia. The formal ceremony, the dinner and the accompanying speeches were at length followed by a dance. Before long Hasluck elbowed aside the drummer, seized the drumsticks and played for more than an hour with great skill and vivacity.[29] It was a performance much at odds with the media image of a formal and stuffy politician.

This knowledge of Northern Territory grassroots informed his handling of the Territory's politics. Ronald Withnall, who was appointed Crown law officer for the Northern Territory in 1954, saw Hasluck as introducing stability in the Legislative

(Ethel) Meernaa and Patience Hasluck, Paul Hasluck's parents.

HASLUCK COLLECTION

Paul Hasluck's brother Lewis and Lewis's dog Nip on his Swan Valley block, c. 1926.

Paul and Alexandra Hasluck's honeymoon in England: sketch from
Alexandra Hasluck's journal, 1932.

Paul and Alexandra Hasluck on their wedding day, 1932. The bride did not wear the traditional submissive veil.

Paul, Alexandra, Rollo and Nicholas Hasluck in the garden, 2 Adams Road, Claremont, 1949.

Paul Hasluck and Alan Renouf at the United Nations, 1946.

Hasluck collection

Paul Hasluck with Dr H. V. Evatt (centre) and John Beasley,
High Commissioner to the United Kingdom, 1946.

Paul Hasluck and Gavin Long, general editor of the
Official History of Australia in the War of 1939–45.
HASLUCK COLLECTION

The Moseley royal commission crossing the Fitzroy River, Kimberley district; from left, Henry Moseley, Paul Hasluck, Arthur Bell and the Dodge utility.

Hasluck as Minister for Territories travelled extensively to
village communities in Papua New Guinea.
NAA: A1200, L18912

As Minister for Territories, Paul Hasluck enjoyed
meeting the stockmen on cattle properties.
HASLUCK COLLECTION

Paul Hasluck with General Nguyen Khanh, Prime Minister of South Vietnam, 1964.

HASLUCK COLLECTION

Sir Donald Cleland, administrator of Papua New Guinea, 1952–66.

NAA: B579, Cleland/Donald

Sir James Plimsoll, secretary to the Department of External Affairs, 1965–70.
NAA: A1200, L52865

'Eski' (Cecil) Lambert, secretary to the Department of Territories, 1951–64:
'Watch me while I clean up this mess'.

NAA: A8947, 41

Paul Hasluck as number one ticket-holder of the Claremont (Australian Rules)
Football Club with Denis Marshall and Lorne Cook, 1969.

The Sumatran tiger presented to Paul Hasluck by President Soekarno of Indonesia is now permanently housed as the mascot of Claremont Football Club.

Hasluck collection

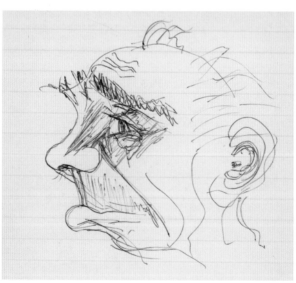

Paul Hasluck sometimes whiled away long cabinet meetings by drawing sketches of his colleagues: here Harold Holt ('Picture of a Treasurer – promising a million') and William McMahon.

NAA: A2668

Paul Hasluck and grandchildren at a picnic in the grounds of
Government House, Yarralumla, c. 1970.
HASLUCK COLLECTION

Governor–General Sir Paul Hasluck swears in
William McMahon as prime minister, 1971.
NAA: A8947, 57

Governor–General Sir Paul Hasluck and Prime Minister Gough Whitlam
with Queen Elizabeth II during the 1973 royal visit to Australia.
NAA: A6180, 22/10/73/3

Sir Paul Hasluck in the robes of a Knight of the Garter.

HASLUCK COLLECTION

Paul Hasluck in relaxed retirement, late 1980s.

HASLUCK COLLECTION

Paul Hasluck on his block at Paulls Valley, 1991.

Council. Previously, the practice had grown up of changing the official members in the Legislative Council according to the nature of the business that had to be transacted, 'and this attitude...which regarded the Legislative Council as being no more than a pale extension of Canberra, was completely stopped as Paul Hasluck understood what was going on'.[30] The official members now gained experience in the handling of government business.

At the same time, from the mid-1950s the Legislative Council became more assertive, its elected membership enlivened by such prominent identities as 'Tiger' Brennan[31] and the young Alice Springs lawyer Dick Ward.[32] They voiced criticism of Eski Lambert, whom they saw as the epitome of the 'Canberra-knows-best' bureaucrat, and of Hasluck as the influence behind Lambert.[33] Hasluck privately welcomed the agitation for self-government as proof of a dawning sense of political responsibility among Territorians. If the Territory produced a few local Washingtons and Jeffersons, he had no objection to playing the role of the British Prime Minister, Lord North. As he recalled:

> At last the Territory was thinking of its future and not dwelling on the grievances of the past, and even if some of the old 'bulsh–artists' climbed on the wagon of constitutional reform it was a worthy cause and a commendable agitation.[34]

Almost without exception the elected members urged that the Northern Territory should free itself from Canberra's apron strings and enjoy a form of self-government similar to the Australian states, but problems loomed. The Territory could not support itself financially without massive federal funding. There were not yet enough voters to make up the numbers for even one federal constituency. The future of the Aboriginal people had yet to be determined. Much of the land in the Territory was held under pastoral lease or as reserves under Commonwealth legislation. Nevertheless, Nelson was to enjoy a parliamentary career lasting seventeen years, echoing the Legislative Council's complaints and accusing Canberra of neglect and timidity.

Throughout his regime as minister, Hasluck's constant long-term goal was to advance the Northern Territory economically and socially until it could be included as an equal among the Australian states.[35] Western Australia in the nineteenth century set a precedent. For more than twenty years, from the end of convict transportation in 1868 to the coming of self-government, its economic backwardness and small population condemned it to the status of a Crown colony whose legislature's powers were restricted. Self-government was granted only in 1890, when autonomy was followed almost immediately by a transforming goldrush. Versed as few others in the history of that period, Hasluck could find parallels in the Northern Territory of the 1950s. In fostering political maturity and responsibility, his first aim was to create a system of local government whose powers might be extended as councils gained experience.[36] When legislation was introduced into the Legislative Council in 1953, however, it was opposed by those who feared they would have to pay rates for amenities instead of enjoying them as government handouts. It was not until 1957 that the Darwin Municipal Council came into being.

Nelson continued to thump the drum for greater self-determination. In October 1955 he demanded an increase in the number of elected members in the Legislative Council so that they formed a majority. He complained that the official majority reflected Canberra's views rather than those of the Territorians.[37] Hasluck was unapologetic in insisting that an official member adhere to the official line:

> While he has not renounced all right to private opinion nor bound himself to accept the directions of an Administrator or a Minister, what he has done, by the acceptance of office, is to limit voluntarily his freedom for independent action by accepting certain other obligations.[38]

This principle governed his own conduct as a member of parliament and a minister. While he expected the official members to yield in time to an elected majority, he knew that the Legislative Council was subordinate to the Commonwealth parliament and should not have power to reject its policies. Hasluck asserted that constitutional change was less urgent than economic and social development.[39] Meanwhile, cabinet would have to be persuaded before any major change could take place.

The Legislative Council tried to force his hand by establishing a select committee on constitutional reform. Its report, tabled in November 1957, recommended the establishment of an executive council responsible to the Legislative Council, the creation of an annual budget for presentation to the legislature, and an increase in the number of elected members. Presenting the report, the Crown law officer, Ronald Withnall, admitted that 'however benign a distant administration may be, the physical fact of its separation…must inevitably lead to inefficiency'.[40] Canberra seemed slow to respond to the report;

Hasluck rejected Lambert's first draft of a submission to cabinet, and while another version was under preparation in April 1958 the six elected members resigned from the Legislative Council en bloc. All of them enhanced their credibility by being returned at the ensuing by-elections. Hasluck was not much impressed by this grandstanding. He explained it as due to the 'Darwin climate', provoking the *Sydney Morning Herald* to describe him as 'extraordinarily cavalier'.[41] But Hasluck thought the resignations were more of an embarrassment to the administrator, Archer, than to Canberra.[42]

Hasluck's submission to cabinet recommended examination of the proposals to enlarge the Legislative Council and establish an executive council, and proposed that when Canberra wanted to amend ordinances passed by the Legislative Council the amendments should be referred back to the Legislative Council. In the House of Representatives, Hasluck admitted the frustration of members of the Legislative Council and affirmed his commitment to political evolution, but stressed the need for the Commonwealth to retain control of lands and Aboriginal policy. Cabinet accepted these recommendations on 8 May, and invited the members of the Legislative Council to a round-table conference in Canberra with Hasluck and two other ministers.

This meeting took place on 24–25 July 1958 and formed the basis for a series of recommendations: the creation of an executive council; the enlargement of the Legislative Council in line with increasing population, including a new category of nominated non-official members who would be chosen by the administration; and the establishment of a budget.[43] After a delay caused by a federal election, Hasluck took these recommendations to cabinet in February 1959. All were accepted except the proposal for a budget. As Hasluck had expected, cabinet rejected any increase in the financial powers of the Legislative Council on constitutional grounds, but the federal member was granted the right of speaking and voting in the House of Representatives on issues affecting the Territory.

During March and April 1959 Hasluck piloted the necessary legislation through the House of Representatives. Nelson predictably condemned the reforms as 'totally inadequate', and Gough Whitlam supported him. Another Labor member, Gordon Bryant, conceded that Hasluck had taken steps that other members of parliament would have been reluctant to take.[44] The bills were passed and became law, but discontent continued to simmer. The three non-official nominees in the Legislative Council often showed their independence by siding with the elected members against the administration. Canberra's right to veto ordinances remained a source of grievance.

This last issue came to a head in 1961, when Hasluck refused assent to two ordinances passed by the Legislative Council. One reduced the penalty imposed on individuals providing alcohol to Aboriginal people from mandatory imprisonment to a fine for a first offender. The other authorised the licensing of betting shops in the Territory. Considering the social problems implicit in both pieces of legislation, Hasluck's decisions were understandable, but the Legislative Council saw its authority as undermined. In March 1961 it passed the ordinances a second time, and Hasluck vetoed them a second time. The Legislative Council responded in April by resolving to seek the abolition of the Commonwealth Government's right to withhold assent from legislation dealing with the internal affairs of the Territory.

Hasluck remained unmoved; the Legislative Council, he minuted, appeared 'to have set out to flout the Government'.[45] When the Legislative Council sent a delegation in October 1961 to Canberra, where he met them with the Attorney-General, Sir Garfield Barwick, the Territorians came away convinced that Canberra meant to keep them 'in a state of arrested development…as a puppet legislature'.[46]

Emboldened by the Menzies government's near-defeat in the federal election of December 1961, the Legislative Council passed a censure motion and remonstrance to the Commonwealth parliament in April 1962. It complained that it had not been accorded 'the respect and dignity due to a legislative body created ostensibly in the British Parliamentary tradition'.[47] Some of the complaints were trivial – that Hasluck communicated with the Legislative Council through the administrator instead of directly – and others contentious – that the Commonwealth had not done enough for the economic development of the Territory. They were most incensed by the minister's willingness to exercise his right of veto and at the continued failure – which was not Hasluck's fault – to devolve more financial responsibility to the Legislative Council. These complaints were taken up gleefully by a resurgent Labor opposition, but nothing substantial resulted during the remainder of Hasluck's time at Territories.

In 1963 the Legislative Council pressed its demands harder. As well as asking for full voting rights for the Northern Territory federal member and for a larger Legislative Council with more elected members, the Territorians now wanted an independent public service separate from the Commonwealth, and the power of raising and spending finance without being answerable to the federal parliament. Another delegation came to Canberra on 24 October 1963 and met Hasluck, Barwick and the Treasurer, Harold Holt. The Commonwealth ministers yielded to none of the delegation's demands, though Hasluck proposed a more extended conference in 1964 if the Menzies government won the next federal election. But by that time he had gone to another portfolio, leaving members of the Legislative Council to reflect that 'despite the extremely slow progress of constitutional development' he was clearly a better minister than his successor.[48] 'Tiger' Brennan spoke of Hasluck as a 'good old uncle', claiming that 'he was the only Minister who has done any good for the political advancement of the Territory'.[49]

Hasluck never wrote a substantial account of his stewardship of the Northern Territory except in the context of national Aboriginal policy, and he may not have considered it as among the most outstanding of his political legacies. It might be argued that the Northern Territory would inevitably have progressed during the 1950s because of the general advance in Australian prosperity and because the events of the Second World War had alerted the Australian people and government to the dangers of neglecting northern Australia. Even so, Hasluck can be credited with providing the Northern Territory with a sound administrative structure and good governance. During his regime, improved infrastructure was provided for the staple pastoral industry, and opportunities for diversifying the agricultural and mineral sectors of the economy were encouraged. Not all were successful, but some useful foundations were laid for the future. Perhaps the most lasting legacy of the Hasluck years was the least tangible. It was the improvement of the morale and the self-concept of Territory's people, nonetheless real if not readily quantifiable. Towards the end of his life, returning to Darwin, Hasluck was greeted as 'the best Minister we ever had'. The tribute was deserved.

Chapter 15

Papua New Guinea

'I knew little about Papua and New Guinea and had taken little interest in them.'[1] Thus Hasluck admitted his ignorance when he assumed ministerial responsibility for those territories, and in this he was like the vast majority of his fellow Australians. As a political unit, Papua New Guinea was created only in 1949. Although the western half of New Guinea was claimed by the Dutch early in the nineteenth century, the remainder was unoccupied by any European power. The Australian colonies, notably Queensland and Victoria, tried to persuade the British Government to annex it, but the Union Jack was raised over the south-eastern quarter only in 1884, after Germany claimed the north-east. Control of British New Guinea (renamed Papua) passed to the new Commonwealth of Australia in 1906. On the outbreak of the First World War in 1914, Australian forces captured German New Guinea, retaining it after the war as a mandate from the League of Nations. The territories of Papua and New Guinea were administered separately. For more than thirty years, Papua fell under the largely benign autocracy of Sir Hubert Murray, whose imprint had remained strong after his death in 1940. During the Second World War, Papua and New Guinea were invaded by the Japanese but were recovered by Australian and American forces. In the process, the territory came to the forefront of Australian political consciousness for probably the first time. In 1949 Papua and New Guinea were combined as a single unit administered by Australia as a trust territory for the United Nations, which from time to time would send a mission to assess its progress towards eventual self-determination.

Hasluck inherited a Papua New Guinea extending over 475,368 square kilometres, of which only two-thirds was classified as under effective administrative control. A mountainous country covered with tropical vegetation, with communications that had only been recently improved by aviation, Papua New Guinea was divided among more than 200 clans with no common sense of nationality and in many cases only recent contact with the wider world. It was Australia's responsibility to weld them into a functional nation with adequate levels of health, education and economic infrastructure. When Hasluck became minister in 1951 it was possible to imagine that it would take two or three centuries to achieve this task. Soon it became apparent that because of pressure from the outside world mediated through the United Nations, Australia had only two or three decades.

The major priorities were economic development, social welfare, education and improving the quality of the administration. The public service at Port Moresby was a mixture of 'befores' – old hands with recollections of Sir Hubert Murray's pre-war administration, which they were apt to remember with nostalgia – and more recent recruits, whose interest in Papua New Guinea in many cases was kindled by wartime experience. Their quality was mixed. On taking office Hasluck was dismayed at the colonialist attitudes among the officials, with

Australian men in white ducks giving 'repertory club performances of a pukka sahib who has just come in from a damned awful day of taking up the white man's burden' and their wives who 'had once read a Somerset Maugham novel about planters in Malaya and had sincerely admired all the things that made the author smile'.[2]

He was considerably more impressed with the patrol officers and other field staff who were dealing with villages in the inland mountains and forests. On his first visit to the territory in July 1951, he wrote to his wife: 'Although Moresby may have more than its quota of dead heads and feeble hands, there is no doubt whatever about the quality of these men in the field'.[3] His admiration for the patrol officers in the front line of contact continued throughout his time as minister. When two patrol officers and two Papuan policemen were killed at Telefomin on the upper Sepik in November 1953, he responded with sympathy and practical help for their families, even to the extent of suggesting the award of posthumous medals to the victims.[4] But although he admired some of the individuals in the Port Moresby bureaucracy, he was less impressed with them as a group. Several years after taking office he still complained 'at the delays and the ineptitude and indeed the lack of basic craftsmanship of the service', and claimed that, with a few exceptions, the officials were not used to thinking for themselves and were 'almost totally deficient in the techniques of administration'.[5]

The fundamental change had to be made at the top. At first Hasluck looked forward to working with Keith Murray as administrator, although he knew that Percy Spender, when minister, had formed reservations about him. Spender considered the territory little better than 'comatose'.[6] Originally, Hasluck hoped that when the experienced Murray was reinforced by a younger and well-qualified coadjutor in Donald Cleland, they would form a team that might energise the territory administration. This was the line Hasluck took in March 1952, when he had the opportunity of presenting his ideas on Papua New Guinea policy to a meeting of Liberal Party members. 'It was a very useful meeting, part of its use being the education of fellow Ministers', he told Alexandra. He enjoyed refuting the ideas of a longwinded Senator Kendall,[7] 'and at the end I had Kendall feeling that he and I were fellow crusaders in a great cause'. But already there were signs of his growing disenchantment with the media: 'The press reports of the meeting were miles astray'.[8]

Closer acquaintance with Murray proved less satisfactory. Hasluck found 'old mopoke Murray'[9] reserved to the point of secretiveness in communication, and his tardiness in response to correspondence suggested that age was slowing him down. He was only sixty-two, but the tropics were believed to sap energy. Murray also seemed too fixated on the quasi-vice-regal aspects of his post. (He was still flying the Union Jack at Government House until Hasluck insisted it be replaced by the Australian flag.) Murray for his part found Hasluck too interfering. They could not work together, and in May 1952 Hasluck informed Murray he must relinquish his appointment as administrator. It was a disagreeable task, and Hasluck, who appreciated Murray's 'loftiness of purpose', was not a good butcher. His brusqueness hurt Murray, and Murray's wife never forgave him.[10] Some blamed Lambert, but the decision was entirely Hasluck's.

Probably Hasluck underestimated the respect in which Murray was held, especially after his leadership following the Mount Lamington volcano eruption of 1951. His senior officials were shocked and dismayed by the news. They considered Murray 'the victim of the whims of politicians'. William Groves, the director of education, rejected the idea that Murray was too old for the job, recalling that Sir Hubert Murray had died in harness at the age of seventy-seven.[11] The local clergy, who got on well with Murray and feared his removal signalled a change in the government's attitude to Christian missions, raised public protest. A roneoed paper aimed at Indigenous readers, the *Papuan Times*, read: 'Many people in Papua and Australia feel that it is a mistake. Some have appealed to leaders in the Government and to the Governor-General'. The Indigenous people were urged to 'tell the Commonwealth parliament that we do not believe in the idea of a new Administrator at this time'.[12] From Canberra, Nugget Coombs sent a handwritten letter to Murray:

> I was profoundly disappointed to hear that you were not to continue in your work in the Territory. The decision is an unhappy one for the welfare of the people there.[13]

It is probably no coincidence that from this time onward a coolness seems to have developed between Coombs and Hasluck, and although they continued to meet socially, their old habits of consultation ceased.

However admirable Murray's personal qualities, a change was needed. As Porter says:

> Murray's replacement...reflected a transition from an era in which emphasis was placed on the outward signs and practices of colonial control to one in which policy initiatives, focused administrative effort and increased expenditure would be

directed to bringing about change…in the pace and extent of Administration activities.[14]

A judicious commentator on the history of Papua New Guinea, Donald Denoon, has written: 'Hasluck incited heads of territory departments to propose and implement projects. This approach unleashed a great deal of energy'.[15] Murray's successor, Cleland, proved a loyal, competent and long-suffering administrator, and Hasluck was able to keep a balance between Cleland as the man on the spot and Lambert the Canberra bureaucrat.

An early issue that confronted them was land policy. Most of the existing records had been lost during the war, and the establishment of accurate native titles, as well as the urban lots in centres such as Port Moresby and Rabaul, was a complex task that took several years. Meanwhile, the administration was under pressure to allow the alienation of land to expatriates. Ex-servicemen who had served in Papua New Guinea were attracted by the country's potential for tropical agriculture, especially coffee-growing. About a thousand non-Indigenous settlers were arriving each year, and for Hasluck that was quite enough.[16] He was aware that if a significant settler population were established in Papua New Guinea it would be more difficult for Australia to withdraw easily when the time came for independence. A young member of parliament, Gough Whitlam, pressured by ex-service associations to promote soldier settlement in Papua New Guinea, approached Hasluck as minister and was glad to find that 'he was against it'.[17]

After several years of persistent lobbying, Hasluck eventually authorised an ex-servicemen's credit scheme that was passed by the Papua New Guinea Legislative Council in 1958. Although the question had not previously been raised, Hasluck was asked by the Australian delegation to the United Nations whether the scheme would be applicable to Indigenous Papua New Guinean ex-servicemen. He immediately ruled that they were indeed eligible, and instructed Cleland to ensure there was no discrimination.[18] Years later he found satisfaction in learning that a visiting Australian diplomat had told the first Chief Minister of Papua New Guinea, Michael Somare:[19]

> At least you can enter on self-government without any fear of having to argue with an Ian Smith[20] in New Guinea. Do you know why? Simply because of Paul Hasluck and nothing else.[21]

Hasluck was intensely concerned with the quality of schooling in Papua New Guinea. Above all, his aim was universal primary education. A common culture was needed to reduce the risk that regional and clan loyalties would prove too powerful for the survival of a unified Papua New Guinea. His hope was that 'the expected and desirable course of change' would result in a blending of Western and Indigenous cultures to create a common nationalism 'with a common language, strongly influenced by Christian teaching and Australian social, economic and political practice, but preserving and enriching all that is best in their native cultural heritage'.[22]

Hasluck gave priority to creating a widespread grounding in primary education. Without this, secondary and tertiary education would be confined to urban elites who would work the political system to their own benefit. He wrote:

...I have made it an aim of our policy that the people in the
outlying areas, such as the Sepik and the Fly River Delta,
have to be brought up to a level of education comparable
with that of the natives of Port Moresby or New Britain so
that they are not left behind in the eventual progress towards
self-government and placed in a position of subservience to
the more fortunate of their fellow-countrymen. We are not
labouring in Papua and New Guinea simply to hand over its
destinies to a few 'smart boys' and 'shrewd heads' from Moresby
and Rabaul. Similarly, we have to ensure that women are not
left behind in the general progress.[23]

In this he was at one with the Papua New Guinea director
of education, William Groves, an anthropologist whose experience in the country went back to Sir Hubert Murray's era.[24]
Appointed in 1946, Groves had to create all the necessary infrastructure of an educational system from the raw materials of
a pre-literate society. Cautious about the impact of rapid change
on communities, his education policy has been described as
having

a strong agrarian flavour, stressing the preservation of village
life while encouraging western standards of health, nutrition
and social mores...He aimed to achieve a form of universal
primary literacy among Papua New Guineans which was
sensitive to the maintenance of traditional cultures and values.[25]

When Hasluck took office he found Groves embattled on
several fronts. Some elements in Canberra accused him of communist sympathies, but this was groundless. Although Groves

had progressive ideas he was curiously ineffectual about arguing his case and securing resources. According to Hasluck (and Cleland shared his view):

> I wanted him to make a bigger bid for education in the
> estimates. Groves however wanted me to listen to his
> enthusiasms about visual aids in education, the merits of the
> Oxford readers prepared for African countries and the value
> of some ideas he himself had formulated about educational
> methods in dependent territories…I never succeeded in one of
> the many attempts I made to have a down-to-earth talk with
> him about the administration of his department.[26]

Nearly all the schooling was provided by religious missions, and their standard was variable. Many of them, thought Hasluck, gave the people

> some chance of being converted from paganism to Christianity
> but little chance of acquiring a skill that they could use for
> further advancement in learning or for doing good on earth.[27]

Groves disliked the mission schools and wanted to build up a competing system of secular education, especially as a means of expanding teacher education. Hasluck thought the quickest way of expanding primary education in Papua New Guinea was to fund the existing mission schools so that they could raise their standards. Much of their instruction was given in local languages, but Hasluck particularly stressed the need to use English as the standard language of instruction in schools because it would provide a common bond, unifying Papua New Guinea's many clans into a sense of national identity. He did not favour reliance on the picturesque 'pidgin' vernacular, believing it less versatile than standard English.[28]

He was also insistent that women be educated to the same level as men. In 1955 he instructed the administration to start a three-year program increasing the proportion of girls in its schools, but progress was slow. During that period the proportion rose only from 19 per cent to 23.8 per cent. When a scholarship scheme was initiated in 1953 to enable Papua New Guinean students to undertake secondary schooling in Australia, the results were mediocre, and inadequate primary schooling was blamed. This reinforced Hasluck's belief that priority should be given to wresting funds from the Commonwealth to keep on expanding primary education. As he put it to Lambert:

> A total of 400,000 children cannot be educated without spending very large sums, but the size of the job and the present and prospective limits to our resources require us to do some very careful and far-sighted planning. In 1955–56 the State of Victoria spent…£23 million to educate approximately 318,000 children in Government schools. When the PNG education system is fully established, will we be able to keep it down to a half, or a third, or a quarter of that cost?[29]

To the House of Representatives in 1957 he spoke of 'the rather distant future when education from elementary level to the university level will be provided by the Territory itself'.[30]

When Groves retired in 1958 it proved difficult to find an outstanding candidate among the outside applicants for the directorship of education, and eventually the job was given to an internal appointee, the experienced chief inspector of schools, Geoffrey Roscoe. Fortunately, he turned out to be vigorous and practical, and the recruitment and training of teachers started to advance substantially. It was just in time to deflect Australian and international criticism about Papua New Guinea's rate of educational progress.

Hasluck was more impressed with the energetic and enterprising director of health, John Gunther.[31] Originally critical of Hasluck for removing Murray, Gunther came to find him a strong source of support. Gunther's challenges were formidable, since as well as providing services for remote communities and protecting the many recently contacted communities from introduced diseases, he needed to build up medical staff almost from scratch. He employed refugee doctors from Europe at a time when they had difficulty securing acceptance in mainland Australia. He trained expatriate and Indigenous medical assistants, sending the latter to the Central Medical School at Suva, Fiji, until it was possible to establish a Papuan Medical College in 1958. Not without settler opposition, he broke down the system of racial segregation in hospitals, supplementing district hospitals with aid posts and medical patrols that brought most people within a day's walk of medical care. By 1955 more than 1,500,000 inhabitants of Papua New Guinea were served. Historian Hank Nelson has written:

> The department concentrated on readily diagnosed diseases
> with known cures, vaccinated widely, and introduced maternity
> and child health clinics and mobile units, and a malarial control
> policy (including controversial insecticide spraying). Permitting
> briefly trained staff to treat patients, and by-passing other

safeguards observed in advanced countries, involved risks, but Gunther argued that overall the policies had saved thousands.[32]

After two unsuccessful appointees who did not stay long, Gunther was made assistant administrator in 1957, proving a valuable colleague to Cleland, who had suffered a coronary incident a year earlier.

By 1957 Hasluck had settled down to the routine of being what he himself described as an 'inspector-general', descending upon the territory for a ceaseless round of visits. As in the Northern Territory, he flew to every accessible corner of the territory, forming opinions about the men on the spot, and noting matters to be sorted out in Canberra. Personal comfort mattered little to him. The story is told that at one remote airstrip the official party found a woman with a seriously ill child who needed to be flown to hospital. To make room for them, Hasluck volunteered to remain behind at the airstrip. When the aircraft returned they found the minister placidly sitting on a log reading his favourite Racine.

A diary survives from 1957 in which he noted that in flight from Canberra he 'read the departmental papers prepared for the Territory tour and champed and fretted at the delays and uncompleted action on the part of the Administration'.[33] Arriving in this mood, he grumbled at 'the so-called Government House and the people going out in cars soliciting salutes from the constables on duty' but praised the patrol officers and other front-line staff. 'We have more hope of getting sound sense from the A[ssistant] D[istrict] O[fficer]', he wrote, 'than from the people on top'.[34] He was vigilant in guarding against developments that might alienate the white minority from the Papuan people. The building of roads suitable for motor traffic might have the unintended result of creating

> a separation and perhaps a tendency for the European to speed
> past on his journey instead of stopping to talk as he did when
> he walked from village to village by the old trails.[35]

At Wewak he was appalled at the condition of the Indigenous hospital. 'It is scandalous that a commencement should have been made with a contract for a new European hospital before the native hospital was put into permanent quarters.'[36]

In a fortnight's tour he listed in a diary more than a dozen separate issues requiring attention. Shortly after his return to Canberra, Cleland incautiously asked him if there were any matters that were of concern to the minister. He received a tremendous rejoinder:

> Among those matters I may mention the long continued
> failure of the Administration to establish adequate financial
> controls in the Territory; the repeated inability to produce
> a satisfactory programme for housing until special insistence
> was sent from Canberra, and the failure to realise the housing
> programme; the apparent unsatisfactory control in respect of
> the Wau hospital, the Wewak hospital and the Lae sawmill;
> the general standards in the Sepik district; the wide gap which
> seems to me to exist between the higher levels of the service
> and the middle and lower levels; the fact of your advocacy for
> the promotion as Assistant Administrator of the Director of
> Civil Affairs when weighed against my own strong impression
> that some of the major imperfections in the Administration

are occurring in the Department of Civil Affairs; the long
continued inability of the education department to measure
up to my minimum requirements; repeated signs on files
which are placed before me of a falling off in the promptness
with which the Administration attends to matters referred
to it for urgent attention; a failure to correct fully what I
regard as a lack of balance between the attention given to the
centres of population and the 'luxury' items on the one hand
and the more pressing needs of the mass of the population
and the outlying districts on the other hand; the slowness
in implementing policy decisions in relation to a number of
matters such as the advancement of women, uniformity of
development, corrective establishments, introduction of cattle,
extension of village agriculture and housing and social care for
mixed-bloods.

Hasluck concluded disarmingly:

I appreciate that there are many difficulties in the way and
that you suffer from many handicaps in the non-availability of
material both human and inanimate. My criticisms are always
made against a standard of perfection.[37]

During this visit, Hasluck encountered the first rumblings
of a movement among parts of the expatriate community that
would give him trouble during the next two years. At Goroka
he met a few expatriates who were:

apt to parrot the usual phrases about 'a namby-pamby attitude
towards the natives' and 'give us a chance to develop this

304

country.' An R.S.L. official from N.S.W. named Yeo recently visited here and I fancy has spread a good deal of such talk.[38]

Discontent among the expatriates found a focus in the issue of taxation. For some years it was apparent that Papua New Guinea required a more coherent taxation system than the present practice of imposing levies on exports. The income from this source fluctuated with the markets, and bore harder on smaller producers. The territory's budget had grown from £4.5 million to £17.5 million in a decade, and it was an essential part of preparation for independence that Papua New Guinea should collect more of its own revenue. The finances must be placed on a sound basis before more progress could be made towards constitutional change. Unfortunately, this argument was not sufficiently publicised nor appreciated in Papua New Guinea. Meanwhile, Hasluck excited some unpopularity in the territory by a speech to the summer school of the Australian Institute of Political Science in January 1958. He said that Europeans engaged in business in Papua New Guinea should appreciate that there were artificial elements in its seeming prosperity:

> Much of what they are selling over their counters, whether
> to Europeans or to natives, is being financed by increased
> Government expenditures in the Territory. They are gleaners
> of a harvest sown and reaped by the toil of others, and if it
> is a poor harvest they will glean less. And I say quite bluntly
> that many of the people who come to me in the guise of solid
> pioneers and frontiersmen of private enterprise in Papua and
> New Guinea are merely locusts in the sense that they are not
> gathering what they have sown.[39]

As Ian Downs comments:

> Those who may have deserved the Minister's scorn were stung
> by his remarks but there were those who, having invested huge
> sums in the Territory, had every right to feel offended.[40]

So it was that many of the expatriate community in Papua
New Guinea were in a fault-finding frame of mind even before
Hasluck submitted to cabinet in March 1958 a proposal for the
abolition of various forms of indirect taxation and the introduction of income tax. Its introduction then had to be delayed
until 1959 because administrative arrangements had not been
worked out. The scheme was meanwhile publicised in Papua
New Guinea to allow for public information and comment,
but the Port Moresby newspaper the *South Pacific Post* led many
among the expatriate community to complain that there had
not been enough consultation.[41] Not for the last time in his
career, Hasluck apparently thought it sufficient to publish the
case for a government policy without following it up with
advocacy and persuasion.

By the time the scheme was approved by cabinet in February
1959, a formidable attack had been mustered by a body calling
itself the Taxpayers' Association of Papua and New Guinea.
Its members urged postponement of the measures pending a
full inquiry into the impact of the legislation. Hasluck commented: 'It seemed to me that they identified the economy of
the Territory with their own personal fortunes'.[42] Some of the
official members who sat in the Legislative Council were sufficiently unhappy with the consultation process to write to the
Governor-General, Sir William Slim, suggesting they should not

have to support the tax legislation, but 'Slim held strong views on the duty of official members to support the Government… inside the Council and in public'.[43] The officials fell into line, though as Hasluck noted they were conspicuously silent when the issue was debated in the Legislative Council.

Eventually the Legislative Council approved income tax by a margin of fifteen votes to twelve, the minority consisting of all the non-official members, nominated and elected. The three elected members resigned, and after the ensuing by-elections in September 1959 the three newcomers who replaced them each made a maiden speech attacking the government and then resigned in their turn. Meanwhile, an appeal was launched in the Supreme Court, arguing that the Legislative Council was improperly constituted in the absence of elected members. It was further urged that the administrative union between Papua and New Guinea was invalid. The court did not accept either argument. The cooler heads among the taxpayers saw no virtue in pursuing the constitutional argument further, and although a minority appealed to the High Court about the validity of the tax legislation, their case was lost in August 1960.

The attack from the business lobby found its voice in the House of Representatives with two Liberal members, Roy Wheeler and Malcolm McColm. Both had entered the House of Representatives at the same time as Hasluck in 1949, but had subsequently languished on the backbenches without promotion. McColm, in pre-war life a jackeroo and buckjumper with a good air force record from 1936 to 1946, had never adjusted to the routine disciplines of parliamentary life. His ally was described by Menzies as 'the curious Mr Wheeler, whose idea of getting support is to attack his government at every opportunity'.[44] In March and April 1959, Wheeler had supported demands for a public inquiry into the administration's developmental policies in Papua New Guinea. During the parliamentary recess McColm was one of a parliamentary delegation that toured Papua New Guinea. He informed the administrator, Cleland, that he intended to stir things up at the next parliamentary session.

Wheeler and McColm made their move during the budget debate in August 1959. Wheeler cited Hasluck's 'locusts' speech of January 1958 as showing an enmity to the private sector. He asserted that permissive occupancy left investors uncertain of their rights, and praised the role of large companies in promoting the economy. He claimed that 'Many officials regard the private traders and the settlers as interlopers in their island paradise', and that what he called 'detribalized natives' were 'building up Harlems' in Port Moresby and Rabaul.[45] McColm, having published an article in the *Sydney Morning Herald* criticising the administration's lack of communication with the wider public,[46] was even more forceful in debate. 'We in this Parliament are very much in the dark' about Papua New Guinea, he told his colleagues. There was 'tremendous resentment' against Hasluck; 'his period of usefulness in his present position has come to an end'. Hasluck stood accused of ignoring the advice of the well informed about taxation in Papua New Guinea. He exhibited 'too much theory' and 'not enough practical knowledge' and 'a complete lack of good public relations'.

Hasluck waited a month before his counterattack. He made no public response to Wheeler and McColm, although his emotions showed in a letter to Alexandra:

I'm fighting my single-handed and unsupported battle over here against the biggest and most unscrupulous pack of liars who have deliberately set out to destroy me...By the way, in my troubles I keep on remembering your words: 'Well, no wonder you're unpopular. You can't expect people to like you.' Nowadays I don't even have a horse to whinny at me... I am as miserable as hell...and, except in this letter and on the telephone last night, I go on pretending to be cheerful and calm...[47]

When he replied to the critics it enabled him to make what was perhaps the most explicit statement of his political philosophy he ever made:

In my own view, the method of liberalism in the field of commerce and industry is to leave the way open for the individual to exercise his energy and initiative and to take responsibility for his own judgments, but, in my view, liberalism certainly does not mean that any one can be as greedy as he likes. Liberalism, in my view, when it emphasizes the importance of the individual, does not mean unbridled opportunity for the strong to do whatever they wish to do; it means expanding opportunity for every person, weak or strong. This means limiting the power of the state – and this is what socialism does not do – and it also means making the ambitions of the powerful subject to the interests of the whole community and the preservation of the rights of the humblest member of it. The liberal respect for property, which is again one of the ways in which liberalism differs from socialism, is a respect for a small property no less than a respect for a large property and this respect means the constant protection of the small man and not merely an encouragement to the strong. That is my view of liberalism and, applying liberal principles to Papua and New Guinea, I assert that the private enterprise of every native villager is just as sacred to liberalism as is the private enterprise of any European who may have established a business there; no more and no less.[48]

The goal for Papua New Guinea, he said, was a self-supporting economy. Meanwhile he called for 'a calm and clear view of the task in hand' and hoped they would stop thinking of Paul Hasluck 'as the personification of all the things they dislike'.[49] The backbenchers rallied to him. Richard Cleaver, one of his Western Australian colleagues, wished the speech had been released in advance. The independent-minded Harry Turner told the House that McColm and Wheeler did not speak for him; Paul Hasluck deserved their trust. Ewen Mackinnon also expressed great respect for him, and said he had irritated 'the hip pocket nerve'.[50] The Labor opposition added its voices. Gordon Bryant said that Hasluck was 'remarkably humanitarian', at which Leslie Haylen interjected: 'That is the result of his earlier training as a public servant under a Labor government', and Whitlam added: 'He is a benevolent despot'.[51]

The debate revealed that there were still Australian politicians who believed it would take decades or even centuries before Papua New Guinea would be ready for independence. If it came prematurely it would surely be followed by a descent into anarchy or by a takeover by some foreign power hostile to Australia, acting either directly or through a puppet regime. Within Papua New Guinea, however, the income tax controversy had raised the level of political consciousness, if only from resentment against what the *South Pacific Post* called 'the Canberra dictatorship'. As Downs put it:

> Expatriates were put in a frame of mind to agree that it would be better for the indigenous people to be given political representation at a level related to their number rather than their readiness to govern.[52]

But Hasluck, although preparing to take the next step, wanted to wait until the High Court challenge was out of the way.

Another pressure for the decolonisation of Papua New Guinea came from the west. The western half of New Guinea had formed part of the Dutch East Indies administratively, but its people were for the most part ethnically distinct from Indonesians.[53] When Indonesia achieved independence at the end of 1949, the Dutch contrived to retain possession of West New Guinea. Before long this promised to become a source of diplomatic strife with potential for escalation. Dr Achmed Soekarno, the charismatic President of Indonesia, found a ready-made grievance in this lingering Dutch presence, insisting that his republic should include all the territories formerly part of the Dutch East Indies.[54] During the 1950s, Indonesia sought United Nations support for their claim on what they termed West Irian. Australia preferred the Dutch to stay. If the Dutch went, said Menzies in one of his more apocalyptic moments, communist infiltrators might cross 'the long, indefensible, purely technical' frontier between the two halves of New Guinea.[55]

Hasluck insisted that the subject be approached 'unobtrusively and with discretion'.[56] From 1953 the Dutch in the west and the Australians in the east built up measures of practical cooperation in such fields as agriculture, quarantine, health and education. Both administrations were working towards self-government for the Indigenous people, but as 'a very long-term aim indeed'.[57] In 1955 Hasluck informed Cleland that 'the measure of co-operation has not been as full as we hoped to see', but in his memoirs he implied he had to restrain Port Moresby from overenthusiasm about dialogue with the Dutch. In practice Cleland was equally cautious, although he recognised that the Dutch in their last-minute efforts at rapid development set a very high standard.[58]

By 1957 the pace of decolonisation was accelerating around the world. In the United Nations the newly independent Afro-Asian nations tended to form a bloc that, together with the Soviet Union and its satellites and the Islamic powers, turned an increasingly critical scrutiny on the remaining colonial territories. Hasluck deplored this tendency, but it had to be confronted. He considered that

> to serve Australia's interest and to help our own work in New Guinea to succeed we should encourage the Dutch to stay in West New Guinea and to do more than they were doing.[59]

In July 1957 Hasluck and Cleland visited the Dutch administrator at the West New Guinea capital, Hollandia (now Jayapura), and in November Menzies, Casey and Hasluck met with Dutch senior officials in an attempt to coordinate the timetables of the two halves of New Guinea in progressing along parallel lines of development towards self-government for the indigenes. Both nations endorsed the concept in February 1958. Hasluck saw the aim as 'advancing the peoples with common practices and mutual understanding, so that, when each was independent, they could eventually join as one people in one nation'.[60] Of course, if the unity of all New Guinea became an internationally accepted notion, it would thwart Indonesia's aspirations.

Others were thinking along similar lines. At the Australian Institute of Political Science summer school in January 1958, John Kerr and John Andrews[61] raised the idea of a Melanesian federation including the two halves of New Guinea, the Solomons, and possibly other south-west Pacific territories. Although the idea was taken seriously enough to warrant exploration by staff of the Department of Territories, Hasluck tried to hose down attempts

> to know the perfect plan for the future. If the Indonesian claim succeeded, I did not want them to have a ready-made case for having East New Guinea too because of its 'affinity' with West New Guinea.[62]

Though some members of cabinet spoke of giving the Dutch unqualified military backing, the government decided in January 1959 to give priority to keeping Indonesia non-communist and friendly.[63] In February the Indonesian Foreign Minister, Dr Subandrio, visited Canberra, and Australia pledged to accept any agreement that Indonesia and the Netherlands worked out between them. But the joint declaration was attacked in parliament and the press, and seemed to have little practical effect.

Indonesia continued to agitate for possession of West New Guinea, and this spurred the Dutch into accelerating the rate of change in their half of the island. Early in 1960 the Dutch

Undersecretary for New Guinea Affairs gave a press conference in which he was quoted as saying that Dutch New Guinea would have its first local parliament, adding that the Netherlands would be prepared to 'pull out' of New Guinea whenever the United Nations ended Australian trusteeship over the eastern half of the island.[64] He later said he was misquoted, but speculation simmered about the future of New Guinea. In May 1960 Hasluck, accompanied by the department's assistant secretary Dudley McCarthy, visited The Hague. They found the Dutch complaining that their allies, the United States and Britain, were deserting them in the face of 'the scandalous and outrageous conduct of Indonesia at all stages', and suggesting that they might have to grant self-government to the people of West New Guinea prematurely. The Dutch thought Indonesia would not dare to invade a newly independent nation. Hasluck responded:

> I made the point…that for the Dutch to introduce self-
> government before the people were in fact able to exercise
> it would simply mean leaving the way open for someone
> else, probably Indonesia, to walk in… [T]he course of events
> might not be an immediate invasion, but, following the
> pattern of eastern Europe, a stirring up of trouble, a collapse of
> government, a local rising, and a moving in to restore order.[65]

He urged economic development

> both to ensure occupation and income for the people of a
> kind that would sustain the higher standard of living to which

we were advancing them and in order to support to a greater
degree from local sources the services that were being provided.

But he sensed that the Dutch were giving up, and might follow
the example of their Belgian neighbours, who were in the
process of abandoning the Congo to its warlords.

From The Hague, Hasluck went to London to join
Menzies at a conference of Commonwealth prime ministers
in June. It was an opportunity to assess whether the British
Government was shifting in its view of the desirable pace of
decolonisation. In February 1960 the British Prime Minister,
Harold Macmillan, dismayed the white supremacists of the
South African legislature by telling them the winds of change
were blowing across the colonial world and might not be
resisted. The conference gave a plain signal that decolonisation
was accelerating, but Menzies and Hasluck were reported as
drawing different conclusions from it. Hasluck proceeded to
Washington, where he allegedly told the *New York Times* that
Papua New Guinea would not be ready for independence for
thirty years.[66] This was immediately picked up by the *Sydney
Morning Herald*:

> To declare…that Papua–New Guinea will not be ready for
> self-government for 30 years is doubtless accurate enough. It
> would be extremely foolish, however, to suppose that Papuan
> or world opinion will be prepared to wait for that period. Mr
> Hasluck is no better qualified than King Canute to turn back
> the tide, and the tide is setting strongly against the perpetuation
> of colonial rule.[67]

Menzies, on the other hand, immediately on returning to Sydney informed a press conference that although

> many of us might have thought that it was better to go slowly in granting independence so that all the conditions existed for a wise exercise of self-government, I think the prevailing school of thought today is, that if in doubt, you should go sooner, not later.[68]

The media may have seen Hasluck as lagging conservatively behind his Prime Minister, but there was no difference between them. Although Hasluck believed the Australian Government was ahead of the game in responding to local demands for self-government, he was convinced that the time was now ripe for the next stage in the evolution of the Legislative Council. On 28 June Hasluck made a statement stating explicitly that, as soon as the High Court had ruled on the constitutional issues mounted by the protesters against income tax, the government would take the next step in the evolution of the Legislative Council into a full parliamentary body.[69]

When the High Court ruled against the challenge, Hasluck was ready with a submission to cabinet to enlarge the Legislative Council. The membership was increased to consist of the administrator, fourteen officials, ten non-official nominees and twelve elected members. Although cabinet did not go quite as far as he wished, it approved an increase in the number of elected members from three to twelve, half of them to be Indigenous, as well as providing for at least five Indigenous members among those nominated for the council. There would be a common electoral roll, and the Executive Council would be replaced by a new Administrator's Council on which both native and non-official members would serve. As Hasluck saw it, 'we had prepared the way for a more rapid and direct evolution towards self-government'.[70] The proposals came before the House of Representatives in September 1960 and passed with bipartisan support in October, although Labor spokesmen considered Hasluck had not been adventurous enough. (In reality, Hasluck himself would have gone further but the original proposals were watered down by cabinet.)[71] The new Legislative Council was elected in 1961.

Menzies and Hasluck wanted to avoid stirring up feelings of insecurity among either the Indigenous or the expatriate inhabitants of Papua New Guinea. Hasluck went to Papua New Guinea in July 1960 and lost no time in spelling out his priorities to an audience in Port Moresby.[72] Political advances, he said, could follow only after social and economic improvements. 'These changes are not made by the stroke of a pen or the passing of a resolution but by hard work year after year.' He had three large meetings with leading Indigenous representatives in Port Moresby, Rabaul and Lae, and told them:

> So long as you need our help you can depend on us to give it. So long as you want us to stay you can depend on us not to desert you.

He recalled: 'It was heartening to hear the deep murmurs of approval and to feel the fervour of the handshake of each native leader at those meetings'.[73] No doubt it was also consoling when some Conservative members of the British parliament visited Papua New Guinea in October and 'came away deeply impressed by the great effort you have been putting into the territory'.[74]

Ian Downs, once a patrol officer and then a planter before becoming a prominent figure in the Legislative Council, wrote a substantial history of postwar Papua New Guinea, and although he and Hasluck had not seen eye to eye on a number of issues, his verdict showed considerable insight:

> Hasluck had been the sole catalyst for change in Papua–New Guinea but he had always been a perfectionist. Change must necessarily occur slowly and with care so that it would be proved right in every particular. However, he could change pace or direction to meet political imperatives and on these occasions he offered explanations that justified change as a variation of his own original theme. In scores of speeches he kept sufficient options open to allow room for change. He could be privately persuaded to change his views if given an opportunity to make all changes in his own name. His own views in areas where he lacked expertise were not formed until he had consulted experts. His ministerial record was so good that few Australians ventured to share the stage or even to ask questions. Hasluck seemed to have asked nearly every question himself in his quest for what was best and to have acted on most of them to public satisfaction.[75]

Chapter 16

Time of transition

From about 1958 Hasluck was growing discontented with his lot. As the Menzies government was returned with an undiminished majority in that year he might have hoped for promotion. Several senior ministers had retired, including Philip McBride as Minister for Defence. This was a portfolio that attracted Hasluck, but it went to the Tasmanian Athol Townley,[1] who had entered cabinet at the same time he did, but who had not distinguished himself except as a youngish man to whom Menzies had taken a paternal liking. Hasluck seemed destined to serve out his time as Minister for Territories, wondering if he was thought incapable of anything else. 'Territories killed me politically', he later wrote, 'and I knew all the time that it was killing me, but what else could one do but stick at a job that no one else wanted'.[2] Hasluck has claimed that long service in the Territories portfolio had stifled all personal political ambition in him, and W. D. Forsyth thought that Menzies must be aware of the harm to Hasluck's prospects of higher office.[3]

It was not just that his fights in the Northern Territory and Papua New Guinea, especially the latter, had earned him the animosity of some members of his own Liberal Party. He felt the pressure keenly, and at the height of the taxation controversy in Papua New Guinea had described himself to Alexandra as 'the loneliest and most hated man in Australia...Does anyone ever want to give me anything at all or do they only want to take from me?'[4] He added: 'But you have been so nice and helpfully understanding this year love!' Before long, however, Alexandra Hasluck was once more resentful of the priority her husband gave to his working life. From Port Moresby he tried to reassure her:

> Work is work and has to be done as best I can do it (unless you really want me to chuck the whole thing overboard and come back to doing nothing), but, though, having a job to do I do it as best I can, and though this has meant neglect of you by me and also some neglect of me by you, there is nothing but my work as your rival.[5]

In his own home state of Western Australia his position had not been eased by the accession to power in 1959 of a Coalition government headed by David Brand[6] and including Charles Court[7] as a senior minister. Eager to promote the mineral resources of their state, and impatient with an embargo on the export of iron ore that the Commonwealth did not lift until late 1960, Brand and Court found Hasluck and his federal colleagues insufficiently zealous in the Western Australian cause. He, for his part, found them parochial, given to posing as 'the champions confronting a wicked dragon from the East'.[8] Alexandra Hasluck once told Court: 'You know, you think more highly of him than he does of you'.[9] It was not surprising that the annual state meetings of the Liberal Party were often uncomfortable for Hasluck.

In January 1960 Casey retired as Minister for External Affairs. Hasluck must have permitted himself a hope that he would be the chosen successor, although for the public record he later wrote:

> I might have been considered, but affairs in Papua–New Guinea had reached a stage in 1960 where several jobs had to be completed before I could leave the portfolio of Territories.

A well-informed observer has asserted that Menzies sounded out Sir Arthur Tange, the secretary of the Department of External Affairs, about appointing Hasluck as minister, and that Tange said the department would not welcome him.[10] Menzies then took the position himself.

It is remarkable that Menzies sought the advice of a public servant, even one as powerful as Tange, and Tange's reasons remain unknown. Perhaps he considered that Hasluck's interventionist style in Territories would not go down well in External Affairs. Perhaps he saw difficulties in that Hasluck would be dealing with former colleagues such as Hood, with whom he had been at odds in the 1940s. Or perhaps, having built up a strong personal dominance within the department, he did not relish working with a minister who believed his own past experience entitled him to challenge Tange's own expertise, and who had shown himself willing to rap Tange over the knuckles when both were more junior.[11] Even if the story was no more than Canberra gossip, it would have got back to Hasluck, and this would help account for his strained relations with Tange during the next five years.

Some years later, Menzies admitted to Hasluck 'what a mistake he had made' in not appointing him to External Affairs in 1960.[12] At the time, however, another formidable rival had appeared on the scene. In 1958 the eminent Sydney lawyer Sir Garfield Barwick[13] entered the House of Representatives, becoming within a few months Attorney-General. With a sufficiency of energy and ambition, Barwick was seen by some as a potential rival to Harold Holt as Menzies' eventual successor. More disturbingly for Hasluck, he was appointed acting Minister for External Affairs once or twice during the absences of the ageing Casey, and showed a candid liking for the job. While Menzies acted as his own External Affairs Minister, he increasingly made it a practice to forward important communications to Barwick for advice.[14]

After this setback Hasluck's disappointment was beginning to show. He should not have been surprised that the possibility of his departure provoked some colleagues to cast calculating eyes over the Curtin seat in the House of Representatives. It was the safest of Liberal seats in Western Australia, especially after a redistribution in 1955. At each of the general elections between 1951 and 1958, Hasluck polled between 24,000 and 26,000 first-preference votes against opponents (the Australian Labor party in 1951, 1954 and a walkover in 1955, then both Labor and Democratic Labor) whose total remained stuck at 14,000 to 15,000.[15] Hasluck was not obliged to spend much time nursing his electorate, but his campaign organisation was never less than thorough. Even in his busiest years as a minister he remained accessible to requests for help from individuals in his constituency.[16]

In November 1960 his colleague Gordon Freeth came to him with news that Senator Shane Paltridge[17] was intriguing for a seat in the House of Representatives. A senator since 1949, Paltridge was known to have ousted a friend of Hasluck's,

Seddon Vincent, from the leadership of the Western Australian Liberal team in the Senate. Now, observing the rivalry between Holt and Barwick, he thought it possible that if he went to the House of Representatives he might be an acceptable compromise candidate as Treasurer and deputy leader of his party. He had his eye on the marginal Liberal seat of Swan, but if Curtin fell vacant it would be a much safer prize. This story persuaded Hasluck that he was not ready to retire from politics after all. He stayed on to fight the federal election in December 1961, holding his seat by his customary margin at a time when the Coalition as a whole almost suffered defeat.[18]

Once again he was disappointed. Menzies had come to realise that at the age of sixty-seven he should not carry both the prime ministership and the External Affairs portfolio. He offered External Affairs to Sir Garfield Barwick, who would combine this office with his post as Attorney-General. An informed source has suggested that Menzies preferred not to appoint ministers to a field in which they claimed superior expertise, and found it useful to have in cabinet someone such as Hasluck who could offer authoritative comment on proposals put forward by the Minister for External Affairs.[19] Alexandra Hasluck reported to a friend that her husband was 'more fed up than ever' with Menzies and in a very restive mood.[20] Apparently he gave serious thought to putting his name forward for the post of Ambassador to Rome.[21] But, although Curtin was a safe seat, it was no time to subject the Coalition to the disruptions of a by-election. After ten years in Territories, Hasluck resigned himself to soldiering on in the post indefinitely, once more loyally assuming the role of model prisoner.

323

Few colleagues seem to have perceived his discontent. To many it appeared that he had built up the Department of Territories into his personal fiefdom, from which he repelled criticism and interference. Labor's Gordon Bryant put it thus:

> The Territory of Papua and New Guinea, I know, is the
> brightest jewel in the crown of the Minister for Territories...
> He is the Minister in charge of an area twice the size of Victoria.
> He has under his command in Papua and New Guinea alone
> the equivalent of almost the total population of Queensland.
> Add the 500,000 square miles of the Northern Territory and he
> becomes an Australian Caesar. He has an empire of his own...
> this one man – this Minister – has responsibilities equivalent to
> those of the Parliament of Queensland...
>   I am prepared to admit that, compared with some of
> his colleagues, the Minister for Territories has made a real
> contribution to government...But this job is beyond the ability
> of one man.[22]

The trouble was that whenever anything contentious happened involving Papua and New Guinea, Hasluck was seen as personally responsible, even if the misadventure was not of his own making. One such misadventure was the Gluckman affair.

During Hasluck's absence overseas, the Department of Territories received an application from a visiting academic at the Australian National University seeking permission to visit Papua New Guinea. He was Professor Max Gluckman, an internationally eminent anthropologist, Manchester-based but of South African origin. Like many South African intellectuals of his generation he had been drawn towards the Communist

Party as a reaction to the racial inequality of the regime, and like many communist intellectuals he had severed his connection with the party after the Soviet Union's brutal suppression of the Hungarian rising in 1956, though remaining a man of the left. After lingering in Canberra for several weeks, the documentation was forwarded to Port Moresby, where the application was vetoed because Gluckman was seen as a security risk. Gluckman was known to be an authority on African trade unions, and the authorities may have feared he would spread unsettling ideas among the workers of Papua New Guinea.

Hasluck himself was unlikely to share those fears. In previous cases he had shown himself willing to grant academics access to the territory provided they were vouched for as responsible scholars. In 1959 he overrode doubters to allow two anthropologists, Arnold and Scarlett Epstein, to work in the politically sensitive Tolai region of New Britain despite their known socialist beliefs. Once a formal recommendation had been made from Port Moresby, however, it was a serious matter to reverse that decision. In this case it turned out that the black mark against Gluckman came from British intelligence, probably acting on advice from South Africa.

That brought the Prime Minister into the picture. A cornerstone of Menzies' foreign policy was support for great and powerful allies, specifically the United States and Britain, who would give Australia access to diplomatic and military intelligence that was otherwise inaccessible. It was unthinkable that Australia should imperil that access by casting doubts on the accuracy of that information. If British sources deemed Gluckman unsafe, then he was unsafe for Papua New Guinea. When news of the ban was reported in *The Age*, protest followed.

University staff complained of the affront to a distinguished scholar. In a debate on the adjournment on 31 August, the Labor opposition asked awkward questions, and two of the hardened Cold War warriors on the government side, Sir Wilfrid Kent Hughes and William Wentworth, attacked the cover-up. It was playing into the hands of the communists, said Wentworth, to call a distinguished scholar a security risk without supporting proof.[23] The *Sydney Morning Herald* reported that Hasluck, having seemed more than usually self-confident when the debate began, 'was badly rattled and very unhappy when the Opposition had finished with him'.[24]

The controversy spread as far as the British media. *The Economist* ran a long story from its Canberra correspondent suggesting that, while the administration cannot have thought that Gluckman could start a revolutionary organisation in Papua New Guinea in less than three weeks, it may have feared 'that after his return he might make speeches or write articles critical of Australian policy, thereby presenting its Afro-Asian critics in the UN Trusteeship Council with fresh ammunition'. With his scholarly background, Hasluck might have been expected to credit Gluckman

> with the desire to pursue anthropology rather than revolution.
> Mr Hasluck, however, has his ideals and plans for New
> Guinea and would like to guard it from contamination like an
> ambitious mother preserving her daughter from the beatniks.[25]

Hasluck was taking the heat for a controversy that was not of his making. The argument continued a few days more, because Gluckman applied for permission to enter Dutch New

Guinea, and on 5 September the Dutch Chargé d'Affaires in Canberra, Dr Insinger, announced that permission would be granted, adding gratuitously: 'Professor Gluckman is a man of outstanding qualities and of great international reputation. We welcome all such outstanding scientists'.[26] That earned him a roasting from the secretary of the Department of External Affairs, Sir Arthur Tange. Gluckman decided not to pursue the idea. His last words before leaving Australia were: 'It would have been profitable for all of us if Paul Hasluck, Donald Cleland and I sat down together to talk'.[27]

Hasluck himself was glad when the controversy subsided. His attitude was clearly expressed in 1962, when ASIO approached him with a proposal to set up a similar agency in Papua New Guinea. Hasluck threw cold water on the idea, writing to Cleland:

> To my mind, the fatal flaw in the approach of the security people is that they tend to relate everything to the subversive influence of this or that person, and consequently they fall into the error of thinking that if you ignore or silence the subversive influence all will be well.[28]

Later he reflected:

> In my own view there were insufficient grounds for refusing the permit, and the incident would never have occurred if the application had been handled in a straightforward way at the appropriate level…My view of the Gluckman case is that it showed that any report from a security organisation should be received only as information and not as 'advice', and should

be weighed by a responsible authority against all other available information and not be handled at a junior level.[29]

The great mischief of the Gluckman affair was that it coloured international perceptions of Australia's role, and specifically Hasluck's role, in shielding Papua New Guinea from the justified scrutiny of the international community. This was a matter of concern because the future of Dutch New Guinea continued to fester as the Indonesian Government kept up its bellicose language. In February 1961 Hasluck received advice that in the event of open hostilities between Indonesia and the Netherlands, the Dutch would at once arrest all Indonesian sympathisers, and refugees might begin to head for the Australian territory.[30] In April, representatives of the Netherlands and Australia visited both halves of New Guinea, and Hasluck was obliged to quash media speculation that Australia had a military commitment to the Dutch if hostilities broke out. His own first priorities were to press forward with the accurate mapping of the frontier and to establish a chain of patrol posts in the border region, not least to ensure effective quarantine.[31]

After the federal election of December 1961, Sir Wilfrid Kent Hughes, a former cabinet minister and disgruntled backbencher, urged that Australia should stop appeasing the Indonesians and form an alliance with the Dutch to defend West New Guinea. He found support in the emboldened Labor opposition and the *Sydney Morning Herald*. Menzies, who thought it 'sheer lunacy' to get into hostilities with a large Asian neighbour, conjectured that Kent Hughes might vote with Labor on the issue and bring down the government.[32] But the time had passed when an alliance with the Netherlands was feasible. Under the recently elected Kennedy administration, the United States considered the Dutch position untenable. The first priority was to secure Indonesian goodwill. Realism brought the Dutch to a speedy acquiescence, and on 15 August 1962 the Netherlands flag was hauled down in West New Guinea. Control passed to an interim United Nations administration, which handed the territory (now to be known as West Irian) to Indonesia with a proviso that an 'act of choice' in 1969 should seek the views of the Indigenous people. It was a hollow promise.

Meanwhile, the United Nations Trusteeship Council sent a delegation to inspect progress in Papua New Guinea. This was a triennial event, and the visits in 1953, 1956 and 1959 had all produced little or nothing that could be seen as controversial. By 1962, however, the critics of colonialism were growing more vocal in the United Nations General Assembly, and Australia could expect a keener scrutiny of its role as trustee. In February 1962 Hasluck was confronted with a proposal to set up a United Nations information centre in Port Moresby. He minuted:

'The Centre' is bound to grow. The 'Empire building' talents of a national public servant are childish fumblings compared with the Empire Building talent of an international public servant. Start as modestly and humbly as you can manage. Offer as little as decency permits.[33]

But it was a more formidable task to deal with the delegation that arrived in Port Moresby a few weeks later.

The leader of the delegation was Sir Hugh Foot from the United Kingdom. He had made his career in the British Colonial Office as an authority on the process of decolonisation, and although he came from a family with a tradition of radicalism, his attitudes were those of some upper-class Englishmen towards the colonial Australians.[34] 'We've come to put you chaps into a gallop', he told the Clelands when he arrived in Port Moresby.[35] Of Hasluck he wrote:

> He has been the District Officer of New Guinea. I at once recognised in him the characteristics which I know so well in District Officers elsewhere, a passionate devotion to the well-being of the people under his charge, a dedicated determination to serve them well – and an intense suspicion of interference from any outside authority.[36]

He added: 'We were specially grateful to him for the great effort of patience and forbearance which he made in dealing with us'.[37]

His Australian hosts were less complimentary. Hasluck thought Foot an 'actor – the sort of actor who always tried to upstage other members of the cast'. Ian Downs complained that 'He created a misleading impression that the advice of his mission had saved Australia from a serious national crisis'.[38] In Robert Porter's view the visiting mission to Papua New Guinea 'has been considered a major catalyst in focusing both Australian and international attention on the government's efforts there'.[39] Among its more significant recommendations were: that Papua New Guinea should have a legislature of 100 elected members; that traditional land tenure systems should be replaced with 'a new and modern system of land-holding'; and that faster progress should be made in higher education. Some of these recommendations, such as the call for a new system of land tenure, were quietly ignored as impracticable, but there was soon to be progress in the system of government and in higher education.

Both Hasluck and the Clelands showed that many of the visiting mission's recommendations covered proposals that were already in preparation. This may simply have been intelligent anticipation of the directions the visiting mission was likely to take. Dame Rachel Cleland related that at his farewell lunch at Port Moresby, Foot said to her:

> Tomorrow I have to make a start on achieving the impossible. To make a report which will reconcile the expectations of the United Nations with the views of the Australian government.

'It's easy', she replied, suggesting that he should identify developments that were already in the pipeline, such as the university, liquor legislation and the creation of a common roll.[40] It may be that the main value of the commission lay in convincing Hasluck's cabinet colleagues that they must accept faster change. Hasluck himself, without drawing attention to the fact, was already abandoning his long-held conviction that it required twenty or thirty years to attain self-government. In a speech to the Economic Society of Australia and New Zealand in October 1961 he acknowledged:

> Political pressures are likely to bring about political independence in Papua and New Guinea within a shorter time than the Australian Government would have wished if its objective of preparing the people and the economy were to be properly realised...yet because the transformation of a people is taking place, we will have to recognise...the people will assert

their own preferences, commit their own follies, and exercise their own wisdom. We may still be paying when we have lost any hope of choosing what we pay for.[41]

Before the arrival of the visiting mission, Hasluck encouraged the Legislative Council to set up a committee on constitutional change. Its report, approved by the council in October 1962, did not go so far as endorsing the visiting mission's target of 100 elected members, but provided for a House of Assembly of ten officials, ten non-Indigenous representatives elected from a common roll, and forty-four elected members. The Commonwealth parliament approved these proposals in May 1963, leaving the administration with the task of compiling the common roll. Of about a million names on it, only about forty per cent had experience of voting. As Hasluck wrote,

> The others knew little about it and lived in thousands of
> villages and hamlets in remote parts on the mountainous
> regions. A mammoth educational effort was made with some
> novel methods.[42]

Also in 1961, well before the visiting mission, Hasluck had set up an interdepartmental committee to investigate the question of tertiary and other forms of higher education. The group recommended that, following a model employed with several new Australian universities, such as New England, Newcastle and Townsville,[43] a university college should be set up under the aegis of an existing major university. The Australian National University was suggested. Unfortunately, the chair of the committee, Lambert's deputy John Willoughby, died unexpectedly.

After Willoughby's death, matters drifted for a while. As Hasluck put it, 'too many cooks were eagerly stirring too little broth'.[44] The Australian National University decided against accepting the role of overseer, so in October 1962 Hasluck moved to appoint a commission, chaired by Sir George Currie, who as Vice-Chancellor of The University of Western Australia had known Hasluck during his years there as an academic. The other members were Professor Oskar Spate of the Australian National University, whom Hasluck had found a wise adviser on Papua New Guinea, and John Gunther. Their report, tabled in March 1964, led to the creation of the University of Papua New Guinea.

While these initiatives were maturing, Hasluck felt pressure from an unwelcome source. Conscious of the increasing urgency within the United Nations to hasten the process of decolonisation, the Department of External Affairs under Barwick and Tange took the view that Hasluck's gradualist approach towards autonomy for Papua New Guinea was a luxury Australia could not afford. More than once the sceptical Tange was heard to complain that he did not know what Hasluck was doing.[45] From the viewpoint of those in External Affairs, it was important to produce an elite with secondary and tertiary educational backgrounds who might provide leadership in an independent nation, and this ran contrary to Hasluck's priority of establishing the widest possible spread of uniform primary education before concentrating on more advanced levels.

Tange, moreover, visited Papua New Guinea in August 1962 and concluded that Hasluck's preference for social services such as health and education was achieved at the expense of commercial and strategic infrastructure such as roads and ports. The 'hand-out' sector, he thought, was out of balance with 'the generative side of the economy'. Rather inappropriately, he compared Australia's policies in Papua New Guinea with France's in Algeria a few years earlier, implying that they might result in a similarly traumatic war of independence.[46] This was inept, since Hasluck's policies had ensured that a settler caste was not established in Papua New Guinea, whereas Algeria contained a minority of colonists, some of second- or third-generation residence. Rhodesia (now Zimbabwe) would have been a more appropriate comparison. It was not surprising that there would be a coldness in future relations between Hasluck and Tange.

During 1963 Hasluck gave a good deal of thought to succession planning in the Department of Territories. Lambert, increasingly handicapped by deafness, was due to retire in 1964 at the age of sixty-five; Cleland would follow two years later. Two of Lambert's senior deputies, Edward Foxcroft and John Willoughby, died unexpectedly while both comparatively young men in 1962, so there was no obvious replacement for Lambert within the department. Looking further afield, Hasluck made his first approach to Sir James Plimsoll in the Department of External Affairs, who was highly regarded and had been Australia's representative on the United Nations Trusteeship Council with oversight of decolonisation since 1959.[47] Hasluck wanted him as deputy secretary with the expectation of taking over on Lambert's retirement. Plimsoll, though he confessed he might have been tempted by Cleland's post as administrator, did not consider himself cut out for the routine of a departmental head. Hasluck then fixed on John Gunther, who from being an effective director of health in Papua New Guinea had shown skill in managing the business of the House of Assembly in

Port Moresby. Gunther's qualities of energy, decisiveness and profound local knowledge would make him an admirable successor to Cleland. Until Cleland retired he could deepen his qualifications by serving for two or three years as Lambert's successor in Canberra, thus gaining a firm grasp of the inner workings of the Department of Territories.

The decision did not rest with Hasluck alone, however. The Public Service Board had an advisory role, and it was chaired by Frederick Wheeler,[48] of whom it has been written: 'Wheeler and Hasluck had some history…including a shattered glass door – PMCH leaving a room in annoyance at FHW's persistence in argument'.[49] Hasluck was much more proactive than most ministers in suggesting possible names and making inquiries about them. Of the two recent replacements as Lambert's deputies, Malcolm Booker (seconded from External Affairs) and Robert Swift, the latter seemed a possibility to Hasluck but would seem a stronger prospect after more experience. He was less impressed with Booker, who returned the dislike.[50] Wheeler wanted consideration given to candidates from other departments. 'Mr Hasluck stressed the need for an appointee who could get things done.'[51] Hasluck also urged a search outside the Commonwealth public service. Several names were canvassed, but Hasluck kept coming back to Gunther. The Public Service Board was not convinced, and the matter was still unresolved when at the end of 1963 Hasluck was at last liberated from Territories.

After two years of governing with a one-seat majority in the House of Representatives, Menzies judged the time was ripe for a House of Representatives election in November 1963. He was rewarded by a convincing victory. The Australian Labor Party did not nominate a candidate for Hasluck's seat of Curtin, and against a Democratic Labor Party opponent he scored his biggest win, with 78.8 per cent of the vote.[52] When Menzies reshuffled his cabinet, Hasluck was at last released from Territories and became Minister for Defence. Athol Townley, the previous minister, was to go as Ambassador to Washington (but he never went, succumbing to a fatal illness at the end of 1963). Hasluck's appointment was well received. The greatly respected Department of Defence secretary Sir Frederick Shedden, now in retirement, wrote: 'you certainly have all the qualifications for a most successful period of office in this important post'.[53] Shedden's successor, Edwin Hicks, was an experienced public servant in the Lambert tradition, adept at solving problems but not regarding it as his business to initiate policies.[54] A critic in External Affairs wrote him off as 'a tough but journeyman head of department who was a renowned 8.30–4.51 five-day worker',[55] but he won Hasluck's trust and is remembered in Canberra as able to manage Miss Dusting.

Hasluck did not hold back from making public comments on foreign-policy issues. Asked in March 1964 to speak to the students at the Australian National University's School of General Studies[56] on the subject 'Is Australia part of Asia?', he asserted that Australia would do best in its dealings with Asian nations by developing its own clearly defined sense of national aims and priorities. He asked

> if those who insist that Australians are Asians hope, by so
> saying, to miss the consequences of being a white people
> in a coloured area. Worse still, is there an element of false
> patronage? Are people saying 'We are just inferior people, like
> you Asians'.[57]

Our Asian neighbours, he said, would find such attempts offensive or comical. Some newspapers, the Melbourne *Age* in particular, misreported his speech as a repudiation of Asian culture.[58] Reactions were immediate. The Employers' Federation telegraphed their concern to Prime Minister Menzies, and several academics were poised to protest until the actual text of Hasluck's address became available. The respected sinologist Patrick Fitzgerald pointed out that 'Asia' was an entirely European concept. 'There was no common notion of Asia as opposed to any other part of the world linking, for example, the Chinese, the Arabs and the Indians.'[59] Sir Keith Hancock found Hasluck's comments 'realistic, humane and timely. It is not only the young who are dangerously muddled about Asia'.[60] Despite this welcome support from eminent academics, the episode, coming after the Gluckman affair, served to confirm Hasluck's poor opinion of much contemporary journalism.

The opportunity he had dreamed of came unexpectedly in April 1964. The Chief Justice, Sir Owen Dixon,[61] wished to retire, but did not want Barwick to succeed him in the post. He timed his resignation at a moment when Barwick was about to leave on an extended ministerial tour overseas and might be unavailable for appointment. Menzies nevertheless offered Barwick the Chief Justiceship, demanding an immediate response. When Barwick accepted, a successor had to be found for External Affairs. Some of the Victorian Liberals lobbied for Harold Holt, in the belief that after five years as Treasurer a spell of experience in foreign affairs would strengthen Holt's claims to succeed Menzies.[62] But Menzies realised that Hasluck could no longer be passed over. In his place as Minister for Defence another Western Australian was appointed, Shane Paltridge.

Despite a period of coolness when Paltridge had coveted the seat of Curtin, he was the sort of 'plain blunt Aussie' character who tended to appeal to Hasluck. They were to work together closely for the next year and a half. Theirs would be the responsibility during one of the most critical episodes in Australian defence and foreign policy.

Chapter 17

Indonesia and Vietnam

Hasluck's arrival at the Department of External Affairs has been seen by some writers as a significant shift away from the directions taken by his predecessor, Barwick. If so, it was a shift in style rather than basic policy. Both were more instinctively sympathetic than Menzies to the importance of building up constructive relationships in Asia. Both gave high priority to the containment of an unpredictable China. Both favoured treating Indonesia with a nuanced tact that would not alienate their volatile neighbour. 'I am not introducing any change in the foreign policy of this Government', Hasluck informed the House of Representatives. 'The foreign policy is that of the Government, not of a person.'[1] This policy came at a cost. The young backbencher Hasluck had been prepared to raise doubts and ask questions: did Australia need an ANZUS-type alliance; might it not be sensible to give diplomatic recognition to the People's Republic of China? After thirteen years as member of a ministerial team, Hasluck was schooled to stick doggedly to the official government line, no matter what his private thoughts might have been.

His style as a minister differed from Barwick's. As an officer of the department Hasluck had suffered too much from Evatt's capricious and personalised style of leadership. In reaction he went to the opposite extreme of insisting too rigidly on formal procedures. He seldom left the ministerial office in Parliament House to visit his department. The staff remembered Barwick's habit of strolling along the corridors in his shirtsleeves, pausing to crack a joke or put his head around someone's office door for a moment's chat. After ten years in Hasluck's service, Miss. Dusting had become a formidable guardian of her employer's privacy, protecting him sedulously from unplanned callers. Hasluck felt he needed this privacy, as he had brought with him from Territories the habit of giving personal attention to as many as possible of the departmental files. Barely possible in Territories as that department's responsibilities grew, it was an impossible aim in the wide-ranging ambit of External Affairs. Eventually Hasluck hampered his capacity for constructive analytical thought about the problems of foreign policy by his insistence on mastering the day-to-day detail of departmental issues without allowing himself time for wider strategic considerations.

It might have been otherwise if his relations with his departmental head, Sir Arthur Tange, had been easier, or at the very least if their complementary qualities had produced a partnership such as Hasluck had enjoyed with Lambert. Nine years younger than Hasluck, Tange was appointed secretary of the Department of External Affairs in 1954 at the age of forty. The two men first met in Perth in the late 1930s, and were colleagues in the formative years of the United Nations, but Hasluck's written reprimand when Tange breached protocol still rankled.[2] Tange's long experience as departmental head fostered an already formidable self-confidence, and his junior officers regarded him with awe and respect.[3] He did not hesitate to disagree with Hasluck's priorities over Papua New Guinea, believing that a concentration on health and education had led to neglect of infrastructure such as roads and communications.[4] This might not have prevented them from working together subsequently, but Tange was also rumoured to have vetoed Hasluck's appointment to External Affairs in 1960, and the issue was never resolved between them.

If only Hasluck had been able, as in similar circumstances at a later stage in Tange's career Malcolm Fraser was, to invite him to address their issues over an informal whisky, things might have run more smoothly. But the characteristic the Clelands had noted, Hasluck's avoidance of one-to-one verbal conflict, was becoming an ingrained habit, and the blunt and forceful Tange was not an easy man to confront. Tange himself asserted

> that Hasluck was invariably abrupt, nervous and frosty, and if he were offered policy advice he would freeze up, rustle his papers, and make non-committal noises to bring the meeting to an end.[5]

Peter Edwards makes a valid point when he argues that, in attempting to avoid Evatt's over-personalised and often chaotic style of leadership, Hasluck went to the opposite extreme. He insisted on an almost pedantic correctness in what he considered the proper roles of minister and departmental officer to a degree that was almost unworkable.[6] And Tange was not the man to adapt patiently to a new regime in the hope of building up trust.

It did not help that one of Hasluck's first actions was to inform Tange that his time as departmental head was to finish, and he would exchange positions with the High Commissioner to India, Sir James Plimsoll. A belief had grown up in official circles – though in fact no such policy was ever formally enunciated – that the headship of the Department of External Affairs should be rotated among senior diplomats every five years or so. Tange had served that length of time when Menzies took over as Minister for External Affairs. Menzies came to consider Tange an over-mighty subject, and formed the view that it was time for him to give way to another senior diplomat. Barwick, however, enjoyed working with Tange – with whom his relationship was like that of a skilled barrister using a first-class solicitor to furnish him with arguments – and during 1962 and 1963 he managed to dodge the issue. When Hasluck became minister, Menzies made it clear he wanted Tange to go soon, transferred to New Delhi. This was confirmed by cabinet on 19 May.

Many, including Tange himself, believed Hasluck was getting rid of his too-powerful departmental head to make way for a more tractable successor. Hasluck was too reticent to explain that he was merely the messenger reporting a decision already made by Menzies. Unfortunately, Plimsoll's term of service at Delhi was not due to end until April 1965, so for nearly twelve months Tange lingered in Canberra, alienated from his minister. In those twelve months Australia would implement its most important measures in foreign policy since the Second World War. It is odd that in such a dysfunctional situation neither Menzies nor Hasluck himself made any move to bring Plimsoll to Canberra earlier. Plimsoll himself felt that an early return would be discourteous to India.

Tange was displeased when Hasluck's first communication to him came in the form of a message from Miss Dusting advising that the new minister was about to depart for Western Australia for several days, and communications did not improve subsequently. Although Hasluck was provided with a liaison officer, Don Kingsmill, to manage communications from within the department, he preferred Miss Dusting to serve as a gatekeeper and dispensed with Kingsmill after a few months.[7] Hasluck insisted that when he was abroad she should receive copies of all submissions sent to him and all correspondence sent by him from overseas, explaining that she served as his 'official memory'.[8]

Miss Dusting even suggested that during Hasluck's absences overseas Tange's submissions to the acting minister (who happened to be John Gorton) should be routed through her office, but although Tange was willing to send her copies of his submissions to be filed in her office, he firmly drew the line against using her as the channel of communication with Gorton. Throughout the time until Tange departed, her presence as trusted private secretary continued to impede the smooth flow of departmental business, partly because she would take no instructions from Tange. A venerable Canberra anecdote relates that when Tange wanted to discuss a number of matters with his minister, and the only opportunity arose when they were travelling to the airport, he was frustrated because Hasluck insisted that Miss Dusting sit beside him, relegating Tange to the back seat where conversation was impossible.[9] The lack of communication between minister and departmental head showed neither at their best, and damaged the effectiveness of both.

Part of the trouble was systemic. In his previous portfolios Hasluck had worked with experienced public servants – Lambert in Territories and Hicks in Defence – who saw it as their job to carry the minister's policies into effect, and perhaps through their command of the administrative process to have an influence on the shaping of those policies, but always with the minister having the last word. Neither of them experienced Miss Dusting as creating difficulties in their access to Hasluck. The culture of the Department of External Affairs was different. Under Tange its officers had developed an assured professionalism that might sometimes seem to exclude outsiders. Hasluck, who had felt himself an outsider when he was an officer of the department in the 1940s, wrote that External Affairs 'had the attitude that foreign affairs was a mystery in their own keeping', with 'the attitude to Cabinet that bright young men have to their parents: "It's no use trying to explain it to you. You would not understand"'.[10] To his son Nicholas he wrote:

> Regarding foreign affairs, it seems that every comma requires
> a conference between three departments, and to make a choice
> between one verb and another requires the presence of the
> Chiefs of Staff. Then the chances are that I will cross out the
> whole sentence.[11]

Tange was not the man to win Hasluck to a more sympathetic understanding of the department's ethos.

Tange's resentment smouldered for decades. In 1969 he told William McMahon, then the newly appointed Minister for External Affairs:

> Men who for years had been encouraged to apply freshness of
> thought to problems created by Australia's environment, and
> who happily gave up more leisure than most to do it, found
> themselves shut off, discouraged, from expressing themselves
> and frequently rebuked.[12]

In retirement Tange judged those months to be 'the most frustrating and unproductive era in his career'.[13] Some members of the department, such as Gary Woodard, found it easier to identify with Tange than with their remote minister,[14] yet others formed a different impression of Hasluck. Plimsoll wrote: 'With you as Minister there was a genuine two-way traffic of ideas, and the formation and enunciation of policy bore very much your imprint'.[15] Walter Crocker wrote: 'I, like most of our Ambassadors, valued your firm and masterly control of your subject and your Department'.[16] Perhaps that was the trouble. Where Barwick had been content to fire the bullets Tange provided, Hasluck wanted to mould his own bullets.

Hasluck gave no credence to suggestions that the Department of External Affairs was divided over the Vietnam issue:

> while of course there were differences of opinion from time to time on methods and procedures and wording of telegrams and so forth…generally the Department had always seemed to go along with him. He of course was always meticulous on acting through the head of department and not trying to cultivate direct links between the Minister and other members of the Department.[17]

Departmental officers who travelled overseas with Hasluck formed a different view of their minister. He revived the practice of convening regional meetings of heads of mission. Hasluck himself reflected once while in Taiwan:

> I always seem to be liked by foreigners and disliked by Australians. The only refreshing thing about these trips is to

345

find that one can earn respect by saying something reasonably intelligent and understanding what others are talking about, and you do not have to earn it by using Christian names of persons whom you are meeting for the first time and setting out to prove that you are as stupid as they are.[18]

Hasluck took office at a time when two gathering crises dominated Australia's relations with South-East Asia. Nearer to home, and in the eyes of many Australians the more worrying problem, was Indonesia. Its leader, Soekarno, had not been appeased by the acquisition of West New Guinea, and soon began to harp on another grievance. In the process of withdrawing from their colonial empire, the British developed an enthusiasm for federations, and in 1963 they granted independence to a Malaysian federation comprising the former colonies of Malaya, Singapore, Sarawak, the Brunei protectorate and British North Borneo (now Kalimantan). The three latter provinces straddled the northern shore of Borneo, the largest island in the Indonesian archipelago. Perhaps feeling that Indonesia had not been sufficiently consulted, perhaps recalling that in previous centuries Borneo had been ruled by kingdoms based in Java, Soekarno embarked on a campaign to 'crush Malaysia', which he sought to depict as a puppet of continuing Western imperialism.

Indonesian patrols began to infiltrate the Malaysian border in Borneo, and in one engagement Malaysian servicemen were killed. Malaysia called for allies in maintaining its integrity. The United Kingdom urged the commitment of an Australian battalion to reinforce British forces already in the region. The Australian Government was reluctant to comply, but in March 1964, while Hasluck was Minister for Defence, Australia committed itself to supplying Malaysia with ammunition, small landing craft and engineering equipment.[19] After a Defence mission assessed Malaysian needs, Hasluck announced in mid-April that Australia would additionally send minesweepers, helicopters and an engineering squadron.[20]

Yet at the same time there was an ambiguity in Australia's relations with Indonesia, as if both sides realised that beneath the noisy posturing it was desirable to maintain diplomatic links.[21] Barwick as minister sedulously tried to avoid raising the temperature. Australian aid projects to Indonesia continued, and Australia avoided needlessly provocative statements on Indonesian affairs. When he moved to External Affairs, Hasluck continued this line, trying to steer a middle course between the possibility of belligerence on the part of Malaysia and Britain, and an excessively conciliatory approach by the United States, following on from their attitude towards West New Guinea. In any case he believed that Indonesia was not the most pressing threat to Australian security and would not become so unless pushed further towards communist alignment. This, he believed, depended on curbing the growth of communist influence elsewhere in South-East Asia, especially at the southern borders of China.

Since the communist regime under Mao Zedong consolidated its hold in China in 1949, Hasluck's view of its intentions had hardened. At first he thought it possible that Mao's China might be accommodated in the developing diplomatic networks of East Asia and the Pacific, but he soon came to believe that China wanted to establish hegemony throughout South-East Asia.[22] This made him a follower of 'domino theory', the belief that an aggressive power driven by a militant ideology would never be content with dominating its immediate neighbours, but unless stopped would embark on a career of conquest after conquest. Specifically he believed that China, unless deterred, would lay claim not only to Taiwan, but also to Vietnam, Cambodia, Thailand, Malaysia, and parts of India, the Soviet Union and the Philippines.[23]

'Domino theory' has fallen into discredit, but it was an understandable concept for a generation who had seen Hitler's Germany begin with the annexation of German-speaking Austria and Sudetenland in 1938, and within three years extend its grasp over much of continental Europe before making an assault on Soviet Russia. Hasluck's history of Australia at war between 1939 and 1941 showed how slowly the potential Japanese threat had been recognised, so that his brother Lewis and many others were sent underprepared to confront the rapid Japanese thrust south across Malaya and Indonesia to New Guinea in the early months of 1942. Many feared that Australia itself would be invaded, and Hasluck vividly remembered the sense of panic close to the surface of many Australian minds at that time, not least in Canberra. Those who lived through those years could readily argue that in the 1960s it was wise to follow policies of forward defence against potential aggressors.

After the war the Soviet Union in its turn used its strength to set up satellite regimes in much of Eastern Europe, calling a halt only when uneasily contained in the 1950s by a balance of power in Europe supported by American might. Only Marshal Josip Broz Tito in Yugoslavia managed to escape Russian hegemony. The Cold War, as it was called, dominated the diplomacy of the 1950s, but eventually the Russians came to show themselves increasingly amenable to conventional diplomatic and military modes of transaction, though they bargained very toughly. As crisis followed crisis without resulting in a world war – the Hungarian rising and the Suez episode in 1956, the confrontation over Cuba in 1962 – it was arguable that potential aggressors should be restrained, not by appeasement but by quickly assuming a posture of forward defence.

The records of Nazi Germany, Japan and the Soviet Union could be interpreted in more than one way. It was possible to believe that in each case an ambitious leadership – Hitler, the Japanese military, Stalin – had set out with a predetermined plan of limitless conquest. But it was also arguable that originally their aims had been limited, only to go on growing as they discovered how easy it was to overrun their neighbours.[24] Their ambitions, notably Hitler's in the late 1930s, had been fed by the realisation that the Western democracies preferred to yield concessions rather than let a crisis escalate into war. In September 1938 the British Prime Minister Neville Chamberlain had flown to Munich to cut a deal allowing Germany to annex part of Czechoslovakia in return for 'peace with honour', only to see Hitler embark on further conquests within six months. Thirty years later, Chamberlain and his colleagues were still labelled as 'guilty men' for following a policy of appeasement. As W. J. Hudson observed:

> The scars of Munich are a long time healing and one feels
> that some participants in foreign policy debates are fearful
> that flexibility in the face of what is seen as totalitarianism
> may lead posterity to place them in the same category as the
> appeasers of the late 1930s.[25]

China under Mao seemed much less predictable. In the fifteen years since Mao took power in 1949, China's record had been less aggressive than either Nazi Germany or Soviet Russia in their heyday. The Korean War of 1950–53, when communist North Korea invaded the South, could be seen as a Chinese try-on using North Korea as catspaw. When United Nations intervention pushed the North Koreans back towards the Chinese border, the Chinese were quick to intervene, but they supported the truce that left the two Koreas divided in roughly the same proportions as before. Since that time China's expansive tendencies had been limited to a successful invasion of Tibet, over which China had claimed suzerainty since long before the communist regime, and to consolidating a hold on the inland around Mongolia, in the process causing friction with the Soviet Union. Years of tension with the anti-communist Chinese regime in Taiwan had never quite escalated into warfare. A clash at the Himalayan border between China and India caused international alarm in 1962, but after a few days the dispute subsided into a diplomatic wrangle. China in practice had so far avoided a full-scale war, but the language of international revolution employed by Mao's regime against what it perceived as the hostile Western world was dismayingly bellicose, and had to be taken seriously.

Nor could Hasluck be expected to show much empathy towards a regime that suppressed dissent rigorously, despised the scholarship of the past, and was given to parading its nonconforming intellectuals in dunce's caps before jeering mobs before sending them off to toil in the collective farms. Hand in hand with his realist views of international relations as grounded inescapably in power politics, Hasluck cherished an idealistic hope that in the conduct of their diplomacy, nations should uphold the core values of civilised governance. These included respect for the rule of law and property rights, probity in the conduct of public administration, and respect for the rights of the individual.[26] Probably it was the very unpredictability of Communist China, its apparent disrespect for these values and practices, that convinced Hasluck that Australia and its senior allies had to deal with an unscrupulously aggressive regime.

By 1964 his distrust of China was implacable. In holding these views Hasluck was at one with his predecessor Barwick, who had written earlier in 1964:

> We must accept, I believe, for the present that China constitutes the greatest threat to the security of the region in which we live. The presence of a super-power…which…is in reach of becoming a nuclear power, cannot fail to give cause for concern…That she should consciously isolate herself from world influences increases the potential that the situation presents. It is said that all this could be changed if China were now brought into the family of nations and given her rightful place as a great power. I wish it were as simple as that.[27]

To an old friend who suggested that it might be constructive to admit China to the United Nations, Hasluck replied:

> My own feeling is that we should not rush to admit China to the United Nations on terms which China dictates unilaterally but that the terms on which China should be admitted should be laid down by the United Nations itself before admission takes place.[28]

Hasluck was, however, far from sharing the lingering view that some day the communist regime in China might be overthrown:

> The rest of the world, and not China's neighbours alone, has an immense problem of finding a way to live with China. No one but a fool would think that China can be ignored or destroyed or reduced or forced to become something else other than China. The problem is to come to terms so that China and other nations can live alongside each other in the same world.[29]

Vietnam seemed the crucial test case. The old French Indochina, which Hasluck and his wife had visited in 1938, had not survived nationalist resistance after the war. By the Geneva Treaty of 1954, the former French colonies were divided into four new nations: Laos, Cambodia, and a divided Vietnam. North Vietnam (the old kingdoms of Annam and Tonkin) fell to a communist regime under the successful leader against the French, Ho Chi Minh, while the South took the form of a parliamentary democracy dominated by various factions and families. The President, Ngo Diem Dinh, member of a Christian minority in a largely Buddhist society, exercised an uncertain authority. A guerrilla movement, the Viet Cong, claiming to fight on behalf of the peasantry against corruption, began to trouble the South Vietnamese regime in the early 1960s, encouraged and supported from North Vietnam. Some thought that behind North Vietnam the manipulation of China could be discerned.

Shortly before Hasluck became Minister for Defence at the end of 1963, President Diem was assassinated in a military coup. He was replaced by a series of unstable political alliances that seemed unable to stem the incursions of the Viet Cong. If South Vietnam fell into the hands of a communist regime, and if that regime proved to be China's obedient client, the balance of power in South-East Asia would tilt, perhaps uncontrollably, against the interests of Australia and its allies. The stabilisation of the balance of power required, as it had in Europe, the active intervention of the United States. This could not be taken for granted. It was only two years since the United States had colluded in giving up West New Guinea to Indonesia, despite Australian misgivings. Of the other major Western powers with a stake in the region, France was eliminated after its defeat in Vietnam in 1954, and the British were labouring under financial pressures that might soon oblige them to abandon their role 'east of Suez'. Australian security, in the eyes of those who thought as Hasluck did, was best served by the involvement of the United States in Vietnam.

Hasluck believed that, whatever local discontents might motivate the Viet Cong, they were serving consciously or otherwise as instruments of Chinese expansion. He could never be convinced by the argument that, however much the North Vietnamese might share the Marxist vocabulary of Mao's China, they had a long tradition of resisting pressure from their over-mighty neighbour. He could recognise that 'Annamite aggressiveness and the desire to dominate their neighbours' motivated the North Vietnamese, but he believed that essentially they were puppets, the agents of the Chinese push for hegemony in South-East Asia.[30] Hindsight would suggest that Hasluck should have been more open to the possibility that North Vietnam's interests were not identical with China's, but it could not be confidently predicted that Ho Chi Minh might become an Asian Tito. Experience suggested that in the communist world nations that attempted to take an independent line, such as Hungary in 1956, would be quickly suppressed.

Critics have argued that Hasluck should have paid more attention to the Australian Ambassador to Saigon, David Anderson, who in September 1964 urged caution in Australian aid policy because of the possibility that South Vietnam might lurch towards neutralism or seek accommodation with the Viet Cong. Canberra responded in a way that made Anderson believe he had received 'a ministerial rebuke'. But Joan Beaumont has shown that Hasluck drafted a reply to Anderson explaining that, while Australian policy was designed to produce a stable anti-communist government receptive to an American presence in South-East Asia, he wanted 'heads of mission to report... accurately and clearly, according to their own observation and their own understanding of local events'. It was the government's responsibility to assess this evidence and use it in formulating policy. Anderson was not in any way 'under correction or reproof'.[31] Inexplicably, Tange failed to pass these comments on to Anderson, leaving him and other heads of mission under the impression that candid comment was unwelcome.

For many Australians, the American alliance was based straightforwardly on loyalty to a great and powerful friend. At a later stage in the Vietnam War, a group of Australian writers optimistically sought to enlist Alexandra Hasluck's support for a statement calling for an end to hostilities.[32] She explained why she could not agree:

I still remember the days of 1942, when Australia, in dire need, asked America for help and got it immediately, with no strings attached. Because of that, my younger son was born free, not in Japanese-occupied Australia. I believe in the payment of a debt, and therefore if America asks Australia help, it is our duty to give it.[33]

Her point of view was not uncommon among those of her generation, but it was not shared by younger Australians, who had no memory of the sense of Japanese threat.[34] Paul Hasluck's view was less unquestioning. Contrary to what some historians have asserted, Hasluck never followed the United States' line blindly. He wrote: 'We also need to show that we reach conclusions for ourselves and do not simply support whatever America says or does'.[35] He disliked America's growing cultural hegemony, complaining to his wife: 'Really America has contaminated the whole of Western Civilisation throughout the world'.[36] But in the circumstances of 1964 it was no time to weaken the American alliance.

Three weeks after Hasluck became Minister for External Affairs, President Lyndon B. Johnson of the United States requested Australia's support in expanding a military presence in the region. 'We could gain U.S. goodwill if, having promptly decided to do something ourselves, we supported U.S. efforts in other capitals to get more flags in Vietnam', Hasluck minuted in May 1964.[37] For the present it was enough to send more military instructors and six transport aircraft, but the decision gave Hasluck credibility in his attempts to secure wider international involvement in Vietnam. Instead, and with characteristic caution, he began to develop an initiative that until a few years earlier would have seemed unthinkable.

During the 1950s Australian foreign policy under the Menzies government assumed the monolithic solidarity of the communist world. Hasluck was prepared to move ahead of this perception. In recent years a number of issues had arisen to cool Sino-Soviet relations, and he considered the Soviet Union open to arguments based on balance of power as a key factor in the conduct of international relations. 'In the past fifteen years we have succeeded in keeping out world war because the United States and Russia have managed to reach a détente through both nuclear weapons and diplomacy', he argued. 'But we are witnessing the emergence of a third power which is purposeful and by nature aggressive.'[38] Hasluck was not the first to offer this analysis, as officers of the Department of External Affairs had raised it in their briefing notes for Sir Garfield Barwick's aborted overseas tour earlier in 1964. In June he authorised Tange to instruct intelligence agencies to cease referring to communist threats and to define them more accurately by national origin. Writing to John McEwen, Hasluck expressed a cautious hope that improved trade relations with the Soviet Union might be followed by Soviet restraint on Chinese aggression: 'although this hope is a faint one the rewards are so great that I think that we should nourish it'.[39]

In his first ministerial overseas journey in June 1964, Hasluck visited Indonesia, Malaysia, Thailand, Cambodia, Laos and South Vietnam. His first priority was Indonesia, where he had an hour's conversation with Soekarno and several hours with Subandrio and Nasution, the Foreign and Defence ministers. 'Djakarta was depressing in many ways but very illuminating', he told Alexandra. 'We talked plainly, but they seemed to set themselves out to be friendly.'[40] Apparently Soekarno afterwards said that Hasluck (unlike Barwick) did not lecture him. 'He tells me what he thinks and lets me tell him what I think.'[41] During their conversation Hasluck confronted the delicate task of complaining to Soekarno about the Indonesian Ambassador to Canberra. Soekarno heard the complaint with the Ambassador sitting at his feet, expressed an apology, 'and proceeded to give the recalcitrant Ambassador a substantial kick in the rump closely followed by another'.[42] As part of the apology Soekarno presented Hasluck with a large taxidermal tiger.

On returning to Canberra Hasluck faced the problem of disposing of the gift, and remembered that he was the number one ticket-holder of his local Australian Rules football club, Claremont, which by a happy coincidence is known as the Tigers. Protocol forbade him from disposing of an official gift into private hands, but with a minimum of publicity the tiger could be placed on permanent loan with the Claremont Football Club.[43] The problem of freighting the beast from Canberra to Perth was solved when Sir Robert Menzies offered to take it as cargo in the VIP aircraft on his next visit to Western Australia. Unfortunately, nobody had thought to inform Dame Pattie Menzies about the arrangement, and during the journey while visiting the powder room she was startled to be confronted by the snarling fangs of a ferocious beast. Hasluck was abject in his apologies, but Dame Pattie was 'very facetious about the whole business'.[44] On the day of the tiger's arrival, Claremont won the Western Australian premiership by four points, and Hasluck wrote: 'I dared not give it to Claremont that night as it would have been hugged to death by the stampeding thousands'.[45] A fortnight later he conjectured: 'I imagine it has had more glasses lifted towards it in the club room than any other dead and stuffed animal in local history'.[46] Despite this agreeable episode, he told his wife: 'I do not feel optimistic about Indonesia'.[47]

He returned from his visit to South-East Asia wondering, as he told Menzies, 'whether enough hard thinking has been done and precise answers found to questions such as the nature of the enemy and the situation with which we have to deal'. He recommended that 'we must make a conscious effort to improve our own assessment of the situation'.[48] A critic has commented that 'he never concentrated the necessary resources on the task or wrestled with the problem of how a small department constrained by an unsympathetic Treasury could create more analysts in depth and theoreticians', adding: 'Indeed, instead, scarce resources were dissipated on new overseas posts, the number increasing by 40 per cent from 1965 to 1970'.[49] This criticism is not entirely well founded. Twelve years at Territories had left Hasluck with experienced skill in cajoling funds from Treasury and cabinet, but when largesse arrived it was not always directed at the priorities External Affairs would have preferred. But undeniably he would have done well to make himself available to a wider range of input about policy than he was receiving.

In July 1964 he accompanied Menzies to the Prime Ministers' Conference in London. There he conferred with British ministers and officials who were piqued when Hasluck told them 'we did not expect Britain to assist in the defence of Australia and frankly did not believe that she would have the capacity to do so'. The British contended that, unless seriously threatened at home, they would still have a significant capacity to assist in Australia's defence. Given the uncertainties about American policy in Indonesia, Britain might show greater readiness to help, 'whatever our treaties with the United States might say'.[50] After this exchange Hasluck flew to Washington, and met members of the United States administration, including President Johnson.

He made a good first impression. The national security advisor, McGeorge Bundy, found Hasluck closely in agreement when he emphasised the importance of building up the social and economic foundations of South Vietnamese society. Bundy considered Hasluck 'a vast improvement on his predecessor', with 'a much more sophisticated view on Indonesia than the Prime Minister'.[51] Some of the Americans saw him as a possible successor to Menzies. But one senior American official warned him that it should not be taken for granted that China and North Vietnam were firm allies, a piece of advice too often forgotten in subsequent months.[52]

Meanwhile, Indonesia continued to harass Malaysia. Early in September, Indonesian paratroops landed on the Malayan mainland, where Australia had an established defence commitment. Hasluck urged that Malaysia should appeal to the United Nations Security Council before considering a military response. Fortunately, the Malaysian Government thought the same, and the paratroops were soon rounded up. Later in September, Hasluck spent an entire weekend in his office monitoring a crisis when Britain asserted its right to send warships through what Indonesia regarded as its territorial waters in the Sunda Straits.[53] A face-saving compromise was achieved, but such events made it harder for Australian public opinion to accept Hasluck's view that Indonesia was a lesser threat than Vietnam.

Between July and September events had not progressed helpfully in Vietnam. The South Vietnamese Prime Minister wrote to thirty-four heads of government appealing for help against North Vietnam. It was no use hoping that the United Nations would call for action against North Vietnam as it had against North Korea in 1950. North Vietnam's incursion was less flagrantly obvious than the North Korean invasion of the South in 1950, and since that time the United Nations had grown to include a large number of Afro-Asian nations that would not necessarily side with the Western powers. Tension rose early in August in what became known as the 'Gulf of Tonkin incident', when North Vietnamese patrol boats clashed with American warships. Each side blamed the other for opening fire, but the effect was to stimulate Congress to vote for more American military aid.

Against this background, in the House of Representatives on 11 August 1964, Hasluck set out his doctrine that the Vietnam conflict was part of a clash of international power groupings. 'North Vietnam, which possesses the largest army on the South-East Asian mainland, and which has behind it the even greater power of mainland China, has been active in war, infiltration and subversion in South Vietnam and Laos', leaving 'no current alternative to using force as necessary to check the southward thrust of militant Asian communism'.[54] Arthur Calwell and Gough Whitlam, the leading figures in the Labor opposition, were unconvinced. They complained that Hasluck's overemphasis on a military solution ignored the social and political factors behind the strife in Vietnam. The conflict might still be explained as a civil war; Hasluck had not given adequate evidence for his view of China as the driving force.[55] But Hasluck felt sure that the government took the honours in the debate.[56]

He had not persuaded the doubters. A few days later Hasluck received 200 copies of an advertisement by the Women's International League for Peace and Freedom describing the United States presence in North Vietnamese waters as provocative and calling for a negotiated solution. Against departmental advice he sent a signed letter to each of the signatories to the advertisement putting the government's position. 'In my political experience', he minuted, 'the cheapest and most effective propaganda is bought with a fivepenny stamp'.[57] During the rest of Hasluck's time at External Affairs he found himself confronting a persistent and growing chorus of criticism of Australia's involvement in Vietnam. He continued to believe in sending an individual response to each critic, and an officer of the department was kept busy with the correspondence.[58]

Hasluck gave no ground to these criticisms. China must be contained, and South Vietnam was the test case demanding a military solution before all else. If the communists triumphed in Vietnam it would become more difficult to hold the line in Indonesia and the intervening nations of South-East Asia. As events turned out, it was another ten years before Saigon fell to the communists, and it could be argued that this decade of breathing space gave such nations as Malaysia, Thailand and Indonesia the opportunity of establishing an economic and social stability that dimmed the appeal of communism. Nothing in Hasluck's public or private utterances in 1964 and 1965, however, suggested that he gave thought to this contingency, still less to the possibility that by the time Mao died in 1976 China would have reached a point of rapprochement with the United States and its allies such as Australia.

Political scientist Henry Albinski once observed:

Drawing upon Hasluck the historian, Hasluck the analyst and policy maker placed priority on broad perspectives and attention to essential national interest. Hence his insistence on long-term perseverance in Vietnam.[59]

Hasluck's historical education included knowledge of the period after the Napoleonic Wars, when the Congress of Vienna ushered in an era during which European nations sought stability by maintaining a balance of power among contending players. In the United States the young Henry Kissinger attracted notice through his influential study applying the lessons of the early nineteenth century to current international politics.[60] Hasluck was not influenced by Kissinger, but he was similarly alert to the balance-of-power principle. Just as the British in 1815 had sided with the old enemy, France, to restrain the potential influence of Russia, Prussia and Austria, so it might be possible to look to the Soviet Union to serve as a possible restraint on China.

The Russians were troubled both by tensions along their Asian frontier with China and by competition for influence in Africa.[61] The Soviet Union leader, Nikita Khrushchev, was thought to give priority to mending his fences with the United States after the Cuban crisis of 1962, 'and saw Vietnam as closely allied with his rival, Mao Zedong'.[62] It was expected that the split would be formalised at a world congress of communist parties in December 1964. Hasluck was accordingly ready to raise the subject when the Soviet Union Ambassador paid him an unsolicited visit on 14 September. He suggested that

> whereas there had been two clearly defined power blocs, China was now emerging as the third great power bloc and this must be a fact that caused as much concern to the Soviet Union as it did to us.

The discomfited Ambassador 'laughed off the reference and spread his hands. When the unintelligible sounds ceased I understood him to say that not everything could be settled by force'.[63]

On 15 October, Khrushchev was overthrown by a junta whose most significant members were Leonid Brezhnev, Andrei Kosygin and Andrei Gromyko, the last of whom was Hasluck's old sparring partner from the early years of the United Nations and still Foreign Minister. This change did nothing to discourage Hasluck's plan to sound out the Russians. Four days later, on 19 October, he left Australia for a six-week world tour, accompanied by his wife. After seventeen years he was returning to the powerhouses of international diplomacy.

Chapter 18

The year of living dangerously

Their first European stopover was at Rome. There the Haslucks had an audience with Pope Paul VI, 'a quiet, humble, kind and holy man'. Hasluck wrote,

> As a Protestant I cannot give him the near divine character that a Catholic would give, but as a fellow human being he warmed my heart and simplified my mind as few people have done.[1]

From an Italian minister who had been in Moscow at the time, Hasluck received a first-hand account of Khrushchev's overthrow. His conversations with the Italian Foreign Minister, Giuseppe Saragat,[2] somehow moved to discussion of Machiavelli, Hasluck expressing admiration for his realistic description of how politics worked, and Saragat suggesting that Machiavelli was not like an Italian at all ('the Italians are not a cunning people') but more like an Elizabethan Englishman.[3] 'The greatest stimulus I ever get', Paul Hasluck commented, 'is to meet clear, trained professional minds that carry lightly the inheritance of Western Civilisation'.[4] Both the Haslucks enjoyed a solid intellectual level of conversation; Alexandra reported that she found 'All the men very attentive and easy to talk to. Their talk was of ideas, books, paintings – *never* of sport'.[5]

The Australians proceeded to Moscow for three nights and two days. Gromyko made time for two long discussions with Hasluck on 28 and 29 October 1964, the second time accompanied by Kosygin. Hasluck later recalled:

As it happened he was the first Foreign Minister to call on Kosygin after Kosygin had become Prime Minister in Russia... He got the strong impression that Gromyko was very anxious to be there as this would be his first impression of what line Kosygin was going to take now that he had reached the top... Early in the conversation there was some reference to...the Sino-Indian dispute and Kosygin emphasized Russia's position of neutrality...Hasluck said he welcomed the Russian attitude of neutrality and was very grateful that they had been neutral on the right side. When this came through from the reporter, Kosygin laughed out loud.[6]

Sharing a memory with Gromyko of Evatt's attempts at San Francisco in 1945 to curb the role of the great powers, Hasluck took some pains to stress that Australia now looked to major players such as the United States and the Soviet Union to take a lead in working for stability. They should uphold the integrity of smaller nations at a time when China was an aggressive and expansionist influence in South-East Asia. He saw ideology as a less important factor than national self-interest – a view shared by the United States Ambassador to Moscow at that time – and implied that the Soviet Union could use whatever influence it possessed with Beijing to restrain North Vietnam and the Viet Cong. Kosygin and Gromyko refused to accept that China was an aggressive threat to world peace, and it emerged that there was now no prospect of a Sino-Soviet split. But Hasluck came away from the interviews satisfied that the new Soviet leadership was made up of balanced human beings with whom it would be possible to form closer political, economic and cultural relations.[7]

Gregory Clark, who acted as interpreter for some of these discussions and was growing disenchanted with the Department of External Affairs, has painted an influential picture of Hasluck as a diplomatic naïf, pestering the Russians with a hastily conceived proposition that had no hope of a good reception.[8] This assessment conflicts with the official reports composed after the interviews. Hasluck himself thought the visit successful. He found Kosygin and Gromyko thoughtful and measured in putting their point of view, without any hectoring stridency. 'It will be a help to the world if we now have people at the Kremlin who will occasionally listen to others and habitually think over matters', he wrote.

> One cannot be optimistic. It would be foolish to nourish illusions about the Soviet Union but so far as foreign policy is concerned I am very hopeful that the change in government there may on the whole be to the good.[9]

Hasluck's account of Kosygin and Gromyko was given considerable weight in Paris, London and Washington. He was the first Foreign Minister to visit Moscow after Khrushchev's fall, and as a representative of a credible middle-ranking power it was appropriate that he should probe the intentions of the new Soviet leadership. Far from treating him as the bumbling amateur of Clark's interpretation, European leaders thought well of him. Dr Ludwig Erhard, the Chancellor of the German Federal Republic

(West Germany), was 'greatly impressed' with Hasluck's 'grasp of essentials'.[10] In Paris the Foreign Minister, Maurice Couve de Murville, was sufficiently approving of Hasluck's French to arrange for him to have a half-hour interview with President de Gaulle, during which the President spoke French but Hasluck discreetly replied in English.

Couve de Murville himself poured cold water on Hasluck's thought of using the Russians to restrain the Chinese. When Hasluck argued that China's aggressive actions were exerting pressure through fear on its weaker neighbours, Couve de Murville disagreed, saying that 'China has three aims, to protect herself from external aggression, to achieve international acceptability and to develop its resources'. He rejected the domino theory, and with the wry realism of a defeated colonial power suggested that

> although North Vietnam was receiving help from China, if peace were achieved by a process of neutrality North Vietnam would be resistant to China. The Chinese would be eager for a settlement with the United States.[11]

Events were to justify Couve de Murville, but Hasluck was unable to heed his insights. It was soon to emerge, as the war in Vietnam escalated, that the Soviet Union found itself competing with China to maintain influence in Hanoi, and its self-interest would not be served by volunteering to act as peacemaker.

In the United Kingdom a new Labour government under Harold Wilson had just come to power after thirteen years of Conservative rule. Its majority was small, and its intended Foreign Secretary, Patrick Gordon Walker, had failed to win a seat at the election, so it was too early to foretell its attitude to developments in East and South-East Asia. Preoccupied with the problems of Britain's faltering economy, the Wilson government was suspected of wishing to scale down Britain's commitments in East and South-East Asia, although this option was not open while the confrontation with Indonesia persisted. The British had to resign themselves to Australia's unwillingness to commit forces against its neighbour Indonesia, and the Australians had to recognise that as co-chair of the Geneva agreement of 1954 that had been intended to settle the future of Vietnam, Britain would be slow to take sides in that conflict.

In Washington a presidential election had just confirmed President Lyndon B. Johnson in office with a handsome majority, but it was unclear how far the United States was prepared to extend its commitment in South Vietnam. The State Department was apparently ill prepared for Hasluck's visit, but he impressed the Americans as 'informed and articulate but businesslike' in conversations with the Secretary of State, Dean Rusk; the Secretary for Defense, Robert McNamara; and other senior officials. Hasluck urged victory in Vietnam as a top priority ahead of all other South-East Asian problems, including Indonesia. He assured the United States of Australia's readiness and willingness to provide increased involvement in Vietnam, militarily and otherwise. The Americans agreed that 'if there is to be any stepping up of American military efforts in South Vietnam, then the United States government will be looking for Australian support'. When Hasluck left the United States, the Australians still had no firm idea whether, or when, the call would come. But the senior members of the State Department had formed a good opinion of Hasluck. William McGeorge

Bundy later described himself, Dean Rusk, Hasluck and the Australian Ambassador, Keith Waller, as 'low-key people' who trusted each other and got on pretty well together.[12]

Menzies' biographer Allan Martin comments that in the closing months of 1964 'the triumvirate – Menzies, Hasluck and Paltridge – came to be of crucial importance in the final shaping of foreign relations'.[13] Woodard and other commentators have suggested that Hasluck was subservient to Menzies to the extent of spurning departmental advice when it conflicted with the Prime Minister's goals and prejudices.[14] It was certainly Hasluck's ingrained practice to subordinate his own views to those of a higher authority as long as he tolerably could, but at this phase of policymaking over Vietnam he was in entire agreement with Menzies. Both saw China as a potential aggressor, the limits of whose aggression could not easily be calculated. Menzies perhaps was too old and too set in his ways to entertain a more nuanced approach. Hasluck, even while he cut himself off from full exposure to departmental advice, was eventually to show a greater caution in committing Australia to the war, but by that time it would be too late.

Hasluck returned to Australia to find that during his absence the federal cabinet had decided to introduce conscription for national service. For the first time this included liability to serve overseas. During the two world wars only regular soldiers and volunteers had gone overseas, although after Japan entered the Second World War national servicemen had been obliged to serve in Papua New Guinea and adjacent islands south of the Equator. Under the 1964 legislation, all twenty-year-old men had to register for the call-up, but only a proportion would be required, and these would be selected by a ballot conducted twice each year. Hasluck did not dissent from this measure. Few if any members of cabinet realised how much this plan of conscription by lottery increased the potential for controversy over Vietnam.[15]

Shortly afterwards, the United States Government sounded out the Australians about the possibility of Australia sending another 200 army advisers to Vietnam, together with 'such ground forces as Australia and New Zealand might be able to provide'.[16] The request was considered on 17 December by the Foreign Affairs and Defence Committee of cabinet, a recently constituted inner group comprising Menzies, McEwen (Deputy Prime Minister), Holt (Treasurer), Hasluck and Paltridge (Minister for Defence), soon supplemented by McMahon (Minister for Labour and National Service). This committee was empowered to take decisions without reference to the rest of cabinet. Instead of responding to the request for advisers, the committee indicated that Australia would be willing, if formally requested by the Government of South Vietnam, to send a battalion of ground troops to Vietnam.[17]

Historians have agreed in identifying this as the moment when Australia's traumatic involvement in the Vietnam con-flict became virtually inevitable. The decision went beyond the advice offered to Hasluck by officials of the Department of External Affairs. On 15 December, Tange had submitted a memorandum recommending that cabinet should not come to any specific decisions about military or civil aid without further study: 'The specific possibility of introducing ground forces needs the most careful study. It is at present far from clear what role they would have'.[18] On the other hand, the chiefs of staff of the armed forces, chaired by the hawkish Air Marshal Sir Frederick Scherger,[19] told the cabinet committee that despite

Australia's other commitments in the region a battalion could be found for service in Vietnam. Tange was deeply chagrined that cabinet preferred this 'low quality advice', giving 'military judgments on what was essentially a strategic question', rather than the cautious view from within External Affairs. Thirty years later he still blamed Hasluck for failing to communicate the department's arguments to his cabinet colleagues.[20] But Hasluck always took the position that he as minister was the gatekeeper who sifted departmental advice before deciding what should be submitted to cabinet.

Hasluck's Christmas holidays in Perth offered no respite from the international situation. With Menzies away on a recuperative overseas trip, it fell to Hasluck to monitor Australia's foreign policy, and it was becoming no easier to balance the conflicting demands of the Vietnam and Malaysian crises. Australia's commitment to send troops to Vietnam was not yet inevitable. The political situation in South Vietnam was deteriorating, but although President Johnson had secured a second term of office, it was still impossible to judge the intentions of the United States. From Washington, Waller wrote on 22 December that 'the signs of a robust and possibly successful American policy in South Vietnam are vanishing rapidly'.[21] Hasluck responded by asking for careful and constructive discussions about the future, but Waller replied that William Bundy considered

too much speculation was involved for there to be any profitable discussion…If the position turned out very badly, the first priority would be to shore up Thailand and in this task the United States would need help. The shock would also be felt in Malaysia…[22]

The confrontation between Indonesia and Malaysia showed no sign of abating. In January 1965 Indonesia, taking umbrage at the election of Malaysia to the Security Council, walked out of the United Nations. The Australian cabinet decided on 27 January to commit a battalion to Borneo, even though it meant stretching military resources if Australia had to cover the commitment of a battalion to Vietnam. To Waller, Hasluck wrote,

I am also moving towards the view that in the coming years the interaction between events in Vietnam and in Indonesia will increase with disturbing effects unless each of these situations, now apparently separate, can be cleared up more quickly.[23]

At the same time, he expressed the fear that the United States would slip into 'negotiation by default' in Vietnam before communist aggression had been seen to fail.

Although Hasluck hoped personal contacts would 'bring certainty to American policy and planning',[24] neither Waller nor Renouf at the Washington Embassy nor Paltridge on a visit to the United States in February could provide that certainty. American aircraft were escalating their strikes against Viet Cong strongholds in North Vietnam, but their targets had not yet extended to Hanoi or other regional centres. The United States had yet to make a major commitment of ground forces, and might still accept the British preference for a further round of negotiations. Hasluck was convinced that talks would be futile unless backed by a show of strength. He no longer hoped that the Sino-Soviet split would lead the Russians into backing negotiations as a means of checking China's influence in South-East Asia. Instead the Soviet leader, Kosygin, visited

Hanoi in February in a show of support. It could be thought that the communist bloc was reuniting, but in fact Kosygin was ensuring that North Vietnam, with its habitual mistrust of its giant neighbour China, would look to the Soviet Union as its patron.

Day followed day without a lead from Washington. When an American official, Michael Forrestal, visited Canberra in February, Hasluck could only reiterate that Australia was able and willing to provide a combat battalion if required. He apparently took no notice when Tange, still lingering in his role as head of department, expressed strong opposition to 'Australian participation in Vietnam in the form of Army units, simply for the purpose of improving our case for having a voice in policy'.[25] At last, in late February the Americans said they were ready for military staff talks at Honolulu. Sir Frederick Scherger, would represent Australia.

This caused concern among the departmental officers in External Affairs. Scherger was known to be a bellicose Cold War warrior, but he was also very well regarded by Menzies, by whom he was promoted to the rank of air chief marshal in 1965; Scherger was the only senior officer of the armed forces whom Menzies considered at all appointable if an Australian were to be Governor-General.[26] The External Affairs officials were concerned to ensure that the staff talks did not commit Australia further, but Hasluck took the view that the talks were wholly military in character. The time for political advice would come when cabinet received Scherger's report. Hasluck was procedurally correct, but he may not have known that Scherger probably went with Menzies' authority to make a firm offer of a combat battalion.[27]

When parliament met in March 1965, Hasluck delivered a major speech setting out his view of international relations as grounded in power politics. 'We might like it otherwise, but we cannot ignore the fact.' Although humankind was creeping towards sanity about the use of nuclear weapons, there was a global struggle that could be contained only when nations accepted agreed principles of international conduct. (The Soviet Union could be seen as more or less conforming to this under-standing, but Communist China was less predictable.) This struggle could not be regionalised, although Australia's interests were necessarily and immediately concerned with East and South-East Asia. The United States could not withdraw from South Vietnam 'without necessarily considering the world-wide impact of such a withdrawal on the broader strategies of world politics'.[28] An experienced academic commentator, Gordon Greenwood, praised the speech:

The impressive logic of the argument, the cohesive comprehension, the personal perception, and the effective blend of realism and positive thinking must rank this as among the best, perhaps *the* best foreign affairs statement ever made in Parliament.[29]

It was a generous tribute from one historian to another; but some months later Arthur Calwell made a pertinent comment:

[Hasluck's] great fondness for his world power struggle theory...I suspect derives from his desire, as an historian – and a very distinguished one – to provide a consistent and self-contained philosophical basis for his activities and attitudes, in a Department which works in a sphere that is full of inconsistencies and contradictions.[30]

In the messy world of diplomacy, Calwell suggested, solutions could not be reduced to world power struggles. He may have put his finger on a major reason for the tensions between Hasluck and some of his departmental officers.

Meanwhile, the United States committed itself to escalating the ground war in Vietnam. In March the first marines landed at Da Nang. This sharpened the need to define the role of the allied forces in Vietnam. Would an Australian battalion be limited in its role to security and conventional combat duties, or would it 'have the job of winkling out Vietcong terrorists and safeguarding hamlets and protecting villages'?[31] The Defence Committee, made up of senior officials from the Prime Minister's Department and the departments of External Affairs and Defence, considered that greater clarity on these issues was needed before the battalion was committed. Their view was reinforced by Sir John Bunting, the very experienced secretary of the Prime Minister's Department. But it would be the hawks who prevailed on 7 April, when the six senior cabinet ministers who formed the Foreign Affairs and Defence Committee met in response to a formal American request for 150 Australian instructors.

Scherger was present and spoke first. He urged that a battalion be sent rather than the instructors as requested. He airily assumed that the United States would not use the Australian forces 'in any way to which we objected'. Hasluck immediately responded, putting the case for delay. He questioned Australia's capacity to be engaged in both Borneo and Vietnam, with the added possibility of an Indonesian threat to Papua New Guinea. Australia should consult with its allies 'to look over the whole South East Asian picture and assess the most useful total way in which our forces could be used'.[32] He was about to travel to a SEATO conference in London, where he hoped to find out more about the attitudes of the United States and Britain, and perhaps also the communist powers.

Hasluck was not repudiating the option of sending a combat battalion, but it was never his view that Australia should offer Washington a blank cheque. There was still some lack of clarity about the purposes for which an Australian battalion would be used, and indeed about the whole thrust of American strategy. Probably Hasluck felt it was time to temper Scherger's eagerness for involvement by reasserting civilian authority. The advice from his own senior departmental officers, such as Patrick Shaw and Gordon Jockel, suggested caution, and they were reinforced by Bunting, whom he respected. Tange was no longer on the scene, having at last been replaced by Sir James Plimsoll, who was also a voice for restraint. Hasluck would have listened to him as he would not have listened to Tange. The case for delay was strong.

Menzies would have none of it. The commitment must be made immediately. Holt backed him up; so did McEwen, although he candidly admitted that political rather than military considerations justified sending the battalion. Paltridge shared Hasluck's reservations, but was soon silenced. To Hasluck's mortification, only McMahon sided with him. Woodard has argued that Hasluck knuckled under because he was dependent on Menzies' good opinion, but this is to undervalue Hasluck's consistent loyalty to the concept of cabinet solidarity, of supporting the majority decision even when it differed from one's own. He was to stick to this principle even with prime ministers Holt and Gorton, whom he respected less than Menzies. But there was a price. As he put it, he sometimes felt that he 'was the wrong driver in the wrong truck'.[33]

Some insight into Hasluck's reservations emerge from the 20 April meeting of the interdepartmental defence committee.[34] There, Plimsoll, representing External Affairs, tried to secure a written assurance that if the Australian battalion in Vietnam were needed for a crisis nearer home, for example in Papua New Guinea, the United States command would facilitate its withdrawal and provide transport. Hasluck, who had spent the crucial years of the war in Canberra, knew that in 1942 after Japan entered the war the Australian Prime Minister, John Curtin, had insisted that troops forming part of the Allied forces in North Africa should be returned to defend their own region. He resisted the British Prime Minister, Winston Churchill, who wanted to divert the Australians to a hopeless campaign in Burma. Plimsoll's request could be seen as anticipating the need to resolve a similar conflict of interest between Australia and its allies in the 1960s, but the proposal was ruled out as impractical by Chief of the General Staff General Sir John Wilton. He considered that such a request, involving an unlikely contingency, would make a bad impression on the Americans.[35]

The decision to send a battalion was not announced to parliament until 29 April, as it was necessary to persuade the South Vietnamese Government led by Dr Phan Huy Quat to issue a formal invitation welcoming Australian troops. It had not arrived when on 29 April somebody in the know – probably McMahon – leaked news of the commitment to the Sydney

Daily Telegraph. Hardly before Quat's request arrived, Menzies informed the House of Representatives of the decision. Hasluck was off the scene, having departed for the SEATO meeting in London. The public reaction was largely acquiescent. Even in the universities, despite a substantial minority of dissenters, the decision was largely supported. Few foresaw how contentious and divisive the Vietnam commitment would become.[36]

The decision to send troops to Vietnam came at a time when change seemed likely in Australian politics. Menzies, having restored his mastery of parliament, was by several years the oldest and longest serving of Australia's prime ministers. He had been known to say that a politician should think of retiring when he attained the age of seventy, and in December 1964 he reached that milestone. In 1963 the Queen had conferred upon him the distinction of Knight of the Thistle, an acknowledgement of Menzies' Scottish ancestry and an award second only to the Garter in the hierarchy of British knighthoods. He could retire gracefully with his honours thick upon him. For several years it had been accepted that the Treasurer, Harold Holt, would succeed him as Liberal Party leader and Prime Minister. Half a generation younger than Menzies, but with many years of ministerial experience, Holt was expected to provide a modernising look to a ministry grown old in office. Few challenged him overtly, but Sydney Liberals were known to grumble at the apparent stranglehold of the Victorians on the party's leadership, and some wondered if Holt, although experienced, diligent and amiable, had the necessary steel for the office.

If they looked beyond Holt, the next most senior Liberal ministers were Hasluck and McMahon. Both entered the House of Representatives in 1949, and both had held ministerial office continuously since 1951. Hasluck's portfolio of External Affairs was senior to any McMahon had so far held, but even after fifteen years he was still seen as something of a loner in parliamentary life, and remote Western Australia was not an ideal power base for building up parliamentary support. McMahon, on the other hand, had become the senior New South Wales Liberal on Barwick's retirement. He was an assiduous cultivator of the media, all too close to Sir Frank Packer's press, whose holdings included the Sydney *Daily Telegraph* and *The Bulletin*.

In contrast, Hasluck disdained publicity and over the years had developed distaste for his old craft of journalism. Nevertheless, in 1964 or 1965 he had been sounded out about his interest in contesting the leadership after Menzies retired, and had replied that he was not interested for three reasons: one, that he did not want the job; two, that he had no wish to destabilise the party; and three, that his wife thought he would not have the temperament for it. He made a point of telling Holt that he was not a rival for the leadership and would support him, but this did not prevent gossip from asserting that the members from 'the smaller States' were trying to 'whip up enthusiasm for Paul Hasluck'.[37]

Menzies in any case seemed in no hurry. He cruised through his seventy-first year with undiminished dominance, although once or twice Hasluck noted symptoms of ageing in the Prime Minister. Hasluck, after his one moment of doubt about entry into the Vietnam conflict, was perceived by many as Menzies' man, carrying out without question his leader's loyal adherence to great and powerful allies. The reality was more complex. Menzies and Hasluck were both uneasy about the possibility that Britain's financial constraints would force it to withdraw its armed forces from South-East Asia, but Hasluck had the livelier awareness of the need to build up good relations with the emerging Asian powers.

In June, Menzies and Hasluck visited London and Washington, accompanied by their wives. During the English leg of the journey there were some agreeable interludes such as a grand commemoration of the 750th anniversary of Magna Carta. The Haslucks spent a summer Sunday visiting their son Nicholas at Oxford before proceeding to lunch at the manor house of Lord Carrington,[38] recently Britain's High Commissioner in Australia. Here Lord Carrington, whom Alexandra Hasluck described as 'looks like P. G. Wodehouse's Bertie Wooster, but a keen mind', regaled his guests with political comment ('he damns all the Labour Party Ministers as boors and fools', Alexandra reported, 'and really they're not'), and after lunch set them to playing croquet.[39] The main official business in London was a meeting of Commonwealth prime ministers, at which the Australians found themselves parrying growing pressure from the Afro-Asian members to condemn the white minority government in Rhodesia. South-East Asia gained little attention. Most of the Commonwealth countries, though not the Australians, were content with an optimistic British proposal for a peace mission to Vietnam.[40]

Hasluck found that although nearly all the members of SEATO expressed support for South Vietnam, only Thailand and the Philippines favoured military intervention by the United States and Australia, while Pakistan and France were against it.[41] The British Secretary for Defence, Denis Healey,[42] was sympathetic, but warned that many government backbenchers were not, and that Britain's defence policy was heavily influenced by financial constraints. This sounded a warning that would haunt Hasluck's term at External Affairs: Britain might not be able to maintain a presence in South-East Asia for much longer. Australia must either take on increased responsibilities or cling more closely to the American alliance.

Both in London and Washington, Menzies had a simplified and bellicose message explaining Australia's involvement in Vietnam. Australia, he proclaimed, was 'lying in the shadow of an increasingly powerful and belligerent China and an unpredictable and irresponsible Indonesia'.[43] Hasluck's rhetoric was much more nuanced:

> He did not refer to a communist tide sweeping the Timor Sea, but said that a Viet Cong victory in South Vietnam would lead to instability and conflict in Southeast Asia.[44]

Laos would be edged out of neutrality into the communist orbit; communists on the Malaysian border might resume armed insurrection; and the opponents of communism in Indonesia would be discouraged. But, as Edwards wryly comments: 'This more restrained and cogent statement of the Government's position, although reported in the press, attracted less attention than Menzies' bolder statements'.[45]

Other opportunities of putting the government's case presented themselves during the winter parliamentary recess. Unlike every other Australian participation in overseas campaigns – the two world wars, Korea and Malaysia in the past, Iraq and Afghanistan in the future – Vietnam would involve the use in combat of national servicemen who had not volunteered to serve overseas. At the same time, the recent arrival of television in Australian households meant that the civilians at home could gain a much more realistic view of front-line conditions than had ever been possible in the past. Majority support still rested with the government, but public opinion must continue to be persuaded.

During the early months of 1965, American universities had developed the concept of the 'teach-in', mass meetings often lasting many hours in which speakers debated the issues of the Vietnam War. It was not long before the model was taken up on Australian campuses. The first teach-in, at the Australian National University on 23 July, lasted from early evening until 3.30 am. By all accounts it was a civilised and informative exchange of strongly held views between academics, writers and students. In such an academic setting a minister might venture to put the government's viewpoint, and Hasluck agreed to speak at the next teach-in scheduled six days later at the recently established Monash University. It turned out to be a much more emotionally charged occasion. Between 1,500 and 2,000 attended, more than twice the number of the Canberra teach-in. The debate lasted from 3.00 pm until after midnight, and drew extensive television and press coverage. Before an audience consisting largely of students in wet duffel coats and anoraks, the participants spoke under the able chairmanship of Professor D. G. E. Hall, a visiting senior academic with an international reputation as historian of South-East Asia. It seemed a first-class opportunity for Hasluck to argue the government's case in a major public forum.[46]

It was a fiasco. Even Louis Matheson, the judicious and even-handed Vice-Chancellor of Monash University, 'didn't think Hasluck very convincing'.[47] Peter Samuel, a journalist who had spoken in favour of the Vietnam intervention at the Canberra teach-in, reported that Hasluck 'rambled through the most complex, repetitive, and incomprehensible passages to recurrent jeers and sarcastic clapping'.[48] In putting a case that was unacceptable to a significant section of his audience, Hasluck's presentation was too low-key and unemotional, and he was unsettled by the barrage of hostile interjections from 'a group close to the stage of about thirty or forty people who cheered vehemently at statements of Jim Cairns, and hooted derisively at every possible opportunity at Hasluck'.[49] He controlled his temper, but in so doing lost effect. On the other side his main parliamentary opponent, Dr Jim Cairns, adapted quickly to the atmosphere of the forum, and was at his most persuasively eloquent. He made little attempt to refute Hasluck's arguments, but struck an appealing note of moral passion, and had the audience eating out of his hand. He was the star turn of the teach-in, whereas Hasluck's standing had been damaged. *The Bulletin* wrote of him that he had missed his chance of proving himself under difficult circumstances, so that it was 'hard to see him as Prime Minister'.[50]

Hasluck was not given to calculating whether he was building up a reputation as a potential prime minister, but he must have been chagrined by his experience. Outwardly he did not talk about his disappointment, but during the rest of 1965 his outbreaks of bad temper were more frequent than usual, suggesting a man barely suppressing internal pressures. The most memorable episode came unexpectedly in the House of Representatives on a quiet night in September 1965, during a low-key debate on pensions for the armed services. Whitlam, as deputy leader of the opposition, was drawing attention to an anomaly excluding Salvation Army officers who had given service and amenities to the armed forces from participating in veterans' benefits. It was 2.00 am, and Hasluck came in to advise the minister in charge of the bill under discussion that the debate would be adjourned. Never one to resist the impromptu gibe, Whitlam said:

> If the Minister for External Affairs is prepared to deny his parents in voting against justice for Salvation Army personnel who have served with the Forces, then I suppose we need not worry about persons with less propriety and pride voting against all the principles which they so loudly espouse during the daytime and on sacred occasions.[51]

Hasluck was stung; Nicholas Hasluck records that his father

> speaking sotto voce across the table, responded to the effect that it was a filthy form of debate to drag one's father into a current political issue, and that Whitlam's own father would have disapproved.[52]

Whitlam decided that Hasluck needed cooling down, and emptied a glass of water over him. Apologies quickly followed, first from Whitlam, then from Hasluck, who said: 'The remark was made in a personal and direct way. It was not part of the proceedings of Parliament'.[53] Journalists were fond of recalling the fracas for years to come, though the incident was far from the last word on what Nicholas Hasluck has described as 'a complex relationship extending over many years…momentarily reduced to a splash of water'.[54]

Meanwhile, Hasluck as spokesman for the government was trying to parry the impression made by the opponents of the

Vietnam War at the teach-ins. When the opposition moved in parliament for a ceasefire in Vietnam, to be policed by a United Nations peacekeeping force while South Vietnam and the Viet Cong entered into negotiations, Hasluck attempted to respond constructively. He suggested a return to the Geneva agreement of 1954:

> South Vietnam is entitled to its own administrative and territorial integrity, the future relationships between the south and the north are for the two parties to settle through processes of freely reached agreement. That could be a starting point for more widely-ranging negotiations aimed at establishing, with appropriate guarantees, the conditions under which the nations of South-East Asia can have some reasonable confidence in their future, be relieved of their present need to divert so much of their energy to fighting and be able, with help from their friends, to get on with the tasks of political, social and economic reconstruction, completing and consolidating the processes that brought them independence.[55]

An academic critic complained that the goal of returning to the Geneva agreement left important questions unanswered, but suggested the Menzies government had to stick to it because

> the United States government, with which almost the whole initiative in this matter lies, has extremely flexible peace aims and would, in all probability, settle for less than the Australian government thinks desirable.[56]

In retrospect, Hasluck was inclined to believe that the government, in presenting its case to the public,

> relied too much on the printed word and too much on proper
> procedures…All we could do was respond by putting out
> pieces of paper, you know all those pamphlets, putting out
> the documents and hoping that the intelligent sensible people
> would take an hour or so to read the documents and draw their
> own conclusions.[57]

The protest movement showed much more readiness to take advantage of film and television opportunities. It was one of the most pointed examples of the generational difference separating Hasluck and his colleagues from the young critics of the Vietnam involvement.

Other problems of foreign policy crowded in on Hasluck's attention. In August 1965 Malaysia agreed to allow Singapore to secede and become an independent state. This gave rise to fears that the Malaysian federation would fragment, with the Borneo states of Sabah and Sarawak striking out on their own and perhaps falling into Indonesia's sphere of influence.[58] Hasluck told parliament that the Malaysian area would continue to be 'one theatre, operating under one operational system and governed by a common purpose', though he admitted that 'considerable difficulties would be raised for us if it were a matter of entering into possibly different commitments with a variety of authorities'.[59] The main problem was whether any political instability would encourage Britain to withdraw from its Singapore base, but for the remainder of 1965 this did not seem an immediate possibility. Meanwhile, Indonesia underwent a startling shift of direction.

At the beginning of October 1965, following what was thought to be an attempted Communist coup, an army junta led by General Soeharto seized power in Indonesia. Suspected communists and their friends were firmly suppressed – the extent of the slaughter remained unknown for some time – and Soekarno was reduced to a figurehead. Hasluck monitored the situation cautiously. In his first parliamentary statement on 19 October, he devoted himself mainly to stressing that 'On a significant scale political parties and national bodies are reducing or eliminating communist influence within their organisations. The populace', he told a backbencher, 'has had an opportunity to demonstrate in a very emphatic manner its abhorrence of all Communist doctrines'.[60] If the new regime began the work of economic reconstruction, Australia would support the granting of 'genuinely disinterested international assistance' to it.[61] It took time before Indonesia's future directions clarified, and it still required patience and subtlety to ensure that Australia maintained good relations with Indonesia, but the task was easier under the new regime. Few if any in Australia raised the question of whether the setback to the communists in Indonesia lessened the necessity of the Vietnam commitment.

Hasluck was less involved in the crisis developing in Rhodesia (now Zimbabwe), where the white settler minority was staunchly resisting British plans to empower the African majority. Menzies, as the elder statesman of the British Commonwealth, attempted to play the role of mediator, handling much of these negotiations himself. The British Government wanted him to head a mission to Rhodesia in the hope of finding grounds for a settlement, but the Rhodesians rejected the overture. Instead, on 11 November 1965 they made their unilateral declaration of independence, and all that remained for Australia was to consider demands from the Afro-Asian members of the Commonwealth to impose sanctions and penalties on the new regime. Hasluck's position was not made easier by the fact that some of his Liberal Party colleagues, such as Jim Killen and Malcolm Mackay, strongly supported the rebel settlers. Hasluck himself appealed to the House of Representatives to put themselves in the white settlers' place 'and to think of ourselves as having established our homes there'[62] but nevertheless the government banned the export of arms to Rhodesia and the import of Rhodesian tobacco. Australia did not attend the conference of Commonwealth prime ministers that met at Lagos in Nigeria early in January 1966, not wishing to collude in precedents for members of the Commonwealth to intervene in the domestic jurisdiction of fellow members.

Hasluck was still behaving like a man under pressure. In December he visited Vietnam and other parts of South-East Asia, and drew some encouragement from what he saw. The Government of South Vietnam, he thought, now led by Prime Minister Air Vice Marshal Nguyen Cao Ky, was 'more realistic and purposeful compared with some of its predecessors'.[63] Despite this hopeful view, on his return to Sydney he disconcerted reporters waiting for a press conference by marching past them and slamming the door. Two years earlier, in very similar circumstances, Barwick had lost his temper, shouting at the reporters and 'purple with rage'.[64] Barwick's outburst attracted little criticism, but Hasluck was no favourite with the press. Unlike McMahon, who would be his main rival for the deputy leadership of the Liberal Party when Menzies retired, he made no attempt to cultivate the Packer and Murdoch media.

The reaction was predictably critical. *The Australian* wrote that Hasluck was 'arrogant, doctrinaire, patronizing and disdainful of public opinion', and called for his resignation.[65] In the *Sydney Morning Herald* Ian Fitchett thought that Hasluck harmed his reputation 'not so much for his refusal to grant a Press inter-view…as by the petulant and bad-tempered manner in which he did so'.[66]

Some influential people showed greater appreciation of Hasluck. On New Year's Day 1966 he was made a member of the British Privy Council. Originally the body of select advisers to the reigning monarch, the Privy Council had become largely honorific by the mid-twentieth century, except that at that time its judicial committee still had power to hear appeals in some areas from the Australian High Court.[67] The importance of the distinction lay in the fact that, as the London *Times* commented, outside its British members it was usually confined to the prime ministers of British Commonwealth countries.[68] The implication was that in the eyes of the British authorities and of Menzies, who recommended him, Hasluck was of prime ministerial quality.

This was significant because in January 1966 Menzies resigned. Holt was elected without opposition as leader of the party on Hasluck's nomination. The Governor-General, Richard Casey (for at last Menzies had consented to appointing an Australian to the post), swore him in as Prime Minister. Hasluck and McMahon contested the deputy leadership.[69] McMahon canvassed members of the party and worked his contacts with the media. Hasluck did virtually nothing, taking the view that his performance was on the record and his colleagues would vote for him if they thought fit. Even so, he ran McMahon close, but lost the election. David Fenbury, formerly one of Hasluck's senior officials in Papua New Guinea, wrote to commiserate: 'I think they've made a mistake, but time will prove this. Perhaps you didn't trundle your barrow noisily enough'.[70] A ministerial colleague, Leslie Bury, later said that Hasluck's defeat was 'the most serious break in the fortunes of the Liberal Party':

> This was the first time I recalled the Party being subjected to high pressure voting tactics, and people brought in from outside to exercise their influence...I regarded Paul Hasluck as infinitely superior to McMahon as a potential Deputy Leader, and regarded it as a very sad event when he was not elected as Deputy Leader.[71]

Less than a year later, Menzies himself wrote that he was not surprised that the party chose McMahon as deputy leader, but added that if the vote had been for the prime ministership Hasluck would have beaten him easily.[72]

If he had been deputy leader two years later when Holt drowned, he would surely have become prime minister. Fate determined otherwise.

Chapter 19

Elder statesman

Hasluck could not have the same relationship with Holt as he had with Menzies. He could defer to Menzies' seniority, authority and grasp of politics, but he held the new Prime Minister in no such respect. Although he acknowledged Holt's popularity and industry, Hasluck thought him lacking in intellectual depth.[1] At the personal level, Harold and Zara Holt moved in a sophisticated ambience of flash Melbourne café society that the Haslucks disliked. Alexandra Hasluck was critical of Zara Holt's bubbly personality and exuberant dress sense.[2] When the press published photographs of Harold Holt in spear fisherman's outfit with his three daughters-in-law in bikinis, Hasluck's reaction was wowserish: Robert Menzies 'would not have exposed the naked bodies of his family in the newspapers'.[3] But he soon settled down to the role of the experienced old retainer loyally supporting his leader and allowing no word of criticism to escape to the wider world.

Within the Department of External Affairs his working relationship with Plimsoll was close, even though they met only once a week for a discussion. Hasluck tended to use Plimsoll as a virtual deputy. In recognition of Plimsoll's impressive role a few years previously as Australia's representative at the United Nations, he more than once sent Plimsoll to stand in for him at meetings of the General Assembly. Old Tange loyalists among the officers of the department, to whom Hasluck remained a somewhat remote and forbidding figure, complained that Plimsoll's 'conventional ideological convictions and style of conformity to Hasluck's view of the unique relationship between minister and secretary inhibited vigorous debate'.[4] This was a superficial reading of the relationship.

Plimsoll was the soul of correctness as a senior public servant. In his private thoughts he may have dissented from some of Hasluck's views – there are indications of doubts about the Vietnam intervention – but if he tried to influence them, his methods were subtle and tactful in contrast to Tange's confronting style. He was widely reputed to have in his office a capacious bottom drawer into which potentially contentious documents vanished for long periods. Hasluck, vexed at media reports on Australian foreign policy, demanded that the Department of External Affairs have the right to vet material broadcast on Radio Australia. Plimsoll managed to shelve the proposal so effectively that it was quietly dropped.[5]

During Hasluck's time, Australia substantially expanded its overseas representation. New embassies were opened in fourteen countries, mostly in Asia and Africa. Recruitment into the department expanded as a result, but not enough could be done to ensure that the administrative structure of the department was streamlined to meet the increase. Although Hasluck was by now thoroughly experienced in bringing convincing submissions for funding to the cabinet, the response was not always the one that best suited the department's priorities. Whereas Tange, a strong administrator, had held the department together largely through his own experience and force of personality, Plimsoll candidly acknowledged that he had little taste for administration, and he was not backed by a deputy who could have made good this shortcoming. It was not Hasluck's business to deal with the problem, as public-service regulations specified that such matters were the responsibility of the permanent head. As it was, it was only when Sir Keith Waller succeeded Plimsoll as secretary to the department in 1970 that reform was initiated.

Hasluck described himself as cooperating with three senior civil servants – Bunting in the Prime Minister's Department, Plimsoll in External Affairs and Hicks in Defence – in 'nursing' Holt into considered habits of decision-making:

> we worked very closely and agreeably together and, I think, succeeded in avoiding many dangers and turning his thoughts towards reality and, to a steadily increasing extent, towards the major issues.[6]

In fact, it seems he took the initiative in calling them into his office

> and more or less said that they would of course be loyal to the Prime Minister as they were expected to be, but that they might have to wear some decisions which they didn't much like, and they would have to do their best to restrain Holt's impetuosity.[7]

It is significant that they were willing to go along with the idea, and it is revealing that Hasluck identified with the seasoned public servants rather than his fellow politicians. He considered that politicians like Holt tended to think that an easy manner and the establishment of first-name terms were enough to clinch the friendship of foreign leaders. But Holt and Hasluck agreed on fundamentals, notably the need for continuing engagement in South-East and East Asia, and the importance of a forward defence policy.

Within a fortnight of Menzies' retirement, there came a hint that the old certainties of the British Commonwealth might be questioned. On 1 and 2 February, Denis Healey, Britain's Secretary of State for Defence, visited Canberra for talks with senior Australian ministers. His message was reassuring. Britain would remain in South-East Asia, but requested the Australians to consider contingency plans, such as creating British bases in Australia in case Malaysia and Singapore had to be abandoned. The Australians suspected that if such ideas were given consideration, the British might be more ready to quit South-East Asia. Healey speculated about the neutralisation of Vietnam, an idea put forward by France; the Australians thought this would just be a step towards Chinese hegemony. Hasluck told Healey that the West might at some time face the choice of Chinese dominance or making a nuclear attack on China. In his memoirs, Healey subsequently wrote that apart from Hasluck the Australian ministers were not 'over-impressive'.[8]

When on 10 March Hasluck made a long-expected speech on foreign policy to parliament, it was criticised as 'pedestrian and stodgy'.[9] Certainly it introduced no new themes. Never one to consider that if a cause was unpopular it must be wrong, Hasluck continued steadfast in his view that the war was necessary. 'Peking, Hanoi, and the Viet Cong prefer war', he told the House of Representatives. 'Let us face the plain fact. They prefer war. They have chosen war. They have said so in plain and angry words.'[10] Talk of negotiation was futile, as anything short of a military victory would play into the hands of the enemy. 'Peking would be encouraged to push for more, and the hope and resolution of other countries in the region would be impaired.'[11] As opposition to the war became louder – though it was still a minority view as yet – Hasluck became more and more entrenched in his commitment to a cause whose outcome Australia, although a declared participant, would be powerless to influence. As he said in April to the United States Secretary for Defense, Robert McNamara: 'our best "cover" is that we are helping at [South Vietnamese] request, while our real reason is that we simply can't let the Communists succeed'.[12]

Holt, meanwhile, was enjoying his first international travel as Prime Minister. In a ten-day tour of South-East Asia in late April, he presented an image of engagement and vigour that made a welcome contrast to the staid anglophile Menzies.[13] Unfortunately, his increased confidence in his role led to some contentious moments of impulse. In June, on his first visit to Washington as Prime Minister, Holt was so pleased with President Johnson's friendly reception that in a speech made at the formal welcoming ceremony he spontaneously told his audience that he and his country would be 'an admiring friend, a staunch friend, that will be all the way with LBJ'.[14] In using Johnson's campaign slogan, Holt impressed the Americans as a loyal ally, but in doing so he undermined Hasluck's insistence that Australia should never be an unquestioning supporter of the United States.

This was not Holt's only venture taken without consulting External Affairs. In 1949, when Mao Zedong's communists ousted the Nationalist government of Chiang Kai-shek from mainland China, the latter established themselves in the offshore island of Taiwan, where they claimed to continue as the legitimate government of China. During the next sixteen years, Australia was among the Western powers that refrained from formally recognising this claim because of the difficulties it might create in future relations with mainland China. Suddenly, in June 1966, Holt – and not Hasluck – announced that Australia was extending diplomatic recognition to the Republic of China (Taiwan). Canberra folklore asserted that Holt's decision was taken after some generous hospitality from the Nationalist Chinese Embassy. Questioned about this story in retirement, Hasluck

> smiled and said he didn't know if that was true but he
> could certainly say that it was not as the result of a carefully
> considered Cabinet consideration of an External Affairs
> submission.[15]

It would have been impossible at that time to establish diplomatic contact with Communist China while that regime was undergoing the Great Proletarian Cultural Revolution. Launched by Mao in May 1966 with the stated aim of purging Chinese society of the lingering elements of traditional culture and capitalism, the movement led to violent factional struggles and the overthrow of many senior officials whose zeal was considered suspect. China's diplomatic corps was not exempt from this turbulence, nearly all the ambassadors being recalled from overseas. It was impossible to expect any reliable basis on which negotiations could be conducted to ease hostilities with the Western world, and in any case the United States was not yet ready to contemplate any such approach.

No change could be expected until the outcome of the fighting in Vietnam became clearer. During 1966 and 1967 the Americans and their allies still hoped that by increasing their military might they might eventually prevail over the Viet Cong and their allies in North Vietnam. Hasluck was one who continued to assert that the military situation in Vietnam was improving, and that the South Vietnamese Government now had a stable basis. The majority of the Australian public found this line persuasive. Before the general election in December 1966, Hasluck wrote: 'I cannot recall any campaign in which the portents have been so favourable to the Government'. Holt, he thought, had 'not yet commended himself to the middle block of Australian voters as a Prime Minister', however. There was 'some vague sort of hesitation about him' because 'grooming his personality has lessened his authority'.[16] Nevertheless, the Holt government was returned with a majority larger than Menzies had ever achieved.

Meanwhile, uncertainty continued about Britain's intentions in South-East Asia. In June the Government of Thailand, worried about subversion in the border areas with Cambodia and Laos, explored the possibility of support from their partners in SEATO,[17] including the United Kingdom, which were thought to have forces available now that Indonesia was no longer threatening Malaysia. The British were not at all willing, and this provoked Hasluck to ask the British Foreign Secretary, Michael Stewart, in what circumstances they might help. Referring to the suggestion that a British base might be established in Australia, he asked why British troops should be stationed in Australia while 'Australian troops went to Southeast Asia to man the ramparts'.[18] Shortly afterwards, Stewart was replaced as Foreign Secretary by George Brown, but he proved even less sympathetic. On their first encounter in Washington, he told Hasluck very bluntly that Britain was going to pull out.[19] It finally emerged in May 1967 that Britain intended to withdraw the bulk of its forces by 1970 and the whole of them in 1975.

If Britain withdrew, it was not because the Chinese were inhibited by the Cultural Revolution from fishing in troubled waters. In June 1967, Hasluck received a secret and confidential communication from the colonial secretary of Hong Kong, where riots allegedly stirred up by the communists were troubling that British outpost. Hasluck was asked to use his influence to win a statement in support of Britain from the Australian Government, perhaps accompanied by sending a warship to the region.[20] The crisis did not escalate, but the request did nothing to encourage optimism about China. From Australia's point of view this made it more than ever important that the American presence remain in the region.

During 1967 it seemed possible to hope that, despite the war, South Vietnam was consolidating. In January, Air Vice Marshal Cao Ky, now the South Vietnamese Vice President, visited Australia with his wife. To Australian cabinet ministers he 'made it quite clear that should the Chinese ever decide to invade North Vietnam and take over the country, then both North and South Vietnam would unite to deter the Chinese invasion',[21] but this does not seem to have had any influence on Australian assessments of the situation. Later in the year, elections were held in South Vietnam, and the Haslucks attended the inauguration of President Nguyen Van Thieu. There seemed to be an atmosphere of hope, but it was soon to prove illusory.[22]

Hasluck's own efforts were directed to building up constructive relationships with South-East Asia. In 1966 and 1967 he paid four visits to Indonesia and lost no opportunity of urging his colleagues to increase economic aid to the new regime. Supported by John McEwen, he fought in cabinet for an increased budget for overseas aid, but encountered resistance from Treasury.[23] He made every effort to encourage the improving relationships between Malaysia and Singapore with Indonesia and the Philippines. This side of his activities gained far less publicity than the continuing conflict in Vietnam, but in the long run it was to be of more lasting benefit to Australia's interests in the region.

In June 1967, the interminable tension between Israel and its Arab neighbours erupted into what has become known as the Six-Day War, ending in an expansion of the territory controlled by Israel. While supporting the United States and Britain in a generally pro-Israel stance, Australia did not wish needlessly to antagonise the Arab states, which were emerging as significant trading partners. From his departmental officers, Hasluck received advice favouring both the Arab and the Israeli points of view, and he actively worked on improving a rather bland statement of Australia's position drafted within the Department. In the view of an Israeli scholar:

> The process of policy formation at DEA during the 1967
> Middle East crisis can be characterised as professional and
> sophisticated...Hasluck himself proved to be an independent
> and innovative decision-maker, who, while taking into
> account the views of his lieutenants, formulated Australia's
> policies in line with his own perceptions as to the realistic

path – acceptable to both the Arab states and Israel – to the resolution of the Israeli–Arab conflict. In fact, something very like the Hasluck formula was eventually applied in September 1978 when Israel and Egypt, under US auspices, signed the Camp David peace accords.[24]

If Hasluck's chance of leaving an imprint on Australian foreign policy was not turning out as he might have imagined when he entered politics, his personal life seemed to be entering a mellow phase. His two sons were embarked on their careers, though their paths were very different. Rollo seemed to inherit some of the restless entrepreneurial spirit of his great-grandfather, old Lewis Hasluck. After leaving school he tried various jobs before becoming a partner in one of the first licensed nightclubs to enliven Perth's staid world of entertainment. In April 1965 he married a doctor's daughter, Jill Munro, of whose good looks and manners Alexandra approved. Meanwhile, Nicholas, having completed a successful first degree at The University of Western Australia, won a scholarship to Oxford, where he read law at Wadham College. There he became engaged to Sally Anne Bolton, and they were married in a Cotswold church on a winter's day in 1966.

As for Alexandra, as wife of the Minister for External Affairs, she was once more enjoying the role of consort and meeting interesting foreign dignitaries. She told Nicholas in Oxford that she and Paul were 'getting on better than we have done for years'.[25] Sometimes Paul and Alexandra engaged in uninhibited public squabbles, and she still indulged in a sniff of wifely superiority at his rare moments of relaxation. In London, when a night out was proposed with her son Nicholas and his fiancée, instead of a night of high culture Paul insisted on attending *Charlie Girl*, a musical whose composer was a young Western Australian, John Taylor. He said he did not want to see anything he had to think about, and enjoyed himself. But, wrote Alexandra:

> I found it rather feeble, and badly dressed. Nick was v[ery] superior about it, and Sally Anne said wonderingly it must have been on a long time because the dressing was almost old-fashioned and the mini-skirts too long.[26]

On another occasion in New York, Paul and Alexandra dined out at a small French restaurant where 'two female pianists of different ages...played the hit tunes of their generation. In no time at all, Paul was singing his old favourites'. As time went by 'the few patrons were all rather matey', and a convivial evening ended shortly before midnight with Paul kissing the hands of all the women present. The next morning, according to Alexandra,

> a pale and fragile Paul...said he was going for a walk and only wanted black coffee for breakfast...I was sympathetic that he had to pay for his pleasures, but privately just a little amused.[27]

Under the formal exterior of the middle-aged public man there still survived a refreshing touch of the larrikin, but the public saw only the gravitas of one who was maturing into an elder statesman.

In these years Alexandra Hasluck was increasingly afflicted with hip trouble, and found the social duties of a minister's wife trying. She decided to solve the problem by grooming her daughter-in-law Jill, Rollo's wife, as a suitable understudy. Preparing for an ECAFE[28] conference she told Jill: 'Keep in mind that you have had a very good education, you have beautiful manners, you have a splendid background of family and country'.[29] Paul Hasluck seemed not at all displeased with this arrangement. He may have drawn the line at the Holt family's bikinis, but he had no objection to being seen at official functions with a good-looking young woman with a stylish taste in miniskirts. Retired diplomats interviewed nearly forty years later recalled this pleasing sidelight on a senior minister in whom some were detecting a growing crustiness.[30]

This was not entirely surprising. During the second half of 1967, several incidents fed his growing dissatisfaction with Holt's leadership. In September 1967 there was a major debate in the Foreign Affairs and Defence Committee about sending extra aid to Vietnam. As yet not ready to envisage defeat in Vietnam, the Americans were incapable of finding any path to victory other than the commitment of ever greater military force. Holt favoured sending a third battalion as well as an increase in other forms of aid. Hasluck was against the proposal because it would leave Australia with few armed forces to spare in any other direction should the need arise, and he was initially supported by McMahon, Allen Fairhall and Alan Hulme. In the end Holt, who was eager to please President Johnson, won over enough support to get his way. It was decided that McMahon, who had an overseas journey scheduled, should communicate this decision to President Johnson or his senior colleagues,

> but Paul, out of a sense of injured pride, suddenly walked out
> of the meeting feeling that he had been by-passed...and that if

anyone was to convey the news to the President it should have been Paul himself.[31]

He was already vexed at McMahon's habit of interrupting during cabinet discussions.

The issue that touched Hasluck most deeply was what he saw as a slight to his long commitment to Aboriginal policy. In May 1967, Australian voters said yes, by a national majority of more than 90 per cent, to a proposal to amend the constitution by removing two sections that discriminated against Aboriginal people by asserting they should not be numbered in reckoning the population of the Commonwealth. The reform was widely perceived as empowering the Commonwealth to legislate on behalf of Aboriginal Australians, as well as vindicating Hasluck's long-held belief that Aboriginal people should be regarded as Australian citizens on the same basis as those of settler ancestry. Unfortunately, the outcome only served to feed Hasluck's discontent with Holt's approach to governance.

The referendum awoke Holt to the fact that the public was ready for strong Commonwealth leadership. Recognising his own lack of experience in the field, he remembered that Nugget Coombs, the long-serving governor of the Reserve Bank, had gained experience of creating a new administrative agency from scratch with the Department of Post-War Reconstruction in the 1940s. He accordingly consulted Coombs, who

suggested that the Prime Minister as an interim solution should establish a small Council backed by a small but powerful research staff to identify the major problems, to establish communication with Aboriginal groups, and then to submit…plans for a continuing organisation.[32]

Holt seized on the idea enthusiastically, and in November 1967 set up a three-man council chaired by Coombs himself, together with a former diplomat, Barrie Dexter, and the respected anthropologist Bill Stanner, who was shortly to deliver his seminal series of Boyer lectures on 'the great Australian silence'.

Hasluck was not consulted, and he felt the slight keenly.

> When I heard of the decisions it seemed to me that Holt may purposely have excluded me…Perhaps he worked on the principle that if you are getting a new broom, you do not mess about with the old broom.[33]

A few months later, after Holt's death, Dexter wrote to Hasluck suggesting a meeting with him, Coombs and Stanner. If the meeting took place, it led to no convergence between Hasluck's ideas and the line that the three-man council was to develop. Coombs, who had previously accepted assimilation as the goal of Australia's Aboriginal policy, now came around to the view that special measures were required that took more account of the distinctive features of Aboriginal culture. Hasluck's concept of assimilation, he felt, placed too much stress on shaping individuals to fit into mainstream society, and too little on the attachment felt by many Aboriginal Australians to family and country. When governments tried to provide services for Aboriginal people by methods based on European societies, 'they cut across the traditional lines of responsibility and impair the division of labour to which the communities are accustomed'.[34] Special arrangements should be designed to fit their needs.

Hasluck thought that in a multicultural society such as modern Australia

> people can retain most of their cultural identity but not those elements in their culture that may be in conflict with the standards of the society of which they have become members or which may cause disruption in social organization.[35]

He felt that too great an insistence on the separate needs of Aboriginal Australians would in time isolate them from the rest of the community, with a potential for future conflict. Ample provision should be made for social services such as health and education, but these should be allocated on a basis of need without regard to racial background. The debate continues nearly half a century later, with little sign of an ultimate resolution.

Chapter 20

The road to Yarralumla

On the afternoon of 17 December 1967, Paul Hasluck in Canberra phoned his wife in Perth to tell her that Harold Holt had disappeared while swimming in rough water off Portsea, and could be presumed drowned:

> She asked me about myself, and I said that I did not want the
> prime ministership, had too little regard for many members of
> the Liberal Party to wish to lead them, and in any case, I had
> been 'rubbished' so successfully by McMahon and undermined
> so much by Harold himself that I doubted anyone would
> want me.[1]

On the same evening, Hasluck and John Gorton were guests at a small supper party given by the High Commissioner for New Zealand.[2] Inevitably, the talk turned to the unexpected succession crisis for the prime ministership. John McEwen, Deputy Prime Minister and leader of the Country Party, would be sworn in as caretaker Prime Minister. Some speculated that his experience and standing entitled him to be confirmed in the post, but custom dictated that, as senior partner in the Coalition, the Liberals would expect their leader to be selected.

After dinner Hasluck and Gorton discussed the next step. There was no obvious heir. McMahon was deputy leader of the federal Liberal Party, but Hasluck was not the only one of his colleagues who had a poor opinion of him, and McEwen quickly made it plain that the Country Party would not accept him as prime minister. Hasluck was the only other cabinet minister of appropriate seniority, but felt unsuitable because of his age and doubts about his standing in the party. He apparently put it to Gorton that he might, as the senior government minister in the Senate, consider making a bid for the leadership. He could move to the House of Representatives by contesting Holt's safe seat and take over as prime minister.

Within a day or two Hasluck reviewed the situation. Gorton had been in parliament as long as Hasluck, but his rise to the frontbenches had been much slower. Less amenable to party discipline and less predictable in his enthusiasms, he rose nevertheless to the leadership of the Senate Liberals in 1966 after a spate of retirements. He made a good impression on the public, especially through an unusual degree of candour. With a good war record and a larrikin charm, he might be expected to appeal to many voters. But some of his party colleagues thought him unsafe, and this view was shared by the elder statesman Menzies, still vigorous in retirement. Menzies also thought that if Gorton were chosen, the Liberals would be announcing that, despite having a great numerical majority, they could not find a Liberal member in the House of Representatives who was fit to serve as prime minister.[3] Menzies and others put it to Hasluck that it was his duty to throw his hat into the ring. As so often, it took prompting from others to bring Hasluck to the point of decision.

Having convinced himself that it was his duty, he sent a letter to his colleagues announcing that he would be a candidate, and then busied himself with the duties that fell upon him as Minister for External Affairs as a horde of distinguished leaders from around the world descended on Melbourne for Holt's memorial service. Hasluck then went to Perth for the Christmas holidays. While there he received a phone call from McMahon offering his support if Hasluck would confirm him as deputy leader.[4] Hasluck's antipathy to McMahon was too great for him to consider the proposal, although it might have delivered him a useful platoon of New South Wales votes. As it was, McMahon's supporters in New South Wales spread the rumour that Hasluck would oust McMahon as Treasurer, and steered support towards Gorton.[5]

Meanwhile, two more contenders appeared: Leslie Bury and Bill Snedden.[6] Both could be seen as staking claims for the future rather than immediate prospects. Gorton seemed the frontrunner, with Hasluck as his main challenger. From the British High Commission in Canberra, Sir Charles Johnston advised Whitehall that Hasluck was

> a reticent man with a somewhat paternalistic approach to politics and press which makes him regarded as rather remote from the public. He has not deigned to lobby support and seems therefore at a disadvantage with Senator Gorton.[7]

John McEwen, the seasoned old Country Party leader who was temporarily Prime Minister, recalled having only one conversation with Hasluck on the subject. 'Who have you got supporting you, Paul?' he asked. 'More important, who have you got working for you?' Hasluck replied that he did not have anyone working for him, but thought he had good support. McEwen replied that if he wanted to win he should have someone working for him, but, he recalled,

> Hasluck just looked disdainful – or I think that is too harsh a word – but he didn't see it that way...He didn't have to scheme or plan or have allies who were helpers, but the sheer rightness of his policy would win.[8]

Commentators in the media were less sure. *The Age* thought that Hasluck

> would probably make an excellent Prime Minister, given the enthusiastic loyalty of his colleagues. But it is doubtful whether the determinedly colorless Mr. Hasluck could make easy work of inspiring such loyalty or of presenting himself on the hustings as a man capable of spirited leadership.[9]

The *Sydney Morning Herald* opined that 'Mr Hasluck would never let us down, and if he could break out of his self-imposed prison, might prove an outstanding leader'. As it was, 'one cannot help admiring a politician who so resolutely refuses to use the vulgar arts of politics'.[10] Nevertheless, when Hasluck returned to the Eastern States in the New Year, he made appearances on television, as all the contenders did, and performed well enough to convince some colleagues who had previously thought him too formal for the medium. That observant recorder of the political marketplace, Minister for Air Peter Howson, commented that Hasluck 'was now working hard for the leadership and is I think, as a result, gaining a lot of votes'.[11] But Fred Chaney senior told a story that he and Gordon Freeth, who were canvassing for their fellow Western Australian, approached one Victorian they knew had little time for Gorton, and asked him if he would vote for Hasluck. No, he wouldn't, replied the Victorian; he had sought to see Hasluck, but Miss Dusting had turned him away brusquely because he did not have an appointment.[12]

One of Hasluck's disadvantages was that he had not made himself well known to the new members who had been swept into the House of Representatives by the 1966 landslide. Edward St John for one thought him uninspiring, 'a prim, upright little man' with whom he had exchanged only two brief conversations. Malcolm Mackay, from the 1963 cohort, was heard to wish that Hasluck, Gorton and Bury could be rolled into one.[13] A researcher who interviewed nearly half the Liberal members of parliament a few months later found that Hasluck's support was strongest among the older members of the party, especially the cabinet ministers. His critics complained that he was too stodgy and not close enough to the people. He was not well enough known to members from New South Wales and Victoria. Gorton, on the other hand, seemed more decisive and less verbose than Holt, and promised a new energy to colleagues rattled by the recent loss of a seat at a Victorian by-election.[14]

The vote was taken on 9 January. Hasluck's sangfroid was perhaps excessive. Malcolm Mackay recalled that on the morning of the poll he conversed with nobody, but contented himself with retiring to the parliamentary library.[15] Snedden and Bury were eliminated from the count, and Gorton was declared the winner. There have been various estimates of the final tally, Gorton being credited with between 43 and 51 votes, and Hasluck with between 30 and 38. Gorton later said that he had 'won by five', which indicates a 43–38 margin.[16] There was a solid body of respect for Hasluck, including nearly all his cabinet colleagues, but his almost wilful refusal to chase votes told against him. He took defeat calmly, informing Menzies (who had been active in his support) that 'At moments I feel that Alix and I have been lucky to escape a fate worse than death'.[17]

He was now on first-name terms with Menzies, and his comments were uninhibited. He thought the party meeting was far more of a triumph for McMahon than for Gorton. After McEwen's veto, McMahon had seemed finished, but by not quitting he had seemed a model of dignity and loyalty, so that his position was stronger than it had been before Holt died. 'In a wry sort of way I recognise McMahon now as being more clever than I thought he was, although my distrust of him is greater than ever...' Hasluck had 'dark forebodings for the future of the party'. Gorton had been a vigorous Senate leader, but he lacked diligence in matters of detail:

> The qualities he will need now in handling a very fidgety Cabinet and a party room which contains an unusually large proportion of new and inexperienced members and some very shabby older members, whose natural faults are now showing through the tatters of decay, still have to be discovered...I do not know whether Gorton realises it, but in mobilising support he has called up from the shadows some of the beasts that could destroy any leader.[18]

Hasluck adapted to the new regime with the imperturb-ability of a seasoned veteran who realised he had risen as high in

411

government as he ever would. He came increasingly to suspect that Gorton had been contemplating a move to the House of Representatives and a challenge to Holt even before Holt's death, and he thought it likely that the government would suffer from a further outbreak of hostility between McEwen and McMahon. He shared with Menzies his misgivings about Gorton: 'Because he relieved me as Acting Minister for External Affairs I also know of his lack of diligence in departmental detail', though he conceded that Gorton's contributions around the cabinet table showed on the whole 'a far higher intelligence than the average of the Cabinet'.[19] He began to contemplate retirement at the federal elections due in 1969.

From Washington the Ambassador, Keith Waller, wrote seeking Hasluck's personal advice. Having enjoyed the support of Menzies and Holt, Waller thought his relations with Gorton 'far less close', and wondered if the new Prime Minister would want his own man in Washington. Hasluck replied bracingly that as a career officer Waller's first responsibility was to the Minister for External Affairs, serving successive governments and ministers 'with equal loyalty regardless of the political complexion of the Government or the personal oddities of the Minister'. Waller should not even think of stepping down.

> If the Prime Minister were to allow past differences of opinion on other matters to affect his confidence in you in your present post, then it becomes an obligation on both of us to stop him from being silly.[20]

Personalities aside, it remained to be seen if Gorton would bring fresh thinking to Australian foreign policy. Hitherto that policy had been shaped on the assumption that the two major allies, the United States and the United Kingdom, would continue to hold the line in South-East Asia. That now seemed less certain. In Canberra on 12 February, George Thomson, Britain's Secretary of State for Commonwealth Relations, met Gorton, Hasluck and Fairhall (the Minister for Defence) with unwelcome news. Britain's financial position was continuing to deteriorate, and her armed forces would withdraw from South-East Asia no later than March 1971. The Australians responded with 'anxiety and dismay', Hasluck especially criticising this 'little Europe' policy, and these criticisms spilt over into the press.[21] Thomson went back to London with a five-page memorandum forcibly putting the Australian point of view, but, although the deadline for withdrawal was extended to December 1971, the message for the long term was clear. The British legions were leaving, and Australia would have to manage as best it could.

Nor could greater reliance be placed on the Americans as the situation in Vietnam deteriorated. During 1967 the war appeared to have reached a stalemate, although Hasluck asserted that the United States and its allies were winning. He continued to support the bombing of North Vietnam, in the hope that conformity to American policy strengthened Australia's credibility as an ally. This optimism was dented when North Vietnam and the Viet Cong launched what is known at the Tet Offensive at the end of January 1968. They made a series of assaults on most of the major towns in South Vietnam, including a raid on the American Embassy in Saigon. They were repelled, but their show of strength disproved any idea that they might sue for peace.

It was at this juncture that Gorton told a press conference on 2 February that the Australian commitment to Vietnam would never be increased beyond its present build-up to 8,000 personnel. This was consistent with the government's position under Holt, but Gorton made his 'personal statement' without consulting his cabinet colleagues, and the timing led some to speculate that the new Prime Minister would distance himself from the policy of forward defence associated with Hasluck and Fairhall. Later in February, when Hasluck visited Malaysia, Singapore and Indonesia in a round of discussions that included the impending British withdrawal, a new complication arose when the Philippines raised a claim to the Malaysian state of Sabah in north-east Borneo. The certainties that had under-pinned Hasluck's doctrine of forward defence were crumbling.

Hasluck continued to urge the continuation of the bombing campaign against North Vietnam, and to spurn the idea of entering into negotiations, but the Americans were moving in a different direction. As Peter Edwards put it, the Tet Offensive was followed by

> two months of policy paralysis in Washington, culminating in
> an announcement by President Lyndon Johnson on 31 March
> that he would stop the bombing of most of North Vietnam and
> withdraw from the 1968 presidential election.[22]

The Australian Government was informed of this radical shift only the day before. This was neither the first nor the last time Washington would announce a major change of policy without consulting or forewarning Canberra.

Less than a week earlier, Hasluck had been asserting the need to keep up the pressure on North Vietnam. President Johnson's announcement left the Australian Government with the option of either disagreeing openly with Washington or falling into line as gracefully as possible. Did this dilemma come about, asked a leading academic commentator, because the Australian Government failed to anticipate the changes that were overtaking the American public mind?

> Or did it happen because architects of the Australia's Vietnam
> policy such as Mr Hasluck, well enough aware of the new
> mood of American public opinion, decided to continue...out of
> genuine loyalty to the government of South Vietnam and their
> stern belief in the justice of their cause?[23]

In Hasluck's case both factors would have counted, but underlying them was a third, incalculable question. If both Britain and the United States withdrew from South-East Asia, who would replace them in the resulting power vacuum?

Hasluck's policy was unravelling. Holt, despite Hasluck's reservations about his performance in foreign policy, had been broadly supportive of the concept of forward defence with the involvement of Australian forces in Vietnam and Malaysia. Gorton was less predictable. He seemed to give vigorous support to this concept when he visited the United States and South-East Asia in May and June 1968, but some of his statements could be seen as favouring a 'fortress Australia' policy concentrating on the defence of the Australian continent. *Financial Review* journalist Max Walsh argued that Gorton's attitude towards Asia was at best casual and at worst negative, in contrast to that of Hasluck and Fairhall, who had virtually decided policy under Holt:

Both men believe in the merit of a forward defence posture and while Mr Hasluck's theory of international power relationships, spheres of influence, and the dangers of Chinese imperialism may seem to sit uncomfortably alongside Mr Fairhall's hawkish anti-Communism, the ultimate policy conclusions of their approaches was identical.[24]

Malaysia was another possible source of disagreement. The threat from Indonesia had virtually vanished, with power firmly in the hands of the anti-communist Soeharto regime and Soekarno reduced to ceremonial impotence, but the Philippines continued to voice their claim to Sabah. Reports in May suggested that Gorton was less eager than his ministers to assure Malaysia of Australian goodwill. A five-power conference at Kuala Lumpur in June 1968, with Hasluck and Fairhall representing Australia, was unable to defuse the problem. With the outcome in Vietnam still in the balance, no certainty about the British timetable for withdrawal from the region, and the Philippines confining themselves to rhetoric, the Australian ministers could only inform a party meeting that this was no time for a rushed decision. Cabinet was able to agree that Australia would maintain forces in Malaysia and Singapore until 1971, and, if requested, naval and air force units might stay beyond that date, but that was all.

Some thought the differing perspectives between Gorton on the one hand and Hasluck and Fairhall on the other led to a lack of direction in Australian foreign policy. Peter Howson, who had been dropped from the Gorton ministry, grumbled that 'there is no policy on external affairs at present'.[25] Journalists, especially Walsh, continued to speculate that Gorton wanted to oust Hasluck and Fairhall from office.[26] Despite gossip in the corridors of Parliament House this did not happen, and by the end of the year Walsh concluded that they had settled down to a regime of 'peaceful coexistence but mutual lack of enthusiasm'.[27] With the outcome in Vietnam still uncertain, the details of Britain's withdrawal still unknown, and the dispute between the Philippines and Malaysia rumbling along at a low level, all three ministers thought it wise to tread cautiously, making no new commitments and leaving open Australia's options in defence policy. For the rest of the year the government could point to few initiatives in foreign policy, while within Australia the protest movements against conscription gathered momentum.

Accompanied by Plimsoll and the South-East Asian expert Tom Critchley,[28] Hasluck went once more to London in November 1968 for a meeting with his British counterpart, Michael Stewart, now restored to the Foreign Office. A briefing memorandum prepared in the Foreign and Commonwealth Office assessed Hasluck as 'an attractive character of great modesty and integrity':

> Mr Hasluck's hallmark is the earnestness in whatever cause he is advocating. He is friendly towards Britain and undoubtedly values the close and confidential relationship that Canberra enjoys in London. But he is primarily devoted to pursuing a philosophical concept of the Australian National interest which does not invariably coincide with British, American, or any other interests. In particular he is preoccupied with the need to improve Australia's relations with her neighbours in South-East Asia, and is happy to think that Australia is accepted by those

nations as one of themselves in a sense which would never apply to either Britain or America.[29]

The discussions covered a wide range of ground, little of it new. On the apparent thawing of relations between the United States and the Soviet Union, Hasluck agreed that there was less cause for anxiety after the Russian suppression of Czechoslovakia in August 1968, but expressed disappointment that the European powers were 'inward-looking and unwilling to accept responsibility' for assisting the process of détente. For their part the British were disappointed that Australia was slow to sign on to the Nuclear Non-Proliferation Treaty brokered by the United States, the Soviet Union and Britain, and opened for other signatories in July 1968. Although 'Mr Hasluck himself is thought to be comparatively well disposed towards the Treaty', other elements in the Gorton government were keen for Australia to develop its own nuclear potential. As it happened, Australia did not sign until February 1970.

The future of Rhodesia preoccupied the British considerably. It was now three years since Ian Smith's white minority government unilaterally declared independence, and the British Government had made several unsuccessful attempts to come to terms with the new regime so as to secure some prospect of admitting the African majority to a greater share in government. Since Menzies' retirement in January 1966, Hasluck had consistently supported the British negotiations, but this had been at the cost of criticism from members of his own party. Jim Killen openly attacked him in parliament for failing to support the settler minority, and Gorton's sympathies were similarly inclined. During a visit to Lord Walston, the British

Parliamentary Undersecretary for Foreign Affairs, Alexandra Hasluck unapologetically embarrassed her husband by sticking up for Ian Smith and his breakaways.[30]

Beyond Rhodesia there was a persistent problem with South Africa, where after twenty years the apartheid regime seemed securely entrenched. The same elements in the Liberal Party who backed the white settlers in Rhodesia would have liked Australia's ties with South Africa to grow closer, even though South Africa was denounced as a pariah by nearly all the Afro-Asian nations and many in the West. Late in 1968, a South African naval detachment undertaking exercises in the Indian Ocean visited Australia, giving rise to conjectures that the two nations might be contemplating a formal defence alliance. Hasluck assured a concerned backbencher that similar facilities would be given to almost any country in the world, including the Soviet Union. Although the security of the Indian Ocean and the Cape route were vital for Australia's interests, there was no reason for a defence alliance. 'No doubt Killen and his crowd would like it', he added.[31]

The British may have considered that 'Mr Hasluck's visit to London was a marked success',[32] but at home success overseas could not disguise the suspicion that Hasluck was approaching the close of his political career. A younger generation was coming to the fore, among them Bill Snedden, Malcolm Fraser and Andrew Peacock, and the Country Party ministers Doug Anthony, Ian Sinclair and Peter Nixon. McEwen, nearing seventy, could not long defer his retirement. This would leave only Hasluck and McMahon as survivors of the Menzies regime at a time when the Coalition, confronted by a resurgent Labor under Whitlam's leadership, would have to modernise its image. At the elections scheduled for late 1969, Hasluck would be sixty-four years old. Although he himself told parliamentary colleagues that he intended to stand for election again in 1969,[33] an honourable retirement after twenty strenuous years of public life could seem attractive to a man who knew he had a lot of writing left in him.

If indeed Gorton wanted to move Hasluck on, he chose a graceful exit for him. In September 1968 he suggested that Hasluck become Governor-General when Casey retired during the first half of 1969. Hasluck himself certainly never originated the idea. In discussions with Gorton he had canvassed the name of General Sir John Hackett,[34] who although he seemed a reversion to the practice of appointing British military men, had the merit of birth and childhood in Perth, as the son of Sir Winthrop Hackett who owned and edited the *West Australian*. Hasluck would have appreciated that Hackett was a man of culture, a successful university administrator and author; but although approached on several different occasions, Hackett was not interested in a vice-regal appointment in Australia. Rather than look further, Gorton then suggested that Hasluck himself should go to Government House.

Inevitably some would assume that Gorton was taking advantage of the opportunity to kick Hasluck upstairs. But as Hasluck told Menzies:

> You can well understand it was a difficult decision for me to make. The ultimate decision was my own, and it was made after a long and friendly discussion of the whole situation with John Gorton. I am sure that he was just as troubled about losing me from External Affairs as I was in going. But the higher appointment had to be filled, and both of us felt that at this

particular juncture it had to be filled by an Australian, that the person appointed would have to have sensitivity for Australian politics and at least some appreciation of the Constitutional position. There was no question of making a list of candidates after there had been a preliminary survey of the field.[35]

Menzies had mixed feelings about the appointment:

That you and Alex [sic] will have a great success goes without saying; your qualities of statesmanship and scholarship and complete integrity ensure it. The Cabinet will, of course, be weakened by the loss of the ablest Minister for External Affairs that Australia has ever had.[36]

But Menzies was troubled about the ethics of appointing a governor-general who was an active politician because vice-regal impartiality might be undermined.

Of all serving politicians, however, Hasluck was most likely to uphold the impartiality of the governor-general's office. It was a role for which he was suited just because of some of the qualities that had not always served him well in the political arena. His lack of fervid partisanship, his intelligence and integrity commanded respect from his Labor opponents, who could trust him to play fair on constitutional issues. Hasluck's formal manner, which some had considered a disadvantage with the press and television, was entirely appropriate in a governor-general. Alexandra Hasluck was not overenthusiastic about the public obligations that would come to her as a governor-general's wife, but her sense of duty, added to her appreciation of the honour to her husband, secured her consent. She insisted, however, that whenever possible she should have several hours of privacy, 'to be undisturbed and consideration given to my work'.[37]

During the rest of 1968 the appointment was kept secret while Hasluck made several more official visits overseas: to Rome, Canada, the United Nations General Assembly in New York, a Colombo Plan meeting in Seoul, and in November with his wife to Yugoslavia. This was officially a communist regime, but its President, Marshal Tito, had split with the rest of the communist bloc, and Australia maintained a senior diplomat there, Alan Renouf, with oversight of most of Eastern Europe. Tito received the Haslucks at his hunting lodge, where Hasluck, Renouf and Plimsoll shared with him reflections on the role of middle-sized powers on the international stage. While Plimsoll and the Yugoslav Foreign Minister continued their talk, Tito invited Hasluck to drive the Blue Train that was to take them to Belgrade. When Renouf approached Hasluck to suggest he should come back, as Plimsoll's conversation was at an inter-esting phase, Hasluck replied, 'No, no, no, I am having too much fun. Let Plimsoll do it'.[38] The iron sense of duty that had characterised him during seventeen years as a cabinet minister was at last beginning to crack.

Once more he returned to London with Gorton in January 1969. On this occasion, Gorton formally requested the Queen's approval for Hasluck's appointment. According to Alexandra Hasluck, 'Her Majesty asked him could he spare Paul from his present position? The Prime Minister replied, "No, but he is the best for the job, Ma'am"'.[39] The main business of the London visit was a conference of Commonwealth heads of government. With a certain sense of detachment – perhaps the bystander's perspective of one governor-general to another – Hasluck reported on the conference to Casey. This was Gorton's first attendance at a conference of Commonwealth prime ministers, and Hasluck had warned his British colleagues that Gorton would be

> impatient if the entire meeting were to be taken up with Rhodesia…He thought that Mr Gorton's capacity to sit in silence during the tirades of the Africans would be limited but that he would try to make every effort to behave as courtesy required.[40]

As it turned out, Hasluck was able to tell Casey that 'the conference has stumbled along without falling flat on its face':

> The behaviour of the African members – even approaching something that resembles good manners – has been very much better than in September 1966…There has been some posturing and a good deal of exaggeration…but no vulgar abuse and ranting as in 1966…Our discussion of world affairs was rather patchy. Nations who take no responsibility do not learn very much about the realities of world politics. I thought the economic discussion was rather better.[41]

Julius Nyerere of Tanzania had been 'statesmanlike', Pierre Trudeau of Canada turned out to be a 'nonentity', the representatives of India and Pakistan were 'below par', but Lee Kuan Yew 'has spoken plainly and well on two occasions and brilliantly once'. As for his own Prime Minister:

Gorton has done very well. He has turned out to have a good touch in conference work and has spoken well and to the point at the right moment. Indeed, although not doing quite as well as Bob Menzies did in the days of the small and intimate conference and not having his stature, I think he is doing just as well and perhaps better than Menzies did in the days of the larger and blacker Commonwealth, and certainly much better than Harold Holt did in 1966. He has made his impression, and it is that of a firm, intelligent and understanding man.[42]

These do not read like the comments of a man who sensed that his Prime Minister wanted to get rid of him.

On 10 February 1969 it was announced that Hasluck would retire from the House of Representatives, allowing for a brief but symbolically important gap before he took up office on Casey's retirement in April. Sir Robert Menzies was not the only observer to wonder about the propriety of elevating a serving politician so immediately to vice-regal status, but most commentators found no fault with Hasluck himself.[43] Peter Howson recorded that gossip in Melbourne was busy speculating on Hasluck's motives for making the move; Howson hoped it did not signal a departure from Hasluck's effective South-East Asian policy. In subsequent months, as discontent with Gorton's performance grew within the Liberal Party, Howson more than once recorded rumours that Hasluck regretted having quit politics, and thus lost another opportunity of becoming prime minister.[44] But there is nothing in Hasluck's extensive archive to support this. Instead, he sent a friend what he thought an appropriate quotation from his beloved French poetry: 'Heureux qui, comme Ulysse, a fait un beau voyage...'[45]

It was a good time for him to leave the Department of External Affairs. He had staked his credibility on the doctrine of forward defence, as a result of which Australian troops had been fighting beside the Americans in Vietnam. But after the Tet Offensive of January 1968 the Americans appeared to be losing heart for the fight. President Johnson's last decision before the presidential elections of November 1968 was to open the possibility of negotiation with the North Vietnamese. By the beginning of 1969, representatives of North Vietnam and the United States were engaged in 'peace' talks in Paris. Although the American presidency passed to the Republican Richard Nixon in January 1969, it was clear that the new administration showed every sign of wanting to cut America's losses in Vietnam.

This change of tack sat ill with Hasluck's repeated assertions that there should be no parleying with the enemy before they had been effectively checked. He was not insensitive to the shifting political winds in China, where the excesses of the Cultural Revolution had been replaced by the ascendancy of a stable leadership, among whom the pragmatic Zhou Enlai was prominent. Hasluck's rhetoric was moderating. In his last speech to the United Nations General Assembly on 9 October 1968, he defined the greatest task for Australia, as for other nations, as that of 'seeing the mainland of China fitted into the family of nations'.[46] His own frame of mind probably echoed that of Dean Rusk, who had been Secretary of State under presidents Kennedy and Johnson, and in a congratulatory letter to Hasluck reflected:

One day we shall know whether we were right or not; if we get a good result in Southeast Asia there will be little doubt of it. If not, let it be written that, at least, we tried.[47]

425

Historians, aware that the Vietnam War ended in a communist victory, have not always written kindly about Hasluck's record. Critics have cast him as an eager promoter of American and Australian involvement in an unnecessary war.[48] Their criticisms gain in cogency when it is acknowledged that Hasluck and his generation, having lived through the Second World War and the Cold War that followed it, were wary of underestimating the expansionist ambitions of great powers. They failed to absorb the counsel of advisers such as Couve de Murville, and even Air Vice Marshal Cao Ky, who suggested that Vietnamese nationalists of all shades would resist Chinese domination. The policy of forward defence through support of powerful allies has been a consistent thread in Australian foreign policy, and the Vietnam involvement was no different except for two factors. One was that, although Hasluck was a realist in foreign policy, he was slow to recognise – and probably was not given enough information to recognise – that the makers of United States foreign policy were even greater realists, and could switch from enmity to rapprochement with China with remarkable alacrity. The other was that the Vietnam War came at a time when it could become a school for protest for a younger generation whose attitudes on many issues of morality, race and gender were shifting. Twenty years of peace and prosperity had made it safe to raise disturbing questions. Committed as Hasluck was to a cool rationality, he was unprepared for the upsurge of emotion that energised and transformed political discourse. By moving to a vice-regal role that necessarily took him outside politics, he was moving into a situation suited to his personality and his qualities.

Chapter 21

Governor-General, 1969–72

Paul Hasluck resigned from the House of Representatives on 10 February 1969. Far from giving himself a holiday in the interval before he assumed vice-regal office, he spent the next six weeks in Perth putting the finishing touches to his long-delayed second volume of *The Government and the People* for the Official History of *Australia in the War of 1939–45*. Meanwhile, Alexandra Hasluck saw the period of quiet as

> intensely necessary for preparing to leave our house for years,
> and for answering over 255 telegrams and stacks of letters
> literally feet high which had to be delivered to the front door as
> the letter box could not contain them.[1]

In April they went to England for ten days, where Paul received the honours due to his office. He became a Knight Grand Commander of the Order of St Michael and St George during a visit to Windsor Castle. He also became a Knight of the Order of St John of Jerusalem.

In an interview in Perth, Hasluck said he was not happy about leaving his home state but was looking forward to his term as Governor-General. 'At my advanced years', he remarked (he was sixty-four), 'one does not become excited'.[2] All the family's ties were in Perth. The patriarch, Meernaa Hasluck, pleased with his status as the oldest Salvation Army officer in Australia at the age of ninety-seven, survived to appreciate Paul's honours, but he had outlived both his other sons, and died early in 1970. Prominent among a generation of young businessmen who had no recollection of the penurious Depression, Rollo Hasluck's main interests were now in real estate, a thriving pursuit in Perth during the mineral boom of the prosperous 1960s. He had plenty of energy left for the enjoyment of yachting and power-boating on the Swan River, and he and his wife Jill often made a handsome couple in the social pages. Nicholas Hasluck had returned to Perth with his wife Sally Anne, and as well as building up a legal practice was making a reputation as poet and novelist. Grandchildren were arriving, and by 1971 there were four, two in each family. But the vice-regal life limited the time Paul and Alexandra Hasluck could devote to their role as grandparents.

Once established at Yarralumla, the new Governor-General and his wife began to come to terms with managing their establishment. The official secretary, Sir Murray Tyrrell,[3] had been in the position since 1947. During his stewardship, half a dozen governors-general had come and gone, and he tended to exercise his duties with the sometimes too relaxed assurance of an old hand who had nothing more to learn. For the first few months Hasluck and Tyrrell worked together smoothly enough. They combined to push for improved salaries and conditions for Government House staff, whose duties had much increased during the past four years with an Australian as Governor-General.[4]

The Haslucks soon discovered some aspects of Government House to be unsatisfactory. Although the grounds of Yarralumla were staffed by fifteen gardeners, the gardens were neglected and ill tended. When Alexandra Hasluck sent a message to the head gardener requesting a meeting on the following morning at 10 o'clock, he replied that he could not come because he was playing golf. She took the problem to her husband, knowing 'Nothing annoyed him more than people not doing their work properly'.[5] Hasluck promptly contacted the Parks and Gardens staff and improvements were soon made, but it was an issue that should have been dealt with by the official secretary. By the beginning of 1973, Hasluck decided it was time for Tyrrell to go. According to Tyrrell:

> I'd been at Government House too long for his liking, and he couldn't brook someone who possibly knew as much about the situation as I did. But nevertheless he went to no end of trouble to make my official departure – a dinner party...and another reception – an event of some significance.[6]

'All in all', Tyrrell admitted,

> it cannot be denied that he has been and is a first-class Governor-General, but he lacks the ability to attract affection... and this of course is a tragedy for an otherwise man of great intellect, capacity, stamina and nationalist outlook.

He was replaced by David Smith – energetic, methodical and twenty years younger.[7]

Miss Dusting did not follow Hasluck to the Government House establishment. She recalled that Sir Paul farewelled her with the comment: 'Well, I suppose you've had an interesting time'.[8] She was found instead a position in the Department of External Affairs. Her residence included a carefully tended rose garden, and from time to time at weekends an official vehicle would arrive with a load of manure from the Government House stables.[9] As secretary and personal assistant, Hasluck acquired Margaret Atkin, who soon found she was working for a man who was never off the job. Even when he was enjoying a few days of solitude at his block at Paulls Valley, she would go each day in a Commonwealth car from Perth with the day's files and correspondence, and deal with them in that rustic setting.[10] Alexandra Hasluck inherited Lady Casey's personal assistant, Sue Hewitt, and when she retired after a few months she was replaced by a Perth woman, Patricia Daw, who was to remain as a valued companion of both Haslucks for many years.

Another survivor from the Caseys' regime was the English butler, Bryan George, whom the Haslucks came to value highly. The establishment also provided the Governor-General with three aides-de-camp, one from each of the armed services, who served for a period of twelve months. They were seconded to the household staff to organise events and formal procedures, both at Government House and in the wider community. Several were Vietnam veterans, and Alexandra Hasluck noted 'their gaunt faces yellow with atebrin…To me they all looked as if they needed feeding up and looking after'.[11] Paul Hasluck preferred them to wear civilian clothes when they dined with him. They were the officials most likely to feel the brunt of Hasluck's peppery temper, but they found him a considerate employer.

Quickly plunging into the round of official and unofficial hospitality expected of their position, the Haslucks soon put their distinctive stamp on the guest lists. More than the elderly

Caseys, the Haslucks made a point of inviting younger people to Government House. Two months after their arrival they gave a buffet dinner for fifty young Australians who had made their mark in the community.[12] They also took every opportunity of inviting writers, artists and intellectuals whose company offered promise of good conversation. The results were usually pleasing, although on one occasion an eminent historian who had forsworn alcohol was so overcome by his surroundings that he lapsed into old habits with predictable consequences.

Early in June, Hasluck hosted a reception for members of parliament, to which he invited Sir Robert and Dame Pattie Menzies. Menzies reported that his warmest welcome came from the Labor men, 'who all assured me, with a broad grin, that they missed me very much and were glad to do so'. He reported that 'Alex is disposed to be a little sombre but Paul, strangely enough, is enjoying the experience'.[13] Menzies later told Hasluck's diplomatic colleague Alfred Stirling that

> anyone would be proud to set their name to the speeches he writes. Each are full of learning and good judgment. His only mistake was to let John Gorton kick him upstairs.[14]

In her memoirs, Alexandra Hasluck expressed disappointment that she seldom saw her husband alone at Government House. Quite apart from the duties of the vice-regal office, Paul was now seizing the opportunity to catch up with some of his long-delayed plans for publication. In the weeks between his resignation from parliament in February 1969 and departure to Canberra in April he had completed the second volume of *The Government and the People 1939–45*. Although most of the manuscript had been drafted before he entered cabinet in 1951, he chose not to attempt revision of the text in the light of research and publication since that date. With Gavin Long's concurrence he decided that his work should stand as a foundation on which others could build. He tried not to work into his early drafts the insights and shifts of opinion that might have come to him during his long ministerial career. He wrote:

> ...I do not think that truth has suffered from this self-discipline
> although it might be that I could have livened the narrative
> with stronger judgments than I chose to make twenty
> years ago.[15]

In one respect he pulled his punches. His experience in the Northern Territory had brought home to him the scenes of panic that occurred after the bombing of Darwin in 1942, when not only civilians but some service personnel fled from the scene of devastation, and there had been widespread looting. In an uncharacteristic display of partisanship he had once denounced this cowardice as occurring 'under the auspices and the influence of a Labor government'.[16] In his published history he once more showed the judicious restraint of the historian, and although he candidly acknowledged the disorderly scenes after the bombs fell, his criticism of the government goes no further than to suggest that Canberra was 'more badly scared than any other part of the continent' and that by harping on the need for morale the authorities underestimated the resolution of most of the general public.[17]

In general his political judgements were free of the taint of partisanship. He paid generous tribute to Curtin and Chifley, while acknowledging the role of the press secretary, Don Rodgers, in influencing the picture most Australians had of those leaders.[18] He was realistic in recognising the weaknesses of the Coalition parties during 1942 and 1943, which unfitted them for government at a time of national crisis. In a thoughtful 'Epilogue' he paid tribute to the leadership of Menzies and Curtin, the latter especially, while recognising that 'Australians do not take kindly to leaders. "Let us now praise famous men" is heard on the lips of the citizenry much less often than "Who the hell does he think he is?"'[19] He was eloquent about the effects of the war in enhancing Australians' awareness of themselves as a nation. He also noted that 'the war brought opportunity to many people to take heavier responsibilities, to discover undeveloped talents, and to enter on duties that led them to a higher and more active part in the nation's affairs',[20] and maybe there was an unconscious note of autobiography in that observation. It was certainly vintage Hasluck when he wrote: 'The Australian newspapers generally give a poor impression of Australia at war... The basic shortcoming of newspapers is to make the exceptional happening the principal event of the day'.[21]

In 1970 Melbourne University Press, by then under the management of Peter Ryan, who became a close friend, published a reprint of Black Australians, to which Hasluck contributed a new introduction. If the first edition had gone insufficiently appreciated because of wartime constraints, the 1970 publication earned a glowing review from the hard-headed doyen of anthropologists of Aboriginal Australia, John Mulvaney.[22] 'Distinguished by its fluent scholarship, historical insight and human understanding', wrote Mulvaney, 'it was a significant book in 1942, and those rare virtues remain'. The book was worth re-reading nearly thirty years later, and not merely as a pointer to Hasluck's ministerial policies in postwar years – although Mulvaney noted that during that time the practice of spelling 'Aborigines' with a capital 'A' was 'an influence stemming from his own department'. It was a heartening tribute at a time when Hasluck had reason to feel that his achievement in Aboriginal policy was going out of fashion.

Later in 1970, Hawthorn Press published an edition of his collected verse. It was, the newspapers claimed, the first time a serving governor-general had ventured into creative writing. A younger poet, Rodney Hall, offered a frank assessment:

> I suppose the truth is he does it rather well. His command of technique is shaky, his subtlety of nuance is practically nil, and yet the best of these poems is utterly convincing.[23]

If his attempts at major themes were sometimes boring or ridiculous, he achieved a 'vivid authenticity about people'. A Western Australian academic, Bruce Bennett, was more attuned to Hasluck's sense of place. Although he thought that 'The new poems in this book, written as they were in the margins of a relentlessly busy public life, are generally shorter and less ambitious than his prewar verse', he pointed out that 'Hasluck's west appears as a place of inwardness and relief from his outer world of politics and anger'.[24] It was this sense of place that was to find expression in the poetry of Hasluck's late maturity.

Paul Hasluck was prepared to spend a lot of time at his desk in order to keep up with the official documents that came to him from parliament and the Executive Council. He wrote:

Beyond the mastery of papers placed before him officially [the Governor-General] also has the need to keep himself informed about a wide range of subjects. Diligence in business is required of governors-general no less than of Ministers if they are to be more than figureheads on leaky ships.[25]

In his first two years at Yarralumla he had few political crises to confront, but established a routine that ensured the Governor-General was more than a cipher in the executive process. One cabinet minister recalled:

He would not let anything pass that might have adversely affected ordinary citizens, such as acquisition of land or property. He would want chapter and verse and wouldn't put his signature to something. He would send you away, so you'd go and do your homework virtually. 'Come back with a more detailed report of the impact study of this legislation or this sector before I'll sign it.'[26]

When the Gorton government went to the polls in November 1969 he refrained from approving any major new decisions or appointments pending in the Executive Council until the result of the election was clear.[27] Gorton retained office, although with a much reduced majority, and from that time on his leadership was never secure. Both Gorton and McEwen, still the Country Party leader, discussed the restructuring of the ministry with Hasluck at some length, McEwen observing that there would be 'no coalition if Gorton persists with off-the-cuff decisions'. With great candour, Gorton discussed the implications of moving McMahon from the Treasury to External

Affairs, saying that he wanted to get rid of him altogether as deputy leader. Hasluck commented:

> I knew McMahon to be a professional dealer in lies, a seller of government secrets in return for favours, one who had been disloyal to each prime minister with whom he had served, and an intensely ambitious man. He would not change his nature or modify his ambition because of the party room vote.[28]

Gorton continued to have trouble with his backbenchers, especially over the question of offshore mining legislation. The emboldened Labor opposition launched a motion of censure on him in May 1970, which, although defeated, enabled his critics to give tongue at some length. Hasluck declared himself 'mentally staggered' by Gorton's apparent 'inability to appreciate what was happening':

> It was not that he was 'cracking hardy' after having been hit; in private he seemed genuinely still full of confidence and ready to brush aside any suggestion that he had met trouble.[29]

Papua New Guinea became the scene of a potential crisis in July 1970. As the territory progressed towards self-government, various secessionist movements began to emerge in regions that considered their interests to be neglected by Port Moresby. Among them were sections of the Tolai people of New Britain, whose grievances about taxation and land policy were of many years' standing.[30] In January 1970, buoyed by the Labor opposition's gains at the recent election, Whitlam, accompanied by Beazley senior and Bill Hayden, made a tour of Papua New

Guinea. He made much of Labor's wish to bring Papua New Guinea quickly to independence if his party were returned at the next federal elections in 1972, but some thought 'he turned national resentment of expatriates into hatred'.[31] In particular his speech before about 10,000 Tolai at Rabaul was embellished by its interpreters and could be seen as repudiating the administration's policies.

It should not have been surprising that when Gorton visited the territory in July he was confronted by threatening demonstrations at Rabaul orchestrated by the Mataungan Association. One of their techniques was to occupy disputed land and threaten violence if an attempt was made to evict them. Gorton accepted the administration's view that the police might not be adequate for the purpose, so that it would be necessary to involve the army in the shape of the Pacific Islands Regiment. Hasluck's consent was required for this call-out, and he became aware that the departments of External Affairs and Defence and the chiefs of the armed services doubted whether there was as yet a clear threat of domestic violence that would provide a basis for the use of troops.[32] The Pacific Islands Regiment was not experienced in crowd control, and if violence erupted Australia might figure badly in the eyes of the international community. The Attorney-General, Tom Hughes, was also unsure of the legality of the use of troops. As Commander-in-Chief it would be Hasluck's formal responsibility to authorise calling out the regiment. He saw the Governor-General as 'the final check against ill-considered or precipitate action'.[33]

When Gorton, seconded by Minister for External Territories Charles Barnes, came to Government House to urge immediate action, Hasluck insisted on a thorough presentation of the facts and the legal position before he gave his consent. He sought assurances that the Minister for Defence concurred in the recommendation, that the armed forces were sufficient to act effectively, and that no alternative course of action was possible. Hughes was sent to Port Moresby to assess the situation and came back convinced that the administration's request was justifiable. Hasluck accepted the advice, but by this time the Tolai were cooling down. In the end the regiment was not called upon, but for the first time use was made of a provision in the Papua and New Guinea Act enabling powers to be transferred to the administration of the territory by a proclamation of the governor-general's instructions.

Gorton's term of office ended in March 1971, when the resignation of Malcolm Fraser as Minister for Defence provoked a split in the Liberal Party. At a party meeting on 9 March the numbers divided evenly for or against Gorton continuing as leader. Quixotically, he gave his casting vote against himself and was replaced by the 63-year-old William McMahon. Alexandra Hasluck told her son that in the privacy of Government House, Paul was 'rabid' at this outcome, which he saw as due to the machinations of Sir Frank Packer's media. She herself doubted if McMahon had the physical stamina for the job. 'It was all Gorton could do to hold up', she wrote. 'Billy is half blind and tired and skinny.'[34] But the swearing-in ceremony took place with all due propriety, although the body language in the official photographs is revealing.

During the next twenty-one months that McMahon held the prime ministership he did not communicate with Hasluck as freely as Gorton had. Yet it would be unwise to exaggerate the extent of disharmony between Hasluck and McMahon. Both were thoroughly seasoned professionals who understood the niceties of political discourse. There is no reason to disbelieve Hasluck when he wrote, bracketing McMahon with Gorton and Whitlam:

> With all three Prime Ministers our talks were marked by frankness and trust...and I never found any difficulty with any of them in discharging the conventional role of the Crown to discuss, counsel and warn.[35]

Trouble soon arose over the award of imperial honours, since McMahon was given to promising more titles of honour than Australia was entitled to in any one year. The first issue involved Hasluck's home state of Western Australia. A few days before McMahon became Prime Minister, the Liberal–Country Party Coalition that had ruled for twelve years in Western Australia was unexpectedly defeated at the polls. The outgoing Premier, Sir David Brand, himself newly knighted, had been intending to recommend knighthoods for his Country Party deputy, Crawford Nalder, and his dynamic Minister for Industrial Development, Charles Court. Both were appointable by the standards of that time, but the incoming Labor government did not believe in knighthoods and refused to forward the recommendations. Canberra was asked to intervene, but Hasluck thought it improper to interfere with the decision of the state government in office. McMahon was unhappy and in 1972 secured Court's inclusion in the Commonwealth list of knighthoods. Nalder had to wait until the Coalition returned to power in Western Australia.

Meanwhile, McMahon excelled himself by suggesting that the long-serving Premier of Victoria, Henry Bolte, should become a member of the House of Lords. Bolte's support had helped McMahon in his tilt at the leadership of the Liberal Party. It could be expected that if the sometimes contentious and roughshod Bolte was thought fit for a peerage, other senior Liberals would press their claims for a similar distinction. In pouring cold water on this idea, Hasluck's diplomacy was masterly. He wrote to McMahon explaining that while peerages may have been appropriate in Richard Casey's time, they were no longer suitable for younger generations; but if any Australian were to be nominated to the House of Lords none had claims superior to Sir Robert Menzies, and he was old and ill and no longer interested if he ever had been.[36] Bolte had to content himself with becoming a Knight Grand Cross of the Order of St Michael and St George.

Paul and Alexandra Hasluck took readily to the round of formal occasions expected of a vice-regal couple.[37] Twice a year there would be investitures for the recipients of imperial honours. These were usually eminent citizens of mature age, although in the early years of Hasluck's office there were servicemen who had served in the Vietnam War, and the ceremony was always followed by a formal dinner. As a civilian Paul Hasluck was always understandably anxious when inspecting servicemen on parade, and relieved when – as invariably happened – the ceremony was conducted with appropriate decorum.[38] When new ambassadors presented their credentials they would be met by a guard of honour from the armed services. All wearing formal morning dress with decorations, the Ambassador and party would be shown into the vice-regal presence:

He would read an address to the Governor–General, bow and advance to hand his credentials to him, and shake hands. The Governor–General would then hand the credentials to an Aide, and in his own turn, read a short speech of welcome. After that, the proceedings broke up, glasses of champagne were handed round by the footmen, and we would all have a photograph taken.[39]

It is not too fanciful to suggest that, in adapting to the formal choreography of such ceremonies, Paul and Alexandra Hasluck were well served by youthful experience with the University Dramatic Society forty years earlier, as well as a long subsequent career in international diplomacy. Few Australians in public office have been better versed in protocol.

With the modernisation of air travel there were more visits from overseas dignitaries than previous governors-general had encountered. Queen Elizabeth II's first visit during Hasluck's term of office came in April 1970, when she was accompanied by the Duke of Edinburgh and Princess Anne. This was an exercise requiring extensive planning, though planning could not avert a bleak Canberra autumn that took some of the pleasure from two of the major features of the visit: a garden party, and an evening barbecue and dance for 300 young people. The visit was nevertheless accounted a success, and the Queen was to pay two more visits during the Haslucks' occupancy of Yarralumla. In addition, Prince Philip made several short solo visits, and Prince Charles consulted Hasluck about the possibility of acquiring a property in the Yass district, only to decide this might suggest a mistrust of investment opportunities in England.[40] Other distinguished guests included the King and Queen of Nepal; the

Crown Prince and Princess of Japan; the Prince Consort of the Netherlands; President Soeharto of Indonesia and his wife; and the American Vice-President, Spiro Agnew, whom Alexandra Hasluck found 'much nicer and more agreeable' than the media reports suggested.[41]

Paul and Alexandra Hasluck were to meet most of these personalities in one of the most bizarre ceremonies of the twentieth century. In October 1971 the Shah of Iran invited many of the current heads of state to a celebration to mark the 2,500th anniversary of the Persian Empire founded by Cyrus the Great, King of Kings. It took a certain amount of chutzpah to stage this celebration, as the Shah himself was a parvenu, the son of an army general who had seized the throne in 1926, but he sought to identify with Cyrus, who was said to be the builder of an empire 'distinguished...by its tolerance towards all religions and races, and by the comprehensive and beneficial character of administration'.[42] Among the ruins of Cyrus the Great's capital, Persepolis, about 60 kilometres from Shiraz, an opulent tent city was built in which the visiting dignitaries were housed. The festivities included a dinner where the main item was roast peacock – rather tough and gamy, Alexandra Hasluck thought, though the dining tent 'was a marvel. Its sides were adorned with swags of gilded artificial flowers and its ceiling was fluted pink chiffon'.[43] After many speeches the night concluded with a spectacular fireworks display among the ruins. The next afternoon saw a massive military parade, with soldiers dressed in the uniforms of each dynasty from Cyrus until the present day. It was all very opulent, but it left the Haslucks glad to be Australian. Eight years later the Shah was an exile, and Iran was ruled by an oppressive theocracy.

More than any of the ceremonial aspects of the vice-regal position, Hasluck saw value in making public statements that emphasised the unifying role of the Governor-General as 'the highest single expression in the Australian governmental structure of the idea that Australians of all parties and all walks of life belong to the same nation'.[44] Finding there was no easily accessible work of reference that explained the nature of the office to schools or to members of the public generally, he thought of writing such an essay, but instead found an opportunity when he was asked to deliver the William Queale Memorial Lecture to the South Australian division of the Australian Institute of Management in October 1972. The lecture, 'The office of Governor-General', with its combination of scholarship and practical experience, was to become a classic text. Hasluck defined the vice-regal responsibilities thus:

> In affairs of state the Governor-General takes advice from those Executive Councillors whose party has a majority in Parliament, no matter which party it is, but in his public engagements, in his own guest lists and in moving about in the Australian community he is careful to make it plain that he is not the possession of any section, social group or political faction but is in the service of the whole nation.[45]

He soon had the opportunity to put these principles into practice.

Chapter 22

Governor-General, 1972–74

The Federal election on 2 December 1972 brought an end to twenty-three years in office for the Liberal–Country Party Coalition. Hasluck was not surprised, considering the Liberal Party was due for the periodical re-examination of itself that all political parties needed from time to time. Because he was suffering from an eye infection, he was obliged to receive the outgoing Prime Minister McMahon and the victorious Labor leader Gough Whitlam in his bedroom at Government House. McMahon expressed a mixture of disappointment and relief. He said that even if he had won the election he would have retired within two years, but felt that there was too much disagreement and scheming in the Liberal Party, and none of his potential successors was any good. He would resign on 5 December, but was willing to form a caretaker government.

Whitlam thought the new government could not ask the old ministry to process policies with which it disagreed. Instead he suggested that until the full cabinet could be sworn in – a process that might take ten days – there should be a two-man ministry comprising himself and his deputy, Lance Barnard, who with the Governor-General would be the three members necessary to constitute a valid Executive Council. Having carefully considered written advice from Clarence Harders, secretary of the

Attorney-General's Department, that there was no impediment to this constitutional novelty, Hasluck agreed to swear in Whitlam and Barnard as an interim ministry, each holding a dozen portfolios. It was clear that Whitlam had thought out this strategy in advance, even to the point of advising Hasluck that if anything were to happen to either minister, such as an air crash, he should send for Frank Crean as the next most senior frontbencher.

When the full Labor ministry was sworn in, Hasluck is remembered as giving its members 'a very warm welcome', as well as offering some avuncular wisdom. According to Labor member Moss Cass:

> I remember Hasluck offering two pieces of advice, which I think he also felt we would not follow. One was not to chase hares, and the other was to take a holiday, as we had all been through a very stressful time.

Les Johnson remembered: 'He told us to pace ourselves, not get carried away and to get ready for the hard work'.[1] Commentators were bemused at the apparent sangfroid with which Hasluck as Governor-General presided over the reversal of policies with which he had been associated as a minister. Only a few years after he had been denouncing the People's Republic of China as dangerously bellicose, he received with gracious composure its Ambassador appointed after the Whitlam government's change of policy. He also approved legislation bringing Papua New Guinea to a rapid independence, though he did not attend the ceremonies marking that milestone.

Hasluck and Whitlam had clashed in politics, and journalists were forever recalling the episode with the glass of water. But as Governor-General and Prime Minister they soon formed a close rapport, based in part on respect for each other's intellectual cargo. In June 1973 Hasluck noted: 'I have had more conversations with Whitlam in six months than I had in the full term of his predecessors', and Whitlam 'said he enjoyed the rare opportunity for turning over a few ideas with someone who was detached from argumentation'.[2] They could discuss the strengths and weaknesses of Whitlam's cabinet colleagues with great candour. The ministers themselves, none of whom had any experience of cabinet office, found Hasluck a tactful and well-informed mentor. David Smith, newly installed in the office of official secretary, recalled that meetings of the Executive Council often resembled the best kind of university tutorial, with Hasluck offering comments and insights from a long experience of parliamentary government.[3] Hasluck was also pleased to find that, although Whitlam might have expected to find the senior public servants and heads of departments to be habituated to the environment of a Liberal–Country Party government, he was in fact 'learning to appreciate their help and their wise counsel'.[4]

By June 1973 Hasluck felt comfortable enough with Whitlam to offer him some 'fatherly' advice:

> He should start to take some care about preserving his
> resources and watch his programme so as not to put a
> continuous strain on himself. Although he was well and
> vigorous at present he should remember that being a Prime
> Minister was not just a 'sprint' but a 'long-distance' race. He
> not only had to be vigorous, energetic, and in full possession
> of all his powers at the end of six months but at the end of
> six years.[5]

Whitlam admitted that

> he had been accepting too many engagements and denying
> himself weekends. Luckily he never felt guilty about being idle
> and he saw the sense of just sitting in the sun for a few hours.

More than once Hasluck warned Whitlam against alarming too many sections of Australian public opinion, and he was vindicated by a curious constitutional incident in August 1973. In his home state of Western Australia, Labor held office by a precarious one-vote majority in the Legislative Assembly. In June 1973 this margin almost vanished when at a by-election Labor's Brian Burke scrambled home by a majority of only thirty votes in what should have been a safe seat. The swing against Labor was widely thought to reflect Western Australian reactions against Canberra more than dissatisfaction with either Burke or the Labor Premier, John Tonkin. The leader of the opposition, Sir Charles Court, wanted to use the Coalition's majority in the Legislative Council to deny supply to the Tonkin government so as to force an election. This became a matter of concern for the state Governor, Sir Douglas Kendrew, of whom Hasluck commented: 'I formed a low opinion of his understanding of political and constitutional questions, although he was always congenial company when talking about affairs in general'.[6]

Kendrew, a British major general, was about to retire after nine years in office, for the first seven of which he had dealt solely with a Liberal–Country Party government. He was comfortable with its leaders, especially Court, for whom he had a great admiration. He was perturbed by the activities of the Whitlam regime, and thought the existing non-Labor state premiers – Robert Askin in New South Wales, Joh Bjelke-Petersen in Queensland and Rupert Hamer in Victoria – would not stand up to the federal government unless they were led by Court as Premier of Western Australia: 'Court was the only man who could save Australia'.[7] To achieve this end he encouraged Court to defeat supply. If Tonkin then asked for a dissolution of state parliament, Kendrew would refuse and commission Court to form a government. If Court was defeated in the Legislative Assembly, Kendrew would prorogue parliament and authorise supply by royal warrant. Hasluck cautioned Kendrew against using a state political crisis to influence Commonwealth events. Kendrew's responsibility was primarily constitutional, and he would incur legitimate criticism if he was seen to favour Court against Tonkin. As it happened, the Liberals in the Legislative Council refused to block supply, perhaps aware that Tonkin would approach Whitlam to provide temporary funding if the Supply Bill was defeated.[8]

Hasluck's term of office was due to expire in April 1974, and it was expected that the Queen's visit to Australia in October 1973 would provide an opportunity for deciding on his successor. In June 1973 Whitlam asked Hasluck to stay for another two years.

> He talked of the difficulty of finding anyone suitable and also said frankly that he did not want to give the Press any chance of making a story that he was 'trying to get rid of Hasluck' for one reason or another.[9]

Whitlam's proposal meant that Hasluck would be in office when the next general election was due at the end of 1975. As it turned out this would have had momentous consequences for Australian political history and for Whitlam himself. Hasluck would have been seventy-one years old at the end of his extended term, but he would probably have accepted if he had only himself to consider. He told Whitlam, however, that his wife was firmly opposed to the idea, and that they could undertake to stay only for a month or two after April 1974.

Alexandra Hasluck's reluctance was understandable. She told her friends she was 'fed up with the travelling life of a vice-regal couple'[10] and complained that 'Paul has so much more energy than me, and never realises it, which leads to tantrums'.[11] Public ceremonies were becoming increasingly difficult for her because of a deteriorating hip condition. Yarralumla was not a comfortable residence for someone so afflicted; David Smith recalled how, after alighting at the front entrance to the vice-regal residence, Alexandra Hasluck would pause for a moment and square her shoulders before resolutely tackling the great staircase.[12] Her husband had requested Gorton, McMahon and Whitlam in turn to consider installing a lift at Government House, but none treated it as a matter of priority. It was a small detail that would cost Whitlam dearly.

An unexpected personal tragedy also played a part. On the evening of 5 June 1973, Rollo Hasluck collapsed and died in a bar in Singapore, where he was on a holiday with three men friends. At the age of thirty-two, he fell victim to a myocardial infarction resulting from a viral infection. Paul Hasluck received the news from the Department of Foreign Affairs late in the evening, waking Alexandra from her sleep to break it to her. The shock was the greater because Rollo had always been full of vitality, and after some rough weather matrimonially and financially, his affairs were improving; he held a good job in real estate development, and his wife and he had abandoned plans for a divorce.[13]

The Haslucks were private in their mourning, and kept the disruption to their official duties to a minimum. Paul later found an outlet to his feelings in a poem:

> *You do not lie in death alone*
> *For some of me went with you there*
> *And rests forever where you rest.*
> *And you walk with me everywhere.*
> *Thus I, still living, not alone*
> *Will often share with you,*
> *Still bright and active, ever here,*
> *Memories of all we used to do.*
> *In loneliness but not distress*
> *I draw from stores in happiness*
> *Not only consolation but a breath*
> *Of your quick Self beyond the body's death.*[14]

This bereavement meant it was even less likely that the Haslucks would stay on in Government House after the autumn of 1974, although the relationship between Governor-General and Prime Minister was, if anything, growing warmer. Hasluck considered that Whitlam and his colleagues showed greater courtesy towards Government House than either McMahon or his successor as leader of the Liberal Party, Bill Snedden. It was with Whitlam's concurrence that Hasluck was encouraged to think of the question of his replacement. He jotted down some names on a piece of paper, not as potential nominees but as 'examples of the way [Whitlam] might look around':

The names I discussed with him were: Ministerial, Crean and Beazley. Judiciary: John Kerr. Academic: David Derham and Kenneth Wheare. Big Business and men prominent in public movements: Vincent Fairfax and Kenneth Myer. Trade Unions: D. H. Souter.[15]

Hasluck advised against 'promoting' any of the state governors, although there had been a few examples in the years when governors were imported from Britain. The list had some striking omissions. There were no women, although by 1974 feminism was stirring vigorously throughout Australia. There were no judges of the High Court, from which two later vice-regal appointments would be drawn; but as an admirer of the recently deceased Sir Owen Dixon, Hasluck probably saw no member of a bench led by Sir Garfield Barwick as measuring up. And there were no high-ranking members of the armed forces, although they had tended to dominate the Australian-born appointees of recent years. Although he was nominally Commander-in-Chief of the Australian armed forces, Hasluck preferred to emphasise the civilian qualities of the vice-regal office.

Whitlam showed interest in all the names on Hasluck's list, and in the following weeks took soundings. He made his first approach to Kenneth Myer, senior member of an eminent Melbourne family of retailers and a noted philanthropist, but Myer said that for personal and family reasons he was not available. Perhaps, even three decades after the Second World War, it mattered that his wife was Japanese. Frank Crean said, 'Not yet', as he was happy as federal Treasurer, not foreseeing that the next year he would be ousted from that role. The third choice was Sir John Kerr, Chief Justice of New South Wales. Hasluck did not know Kerr well, but they had met over the years because of a shared interest in Papua New Guinea. Kerr had a good presence, and could be expected because of his legal background to appreciate the constitutional responsibilities of a governor-general (though from that point of view Sir Kenneth Wheare, an Australian-born Oxford don who was an international authority on the subject, would have been far preferable). Kerr spent a considerable time haggling over the offer, asking for an unprecedented ten-year term of office equivalent to the time he could have served as Chief Justice of New South Wales, but it seemed increasingly obvious that he would accept.[16]

Perhaps it would not have been necessary for Hasluck to step down, however. Despite increasing pain from her arthritic hip, Alexandra Hasluck had stoically gone through her official duties during the Queen's visit in October, followed by the opening of the Sydney Opera House with its numerous steps to climb. That, she told her friends, 'packed it up for me. I felt I had to get the hip joint removed'.[17] She wanted the operation to take place in the familiar and comfortable surroundings of the St John of God Hospital in Perth, but her consultant, Dr Hector Stewart, advised her that he preferred not to operate until she had reduced her weight by 2 stone (about 13 kilograms). Alexandra was indignant. 'I don't *want* to lose a lot of weight & get weak & wrinkled & old looking & ruin my digestion'.[18]

Although she often complained that Paul was no use in such crises, it was he who suggested she seek a second opinion from Canberra's leading physician, Dr Marcus de Laune Faunce, and, as Alexandra admitted, 'explained the case better than she could have'.[19] Himself a man of comfortable build, Faunce pronounced her perfectly fit to undergo the operation. Then came a highly apologetic letter from Dr Stewart, with the news that Alexandra's records had somehow got mixed up with those of another patient, and she would indeed be fit to undergo the operation on 8 December in Perth. The hip replacement was entirely successful, and although Alexandra had to endure a few tedious weeks on crutches with post-operative pain, by January she felt fitter and more mobile than she had been for a long time. But Sir John Kerr had already accepted the governor-generalship, and there was no going back.

In December 1973, Hasluck and his successor had their first private discussion at Admiralty House. Very little was said of the governor-general's constitutional or political responsibilities. According to Hasluck: 'Kerr was mainly interested in the duties, the expenses, and the conditions of life at Government House and especially what was expected of a Governor-General's wife'.[20] Alexandra Hasluck was writing letters to Maie Casey as a confidante. Henrietta Drake-Brockman, who had previously filled this role, had died in 1968. As a former Governor-General's wife, Maie Casey was uniquely suited to give a sympathetic hearing to Alexandra's feelings. Just as the Caseys had extended a helping hand to the Haslucks when they were new to vice-regal office, Paul and Alexandra in their turn now invited Sir John and Lady Kerr to stay two days at Yarralumla to see how things ran. But at Sir John Kerr's investiture in April, Alexandra was shocked to learn that Lady Kerr could not come as she was in hospital being treated for cancer:

Maie, I cannot imagine how Sir John cld have accepted the position knowing that his wife was practically an invalid...It simply means that he hasn't given thought to some aspects of the position. When I told him that I was Patron or President of some 20 Women's Associations, & that one was expected to visit them sometimes and give a slight speech, he seemed quite dazed. How do men think of their wives' part? I think the women of Australia are in for a fairly arid time.[21]

Even Whitlam was surprised, saying, 'I suppose that the wife is a rather important part of the job'. 'Men never cease to amaze me', said Alexandra, but she was even more amazed when Sir John came to stay at Yarralumla accompanied by his female judge's associate instead. 'I feel it is a little odd', she commented to Maie Casey.[22]

Alexandra Hasluck's comments even hinted that she had some regrets about insisting on her husband's retirement:

I am baring my heart to you, Maie, because I have enjoyed this life on the whole (leaving aside the matter of my poor arthritic leg now completely recovered) & I would not like to see the aura of tradition & ceremony given away. It is often suggested that Sir John Kerr, being a Labor appointee, will be so democratic & do away with formality. Which makes me mad, because if this is done, there will be no particular kudos about being invited to Govt House & it will become just any old neck of the woods, without interest...Whitlam himself, I think, is of a nature to keep up a certain amount of tradition & ceremony, but his wife is not. He will also be almost alone in his Cabinet in standing for a relatively conventional order of things. How long can a man, even if a strong one, stand alone?[23]

She wrote at a moment when it was not certain if Whitlam would remain in office. The Senate, where Labor was in a minority, had rejected several government bills, giving constitutional grounds for Whitlam to request a dissolution of both houses of parliament and a general election. Even if no double dissolution was called, the time had come for an election for half the members of the Senate. To improve his prospects for the half-Senate election, Whitlam proposed the appointment of Vince Gair[24] as Ambassador to the Irish Republic. Gair, a veteran Queensland senator, had fallen out with his colleagues in the Democratic Labor Party, who held the balance of power in the Senate. His departure would create a Senate vacancy that might be filled by a Labor candidate. Hasluck, although he thought the scheme a little too clever, assured himself that it was constitutionally valid and raised no objection, but the manoeuvre was mishandled. Although the Governor-General approved the appointment on 14 March and the Irish Republic endorsed it six days later, it was not until the afternoon of 3 April that Gair wrote to the President of the Senate advising him that he was vacating his seat. By this time the Queensland authorities had issued the writs for the half-Senate election, nullifying the effect of Gair's resignation.[25] Meanwhile, the Coalition and the Democratic Labor Party responded by refusing to pass the government's appropriation bills, thus provoking a dissolution of both houses of parliament.

Hasluck was about to depart for the funeral of the French President, Georges Pompidou, but was unwilling to leave if a political crisis was developing. He pointed out that Whitlam would

> further damage his political reputation if he left any grounds
> for his opponents to say that he had found a pretext for getting
> the Governor-General out of the country while they put up a
> submission for a double dissolution to a deputy.[26]

He went only after receiving a solemn assurance that no action would be taken during his absence.[27] On his return, he was furnished with advice from the Attorney-General's Department that six defeated bills could provide a trigger for a dissolution. On previous occasions, in 1914 and 1951, the Governor-General of the day had been prepared to grant a double dissolution on the ground that only one bill had been twice rejected by the Senate after approval by the House of Representatives. Whitlam could point to no fewer than six pieces of rejected legislation in support of his application. Hasluck took no other advice but granted Whitlam's request, satisfied that supply had been provided and that the electoral rolls and administrative machinery were in readiness. When Whitlam said 'he had not wished to embarrass me by involving the Governor-General in subsequent controversy', Hasluck reported:

> We digressed for some time to consider the need that both he
> and I feel to ensure that the submission he intended to make
> later in the day was such as to do us credit in the eyes of the
> constitutional critic and historian.[28]

During the next twenty-four hours he guided Whitlam through the appropriate procedures, declining to sign the proclamation on 11 April until he had given the royal assent to all the bills passed by the outgoing parliament. Hasluck and Whitlam were unusually conscious of 'the constitutional critic and historian', but it was to turn out that their caution was justified.[29]

The result of the election on 18 May 1974 was ambiguous. The Whitlam government lost a few seats in the House of Representatives but retained a majority. In the Senate the Democratic Labor Party was eliminated, but numbers were even between Labor and the Liberal–National Party[30] opposition, with two independents. This meant that in a joint sitting of both houses the government could pass the legislation in contention. As his last official function Hasluck opened the new Parliament on 9 July 1974. In preparing the Governor-General's speech he was as meticulous a draftsman as ever, demanding the alteration of 'My Government favours a rational national rural policy' as sounding too much like Gilbert and Sullivan. (Whitlam agreed.) He read the speech with 'ceremonial formal facial expression firmly in place'.[31]

That night he was given a farewell dinner by members of parliament, where Whitlam was at his most urbane. After listing Hasluck's numerous fields of achievement, he said: 'There has not been a proconsul of more diverse attainment since Cicero'. He considered Hasluck his most formidable opponent; if the Liberals had chosen him as their leader in 1968 they might have won the 1972 election. The leader of the opposition, Bill Snedden, had, in Nicholas Hasluck's opinion, a most wooden manner...One almost expects to see [the gold watch] in the benign hand of the chairman of directors while the elderly bookkeeper mutters a few words and shuffles off stage to the watering can and the gladioli.[32]

Hasluck in reply stayed with familiar themes. Politics, although it had its share of bad apples, was an honourable profession; the media carried a great responsibility but lapsed too often into inaccuracy. He won a substantial round of applause. Nicholas Hasluck was moved:

> Standing there in a dinner suit, balding, slightly rounded in the shoulders, speaking with a middle-of-the-road Australian accent, a folded serviette held in his strong hands, pugnacious, speaking with recognizable humour rather than facile wit – he looks as though he has plenty of strength left in him. At that moment it is borne into me, how fortunate I am, to see one's father at the peak of his ability.[33]

Nicholas Hasluck was disappointed by the media coverage of his father's retirement. Several reports trotted out the old story of Whitlam throwing the glass of water over Hasluck. One thought his term of office colourless. A more common evaluation was to respect his seriousness of purpose but to find it old-fashioned. 'He's a wonderful chap, but he's living in another century', said the Attorney-General Lionel Murphy. Journalist Creighton Burns wrote in *The Age* that he was 'yesterday's man – a gentleman rather than a player'.[34] But with the passage of years, and experience of other vice-regal performances, there would come a gathering respect for Hasluck's achievement. The perspective from 1989 was summed up by Max Harris:

I don't know how Sir Paul Hasluck fell into the job. For that matter I don't know how he ever chose to fall into politics – he deserved better.

He was, and still is, essentially a writer, intellectual and poet. The only way he knew how to be a politician was to adhere to all the rules and play it by the book. By nature he was not an orator, a perturbator or a backroom powerbroker; perhaps that is how he came to rise to the top of the conservative hierarchy.

It was not in his nature to be a populist...He couldn't be the extrovert good bloke, the common man's figurehead. He wasn't, and isn't, an exemplar of the common man. In any case it wasn't a time for manifest Australianism. We weren't quite ready...[35]

Chapter 23

A vigorous retirement

Paul Hasluck told his son that he saw himself as having five or six years of activity left after retiring to Perth:

> He will not be accepting any positions. He intends to do the things he wants, the things a career in public life have denied him. His present plans are to finish off a work on his years in New Guinea he has already commenced, then to tackle a sizeable autobiographical work, then to do a practical study of Cabinet Government in Australia. He does not intend to be diverted. He makes it very plain...[1]

With Alexandra already established as writer in residence at the Adams Road house, Paul needed to find a working space for himself elsewhere. Fortunately, the perquisites of a retired Governor-General included the right to office space in or close to the central business district. He found premises, at first in an insurance building, later on the third floor of the newly constructed Allendale Square building at the corner of St Georges Terrace and Sherwood Court. With a superb view of the Swan River and an efficient secretary in Patricia Daw,[2] he could soon establish regular working habits.

He punctuated his working life with visits to the sanctuary of his bush block. In the early years of his retirement there was a good deal to be done improving the house and garage. He spent many weekends constructing dry walls from the local stone as a form of bushfire protection, and developed considerable skill at working in this mode. The wildlife included several species of kangaroo and wallaby, goannas and harmless scorpions, but very few snakes; he said he had seen only three in forty years. Because of the lack of surface water the bird life was not numerous, but included treecreepers, honeyeaters and wagtails. He found the bush friendly, and the untroubled environment reminded him of his early formative years in Collie, where he developed his feeling for country and taste for solitude. But he also enjoyed the products of European culture, and listened to classical music, especially the choral works of early masters such as Palestrina, Monteverdi and Johann Sebastian Bach. There was also jazz.

He found no difficulty refraining from comment about the politics of the day, even though the sixteen months following his retirement were among the most turbulent in the history of the Commonwealth parliament. As the Whitlam government confronted crisis after crisis, and as the opposition revitalised itself under a new leader, Malcolm Fraser, Hasluck's successor at Yarralumla, Sir John Kerr, appeared curiously passive. He seemed more concerned with the ceremonial aspects of his position than in taking the keen supervisory interest in political process that Hasluck had exercised with his three prime ministers. He failed to ensure that he met regularly with the Prime Minister, and did not subject the business of the Executive Council to the same detailed scrutiny Hasluck had given it. He raised no objection in December 1974 when Whitlam cut corners in securing the Executive Council's consent to an ill-judged plan to raise loans from unorthodox Middle Eastern sources.

In October–November 1975, when the opposition refused to pass supply through the Senate and Kerr decided eventually to use his vice-regal powers to dismiss the Whitlam ministry, Hasluck maintained an unbroken silence. When Kerr took advice before he acted, as he was entitled to do, his choice of advisers was idiosyncratic. He had no hesitation in consulting old colleagues from the Sydney bar, even if it meant possibly compromising half the members of the High Court who might at some future time be required to pronounce on the constitutional validity of his actions. Apparently he made no move to consult his predecessors as Governor-General, Hasluck, Casey and McKell, although each had long experience of parliamentary politics as well as serving in the vice-regal role. If Casey and McKell might have been seen as too old, Hasluck, both through his practical experience and his magisterial Queale lecture, was uniquely qualified to give him thoughtfully nuanced insights into the problem. In the past Kerr had sought Hasluck's advice. Shortly after taking office he wrote Hasluck a conscientious and thoughtful letter consulting him about the issues arising from the Senate's rejection for a second time of the government's bill on the petroleum industry.[3] He did not keep up this practice, even when a major constitutional crisis was impending. Perhaps Kerr felt that Hasluck might offer advice he did not want to hear.

Hasluck may not have been aware that in one respect Kerr's dismissal of Whitlam on 11 November 1975 served him ill. In March his old colleague from the San Francisco conference, Fin Crisp, seconded by the historian Manning Clark, put Hasluck's name forward for an honorary doctorate from the Australian National University, whose chancellor was Nugget Coombs. Neither of his sponsors came from the same side in politics as Hasluck, but they considered that his distinguished career in scholarship and public service made him well worthy of recognition. The only point at issue was whether he should be offered a doctorate in letters or in law. But when the vice-regal office became embroiled in controversy because of the dismissal, the university authorities took fright. When Crisp was informed that it would not be expedient to award the degree, he angrily resigned from the honorary degrees committee, venting his feelings in a scathing letter. The university never subsequently honoured Hasluck. Approaches were made to him from other universities, including his old alma mater, The University of Western Australia, but he did not accept them.

The repercussions of Whitlam's dismissal lingered into 1977. In March that year Queen Elizabeth II visited Australia and Papua New Guinea as part of a round of celebrations of her silver jubilee. Perth was the last stop on the itinerary. Before departing on the royal yacht *Britannia* the Queen hosted a lunch at which the Haslucks were present, as well as Sir John Kerr, with whom she later had a private audience. In consequence it was decided that Kerr should discreetly retire from the office of Governor-General. When Hasluck visited London in August, the Queen's private secretary, Sir Martin Charteris, took the opportunity for a long and confidential interview with him, seeking an update on opinion in Australia. Buckingham Palace knew that Kerr had been offered lavish sums by the media to reveal his side of the story. Hasluck replied that, although Kerr had shown some weakness for self-justification, and during more than one function at Perth was heard to ask people 'Did I do the right thing?', he could be expected to keep his word.[4]

Hasluck told Charteris that the Governor-General undoubtedly had the right to dismiss the Prime Minister 'if one assumed that Mr Whitlam was in a frame of mind that was unreasonable, arrogant, and indeed close to defiant of any persuasion to conventional courses of action'. The question was whether Kerr had fulfilled the traditional vice-regal function of counselling, advising and warning:

> it seemed to me that in the period leading up to crisis the Governor-General had either acted politically or been neglectful. Of course this view arose from my view that in a constitutional monarchy the wisdom is to avoid confrontation and never let an issue come to a crisis in a political sense...
>
> I said I had always found Whitlam to be an intelligent man and one conscious of the judgment of history as well as immediate advantage...I myself had always found Whitlam responsive to a question or a cautionary word.[5]

Hasluck knew that Whitlam had a poor opinion of Kerr, even when he recommended him for the governor-generalship ('Neither Charteris nor I was quite sure whether or not Whitlam intended Kerr to be his puppet'). This attitude might have been overcome in time:

> If at the time of the 'loans crisis' Kerr had been diligent and attentive to the duties of his office, if he had been available at all times instead of travelling abroad, and if he had called Whitlam to see him more frequently and, in doing this had

established in Whitlam's mind some greater respect for the office of Governor-General and some greater confidence in his (Kerr's) own trustworthiness and wisdom, there would never have been a crisis.[6]

As for the possibility that Whitlam could have telephoned Buckingham Palace recommending the withdrawal of Kerr's commission – a possibility that weighed in Sir Garfield Barwick's advice to Kerr – Hasluck thought it unlikely. Such a momentous step could not be taken on a telephone call. A formal submission to the Queen would be required, backed by support from the Crown's legal advisers, and presented in a form fit for publication.

Before long it became evident that Hasluck's performance of his vice-regal office had left a good impression in a significant quarter. During the previous twenty years the Crown had awarded high honours to two senior Australian statesmen. Casey had been made a life peer and admitted to the highest rank in the knighthood, the Order of the Garter; Menzies, in acknowledgement of his family background, was given the equivalent Scottish award, becoming a Knight of the Thistle. Casey died in 1976 and Menzies in 1978, and it was thought appropriate that another Australian should be recognised. Considerably to his surprise, Hasluck received word in April 1979 that he would become one of the twenty-four Knights of the Garter.

In the previous year Alexandra had also been honoured for services to literature. She was now Dame Alexandra Hasluck, the first woman to be admitted to the highest rank of the Order of Australia. In the same year she published what was to be her last major work of history, an edition of the letters of Audrey

Tennyson, whose husband was a colonial governor at the time of Federation.[7] A valuable and vivid sidelight on the major public figures of the time, the collection was lodged in the National Library of Australia. Professor John La Nauze, a friend of the Haslucks from university days, who had been searching for somebody suitably qualified to edit the correspondence, thought it apt that Alexandra Hasluck, with her experience of vice-regal life, should undertake the project. She began working on it while still at Government House. Although she approached the task with diffidence, she produced an admirable work of scholarly editing, presented in a handsome publication.

At the same time Paul Hasluck was achieving his own impressive record of scholarly publication. He could now concentrate energies pent up during twenty-five years of public service on writing, and he had an able and sympathetic publisher in Peter Ryan at Melbourne University Press. In 1976 *A Time for Building* appeared, his account of his twelve years of stewardship in Papua New Guinea. 'I will try to write only of what I know at first hand and what I did myself, offering my evidence but not completing the story', he began. 'This book will thus be an account given by one witness, not the study undertaken by historians.'[8] This did not prevent some reviewers from complaining that the book gave insufficient credit to other shapers of Papua New Guinea policy, but even the exacting critic Charles Rowley owned that 'it was a really great achievement to have set the Australian relationship with New Guinea in a new direction – sufficiently so that…the colonial tie was not broken in anger'.[9] A university student encountering the book some years later was 'surprised that so literate a book, conveying a great humanity and sincerity of purpose, had been written by an Australian politician'.[10] In consequence Robert Porter was to complete a doctoral thesis and a biographical study of Paul Hasluck.

In 1977 there followed *Mucking About*, an autobiography of his first thirty-five years that presented a loving evocation of the Western Australia of his youth. To this day it remains the most popular of all his works. He also came back to his early interests in Western Australian history. In 1976, as the sole survivor of its inaugural committee, he took part in the fiftieth anniversary celebrations of the Royal Western Australian Historical Society and delivered more than one paper to its meetings. And he took an active interest in the Fremantle Society, which with a fair measure of success fought for the preservation of the port's unusually rich heritage of public and private buildings from the late-nineteenth and early twentieth centuries.

These interests did not mean his scope was narrowing. In 1980 he returned to international relations with the publication of *Diplomatic Witness*, an account of his service in External Affairs between 1941 and 1947. Hasluck had published earlier articles on this period, and in reverting to it he was at least partly impelled by a wish to explore the relationship between a minister, specifically a minister such as Evatt with strong ideas and purposes of his own, and his public-service advisers. He could now write with the authority of one who had seen nearly eighteen years of service as a minister, and for him Evatt was a case study of a minister of potentially great capacity flawed by an inability to use advice and to operate within agreed systems and conventions. Perhaps he was also answering, albeit indirectly, some of the critics of his own ministerial style.

Alexandra Hasluck also ventured into autobiography, and in 1981 *Portrait in a Mirror* appeared. Although it contained some accounts of childhood and university days that complemented Paul's account in *Mucking About*, it went on to cover a public life in which an observant reader could discern some wry sidelights on the personal pressures created by such an existence. Shortly after its publication her health began to break down. She was afflicted by the first of a series of strokes that were to incapacitate her increasingly during the last twelve years of her life. She retained some mobility for a year or two, during which she and Paul celebrated their golden wedding anniversary, but the deterioration continued, and eventually she went permanently into hospital care. Her condition was all the more poignant because, having seen her mother and grandmother succumb to senile dementia in their last years, she had feared a similar fate. During the years of her incapacity, Paul visited her daily.

His working routine had to be modified. As he explained to an interviewer who inquired whether he would write a book on his period as Minister for External Affairs, he had more domestic duties in mornings and evenings, and lacked the energy and the time in an unrestricted way to write as he would like.[11] For the same reason he published nothing about his administration of the Northern Territory. The task to which he gave priority was to set down an account of Aboriginal policy during the period from 1925 to 1965, under the title *Shades of Darkness*. In those years, Australia's objective moved from segregation to assimilation, and Hasluck himself was involved. The debates of the 1980s often showed misunderstanding of the previous generation's approach to these issues, and Hasluck wanted to set the record straight. But younger commentators, while according Hasluck respect for his achievements, considered that 'He was, however, also a man of his time in Aboriginal affairs and by the years of his retirement the times had moved on'.[12]

If he was no longer producing books on a large scale, he was still writing prolifically. Essays, reflections on the past and present, book reviews (done sometimes simply for his own amusement, and not for publication), character sketches of political colleagues, and prefaces to other authors' publications kept him steadily occupied. In most years he took the opportunity of travelling to England for the annual Garter ceremony in April, using the journey to indulge his love of English choral music. In Perth he developed a habit of lunching at the Weld Club, introducing himself to some of the younger members and engaging them in conversation. By all reports this was enjoyed by all parties. He sometimes allowed his irreverent streak a little licence. When Western Australia celebrated the 150th anniversary of European settlement, he recalled that 1829, the year of Captain James Stirling's arrival, also coincided with the publication of Felix Mendelssohn's first symphony. He imagined the two men giving an account of themselves in the afterlife:[13]

> *Now, tell me, Felix, what did you achieve?*
> *'I tossed some semi-quavers in the pond?'*
> *And you – Young Jimmy Stirling, I believe?*
> *'I opened up the way for Alan Bond'.*

Past his eighty-sixth birthday he was still vigorous. In November 1991 he travelled to Darwin to deliver an oration, giving a mellow and appreciative account of his colleagues in the Northern Territory administration. He might have seemed destined to achieve the near-centenarian record of his father. But prostate cancer was diagnosed, and in October 1992 he suffered a severe fall and spent two months in St John of God Hospital, Subiaco. He wrote a wryly humorous account of his infirmities to his former parliamentary colleague Clyde Cameron:

> Through misadventure I am approaching Christmas in the following condition (choose your word):
>> Recumbent
>>
>> Supine
>>
>> Prone
>>
>> Prostrate
>>
>> Flat on my back
>
> Hence no Christmas cards. This brings my greetings, and a promise to write in the New Year.[14]

He was discharged in mid-December, but a few days after returning home he had a second fall with dislocation of a prosthetic hip, and returned to hospital. In poor shape, he was still mentally alert enough to occupy himself with drafting a paper for the Samuel Griffith Society. By some mishap the manuscript went missing on its way to the word processor. When his son Nicholas brought the news it hardly seemed reasonable to ask the sick man to write the whole paper a second time, but the old professional in him rallied. Within twenty-four hours the job was done in his legible handwriting. Then, after three days of acute respiratory failure, he died on 9 January 1993. Characteristically, he had prepared for the event. Some months earlier, he called on the newly appointed Anglican Dean of Perth, who admitted he had scant experience in the conduct of state funerals. Paul

Hasluck explained that he might soon have to conduct one, and, with the assistance of his former secretary, Patricia Pidgeon (née Daw), precise instructions were given.

The funeral service at St George's Cathedral took place on a warm summer's afternoon. The Prime Minister, Paul Keating, attended, as did two of his predecessors, Malcolm Fraser and Bob Hawke. Dame Pattie Menzies was present, escorted by the leader of the opposition, John Hewson. Three of Hasluck's successors as Governor-General, Sir Zelman Cowen, Sir Ninian Stephen and Bill Hayden, also attended, although Sir John Kerr had died two years earlier. Alexandra could not be present, but Paul's sister Rosa was there, as was his old mentor, Professor Fred Alexander. For the most part the service followed the full dignity of the Anglican ritual, and the eulogy by his son Nicholas was appropriately well crafted. But at the end a memory of the man behind the formal Paul Hasluck emerged. As the coffin was borne down the cathedral aisle, four trombonists advanced to the high altar and rendered a spirited performance of 'When the Saints Go Marching In'.

Alexandra lingered for five months more before a merciful release on 18 June 1993. Like Paul she left a carefully prepared will. Most of the arrangements in both wills were straightforward, specifying how the estate and personal effects would be allocated among members of the family. The house at 2 Adams Road was sold, and the purchasers, finding it in need of extensive renovation, demolished it and built another on the site. But the disposal of the block at Paulls Valley gave rise to unexpected difficulties. Observing the accelerating sprawl of Perth's suburbs, Paul had foreseen that in future years it would be valuable to ensure the preservation of an area of the native bushland of the Darling scarp, just as Kings Park in the centre of Perth enabled the survival of 400 hectares of bushland that, if not pristine, at least provided a respectable example of secondary growth. The 35 hectares of Paulls Valley could be preserved as a smaller example of a Darling scarp landscape. Paul had therefore proposed that it should be vested in The University of Western Australia under a trust enduring for seventy-nine years after his death. The four trustees would be Nicholas Hasluck, Patricia Pidgeon, and the university's Vice-Chancellor and professor of botany.

It was an imaginative gesture, symbolising Hasluck's love of the environment and his loyalty to his old university, but it was not welcomed. The professor of botany could not testify that the land in question was of unique ecological importance, though the gift was conceptualised as preserving a block that was typical rather than in any way special. It was uncertain whether the trust could be classified as a charitable trust exempt from rates and taxes, with the majority of legal opinions doubtful. The university baulked at assuming an indefinite financial responsibility, though it accepted Hasluck's bequest of a sum providing for botanical research. It took Nicholas Hasluck nearly four years of patient negotiation before the block was eventually purchased at the end of 1996 by the state government for incorporation into a national park. Hasluck's cottage and garage were demolished, but at the present date the stone walls he built in retirement remain as evidence of his presence.

There is another reminder. At the redistribution of Commonwealth parliamentary seats in 2000 it was decided to create a new House of Representatives electorate in Western Australia, covering a sweep of the foothills of the Darling scarp.

Its borders contained a mixture of semi-rural properties and new suburbs on the expanding east side of the Perth metropolitan area. The constituency was named 'Hasluck' in honour of Paul and Alexandra Hasluck. So far it has proved a marginal seat, veering from Labor to Liberal and back again with every slight shift in voting opinion. We cannot be sure what Sir Paul Hasluck would have thought about this characteristic, but he would probably be pleased that the block at Paulls Valley lies comfortably inside the Hasluck electorate. He would certainly be pleased and feel vindicated by the fact that since 2010 the member for Hasluck has been Ken Wyatt, the first Aboriginal to sit in the House of Representatives.

Chapter 24

An intellectual in politics

It is not quite an oxymoron to speak of intellectuals in Australian politics, but their influence has been limited and their number few. Paul Hasluck was one of the few. If he had never entered politics he would still be remembered as a distinguished historian, poet, cultural publicist and essayist, and an important and early spokesman in favour of Aboriginal rights. This makes him a daunting prospect for the biographer. Precisely because he was a first-class historian who wrote extensively and perceptively on the public life of his time, he was unusually conscious that every minute and memorandum he drafted as a minister, every sentence he wrote in his memoirs, at some time in the future would be read by another historian. Few public figures can have been so conscious of the future looking over their shoulders.

He brought to public life a belief in the rational application of intellect to the resolution of policy, whether in the field of social issues or international relations. Confronted with a problem, whether it related to the status and wellbeing of the indigenous people of Australia and Papua New Guinea, the attainment of a stable balance of power between nations, or the encouragement of the arts, it was the responsibility of the person in authority to take decisions based on a diligent study of all the available facts. In a parliamentary democracy such as the

Australian Commonwealth, public servants would assemble and analyse the relevant data, but decisions would be taken by the cabinet minister who was responsible to parliament, and through parliament to the wider public. If others arrived at different conclusions from the same premises, the differences should be sorted out by civil and intelligent discussion. If the outcome went against Hasluck's preferred position, he would accept it loyally and not seek to undermine those who had overruled it.

His values were consistent. From his Salvation Army background he retained a strong sense of social conscience. Public policy should be attuned to the needs of the less fortunate, who should be helped by education and economic opportunity to achieve a self-supporting independence. The product of a Western Australia that in the early twentieth century placed great value on education as the key to betterment, and great faith in the ideal of the self-reliant yeoman farmer and small businessman, Hasluck sought to provide opportunities of this kind for the indigenous people of Australia and Papua New Guinea. In both, but especially the latter, he upheld the need to develop the human and social resources of the community ahead of the demands of business investment, and this brought him into conflict with sections of his own Liberal Party. His ideas were grounded in belief in a common citizenship, irrespective of race, for all who shared the same environment. If the needs of some groups required special intervention by the government, this should be temporary while they were furnished with the resources that enabled them to become fully participating members of their society.

Like many of his generation, Paul Hasluck took it for granted that for the most part an advanced society would share the values of a common Western civilisation, marked by an infusion of Christian ethics, if not Christian belief, valuing the products of education and culture, but admitting elements of the older traditions of the Indigenous people. As a historian he saw this as a long-term process. His model of a British culture that had absorbed elements of Celtic, Anglo-Saxon, Danish and Norman-French culture into an amalgam that was an improvement on all its different elements was too long term for twentieth-century conditions, but he was far from expecting that all trace of Aboriginality would be eradicated from a homogenous Australian culture; and in Papua New Guinea an infusion of Western culture seemed essential as a glue to bind together the numerous clans and communities. Behind his ideal of communities enjoying a shared national identity there lay an awareness of the environment as a shaping force on all who lived in it. This underpinned his sympathy with Aboriginal Australians. If his own response to the bush was so imaginative and deep, their understanding, the product of many generations, must be stronger. The shared sense of place was the essential foundation of national identity.

But he is not one of the figures Australians remember in their search for national identity. Part of the problem lies with Hasluck's personality, at least those aspects of his personality he chose to display in the conduct of official business. The private man was genial, lively minded, stimulating in conversation, even affording a glimpse at times of a larrikin streak. As a minister his style was often brusque, demanding and aloof. He was not much of a mixer with other parliamentarians, and even when the leadership of his party was at stake he made little effort to muster support. He could be seen as judgemental, and a memoir published after his death contained some tough assessments of former colleagues.

He was even tougher on himself. He was never content with his achievements. As a young man in Perth he was, among other things, a pioneer of oral history, but in later life he proclaimed himself a sceptic about the value of oral history. He was a good journalist, and a critic and publicist who had a dynamic influence on the growth of drama in Western Australia in the 1930s, but he was to define his activities at that time as no more than 'mucking about', and held the profession of journalism in low esteem. Looking back on his political career he often felt that he was 'the wrong driver in the wrong truck': 'I was unable to do many things I would have liked to do and was required to do many things I had no personal interest in doing'. He was usually credited with a good performance as Governor-General, and it is possible that in old age his writings brought him a measure of contentment, but he was never complacent. Somewhere in his early upbringing he must have absorbed too deeply that discouraging text from St Luke's gospel: 'When we have done all that lies within our power to do, we are yet unprofitable servants'.[1]

Another legacy from his upbringing was his difficulty in dealing with emotions and those parts of the human and social condition that are not reducible to rational analysis. Most Australian men of his generation – and perhaps the next and the one after – seemed uncomfortable with strong emotions, and in Paul Hasluck's case this discomfort was sharpened in his early years by his revulsion with the noisy hot-gospelling of some Salvation Army meetings. He lacked an efficient emotional thermostat. Usually relaxed and good-humoured in private, formal and controlled in public, he found himself at times in the grip of an ungovernable anger, apparently built up while suppressing his inner feelings. This was a source of tension in his marriage. It also cramped his effectiveness in public life. He tried to bottle up the resentment and frustration that resulted from the failure of others to understand his arguments, to carry out his requests, to bring the requisite qualities of intelligence and hard work to their responsibilities; but eventually a tart memorandum or an outburst of rage emerged, where a gentle rebuke or comment might have sufficed.

In the long run of history this characteristic is unimportant. Other leaders have been choleric, demanding, and indifferent to their colleagues' reactions. But in an assessment of his achievements it could be argued that his rationality led him to underestimate the place of the emotional – what Arthur Calwell described as the 'inconsistencies and contradictions' – in public affairs. He grasped that in Aboriginal affairs equality of citizenship and the opportunities of citizenship were the first essential for social justice. He may not have fully appreciated that, once this goal was achieved, there was a legacy of emotions built up over generations of racial inequality, and they would take a long time to address. He could argue that a realistic appraisal of international relations called for policies of forward defence that entailed an Australian involvement in Vietnam, without appreciating the shift in values that energised the protesters against Vietnam. In consequence, during his own lifetime he began to seem old-fashioned even in the eyes of some who respected him.

He should be judged in the context of the problems and opportunities of his own time. He grew up in a community with a provincial culture and during the 1930s was a strong influence in widening its perspectives. When Australia was propelled into the international arena by the Second World War and the challenges of a postwar settlement, he played an important part in ensuring his country took a constructive role in the debates. He encountered Aboriginal Australians as a segregated remnant without agency, and left politics when they had secured the status of citizenship. His control of Papua New Guinea at a critical time in its evolution ensured that its people would be united in independence and relatively free of some of the deeper traumas of decolonisation. If his record in foreign policy remains more contentious, he did much to ensure that Australia built up sound ties with the nations of East and South-East Asia. He provided an admirable model of the conduct and initiatives appropriate in an Australian head of state. He was an able historian who left valuable materials for other historians.

It is an impressive record, but there was a cost to his personal happiness. As William Butler Yeats wrote:

> *The intellect of man is forced to choose*
> *Perfection of the life or of the work;*
> *And if it choose the second, must refuse*
> *A heavenly mansion, raging in the dark.*

But for Paul Hasluck there was saving grace in his attachment to the Australian soil:

> *...Where clear skies bless*
> *With fruitfulness, fulfilment and a mood*
> *Of happiness*
> *The place that is my home,*
> *Apples as old as Eden*

Deep in Australian loam
Burden the bough
Where noisily the parakeets return
In coloured flight
And here I read Traherne.
He and the Saxon Sheep are native now.
This is my sacred site.[2]

Notes

ABBREVIATIONS

A&R	Angus & Robertson
ADB	*Australian Dictionary of Biography*, MUP, Melbourne, 1966–present
AGPS	Australian Government Publishing Service
AJPH	*Australian Journal of Politics & History*
ANU	Australian National University
AWM	Australian War Memorial
CPD	*Commonwealth Parliamentary Debates*
CRS	Commonwealth Record Series
CSIR	Council for Scientific and Industrial Research
CSO	Colonial Secretary's Office
CUP	Cambridge University Press
DEA	Department of External Affairs
DFAT	Department of Foreign Affairs and Trade
FCO	Foreign and Commonwealth Office, Australia
FCO	Foreign and Commonwealth Office, United Kingdom
H of R	House of Representatives
ML	Mitchell Library, State Library of New South Wales
MUP	Melbourne University Press
NAA	National Archives of Australia
NLA	National Library of Australia
NTAS	Northern Territory Archives Service
OHA	Oral History Australia
OUP	Oxford University Press
RAHS	Royal Australian Historical Society
SLWA	State Library of Western Australia
SROWA	State Records Office of Western Australia
SWAH	*Studies in Western Australian History*
UQP	University of Queensland Press
UWA	The University of Western Australia

Part I: Years of Aspiration, 1905–51

Chapter 1: Beginnings

1 N. Hasluck, 'The garter box goes back to England', *Quadrant*, vol. 38, no. 9, September 1994, p. 43; see also *The Hasluck Banner*, Freshwater Bay Press, Perth, 2006. I draw the material in this and the following two paragraphs from these sources.

2 S. Trigg, *Shame and Honour: a vulgar history of the Order of the Garter*, University of Pennsylvania Press, Philadelphia, 2012.

3 He did not choose the black swan, after which the river was named, probably because during his lifetime there were no swans, though they have since been re-introduced.

4 P. Hasluck, *Mucking About: an autobiography*, MUP, Melbourne, 1977, p. 9.

5 Ibid., p. 17. As Governor-General attending a public dinner given by the Melbourne Scots, Sir Paul apologised for his lack of Scottish blood. Sir Douglas Menzies replied that as his mother's family originated from the village of Wooler on the English side of the Scottish Border, he should not underestimate the rapacity of Scottish raiders (A. Stirling, Diary, 29 November 1969, DFAT). Paul Hasluck compiled a 'Note on the Name Merna or Meernaa' now in the Hasluck collection. (Here and in all subsequent entries, 'Hasluck collection' refers to the papers, letters, notebooks and journals of Paul and Alexandra Hasluck held by Nicholas and Sally Anne Hasluck and detailed in the Bibliography.) The mistaken attribution of Welsh ancestry is in a Foreign and Commonwealth Office briefing memorandum of 1968 (FCO 24/172).

6 P. Hasluck, *Mucking About*, pp. 11–13.

7 Caedwalla was a son of King Centwine of Wessex, who sent him into exile for some years before he became king between AD685 and 689. I cannot improve on Nicholas Hasluck's conjecture: 'In some private corner of his mind did Lewis see himself as a deposed ruler forced into exile by time and chance?' (information of N. Hasluck).

8 I am indebted to the research notes compiled by Nicholas Hasluck, and also to Mrs Sally Anne Hasluck and my brother, Dr Roger Bolton, for the genealogical material used in these paragraphs. Much of it was unavailable to Sir Paul Hasluck when he wrote *Mucking About*.

9 P. Hasluck to Neville Green, 22 June 1970, states that the Chief Justice of the day commissioned the coat of arms but later had difficulty persuading the Treasury to pay the promised £25 fee (communication from Dr Neville Green; the letter is now in the Hasluck collection). See also P. Hasluck to Neville Green, 24 May 1972, Hasluck collection.

10 SROWA 527/156, CSO 1864/1887. I am indebted to Andrew Morant for this reference.

11 *West Australian*, 20 November 1887; Horace Stirling reminiscences, Battye Library, MSS 2415A, SLWA.

12 E. M. Hasluck, 'Life story and recollections: the early years 1872–1896', Hasluck collection; part published in P. L. Arthur & G. Bolton, *Voices from the West End, Western Australian Museum,* Perth, 2012, pp. 56–63.

13 Ibid.

14 W. C. Best to P. Hasluck, 15 December 1949, Hasluck collection.

15 P. Hasluck, *Mucking About,* p. 19; SROWA 527, CSO 0428/1890.

16 E. M. Hasluck, 'Thirty-four years of full salvation', *War Cry,* 22 June 1929, p. 6; 'Fifty years with the blood and fire in the land of the black swan', unpublished autobiographical MS, Salvation Army Heritage Centre, Melbourne.

17 B. Halse, 'The Salvation Army in WA – its early years: "…Ours is a fast express train"', typescript MS, June 1990, Battye Library, SLWA.

18 P. Hasluck, *Mucking About,* pp. 20, 24; see also E. M. Hasluck, 'Mrs Major E. M. Hasluck nee Patience E. Wooler promoted to Glory March 26th 1954', unpublished MS, Salvation Army Heritage Centre, Melbourne.

19 P. Hasluck, *Mucking About,* p. 20.

20 Electoral roll, 1908. He did not, however, sever his connection with the Salvation Army; in 1905 he was one of the working party that refurbished a pub to become the army's Maylands citadel.

21 P. Hasluck, *Mucking About,* p. 34. The decimal equivalent of a shilling is 10 cents, but 100 years ago its purchasing value would have been more like $10.

22 Ibid., p. 35.

23 Ibid.

24 Ibid., p. 39.

25 *Sunday Times* (Perth), 10 May 1908.

26 E. M. Hasluck, 'Fifty years with the blood and fire'.

27 P. Hasluck, *Mucking About,* p. 50. See also N. S. Coote, *Pioneers of the Collie District, 1880–1930,* Literary Mouse Press, Perth, 1991, pp. 15–50.

28 'Paul Hasluck notes re brother Lewis Hasluck following death in Singapore, World War II', 1945, Hasluck collection (hereafter cited as 'Lewis Hasluck notes').

29 P. Hasluck, *Mucking About,* p. 44; see also P. Hasluck, *The Light That Time Has Made,* NLA, Canberra, 1991, pp. 47–50.

30 P. Hasluck, *Mucking About,* pp. 59–60. His father and one of his sons were stamp collectors, but Paul seems never to have been interested.

31 Ibid., p. 54. A rough diary of the trip kept by Meernaa Hasluck is among the Hasluck collection.

32 Ibid., p. 55.

33 Sphinx Foundation, *Perth Modern School: the history and the heritage,* B+G Resource Enterprises, Cottesloe, 2005.

34 Y. & K. Coate, *More Lonely Graves of Western Australia,* Hesperian Press, Perth, 2000, p. 168.

35 A. Hasluck to Henrietta Drake-Brockman, 13 July 1965, Henrietta Drake-Brockman papers, NLA, MS 1634.

36   P. Hasluck, *The Poet in Australia: a discursive essay*, Hawthorn Press, Melbourne, 1975, pp. 53–5.

CHAPTER 2: APPRENTICESHIP

1   P. Hasluck, *Mucking About*, p. 66.

2   Ibid., p. 62.

3   Ibid., p. 63.

4   Ibid., pp. 68 and 68–72 generally.

5   Ibid., p. 71.

6   Transcript of student record, 'Cultural activities' file, Hasluck collection.

7   P. Hasluck, *Mucking About*, p. 69. See also J. Gregory, 'Education and upward mobility in interwar Western Australia: the case of Perth Modern School' (*SWAH*, vol. 11, 1990, pp. 83–95), a useful article, though I do not entirely agree with its conclusions.

8   E. M. Hasluck, 'Fifty years with the blood and fire'; 'Mrs Major E. M. Hasluck'.

9   These details are taken from 'Lewis Hasluck notes'.

10   'Cultural activities' file, Hasluck collection.

11   'The notebooks of Paul Hasluck, No. 8', Hasluck collection.

12   P. Hasluck, *Mucking About*, p. 74.

13   Herbert Cole Coombs (1906–97), educated at The University of Western Australia and London School of Economics (PhD 1934); Commonwealth Bank 1935–40; director of rationing 1942; director-general of postwar reconstruction 1943–49; governor Commonwealth Bank 1949–68; chair Australian Elizabethan Theatre Trust 1949–68; chancellor Australian National University 1969–76; Australian of the Year 1972; in later life prominent in Aboriginal policy.

14   Testimonials held in 'Cultural activities' file, Hasluck papers. Apart from Parsons and Sharp, they came from a Salvation Army major; the Reverend Tom Allen, a noted Methodist clergyman; and the secretary of the Metropolitan and Suburban Master Bakers' Association.

15   P. Hasluck, *Mucking About*, p. 73.

16   *West Australian*, 22 December 1922.

17   Sir (John) Winthrop Hackett (1848–1916), from 1885 editor of the *West Australian* and from 1912 sole proprietor; member of the Legislative Council 1890–1916; first chancellor 1912–16 and benefactor of The University of Western Australia.

18   Sir Alfred Langler (1865–1928), journalist South Australia 1890–95, Western Australia 1895–1927; succeeded Hackett as managing editor of the *West Australian* 1916–27; negotiated its sale 1926, greatly increasing the value of Hackett's bequest to The University of Western Australia.

19   There is no history of the *West Australian*, though its centenary issue of 5 January 1933 contains a good deal of historical material. An unpublished

manuscript by O. K. Battye is held in the Battye Library, SLWA (MN 1719, Acc. 5192A/27).

20 Dudley Disraeli Braham (1878–1951), *Times* correspondent at St Petersburg 1901–1903 (expelled by the Tsarist government); journalist in Australia 1904–16; editor of the *West Australian* 1916–31; returned to England thereafter.

21 P. Hasluck, *Mucking About*, p. 85.

22 Ibid., p. 91.

23 Extract from 'Issacher', a novel started around 1935 under the influence of the *Chroniques des Pasquier* of the French author Georges Duhamel. The original Issacher was one of the twelve sons of the patriarch Jacob, who according to the Old Testament said: 'Issacher is an ass crouched between two burdens'.

24 P. Hasluck, *Mucking About*, p. 27.

25 I owe this observation to Dr John Nethercote.

26 P. Hasluck, *Mucking About*, p. 83. Curiously, the state electoral roll for 1927 situates him as living with his parents at 3 Keane Street, Midland Junction, although I have found no reference to this in any of his unpublished or published writings, and the Salvation Army records suggest that his parents did not return to Perth until 1928.

27 Ibid., p. 82; see also Chapter 11, 'The feel of the earth'.

28 Leslie Rees (1905–2000), The University of Western Australia 1924–29; University College London 1929–31; drama critic London 1931–35; federal drama editor Australian Broadcasting Commission 1936–66; prolific author of children's stories, and also *The Making of Australian Drama* (1973); AM 1981.

29 Dom Serventy (1904–88), founding member Western Australian Naturalists' Club 1924; Western Australian newspapers 1924–31; BSc The University of Western Australia 1931; PhD Cambridge University 1933; CSIRO staff 1936–66; noted authority on fisheries and bird life; MBE 1973.

30 P. Hasluck, *Mucking About*, p. 84.

31 Personal communication from Dr Rica Erickson. The relationship between Paul and Lewis Hasluck is not unlike that described by George Johnston in *My Brother Jack*.

32 Records of the Western Australian Government Railways held at the SROWA show that Lewis Hasluck was employed in the Locomotive Branch of the Midland Junction Railways Workshop as a labourer on 1 August 1927, becoming a turner's and machinist's assistant in January 1928, and a belt and shaft attendant in January 1933.

33 P. Hasluck, *Mucking About*, pp. 127–30.

34 'The notebooks of Paul Hasluck, No. 8', Hasluck collection.

35 Ibid.

36 P. Hasluck, *Mucking About*, p. 283.

37 'The notebooks of Paul Hasluck, No. 8', Hasluck papers.

38 P. Hasluck, *Mucking About*, p. 84.

39 Malcolm John Leggoe Uren (1900–73), joined West Australian newspapers 1920, retiring 1965; OBE 1965; publications include *Sailormen's Ghosts* (1940), *Glint of Gold* (1948) and *Land Looking West* (1948).

40 Walter James (1905–91), worked on the *West Australian* until 1945, when he tried unsuccessfully to establish a vineyard at Darlington. He returned to journalism in Melbourne in 1948 and lived there until his death, publishing some of Australia's earliest modern volumes on food and wine.

41 The minutes of the Arts Club are preserved among the Hasluck collection. Its members included Roy Nevile, later a Supreme Court judge; Ken Hatfield, later a prominent lawyer; and Colsell Sanders, later registrar and professor of education at The University of Western Australia. All quotations in this paragraph are taken from the minute book.

42 P. Hasluck, *Mucking About*, pp. 141–50; P. Hasluck, 'The founding of the society: some personal reminiscences', *Early Days*, vol. 8, no. 1, 1977, pp. 7–22. The prefix 'Royal' was added to the society's name in 1963.

43 P. Hasluck, *Mucking About*, p. 143.

44 S. J. Hunt & G. Bolton, 'Cleansing the dunghill: water supply and sanitation in Perth 1878–1912', *SWAH*, vol. 2, 1977, pp. 8–24. Traylen had been mayor of Guildford 1914–18, when the Hasluck family went to live there.

45 I have dealt with this aspect of Hasluck's activities in 'Oral history', in T. Stannage, K. Saunders & R. Nile (eds), *Paul Hasluck in Australian History: civic personality, and public life*, UQP, Brisbane, 1998. I hope to publish an edition of the transcripts, which are held in the SROWA.

46 P. Hasluck, 'The founding of the society', p. 15.

47 C. T. Stannage, review of P. Hasluck, *Mucking About*, *SWAH*, vol. 3, 1978, pp. 56–7; J. Gregory, 'Western Australia between the wars: the consensus myth', *SWAH*, vol. 11, 1990, pp. 1–18. I have to declare an interest here; my own view is that Hasluck was largely accurate, however much attitudes have changed since.

48 P. Hasluck, *Mucking About*, pp. 148–9.

CHAPTER 3: 'SKIPPING UP THE STAIRS OF CULTURE'

1 Paul Hasluck's own description of his activities in these years (*Mucking About*, Chapter 16).

2 P. Hasluck, *Mucking About* (p. 99) states that he served for 'more than twelve years', but he was still a vice-president in 1940 when he resigned, despite requests to reconsider his decision, because of the outbreak of war (J. A. K. Tonkin to P. Hasluck, 18 June 1940, Hasluck collection).

3 Leslie Rees, oral history transcript, 28 October 1980, Battye Library, OHA402, SLWA; F. Alexander, *Campus at Crawley: a narrative and critical appreciation of the first fifty years of The University of Western Australia*, F. W. Cheshire for University of Western Australia Press, Melbourne, 1963, pp. 385–6.

4   P. Hasluck, *Mucking About*, p. 150.

5   Ibid., p. 152.

6   *Black Swan*, vol. 13, no. 1, 1929, p. 33.

7   M. Drabble (ed.), *The Oxford Companion to English Literature*, 5th edn, OUP, Oxford, 1985, p. 331; A. Hasluck, *Portrait in a Mirror: an autobiography*, OUP, Melbourne, 1979, p. 113 (hereafter cited as *Portrait*).

8   *Black Swan*, vol. 13, no. 3, 1929, p. 18.

9   She was known as 'Alix' at university, and to a few close friends in later life.

10 Alix Darker to P. Hasluck, 'Tuesday', Hasluck collection. She was less successful when she tried to enlist John La Nauze to play Death, needing 'a gaunt, sallow, sinister-looking person' for the part. Offended, La Nauze refused (N. Hasluck to Joan Pope, 20 May 2006).

11 *Black Swan*, vol. 13, no. 3, 1929, p. 18.

12 P. Hasluck, *Mucking About*, p. 123. This attitude was not uncommon among young men in Perth in the 1920s; see W. K. Hancock, *Country and Calling*, Faber, London, 1954.

13 Gertrude Miller to P. Hasluck, 20 March 1929; Beatrice Page to P. Hasluck, 22 March 1929; Rachel Green to P. Hasluck, 5 December 1929, all in Hasluck collection.

14 P. Hasluck, *Mucking About*, pp. 112–13.

15 A. Hasluck, *Portrait*, Chapter 2; R. L. Whitmore, 'Darker, Walter Bruce (1878–1950)', *ADB*, vol. 13, p. 572.

16 S. Lynam, *Humanity Dick: a biography of Richard Martin, MP, 1754–1834*, Hamilton, London, 1975; W. B. Yeats, 'The colonel went sailing', *Collected Poems*, 2nd edn, Macmillan, London, 1950, pp. 361–4.

17 Alix Darker to P. Hasluck, 'Thursday' [postmarked 14 June 1930], Hasluck collection.

18 Evelyn Darker to P. Hasluck, 16 May 1932, Hasluck collection.

19 L. Rees, 'Feathers from the *Black Swan*', *Artlook*, vol. 6, no. 10, October 1980, pp. 33–5.

20 'The notebooks of Paul Hasluck, No. 8', Hasluck collection.

21 Edward Vidler (1863–1942), emigrated from England 1888; editor *Geelong News* 1890–98, *Tatler* (Melbourne) 1901–1907, head of publishing Robertson & Co. from 1908; founder Australian Institute of Australian Literature 1921–31. William Moore (1868–1937), art and drama critic Melbourne *Herald* 1904–12; to London 1912–19; then journalist in Sydney; published *The Story of Australian Art* (1934).

22 Moore to P. Hasluck, 8 October [1929], Hasluck collection. Best known for his comedy *The Time is Not Yet Ripe*, Louis Esson (1878–1943) was encouraged by W. B. Yeats to develop a national theatre movement in Australia, but he had little success and had almost ceased writing by 1929 (D. R. Walker, 'Esson, Thomas Louis Buvelot [1878–1943]', *ADB*, vol. 8, pp. 440–1).

23 Moore to P. Hasluck, 7 December [1929], Hasluck collection.

24 Vidler to P. Hasluck, 20 January 1930 and 19 November 1929, Hasluck collection.

25 Rees to P. Hasluck, 1 January 1930, Hasluck collection.

26 *Pelican*, 13 June 1930. Reviews were anonymous, and at first some readers attributed these comments to John La Nauze (Alix Darker to P. Hasluck, 'Thursday' [postmarked 14 June 1930]). She herself wrote: 'Darling, it *was* virulent'.

27 *Pelican*, 25 July 1930.

28 Ibid., 5 September 1930.

29 Rees to P. Hasluck, 14 November [1930] and 21 January 1931, Hasluck collection.

30 L. Reece, 'Rees, Coralie Clarke (1908–1972)', *ADB*, vol. 16, p. 67. Coralie Clarke Rees (1908–72), BA The University of Western Australia; scholarship to University of London 1930; married Leslie Rees 1931; collaborated with him on many of his publications.

31 *Black Swan*, vol. 15, no. 2, 1931, pp. 11–20.

32 Moore to P. Hasluck, 20 November [1931], Hasluck collection. Later (16 February 1932) Moore wrote that the Perth Repertory Club 'is not originating anything, and is the only repertory society in Australia which ignores Australian drama. It must be composed of very superior persons'.

33 *Black Swan*, vol. 15, no. 2, 1931, pp. 35–9.

34 P. Hasluck, *Collected Verse*, Hawthorn Press, Melbourne, 1969, p. 97.

35 'Murder Farm' and 'Dialogue between Collaborators', both in Hasluck collection.

36 Moore to P. Hasluck, n.d., Hasluck collection.

37 Elizabeth Caroline (Carrie) Tennant (1899–1989) came to Sydney from England in the early 1920s; established Community Playhouse, Darlinghurst, 1929, with annual competition for one-act plays 1930–32; later an anthropologist and authority on the social aspects of town planning.

38 Moore to P. Hasluck, 14 April 1932, Hasluck collection.

39 Dora Moore to P. Hasluck, 14 April 1932, Hasluck collection.

40 Sir James Mitchell to Sir Granville Ryrie, 1 April 1932, Hasluck collection.

41 A. Hasluck, *Portrait*, p. 120.

42 A. Hasluck, Diary, April–June 1932, Hasluck collection.

43 A. Hasluck, *Portrait*, p. 127.

44 P. Hasluck, *Mucking About*, p. 176.

45 Ibid., pp. 281–2.

46 A. Hasluck, *Portrait*, p. 126.

47 P. Hasluck, *Mucking About*, Chapter 15; 'Geneva International Summer School: an account of the seventh annual session', brochure, Hasluck collection.

48 Ibid., p. 187.

49 C. T. Stannage, review of P. Hasluck, *Mucking About*, p. 56.

50 P. Hasluck, *Mucking About*, Chapter 14; cuttings from the *West Australian*, Hasluck collection.

51 Fred Alexander (1899–1996), born in Victoria; a graduate of Melbourne and Oxford (Balliol College); appointed lecturer at The University of Western Australia in 1924, retiring as professor in 1966; director of adult education, 1941–54; established the Festival of Perth 1953.

52 I draw on several conversations with Fred Alexander, but see A. Hasluck, *Portrait*, pp. 130–1. In *Mucking About* (p. 195) Hasluck states that after returning from his travels he was too late to enrol in 1933, but this is one of the very rare occasions when his memory must have been amiss. His academic transcript at The University of Western Australia (UWA Archives, E01/136) shows he passed two units with distinction in 1933, as well as being granted credit for two units taken as part of his Diploma of Journalism. He was indeed late for enrolment, but Fred Alexander was adept at stretching the rules for a promising student.

53 E. M. Hasluck to P. Hasluck, 12 June 1932 and 19 September 1932, Hasluck collection.

54 A. Hasluck, *Portrait*, pp. 132–3; author's conversation with Sir Paul Hasluck, c. 1987.

CHAPTER 4: ENCOUNTERING BLACK AUSTRALIANS

1 Lionel Yarran, spokesman for the Badjaling Aboriginal people, quoted in A. Haebich, *For Their Own Good: Aborigines and government in the South West of Western Australia, 1900–1940*, University of Western Australia Press for the Charles and Joy Staples South West Region Publications Fund, Perth, 1988, p. 301.

2 P. Hasluck, *Mucking About*, pp. 203 and 202–204 generally; see also P. Hasluck, *Shades of Darkness: Aboriginal affairs 1925–1965*, MUP, Melbourne, 1988, pp. 20–1.

3 Ibid., pp. 206–209.

4 P. H. 'Tales of Old Jupiter', *Black Swan*, vol. 12, no. 3, 1928, pp. 39–41. The provenance of these stories appears to be the district between Mount Barker and the Stirling Range.

5 Alexandra Hasluck remembered how at a costume ball held by the Historical Society, the 82-year-old Hammond 'polked me to a standstill one night during an energetic polka' (*Portrait*, p. 134).

6 Dr James Sykes Battye was State Librarian for sixty years until his death in 1954, and published *Western Australia: a history* (1924), the standard reference of his generation. Auber Octavius Neville was the influential Chief Protector of Aborigines from 1915 to 1940.

7 Hammond to P. Hasluck, 11 July 1932, Hasluck papers, NLA, MS 5274.

8 J. E. Hammond, *Winjan's People: the story of the South-West Australian Aborigines*, Hesperian Press, Perth, 1933 (facsimile edn 1980).

9   This term is now disused as derogatory.

10 Department of Aborigines, Annual Report, 1932, quoted in G. C. Bolton, 'Black and white after 1897', in C. T. Stannage (ed.), *A New History of Western Australia*, University of Western Australia Press, Perth, 1981, p. 143.

11 P. Hasluck, *Black Australians: a survey of native policy in Western Australia, 1829–1897*, 1st edn, MUP, Melbourne, 1942, p. 223.

12 Haebich, *For Their Own Good*, pp. 301–307.

13 P. Hasluck, *Mucking About*, p. 209.

14 Ibid., p. 217.

15 V. Whittington, *Sister Kate: a life dedicated to children in need of care*, University of Western Australia Press, Perth, 1999, p. 329. I draw on this work for the material in this paragraph.

16 Bennett's claims were reported in *Daily News* (Perth), 17 June 1933: 'Natives are virtually slaves'. Her father, Robert Christison of Lammermoor station, was notably humane in his dealings with Aboriginal people.

17 P. Hasluck, *Mucking About*, p. 214.

18 Henry Doyle Moseley (1884–1966), entered the WA public service 1900; AIF 1916–19; magistrate Carnarvon 1924, Northam 1926, Perth 1928–49; chaired many royal commissions and inquiries.

19 *West Australian*, 8, 9 and 10 March 1934.

20 *West Australian*, 18 June 1932.

21 A. Hasluck, *Unwilling Emigrants: a study of the convict period in Western Australia*, OUP, Melbourne 1959, pp. xi–xiv.

22 P. Hasluck, 'At Wyndham', *Collected Verse*, pp. 2–3. Two decades later, on a ministerial visit, he thought Wyndham had deteriorated into 'about the most swinish place I have ever seen...The great working class seems to be able to spend pounds and pounds every night and gets most beastly and disgustingly drunk' (P. Hasluck to A. Hasluck, n.d., Hasluck collection).

23 A. Haebich, 'The formative years', in Stannage, Saunders & Nile (eds), *Paul Hasluck in Australian History*, p. 98.

24 Ibid., p. 99.

25 M. P. Durack, Diary, 5 June 1934, Battye Library, Acc. 7273A, SLWA.

26 P. Hasluck, *Shades of Darkness*, p. 59.

27 Ibid., pp. 59–60. After the publication of Hasluck's reports (of which he approved as 'nothing hysterical, nothing overdrawn'), Durack wrote a letter to the *West Australian* from which these excerpts are quoted.

28 P. Hasluck, *Mucking About*, p. 217.

29 P. Hasluck, 'Kimberley scenes', MS, Hasluck collection, p. 53.

30 'The notebooks of Paul Hasluck, No. 8', Hasluck collection.

31 P. Hasluck, *Shades of Darkness*, p. 61; *Mucking About*, p. 220.

32 I owe this insight to discussion with Professor Tim Rowse.

33 *West Australian*, 3 July 1934; Haebich, *For Their Own Good*, p. 99.

34 *West Australian*, 11 July 1934.

35 P. Hasluck to A. Hasluck, 'Thursday' [probably 1 August 1934], Hasluck collection.

36 P. Hasluck to A. Hasluck, 14 August 1934.

37 P. Hasluck, *Mucking About*, p. 216.

38 'Report of the Royal Commissioner appointed to investigate, report and advise upon matters in relation to the condition and treatment of Aborigines', *Votes and Proceedings*, Western Australia, Parliament, 1935, vol. 1; Haebich, *For Their Own Good*, pp. 322–30, 338–9.

39 P. Hasluck, *Black Australians: a survey of native policy in Western Australia, 1829–1897*, 2nd edn, MUP, Melbourne, 1970, p. 3.

40 Emphasis in original.

41 *West Australian*, 23, 24, 25 and 27 July 1936; published subsequently by the Native Welfare Council as *Our Southern Half-Caste Natives and Their Condition* (Perth, 1936).

42 Haebich, *For Their Own Good*, p. 344.

43 Ibid., p. 352; R. McGregor, '"Breed out the colour" or the importance of being White', *Australian Historical Studies*, vol. 33, no. 120, 2002, pp. 286–302.

44 P. Hasluck, *Shades of Darkness*, p. 23.

45 Judith Brett, quoted in 'Sir Paul Hasluck', *Hindsight*, ABC Radio National, 9 July 2000.

46 He chose not to retain them as his personal property, and they finished up with his personal assistant, Ellestan Dusting. The administrators of her estate presented the collection to AIATSIS (*The Australian*, 19 January 2011).

47 P. Hasluck, *Mucking About*, p. 226.

48 Ibid.

49 A. Hasluck, *Portrait*, p. 131.

50 P. Hasluck, *Mucking About*, p. 280; see also UWA Archives, file E01/136, from which all references to Hasluck's academic transcript are taken.

51 Professor Alexander made this comment to me on the afternoon of Hasluck's funeral, January 1993.

52 J. S. Battye, *Western Australia: a history from its discovery to the inauguration of the Commonwealth*, Clarendon Press, Oxford, 1924.

53 This was eventually published as 'The early years of John Forrest', *Early Days*, vol. 8, no. 1, 1977, pp. 69–97.

54 Academic transcript, UWA Archives, file E01/136.

55 P. Hasluck, *Shades of Darkness*, p. 33.

56 This was E. J. B. Foxcroft (1915–62), whose research, mainly in Victoria, was published as *Australian Native Policy: its history, especially in Victoria*, MUP in association with OUP, Melbourne, 1941. He became lecturer in politics University of Melbourne 1939–42; Commonwealth public servant in various positions 1942–55; official secretary Australia House 1955–58; assistant secretary Department of Territories 1958–62.

57 Examiner's report, 3 June 1940, UWA Archives, file E01/136.

58 Ibid., 18 March 1940.

59 P. Hasluck, *Black Australians*, 2nd edn, p. 3.

60 A. P. Elkin, review of P. Hasluck, *Black Australians, Historical Studies: Australia and New Zealand*, vol. 2, no. 8, 1943, pp. 274–9.

61 H. I. Hogbin, review of P. Hasluck, *Black Australians, Australian Quarterly*, vol. 15, no. 2, 1943, p. 100.

62 Price to P. Hasluck, 31 January 1943, Hasluck collection. Price reviewed the book for the American publication *Geographical Review* (vol. 34, no. 3, 1944, pp. 476–78). (Sir) Archibald Grenfell Price (1892–1977) was master of St Mark's College, Adelaide, 1925–57; MP for Boothby (SA) 1941–43; chairman National Library Board 1961–73; knighted 1963.

63 P. Hasluck, *Black Australians*, 2nd edn, pp. 57–8.

64 Ibid., p. 203.

65 See, for instance, W. K. Hancock, *Australia*, Ernest Benn, London, 1930, pp. 32–33, favouring 'well policed local reserves'. Hasluck thought this view implicit in the resolutions of the Canberra conference of April 1937.

66 P. Hasluck, *Black Australians*, 2nd edn, p. 206.

67 Ibid.

Chapter 5: 'We had to do it ourselves'

1 'Claremont in the 1920s and 1930s – Paul Hasluck's view', in G. Bolton & J. Gregory, *Claremont: a history*, University of Western Australia Press, 1998, pp. 184–93.

2 A. Hasluck, *Portrait*, p. 131.

3 Ibid., p. 140.

4 P. Hasluck, *Mucking About*, pp. 240–1.

5 A. Hasluck to P. Hasluck, 4 August 1934, Hasluck collection.

6 Griff Richards, quoted in 'Sir Paul Hasluck', *Hindsight*, ABC Radio National, 9 July 2000. Richards, together with Bob James, was among the 'one or two he was friendly with' for the rest of their lives.

7 Penton to P. Hasluck, 29 September 1936, Hasluck collection. He placed Hasluck on a level with the British critic V. S. Pritchett and with T. S. Stribling of the Baltimore *Sun*.

8 Memorandum, 1971, Hasluck collection. A variant version is in *Mucking About* (p. 199). His contemporary, the poet W. H. Auden, wrote: 'Only a minor talent can be a perfect gentleman; a major talent is always more than a bit of a cad' (*The Dyer's Hand and Other Essays*, Faber, London, 1963, p. 21).

9 P. Hasluck to Henrietta Drake-Brockman, 13 August 1945, Henrietta Drake-Brockman papers, NLA, MS 1634.

10 P. Hasluck, *Mucking About*, p. 199.

11 He grew a moustache experimentally during his tour with the Moseley commission in 1934, but it became permanent only after Alexandra told him it added maturity to his appearance.

12 Bruce Bennett, quoted in 'Sir Paul Hasluck', *Hindsight*, ABC Radio National, 9 July 2000.

13 P. Hasluck, 'The burden of Habakkuk and the sword of Gideon', *Collected Verse*, pp. 115–40; B. Bennett, 'Poet', in Stannage, Saunders & Nile (eds), *Paul Hasluck in Australian History*, pp. 32–3.

14 P. Hasluck, 'Songs of Australia', *Collected Verse*, p. 112.

15 N. Hasluck & F. Zwicky, 'Poetry', in B. Bennett (ed.), *The Literature of Western Australia*, University of Western Australia Press for the Education Committee of the 150th Anniversary Celebrations, Perth, 1979, p. 157. The Vulgate is the translation originally produced by St Jerome in the late fourth century and accepted as canonical by the Catholic Church.

16 P. Hasluck, 'Breaking point', *Collected Verse*, p. 52.

17 Oral history interview with Don Baker, 30 January – 3 March 1992, NLA, TRC 2194.

18 H. Wright, 'A liberal "respect for small property": Paul Hasluck and the "landless proletariat" in the Territory of Papua and New Guinea, 1951–63', *Australian Historical Studies*, vol. 33, no. 119, 2002, pp. 55–72.

19 'Lectures and radio talks mainly on literary subjects given in 1935, 1936 and 1937 by Paul Hasluck', Hasluck collection.

20 'The notebooks of Paul Hasluck, No. 8', Hasluck collection.

21 Reginald (Rex) Ingamells (1913–55), schoolteacher 1936–45; publishers' representative 1945–55; rejected for a number of academic appointments; founded Jindyworobak movement 1937–41.

22 Ingamells to P. Hasluck, 18 July 1941, Hasluck collection.

23 'The notebooks of Paul Hasluck, No. 8', Hasluck collection.

24 A useful introduction to this period is T. Craig, 'Radical and conservative theatre in Perth in the 1930s', *Studies in Western Australian History*, no. 11, 'Western Australia between the wars 1919–1939', pp. 106–18.

25 P. Hasluck, *Mucking About*, p. 200.

26 A. Hasluck, *Portrait*, p. 137.

27 Craig, 'Radical and conservative theatre in Perth', p. 109; see also comments by David Hough in *A Dream of Passion: the centennial history of His Majesty's Theatre* (His Majesty's Theatre, Perth, 2004).

28 This and other quotations from 'Polygon' are taken from a scrapbook of cuttings in the State Records Office of Western Australia (3499A) but the entries are not dated. Folklore in the Perth drama community credits Hasluck with a review beginning: 'The prompter, occasionally assisted by members of the cast, gave a spirited performance of...' but this is the closest I have been able to find.

29 Albert Kornweibel, interviewed by Joan Ambrose, 31 May 1977, NLA, TRC 541.

30 Craig, 'Radical and conservative theatre in Perth', p. 108.

31 Ibid.; *West Australian*, 20 June 1936.

32 Craig, 'Radical and conservative theatre in Perth', pp. 109, 111; *West Australian*, 29 July 1939.

33 P. Hasluck, *Mucking About*, p. 246.

34   Ibid.

35   SROWA, 3499A/8/1–12 and Battye Library, 10/1–14, SLWA. 'Jaxartes' was probably Alexander Turner, who was to have a long career as drama producer with the Australian Broadcasting Commission.

36   Ibid.

37   SROWA, 3499A/9/1–5. The members of the working party were Hasluck, A. W. Darbyshire, Harold Krantz, Keith George and Sol Sainken, whose friendship for Hasluck evidently survived criticism.

38   Bishop to P. Hasluck, 26 March 1941, Hasluck collection.

39   P. Hasluck, *Mucking About*, p. 247.

40   Green to P. Hasluck, 20 March 1942; Palmer to P. Hasluck, 4 October 1943, both in Hasluck collection.

41   P. Hasluck to 'Beppo', 4 July 1939; 'Beppo' to P. Hasluck, 28 June 1939 and 17 July 1939, all in Hasluck collection. 'Beppo' was the nickname of Colin Badger, then at the Melbourne University Extension Board.

42   Curtin to P. Hasluck, 29 June 1939, Hasluck collection.

43   P. Hasluck to 'Beppo', 4 July 1939, Hasluck collection. The Benedictine Dom William was reportedly engaged on the project for many years. It was only in 1970 that a translation by Father E. J. Stormon appeared.

44   P. Hasluck, *Mucking About*, p. 247.

45   Fryer to P. Hasluck, 25 March 1940; Gartner to P. Hasluck, 31 March 1940; Walter Murdoch to P. Hasluck, 4 April 1940, all in Hasluck collection.

46   A. Hasluck, *Portrait*, p. 135.

47   The journey is described in *Mucking About* (pp. 249–63) and A. Hasluck, 'Diary trip to Saigon', Hasluck collection.

48   P. Hasluck, *Mucking About*, p. 260.

49   Sir George Alexander Currie (1896–1984) served in the Gordon Highlanders 1914–19; BSc and DSc University of Aberdeen; managed a Queensland sugar plantation 1923–26; officer Queensland Department of Agriculture and Stock 1926–29; at CSIR 1929–39; professor of agriculture University of Western Australia 1939–45 and Vice-Chancellor 1941–52; Vice-Chancellor University of New Zealand 1952–62; returned to Australia.

50   Currie to P. Hasluck, 24 December 1940, UWA Archives, file D4727.

51   Meernaa Hasluck to Rosa Hasluck, 10 August 1941, Hasluck collection.

52   P. Hasluck, *Mucking About*, p. 264.

53   Bill Bunbury, quoted in 'Sir Paul Hasluck', *Hindsight*, ABC Radio National, 9 July 2000.

54   Frederick Alexander, interviewed by Bruce Miller (24 October 1976, NLA, TRC 477), confirmed by several personal conversations.

55   Mitchell to P. Hasluck, 18 March 1941, Hasluck collection. For Mitchell as mentor, see P. Hasluck, *A Time for Building: Australian administration in Papua and New Guinea, 1951–1963* (MUP, Melbourne, 1976, p. 66): 'He said it was easy to be a good Minister and even easier to be a bad one. The most important thing was strict care over public expenditure and public appointments'.

CHAPTER 6: CANBERRA IN WARTIME

1   In *Portrait* (pp. 141–6) Alix graphically describes the move.

2   A. Hasluck to Henrietta Drake-Brockman, 11 June 1941, Henrietta Drake-Brockman papers, NLA, MS 1634, series 3, folder 9.

3   A. Hasluck to Henrietta Drake-Brockman, 'Thursday' [March/April 1942], Henrietta Drake-Brockman papers, NLA, MS 1634, series 3, folder 9.

4   P. Hasluck to Henrietta Drake-Brockman, 30 June 1941, Henrietta Drake-Brockman papers, NLA, MS 1634, series 3, folder 9. P. Hasluck to Rosa Hasluck, 11 October 1941 (Hasluck collection), describes enjoyment of a bushman's carnival at Queanbeyan.

5   P. Hasluck to Henrietta Drake-Brockman, 30 June 1941, Henrietta Drake-Brockman papers, NLA, MS 1634, series 3, folder 9.

6   'The organisation of Australia's external relations in the department of Foreign Affairs', in R. G. Neale (ed.), *Documents on Australian Foreign Policy 1937–49*, vol. 1, '1937–38', AGPS, Canberra, 1975, Appendix II, p. 550; R. Porter, *Paul Hasluck: a political biography*, University of Western Australia Press, Perth, 1993, p. 19.

7   A. Watt, 'Hodgson, William Roy (1892–1958)', *ADB*, vol. 9, pp. 321–2; P. Hasluck, *Diplomatic Witness: Australian foreign affairs, 1941–1947*, MUP, Melbourne, 1980, pp. 8–10; A. Watt, *Australian Diplomat: memoirs of Sir Alan Watt*, A&R in association with the Australian Institute of International Affairs, Sydney, 1972, p. 19.

8   P. Hasluck, 'Diary 1941–42', 20 October 1941, 5 January 1942, Hasluck collection; A. Hasluck, *Portrait*, p. 144; P. Hasluck, *Diplomatic Witness*, p. 6. But Alan Watt found Hood quiet, laconic and easy to work with, although 'some family and personal problems hampered the complete fulfilment of his early promise' (Watt, *Australian Diplomat*, p. 26).

9   A. Hasluck, *Portrait*, p. 151. Porter has detected a lonely example of cordiality in a cablegram from Hood to Paul Hasluck while the latter was in Canada, including the phrase 'Family well' (DEA cablegram 19.12.42, p. 11, NAA: M1942, box 3).

10 W. D. Forsyth, 'Recollections of a maverick diplomat', Book 2, Chapter 3, Sir Paul Hasluck papers, NLA, MS 5274, box 71.

11 P. Hasluck, *Mucking About* p. 266; see also W. J. Hudson, quoted in J. Beaumont, 'Paul Hasluck: the diplomat as minister', in J. Beaumont, C. Waters, D. Lowe & G. Woodard (eds), *Ministers, Mandarins and Diplomats: Australian foreign policy making, 1941–1969*, MUP, Melbourne, 2003, p. 136.

12 Beaumont, 'Paul Hasluck: the diplomat as minister', p. 131.

13 Stuart Macintyre, personal communication by email, 6 April 2011.

14 P. Hasluck, 'Diary 1941–42', 20 October 1941, Hasluck collection.

15 Ibid., 12 November 1941.

16 H. J. Lambert to P. Hasluck, 1 April 1941 and 29 September 1941; Richards to P. Hasluck, 17 January 1942, all in Hasluck collection.

17 P. Hasluck, *Diplomatic Witness*, p. 56; P. Hasluck, 'Australia and the formation of the United Nations: some personal reminiscences', *RAHS Journal and Proceedings*, vol. 15, no. 3, 1954, p. 135.

18 P. Hasluck, *Diplomatic Witness*, pp. 43–45.

19 Ibid., p. 45.

20 Patience Hasluck to Rosa Hasluck, 17 May 1942, Hasluck collection.

21 P. Hasluck to Rosa Hasluck, 26 March 1941 [actually 1942], Hasluck collection.

22 A. Hasluck to Henrietta Drake-Brockman, 'Thursday' [1942], Henrietta Drake-Brockman papers, NLA, MS 1634, series 3, folder 9.

23 A. Hasluck, *Portrait*, p. 157.

24 P. Hasluck to Rosa Hasluck, 26 March 1941 [1942] and 5 May 1942, Hasluck collection.

25 A. Hasluck, *Portrait*, p. 156.

26 Ibid., p. 155.

27 Ibid., p. 230.

28 P. Hasluck, *Diplomatic Witness*, p. 62; P. Hasluck, *The Government and the People, 1942–1945*, AWM, Canberra, 1970, pp. 456–9, 524–40.

29 W. D. Forsyth, *The Myth of Open Spaces: Australian, British and world trends of population and migration*, MUP in association with OUP, Melbourne, 1942.

30 [P. Hasluck], 'Report on the Pacific Relations Conference', Mont Tremblant, Quebec, 4–16 December 1942, Hasluck collection; G. C. Bolton, *Dick Boyer: an Australian humanist*, ANU Press, Canberra, 1967, pp. 85–9.

31 'Report on the Pacific Relations Conference', p. 3; Bolton, *Dick Boyer*, p. 84 (see pp. 84–7 for the proceedings of the conference).

32 [P. Hasluck], 'Report on the eighth conference of the Institute of Pacific Relations, December 4th to 14th 1942', NAA: M1942, 5.

33 Ibid.

34 P. Hasluck, *Mucking About*, p. 282.

35 P. Hasluck to Coombs, 29 April 1943, NAA: M1942, 36.

36 Forsyth to Eggleston, 14 May 1943, Sir Paul Hasluck papers, NLA, MS 5274, and William Douglass Forsyth papers, NLA, MS 5700, series 6, folder 2.

37 P. Hasluck to Watt, 5 April 1943, NAA: M1942, 36.

38 P. Hasluck, *Diplomatic Witness*, p. 140.

39 P. G. Edwards, *Prime Ministers and Diplomats: the making of Australian foreign policy 1901–1949*, OUP in association with the Australian Institute of International Affairs, Melbourne, 1983, p. 145.

40 Burton to P. Hasluck, n.d. [May 1943], NAA: M1942, 36.

41 Burton to P. Hasluck, 16 June 1943, NAA: M1942, 36.

42 Edwards, *Prime Ministers and Diplomats*, pp. 146–7.

43 P. Hasluck to J. B. Brigden, 28 November 1943, NAA: M1942, 36.

44 Edwards, *Prime Ministers and Diplomats*, pp. 152–3; P. Hasluck, *Diplomatic Witness*, pp. 131–2; P. Hasluck, *The Government and the People, 1942–1945*,

pp. 608–609; Peter Ryan, oral history interview, 10–11 October 2000, NLA, TRC 4631.

45 P. Hasluck to Brigden, 8 September 1943, NAA: M1942, 36.

46 P. Hasluck to Watt, 30 July 1943; Watt to P. Hasluck, 6 September 1943, both in NAA: M1942, 36.

47 P. Hasluck to Brigden, 28 November 1943, NAA: M1942, 36.

48 Ibid.

49 A good short account may be found in A. Watt, *The Evolution of Australian Foreign Policy 1938–1965*, CUP, London, 1967, p. 73.

CHAPTER 7: TOWARDS SAN FRANCISCO

1 A manila folder of miscellaneous documents in the departmental files is labelled 'Dr Evatt's method of filing'.

2 R. Throssell, *My Father's Son*, Heinemann, Melbourne, 1989, p. 205.

3 In 1926 Canada signed an agreement with the United States without securing British approval, but the treaty concerned the relatively uncontroversial subject of halibut fisheries.

4 Watt, *The Evolution of Australian Foreign Policy 1938–1965*, pp. 73–4.

5 P. Hasluck, 'Australia and the formation of the United Nations', p. 154.

6 Shaw to P. Hasluck, 26 January 1944, NAA: M1942, 36.

7 R. G. Neale (ed.), *Documents on Australian Foreign Policy 1937–49*, vol. 7, '1944', AGPS, Canberra, 1988, p. 601.

8 Porter, *Paul Hasluck*, p. 28; P. Hasluck, 'Australia and the formation of the United Nations', p. 154.

9 Porter, *Paul Hasluck*, p. 29; P. Hasluck to secretary, DEA, 16 February 1944, NAA: M1942, 3.

10 Ric Throssell, oral history interview by Don Baker, 30 January – 3 March 1992, NLA, TRC 2194.

11 Not to be confused with the Beazley family. 'Stabber Jack' Beasley (1895–1949) was a Labor MP 1929–45, leading the Lang faction in bringing down the Scullin government in 1931; reconciled to the ALP and minister in the Curtin government 1941–45; High Commissioner for Australia in London until his death.

12 P. Hasluck, 'Australia and the formation of the United Nations', p. 146. In this version Hasluck dates the dispute at 1943, but it is clear from his *Diplomatic Witness* (pp. 140–1) that 1944 is intended.

13 P. Hasluck, 'Australia and the formation of the United Nations', p 147.

14 Edwards, *Prime Ministers and Diplomats*, p. 147. Administrator and academic John Nethercote has suggested that it was not unusual in the public-service setting of that time for ministers to hear different sides of an argument from different advisers. Menzies operated in a similar manner, not least with Coombs and Roland Wilson.

15 Author's interview with John Burton, 26 May 2004.

16 Paul McGuire, journal, 13 September 1944, Paul McGuire papers, NLA, MS 6453, series 4, folder 2. For this reference I am indebted to Stuart Macintyre.

17 Smith to P. Hasluck, 19 August 1944, Hasluck collection: 'We want you just because you are you!'

18 P. Hasluck to W. Dunk, 25 March 1947, NAA: M1943, 16.

19 Gavin Merrick Long (1901–68) was a journalist with *The Argus* 1926–31, *Sydney Morning Herald* 1931–43; war correspondent 1939–41; general editor, Official History of Australia in the War of 1939–45 1943–63; OBE 1953; member of the Greek Order of the Phoenix (1956).

20 Long to P. Hasluck, 27 August 1943; P. Hasluck to Long, 3 September 1943; Long to P. Hasluck, 13 October 1944; Official War History contract, all in Hasluck collection.

21 P. Hasluck to A. Hasluck, 15 March 1945, Hasluck collection.

22 Smith to P. Hasluck, 8 December 1944, Hasluck collection.

23 A. Hasluck to P. Hasluck, 'Sunday' [20 May 1945], Hasluck collection.

24 Ibid.

25 P. Hasluck, *Diplomatic Witness*, p. 158.

26 Ibid., p. 145.

27 W. D. Forsyth, 'Recollections', Book 2, Chapter 3, William Douglass Forsyth papers, NLA, MS 5700, series 5, folder 22.

28 Francis Forde (1890–1981) was a Queensland MLA 1917–22; MP for Capricornia (Qld) 1922–46; High Commissioner to Canada 1946–51; and a Queensland MLA 1955–57. Curtin defeated him by one vote for the leadership of the Australian Labor Party in 1935, and in 1945 he was Prime Minister for eight days after the death of Curtin and before the selection of Chifley as party leader.

29 P. Hasluck, *Diplomatic Witness*, p. 148; Edwards, *Prime Ministers and Diplomats*, p. 164.

30 P. Hasluck, *Diplomatic Witness*, pp. 149–50.

31 Ibid., p. 145.

32 See ibid. (pp. 152–4) for the manoeuvres leading to this outcome.

33 Ibid., p. 188.

34 Atyeo deserves a good biography. A brief account of his career appears at D. Mandel, 'Atyeo, Samuel Laurence (Sam) (1910–1990)', *ADB*, vol. 17, pp. 40–1. Hasluck's comments appear in *Diplomatic Witness* (pp. 30, 36–7).

35 For Milner, see *Report of the Royal Commission on Espionage*, Commonwealth Government Printer, Canberra, 1955, paragraphs 521–6.

36 R. Hall, *The Rhodes Scholar Spy*, Random House, Sydney, 1991, pp. 118–19.

37 On this see Manning Clark, *The Quest for Grace*, Viking, Melbourne, 1990, pp. 151–3.

38 Telegram, P. Hasluck to his parents, Hasluck collection. Lewis Hasluck's obituary appeared in *Western Australian Railway and Tramway Magazine*, vol. 31, no. 8, 1945, p. 14.

39 P. Hasluck, 'Lewis Hasluck notes', Hasluck collection.

40   P. Hasluck, 'In time of drought', *Collected Verse*, p. 147. The poem was originally published in *Southerly*, vol. 14, no. 1, 1953, pp. 8–19.

41   Author's interview with John Burton, 26 May 2004.

Chapter 8: At the Workshop of Security

1   P. Hasluck to A. Hasluck, 15 March 1945, Hasluck collection.

2   P. Hasluck to A. Hasluck, 20 March 1945, Hasluck collection.

3   Ibid.

4   P. Hasluck to A. Hasluck, 8 April 1945, Hasluck collection.

5   P. Hasluck, *Diplomatic Witness*, Chapter 17 and p. 193.

6   P. Hasluck to A. Hasluck, 17 April 1945, Hasluck collection.

7   P. Hasluck to A. Hasluck, 15 April 1945, Hasluck collection.

8   P. Hasluck to A. Hasluck, 9 April 1945, Hasluck collection. Osbert Lancaster was an English cartoonist famous for gently satirising the English upper classes.

9   P. Hasluck to A. Hasluck, 25 April 1945, Hasluck collection. Lord Burghley (later Marquess of Exeter) competed in the 1924, 1928 and 1932 Olympics, winning the 440 yards hurdles in 1928.

10   P. Hasluck, *Diplomatic Witness*, pp. 190–1.

11   P. Hasluck to A. Hasluck, 24 April 1945, Hasluck collection. Hasluck added: 'I believe his greeting to de Gaulle in France was to say with an air of pleased and encouraging surprise that he had quite a nice country'. Sir John Colville (*The Fringes of Power: Downing Street diaries, 1939–1955*, Hodder & Stoughton, London, 1985, p. 230) has a story of taking Forde to the Prime Minister's country residence in the Chilterns, Chequers, and explaining that the house was Elizabethan. Forde replied: 'There are quite a number of nice houses like that in Melbourne, only we call them Tudor'. See also P. Hasluck, *Diplomatic Witness*, pp. 169–70.

12   P. Hasluck to A. Hasluck, 22 May 1945, Hasluck collection.

13   P. Hasluck to A. Hasluck, 5 May 1945, Hasluck collection.

14   L. F. Crisp, Diary, 29 April 1945, L. F. Crisp papers, NLA, MS 5243.

15   Edwards, *Prime Ministers and Diplomats*, p. 168; J. D. E. Plant, 'The origins and development of Australia's policy and posture at the United Nations Conference on International Organization, San Francisco, 1945', PhD thesis, ANU, 1967, pp. 329–33.

16   Forsyth, 'Recollections', William Douglass Forsyth papers, NLA, MS 5700, series 15, folder 24.

17   Alan Renouf, oral history interview by Michael Wilson, 23 November 1993, NLA, TRC 2981/6.

18   P. Hasluck to A. Hasluck, 5 May 1945 and 1 June 1945, Hasluck collection.

19   Ibid.

20   Ibid.

21   P. Hasluck, *Diplomatic Witness*, p. 201.

22   I am indebted for this point to Jeremy Hearder.

23   P. Hasluck to A. Hasluck, 9 May 1945, Hasluck collection.

24   Ibid.

25   A. Hasluck to P. Hasluck, 'Sunday' [20 May 1945], Hasluck collection.

26   P. Hasluck to A. Hasluck, 26 May 1945, Hasluck collection.

27   P. Hasluck to A. Hasluck, 22 May 1945, Hasluck collection.

28   P. Hasluck to A. Hasluck, 26 May 1945, Hasluck collection.

29   P. Hasluck, *Workshop of Security*, F. W. Cheshire, Melbourne, 1948, p. 128.

30   Ibid., p. 171.

31   P. Hasluck to A. Hasluck, 1 and 18 June 1945, Hasluck collection.

32   P. Hasluck to A. Hasluck, 13 June 1945, Hasluck collection.

33   P. Hasluck to A. Hasluck, 18 June 1945, Hasluck collection.

34   P. Hasluck to A. Hasluck, 25 June 1945, Hasluck collection.

35   P. Hasluck, 'Australia and the formation of the United Nations', p. 177.

36   Watt, *Australian Diplomat*, p. 63.

37   P. Hasluck to A. Hasluck, 29 October 1945, Hasluck collection.

38   P. Hasluck to A. Hasluck, 25 June 1945, Hasluck collection.

39   Ibid.

40   A. Hasluck to P. Hasluck, 26 June 1945, 7 and 17 July 1945, Hasluck collection.

41   P. Hasluck to A. Hasluck, 9 October 1945 and 6 November 1945, Hasluck collection.

42   P. Hasluck to A. Hasluck, 3 July 1945, Hasluck collection.

43   P. Hasluck, unpublished review of Kylie Tennant, *Evatt: politics and justice*, Hasluck collection.

44   P. Hasluck, *Diplomatic Witness*, Chapter 21.

45   P. Hasluck to A. Hasluck, 15 August 1945, Hasluck collection. For the contrary view I rely on a personal communication from Carol Bolton.

46   P. Hasluck to A. Hasluck, 1 September 1945, Hasluck collection.

47   A. Renouf, *The Champagne Trail: experiences of a diplomat*, Sun Books, Melbourne, 1980, p. 16.

48   P. Hasluck to A. Hasluck, 29 August 1945, Hasluck collection.

49   P. Hasluck to A. Hasluck, 22 August 1945, Hasluck collection.

50   Renouf, *The Champagne Trail*, p. 17.

51   P. Hasluck, *Diplomatic Witness*, p. 228.

52   Ibid.; Porter, *Paul Hasluck*, p. 44.

53   Ibid., pp. 230–5.

54   P. Hasluck to A. Hasluck, 4 September 1945, Hasluck collection.

55   W. E. Dunk, *They Also Serve*, W. Dunk, Canberra, 1974, p. 66; Edwards, *Prime Ministers and Diplomats*, p. 180.

56   P. Hasluck to A. Hasluck, 1 September 1945, Hasluck collection.

57   P. Hasluck to A. Hasluck, 15 November 1945, Hasluck collection.

58   Ibid.

59 Alan Renouf, oral history interview by Michael Wilson, 23 November 1993, NLA, TRC 2981/6.

60 Dunk to P. Hasluck, 22 November 1945, NAA: M1943, 1.

61 P. Hasluck to Dunk, 14 December 1945, NAA: M1943, 1.

62 Ibid.

63 Ibid. On 14 January 1946, Hasluck wired Evatt wishing to be considered as Australia's permanent representative on the Security Council. 'The department's proposals are unrealistic and prejudiced.'

64 P. Hasluck to Evatt, 12 December 1945, NAA: M1942, 22; see also Hodgson to Evatt, 14 December 1945, NAA: M1774, 23.

65 P. Hasluck to Dunk, 23 December 1945, NAA: M1942, 22.

66 Ibid.; see also Evatt to Hodgson and P. Hasluck, 20 December 1945, NAA: M1774, 23; P. Hasluck, *Diplomatic Witness*, pp. 252–4.

67 P. Hasluck, 'Australia and the formation of the United Nations', p. 177; Watt, *The Evolution of Australian Foreign Policy 1938–1965*, pp. 94–105.

68 Evatt, quoted in Watt, *The Evolution of Australian Foreign Policy 1938–1965*, p. 85.

69 P. Hasluck, *Workshop of Security*, p. 178.

70 Watt, *The Evolution of Australian Foreign Policy 1938–1965*, p. 105.

CHAPTER 9: RESIGNATION

1   Memorandum, P. Hasluck to Dunk, 19 January 1946, NAA: M1943, 1.

2   P. Hasluck, *Workshop of Security*, p. 3.

3   P. Hasluck, *Diplomatic Witness*, pp. 241–3.

4   Renouf, *The Champagne Trail*, pp. 18–19.

5   P. Hasluck to Dunk (private and confidential), 1 February 1946, NAA: M1943, 1.

6   Stevenson to P. Hasluck, 18 February 1946; Jebb to P. Hasluck, 20 February 1946, both in Hasluck collection. Adlai Stevenson (1900–65), an attorney; Department of Navy 1940–44; temporary appointee to State Department 1945–47; Governor of Illinois 1949–53; unsuccessful Democratic candidate for presidency 1952 and 1956; Ambassador to United Nations 1961–65. Sir Gladwyn Jebb (1900–96), career diplomat from 1924; acting Secretary-General of United Nations 1945–46; Ambassador to United Nations 1950–54 and to Paris 1954–60; then sat in the House of Lords as a Liberal.

7   Renouf, *The Champagne Trail*, p. 24; Renouf, oral history interview by Michael Wilson, 23 November 1993, NLA, TRC 2981/6; P. Hasluck to Dunk, 29 March 1946, NAA: M1943, 11.

8   P. Hasluck to Watt, 12 June 1946, NAA: M1943, 11.

9   A. Hasluck to her mother, Evelyn Darker, 22 May [1946], Hasluck collection.

10 A. Hasluck to Henrietta Drake-Brockman, 30 May 1946, Henrietta Drake-Brockman papers, NLA, MS 1634.

11 Ibid.

12   Ibid.

13   A. Hasluck to Henrietta Drake-Brockman, 11 June 1946, Henrietta Drake-Brockman papers, NLA, MS 1634.

14   A. Hasluck to Evelyn Darker, 6 May 1946, Hasluck collection.

15   P. Hasluck, *Diplomatic Witness*, Chapter 16; the comment about Evatt is at p. 275.

16   Renouf, oral history interview by Michael Wilson, 23 November 1993, NLA, TRC 2981/6.

17   A. Hasluck to Henrietta Drake-Brockman, Henrietta Drake-Brockman papers, NLA, MS 1634.

18   P. Hasluck, *Diplomatic Witness*, p. 277.

19   Ibid., p. 279.

20   Renouf to P. Hasluck, 'Paris/Saturday' [August 1946], NAA: M1943, 12.

21   Renouf to P. Hasluck, 22 October 1946, NAA: M1943, 12; Watt, *Australian Diplomat*, pp. 87–8.

22   P. Hasluck, *Diplomatic Witness*, pp. 282–3.

23   P. Edwards, *Arthur Tange: the last of the mandarins*, Allen & Unwin, Sydney, 2006, pp. 46–7. Edwards cites as his source an interview with Gordon Jockel, then a member of the delegation. Hasluck's good opinion of Tange extended to recommending him for high office (see Chapter X, note 57).

24   P. Hasluck, *Diplomatic Witness*, p. 282.

25   A. Hasluck to Evelyn Darker, 13 May 1946; see also A. Hasluck to Evelyn Darker, 18 August 1946, both in Hasluck collection.

26   A. Hasluck to Evelyn Darker, 30 November 1946; see also A. Hasluck to Evelyn Darker, 12 August [1946], both in Hasluck collection.

27   A. Hasluck to Evelyn Darker, 7 November 1946, Hasluck collection.

28   Ibid.

29   Watt, *Australian Diplomat*, p. 89.

30   Ibid.

31   P. Hasluck to Evatt, 14 December 1945, NAA: M1943, 16.

32   Evatt to P. Hasluck, 17 December 1945, NAA: M1943, 16.

33   P. Hasluck to Evatt, 18 December 1946, NAA: M1943, 16.

34   Dunk to P. Hasluck, 23 December 1946, NAA: M1943, 16.

35   Ibid. and 18 January 1947, NAA: M1943, 16.

36   P. Hasluck to Dunk, 7 January 1947, NAA: M1943, 16. For details see A. Hasluck to Evelyn Darker, 17 February 1947, Hasluck collection.

37   Dunk to P. Hasluck, 13 January 1947, NAA: M1943, 16.

38   P. Hasluck to Dunk, 13 January 1947, NAA: M1943, 16.

39   Dunk to P. Hasluck, 18 January 1947, NAA: M1943, 16.

40   A. Hasluck to Evelyn Darker, 14 February 1947, Hasluck collection.

41   Ibid.

42   *The Times* (London), 14 February 1947, p. 3.

43   Ibid., 25 February 1947, p. 4.

44   P. Hasluck, *Diplomatic Witness*, p. 287.

45 Ibid., p. 288.

46 R. Harry, *The Diplomat Who Laughed*, Hutchinson, Melbourne, 1983, p. 18.

47 P. Hasluck to Evatt, 4 March 1947; Evatt to P. Hasluck, 7 March 1947; P. Hasluck to Evatt, 16 March 1947, all in NAA: M1943, 16.

48 Dunk to P. Hasluck, 25 March 1947, NAA: M1943, 16.

49 Dunk to C. V. Kellaway, 26 April 1947, Sir William Ernest Dunk papers, NLA, MS 1535, box 1, folder 3. I owe this reference to Stuart Macintyre.

50 P. Hasluck to Dunk, 25 March 1947, NAA: M1943, 16.

51 P. Hasluck to Evatt, 27 March 1947, NAA: M1943, 16.

52 Evatt to P. Hasluck, 27 March 1947, NAA: M1943, 16.

53 P. Hasluck, *Diplomatic Witness*, p. 289.

54 Author's interview with Mrs Rosemary Carrodus, 26 November 2009.

55 *The Times* (London), 29 March 1947, p. 6.

56 Swope to P. Hasluck, 7 April 1947; de Rose to P. Hasluck, 29 March 1947, both in NAA: M1943, 16.

57 P. Hasluck to Alexander, 3 April 1947, Hasluck collection.

58 P. Hasluck, note commenting on Kylie Tennant, *Evatt: politics and justice*, Hasluck collection.

59 A. Stirling, Diary, 16 May 1947, DFAT; P. Hasluck, *Diplomatic Witness*, pp. 289–91.

60 R. Donington, 'Doctor Evatt at large', *The Observer* (Sydney), no. 20, 15 September 1958, p. 613.

61 Author's interview with Mrs Rosemary Carrodus, 26 November 2009.

62 R. Harry, *The Diplomat Who Laughed*, p. 81.

63 A. Watt, 'The Australian diplomatic service 1935–1965', in G. Greenwood & N. Harper (eds), *Australia in World Affairs 1961–1965*, F. W. Cheshire for the Australian Institute of International Affairs, Melbourne, 1968, p. 143.

64 A. Hasluck to Evelyn Darker, 17 February 1947, Hasluck collection. The letter is annotated in pencil: '1952. It all happened as I planned, except Minister for Ex. Territories'.

65 A. Hasluck to Evelyn Darker, 23 April 1947, Hasluck collection.

66 P. Hasluck, *Diplomatic Witness*, p. 33.

67 Author's interview with Clyde Cameron, 12 November 2002.

CHAPTER 10: ACADEMIC INTERLUDE

1 P. Hasluck, *Diplomatic Witness*, p. 290; P. Hasluck to Walter James, 11 July 1947, Hasluck collection.

2 P. Hasluck to Walter James, 11 July 1947, Hasluck collection.

3 SROWA, 3500A/1–6, including J. S. Battye to P. Hasluck, 16 January 1947 and P. Hasluck to J. S. Battye, 25 June 1947.

4 P. Hasluck, dedication, *Workshop of Security*.

5 P. Hasluck to Alexander, 3 April 1947; Alexander to P. Hasluck, 15 April 1947, both in Hasluck collection.

6 Frederick Alexander, oral history interview by Bruce Miller, 24 October 1976, NLA, TRC 477.

7 Part of this manuscript is published in P. L. Arthur & G. Bolton (eds), *Voices from the West End*, Western Australian Museum, Fremantle, 2012.

8 Hasluck collection. Later in 1958 he was to add an adjacent block to the property, making a total of about 35 hectares. Apparently he was alerted to this opportunity by the managing partner of a leading Western Australian timber company, Charles Bunning. I owe the information in this paragraph to a number of informants, including Dr Rica Erickson and Mrs Jenny Mills.

9 P. Hasluck to Currie, 8 January 1948, UWA Archives, file E01/136; P. Hasluck to Long, 22 March 1948, Records of Paul Hasluck, AWM68, 3DRL 8051/66.

10 J. D. Legge, 'Bits of autobiography: 2: My war', unpublished MS, by courtesy of the author.

11 Among Hasluck's friends and acquaintances, Fin Crisp became professor of politics at the Canberra University College; Walter Crocker was briefly professor of international relations; and Nugget Coombs served for many years as the influential Pro-Chancellor and Chancellor of the Australian National University.

12 Sir Paul Hasluck papers, NLA, MS 5274, box 31.

13 S. Macintyre, *The Poor Relation: a history of social sciences in Australia*, MUP, Melbourne, 2010, pp. 73, 77, 148.

14 P. Hasluck, opening address, *Promoting the Better Use of Archives in Australia: papers from the 1981 conference of the Australian Society of Archivists*, Melbourne, 23–25 May 1981, Australian Society of Archivists, Canberra, 1981.

15 Ibid.

16 E. Scott, *Official History of Australia in the War of 1914–18*, vol. XI, 'Australia during the war', edited by C. E. W. Bean, A&R, Sydney, 1936.

17 P. Hasluck, 'Problems of research on contemporary official records', *Australian Historical Studies*, vol. 5, no. 17, 1951, pp. 1–13.

18 P. Hasluck to Penman, 14 October 1947, Records of Paul Hasluck, AWM68, 3DRL 8051/66.

19 P. Hasluck to Penman, 8 November 1947, Records of Paul Hasluck, AWM68, 3DRL 8051/66.

20 P. Hasluck to Penman, 6 May 1948, Records of Paul Hasluck, AWM68, 3DRL 8051/66.

21 Hasluck, 'Problems of research', p. 2.

22 Introduction to 'Public addresses and articles (other than speeches in Parliament and official statements)', vol. 1, p. 10, Sir Paul Hasluck papers, NLA, MS 5274, box 37.

23 P. Hasluck to Coombs, 20 October 1947, Records of Paul Hasluck, AWM68, 3DRL 8051/66.

24   P. Hasluck to Menzies, 17 May 1948, Sir Robert Menzies papers, NLA, MS 4936, box 574.

25   P. Hasluck to Gilroy, 11 October 1948, Records of Paul Hasluck, AWM68, 3DRL 8052/81A–E.

26   P. Hasluck to Penman, 27 January 1949, Records of Paul Hasluck, AWM68, 3DRL 8052/81A–E.

27   D. McIntyre & K. Saunders, 'Official historian', in Stannage, Saunders & Nile (eds), *Paul Hasluck in Australian History*, pp. 57–9.

28   P. Hasluck to Wilson, 20 October 1947, Records of Paul Hasluck, AWM68, 3DRL 8052/81A–E.

29   P. Hasluck to Penman, 12 May 1948, Records of Paul Hasluck, AWM68, 3DRL 8052/81A–E.

30   P. Hasluck, *Diplomatic Witness*, p. 128.

31   Eggleston to P. Hasluck, 19 September 1949, Records of Paul Hasluck, AWM68, 3DRL 8052/81A–E.

32   Not the founder of the Palmer United Party, and no relation.

33   P. Hasluck, *Mucking About*, p. 286.

34   Ibid., p. 285.

35   Ibid.

36   I am grateful to Ai Kobayashi, who is writing a biography of Macmahon Ball, for information about material in the University of Melbourne Archives (Registrar's Correspondence, UMA, UM3121949/802).

37   *Daily Telegraph*, 27 January 1949, quoted in Porter, *Paul Hasluck*, p. 72.

38   J. Brett, *Robert Menzies' Forgotten People*, Macmillan, Sydney, 1992.

39   Curtin Divisional Conference, '10th anniversary speech, 26 July 1966', Hasluck collection.

40   Patience Hasluck to P. Hasluck, 5 September 1932, Hasluck collection.

41   A. Hasluck to P. Hasluck, n.d. [March or early April 1949], Hasluck collection.

42   A. Hasluck, *Portrait*, p. 212.

43   Long to P. Hasluck, 22 April 1949, Records of Paul Hasluck, AWM68, 3DRL 8052/81B.

44   Long to P. Hasluck, 20 April 1950, Records of Paul Hasluck, AWM68, 3DRL 8052/81A–E.

45   Johnson to P. Hasluck, 31 October 1949, Records of Paul Hasluck, AWM68, 3DRL 8051/61.

46   G. Long, Diary, 30 September 1949, Records of Gavin Long, AWM67, item 1/12, quoted in McIntyre & Saunders, 'Official historian', p. 50.

47   P. Hasluck to A. Hasluck, 27 February 1953, Hasluck collection.

48   P. Hasluck to Long, 23 June 1949, Records of Paul Hasluck, AWM68, 3DRL 8051/66.

49   Long to P. Hasluck, 6 July 1949, Records of Paul Hasluck, AWM68, 3DRL 8052/228B.

50 P. Hasluck to Long, 16 July 1949, Records of Paul Hasluck, AWM68, 3DRL 8051/66: 'It may be gratifying to know how manfully Bloggins pushed a pen and how many office desks of increasing size were ornamented by the presence of Boggins [sic], but in perspective such chronicles are small beer'.

51 Long to P. Hasluck, 8 June 1950, Records of Paul Hasluck, AWM68, 3DRL 8051/66.

52 P. Hasluck to A. Hasluck, 27 February 1953, Hasluck collection.

53 L. F. Fitzhardinge, review of *The Government and the People, 1939–1941*, *Australian Historical Studies*, vol. 6, no. 21, 1953, pp. 103–105.

54 T. Inglis Moore, 'Australia at war – the political story', *Australian Outlook*, vol. 8, no. 1, 1954, pp. 32–4.

55 M. Harris, 'Man for all seasons at the helm of the good ship Australia', *Weekend Australian*, 10 September 1989.

56 Macintyre & Saunders, 'Official historian', p. 56.

57 P. Hasluck to Penman, 16 July 1949, Records of Paul Hasluck, AWM68, 3DRL 8051/66.

58 *West Australian*, 19 November 1949, p. 13.

59 A. Hasluck, *Portrait*, p. 212.

60 Report of Campaign Committee meeting, 8 September 1949, Hasluck collection.

61 P. Hasluck, *A Time for Building*, p. 3.

CHAPTER 11: POLITICAL DEBUT

1 Percy Spender (1897–1986), MP for Warringah (NSW) 1937–51; junior minister 1940–41; Minister for External Affairs 1949–51; Ambassador to the United States 1951–56; a judge of the International Court of Justice 1956–65.

2 Edwards, *Prime Ministers and Diplomats*, pp. 54–5. Burton soon resigned in order to gain preselection as Labor candidate for the House of Representatives seat of Lowe (NSW) but at the 1951 election was defeated by the Liberal sitting member, William McMahon.

3 Sir Arthur William Fadden (1895–1973), MP 1936–58; leader of the Country Party 1940–58; Treasurer 1940–41 and 1949–58; knighted 1951.

4 Sir Philip McBride (1892–1982), pastoralist; MP for Grey (SA) 1931–37; senator for South Australia 1937–44, MP for Wakefield (SA) 1946–58; various cabinet offices 1939–41; Minister for the Interior 1949–50; Minister for Defence 1950–58; knighted 1953.

5 Fadden to McBride, 2 June 1950, Sir Paul Hasluck papers, NLA, MS 5274, box 33.

6 Cecil Lambert (1899–1974) hated his first name and was always known as 'Eski', apparently because of a boyhood liking for an ice-cream known as 'Eskimo pie' (P. C. Grundy, 'Lambert, Cecil Ralph (Eski) (1899–1971)', *ADB*, vol. 15, pp. 48–9).

7 Lambert to McBride, 6 June 1950, Sir Paul Hasluck papers, NLA, MS 5274, box 33.

8 *CPD*, H of R, 8 June 1950, vol. 212, pp. 87–9.

9 Kim Edward Beazley (1917–2007), MP for Fremantle (WA) 1949–77; Minister for Education in the Whitlam government 1972–75. His son, also Kim Beazley, was the Labor MP for Swan (WA) from 1980 to 1996, and for Brand (WA) from 1996 to 2007.

10 P. Hasluck, *Shades of Darkness*, p. 78.

11 *CPD*, H of R, 7 December 1950, vol. 211, p. 4051.

12 Ibid., 27 September 1950, vol. 209, pp. 28–33.

13 Ibid., p. 30.

14 Ibid., 26 October 1950, vol. 210, p. 1544.

15 Ibid., 29 November 1950, vol. 211, p. 3200.

16 'He threw up his job for a principle', *People*, 28 March 1951.

17 P. Hasluck, 'Speech to the Adelaide University Liberal Union, 25 September 1950', Hasluck collection.

18 Ibid.

19 In his Adelaide speech he cautioned against forcing an onerous peace on Japan: 'The victors grow weary, the vanquished grow more devious' (ibid.).

20 *CPD*, H of R, 27 September 1950, vol. 209, p. 33.

21 Leslie Haylen (1898–1977), journalist and playwright; MP for Parkes (NSW) 1943–63; published autobiography *Twenty Years' Hard Labour* (1969).

22 *CPD*, H of R, 27 September 1950, vol. 209, p. 34 (for Evatt see p. 51).

23 Prichard to P. Hasluck, 20 April 1944 (Hasluck collection), thanks him appreciatively for his mentoring of her son, Ric Throssell, a cadet in the DEA.

24 P. Hasluck, *The Public Servant and Politics*, Royal Institute of Public Administration (ACT Group), Canberra, 1968, pp. 5–6.

25 *CPD*, H of R, 10 May 1950, vol. 207, pp. 2787–90.

26 Ibid., pp. 2790–5.

27 P. Hasluck, Diary, October 1941, Hasluck collection; see also Chapter 16 in this book for the Gluckman affair.

28 P. Hasluck to A. Hasluck, 5 March 1952, Hasluck collection. Clyde Cameron (1913–2008); AWU organiser and senior official; MP for Hindmarsh (SA) 1949–80; Minister for Labour 1972–75; Minister for Immigration 1974–75; Minister for Science and Consumer Affairs 1975; AO 1982; in retirement befriended Hasluck. Daniel Curtin (1898–1980), boilermaker and union official, Sydney; MP for Watson (NSW) 1949–55; MP for Kingsford Smith (NSW) 1955–69.

29 *CPD*, H of R, 20 March 1958, vol. 18, pp. 591–2.

30 *CPD*, H of R, 7 November 1950, vol. 210, p. 2016.

31 Ibid., p. 2020 (for Chifley see p. 2017).

32 Dame Enid Lyons (1897–1982), widow of Joseph Lyons (Prime Minister 1932–39); MP for Denison (Tas.) 1943–51; vice-president of the Executive

Council 1949–51; subsequently a commissioner of the Australian Broadcasting Commission.

33   P. Hasluck to A. Hasluck, 11 March 1951, Hasluck collection.

34   Ibid. Wilfrid Kent Hughes (1895–1970), Victorian MLA 1927–49; cabinet minister 1932–35; prisoner of war 1942–45; MP for Chisholm (Vic.) 1949–70; Minister for the Interior 1951–55.

35   P. Hasluck to A. Hasluck, 6 March 1951, Hasluck collection. Gordon Freeth (1914–2000) was MP for Forrest (WA) 1949–69 and a cabinet minister from 1961; succeeded Hasluck as Minister for External Affairs February–December 1969 (when defeated at an election); subsequently Ambassador to Japan.

36   John Howse (1913–2002), MP for Calare (NSW) 1946–60; never achieved cabinet rank.

37   P. Hasluck to A. Hasluck, 6 March 1951, Hasluck collection. 'Of course', Hasluck wrote, Chifley was 'a shrewd old politician always looking for cracks in the Government'.

38   P. Hasluck, *A Time for Building*, p. 4.

39   P. Hasluck to A. Hasluck, 12 May 1951, Hasluck collection.

40   P. Hasluck, *A Time for Building*, pp. 4–5. The official portraits of the ceremony reveal no trace of dishevelment.

41   P. Hasluck to A. Hasluck, 12 May 1951, Hasluck collection.

42   Ibid. This letter is free of the reservations Hasluck later expressed in *A Time for Building* (p. 5).

43   Ibid.

44   B. D. Castleman, in 'Changes in the Australian departmental machinery of government, 1928–82' (PhD thesis, Deakin University, 1992, pp. 210), writes: 'The decision to consolidate territories administration appears…to have been driven by policy reasons. It is unclear whether administrative logic was also a driving factor in Menzies' mind'. I owe this reference to Dr John Nethercote.

45   Noel-Baker to P. Hasluck, 13 June 1951; McLarty to P. Hasluck, 12 May 1951; both in Hasluck collection.

46   Parsons to P. Hasluck, 11 May 1951, Hasluck collection.

47   Prendiville to P. Hasluck, 18 May 1951, Hasluck collection.

48   Serle to P. Hasluck, 18 May 1951, Hasluck collection.

49   Miles Franklin to P. Hasluck, 15 May 1951, Hasluck collection.

50   Hodgson to P. Hasluck, 17 May 1951, Hasluck collection.

51   Watt to P. Hasluck, 12 May 1951, Hasluck collection.

52   Hood to P. Hasluck, 31 May 1951, Hasluck collection.

53   P. Hasluck to A. Hasluck, 12 May 1951, Hasluck collection.

54   Edward Dunphy (1907–89), President of the Arbitration Court, Western Australia, 1945–49; Justice of the Commonwealth Arbitration Court 1949–56 and the Commonwealth Industrial Court 1956–83; Justice of the ACT Supreme Court 1958–82.

55   A. Hasluck to Henrietta Drake-Brockman, 26 June 1951, Henrietta Drake-Brockman papers, NLA, MS 1634.

56   Ibid.

57   P. Hasluck, *Mucking About*, p. 287.

CHAPTER 12: MINISTER FOR TERRITORIES

1   J. K. Murray, 'In retrospect – Papua-New Guinea 1945–1949 and Territory of Papua and New Guinea 1949–1952' *AJPH*, vol. 14, no. 3, 1968, pp. 320–41.

2   P. Hasluck to Latham, 17 May 1951, Sir John Latham papers, NLA, MS 1009.

3   P. Hasluck, 'Introduction', 'The Northern Territory 1951–63: public addresses and articles (other than speeches in parliament)', Sir Paul Hasluck papers, NLA, MS 5274, box 38.

4   I. Downs, *The Australian Trusteeship: Papua New Guinea 1945–75*, Department of Home Affairs, Canberra, 1980, pp. 55–60; R. C. Thompson, 'Halligan, James Reginald (1894–1968)', *ADB*, vol. 14, pp. 358–9. James Reginald Halligan entered the Commonwealth public service 1911; head of the territories branch of the Prime Minister's Department 1933, assistant secretary 1942–44 and secretary 1944–51; South Pacific Commission 1951–59; OBE 1960.

5   P. Hasluck, *A Time for Building*, pp. 7–8; N. Hasluck, interview with Reg Marsh, 23 August 1988, Hasluck collection.

6   Forsyth to P. Hasluck, 16 May 1951, NAA: M334, 5.

7   Crocker to P. Hasluck, 24 July 1976, Hasluck collection.

8   P. Hasluck to A. Hasluck, 24 March 1952, Hasluck collection.

9   Downs, *The Australian Trusteeship*, p. 285.

10 (Sir) (Jack) Keith Murray (1889–1974), agricultural scientist, foundation professor of agriculture, the University of Queensland, 1927–40; colonel administering army training, Queensland, 1940–43; directorate of research under A. A. Conlan 1944–45; administrator Papua and New Guinea 1945–52; OBE 1959; knighted 1978. He was not related to Sir Hubert Murray, administrator of Papua 1908–40.

11 Francis Joseph Scott Wise (1897–1986), agricultural scientist; MLA for Gascoyne (WA) 1933–51; cabinet minister 1936–45 and 1958–59; Premier of Western Australia 1945–47; administrator of the Northern Territory 1951–1956; MLA for North Province (WA) 1958–71. As a backbencher he introduced the motion that led to the appointment of the Moseley royal commission in 1934, but Hasluck did not know him before 1948.

12 In contrast to the political culture of the present day, Wise was concerned to communicate his intention to his political opponent, the acting Premier, Arthur Watts, 'because we act on a basis of mutual trust and I would not spring anything on him'. Watts wrote Hasluck what reads like a genuinely heartfelt letter of support, but it cannot have escaped him that Wise's departure would necessitate a by-election that the Coalition had a realistic

chance of winning (Wise to P. Hasluck, 27 May 1951; Alexander Reid to P. Hasluck, 29 May 1951; Watts to P. Hasluck, 2 June 1951; Palmer to P. Hasluck, 15 June 1951, all in Sir Paul Hasluck papers, NLA, MS 5274, box 34).

13   Telegram, Driver to P. Hasluck, 27 June 1951, Sir Paul Hasluck papers, NLA, MS 5274, box 34.

14   Hugh Barclay, oral history interview, NTAS, NTRS226/P0001, T306.

15   Harry Giese, oral history interview, NTAS, NTRS226/P0001, T755.

16   Wise to P. Hasluck, 7 April 1961, Hasluck collection.

17   P. Hasluck, 'Pioneers of post war recovery', Sixth Eric Johnston Lecture, published as NT Library Service Occasional Paper no. 28, Darwin, 1991, p. 5.

18   Downs, *The Australian Trusteeship*, p. 74.

19   Coombs to P. Hasluck, 30 May 1951, NAA: M334, 7.

20   P. Hasluck to Coombs, 'personal', 5 July 1951, NAA: M334, 7.

21   Downs, *The Australian Trusteeship*, p. 115.

22   P. Hasluck, *A Time for Building*, pp. 10–11.

23   P. Samuel, 'The Hasluck behind Hasluck', *The Bulletin*, vol. 91, no. 4641, 22 February 1969, p. 33.

24   P. Hasluck, *A Time for Building*, p. 11.

25   Memorandum, 5 July 1962, 'Minister's instructions', NAA: M1776, 22.

26   N. Hasluck, interviewed by Reg Marsh, 23 August 1988, Hasluck collection.

27   Dame Rachel Cleland, 'Comments on *A Time for Building*', Cleland papers, School of Pacific Studies, ANU, Canberra, p. 54.

28   Ibid.

29   Kim Beazley senior, oral history interview 1983–85, OHA 2226, Battye Library, SLWA.

30   Draft letter for minister's signature, 4 February 1953, NAA: M1776, 3.

31   Minute, 4 September 1953, 'Minister's instructions', NAA: M1776, 4.

32   Memorandum, 25 August 1960, 'Minister's instructions', NAA: M1776, 18, 58/143.

33   Author's interview with Sir Walter Crocker, 10 June 2002.

34   Author's interview with Sir Victor Garland, 14 November 2007. My own impression of Miss Dusting was 'scout mistress', but this was probably influenced by knowing of her interest in the Girl Guide movement.

35   Author's interview with Ellestan Dusting, 1 June 2004.

36   H. B. Gullett, oral history interview by Clarrie Hermes and Pat Shaw, 5 March 1984 – 13 December 1988, NLA, TRC 4900/55.

37   Ric Throssell, oral history interview by Don Baker, 30 January – 3 March 1992, NLA, TRC 2194.

38   He told John Nethercote (23 April 1989) that Casey did not prepare adequately even in presenting his own submissions.

39   (Sir) (Oliver) Howard Beale (1898–1983), Sydney barrister; MP for Parramatta (NSW) 1946–58; Minister for Transport and Information

1949–50; Minister for Supply 1950–58; Ambassador to Washington 1958–64; knighted 1961.

40   'Sundry persons, 1958–73', p. 10, Sir Paul Hasluck papers, NLA, MS 5274, box 39.

41   Peter Ryan, oral history interview by John Farquharson, 10–11 October 2000, NLA, TRC 4631.

42   Nelson Lemmon (1908–89), a minister in the Chifley government (1946–49), faced similar problems but lost his seat at the 1949 federal elections; MP for St George (NSW) 1954–55.

43   A. Hasluck, *Portrait*, pp. 214–15.

44   P. Hasluck to A. Hasluck, 13 January 1961, Hasluck collection.

45   G. Long to J. Fisher, 16 November 1961, AWM93, item 50/93/3/9/2A, quoted in Macintyre & Saunders, 'Official historian', p. 52.

46   P. Hasluck to A. Hasluck, 29 July 1951, Hasluck collection.

47   P. Hasluck to A. Hasluck, 24 March 1952, Hasluck collection. The social historian of Norfolk Island would find this document of interest.

48   A. Hasluck, *Portrait*, pp. 216 and 214–29 generally.

49   Personal communication from Mary Ciccarelli, daughter of Sir Shane and Lady Paltridge.

50   P. Hasluck to A. Hasluck, n.d. [probably 7 July 1953], Hasluck collection. In a second letter written later that evening he added: 'The one thing that I forgot to put in is that I love you…but then, as you always say, I have a funny way of showing it'.

51   *CPD*, H of R, 8 October 1953, vol. 1, pp. 1154–6.

52   P. Hasluck, *The Chance of Politics*, Text, Melbourne, 1997, p. 50.

53   A. Hasluck, *Victorian and Edwardian Perth from Old Photographs*, pictures selected by Mollie Lukis, John Ferguson, Sydney, 1977.

54   P. Hasluck to A. Hasluck (n.d. [January 1954], Hasluck collection) describes a meeting with the Earl of Munster, a visiting junior British cabinet minister and illegitimate descendant of William IV. Georgiana Molloy's husband was thought to be an illegitimate son of William's brother, the Duke of York, and Paul speculated on the likelihood of a connection.

CHAPTER 13: ABORIGINAL POLICY

1   Porter, *Paul Hasluck*, p. 195; *CPD*, H of R, 8 June 1950, vol. 208, p. 3977.

2   Charles Duguid (1884–1986); see R. Kerin, *Dr Do-Good: Charles Duguid and Aboriginal advancement, 1930s–1970s*, Australian Scholarly Publishing, Melbourne, 2011.

3   P. Hasluck to Elkin, 4 May 1951, Papers of Professor Adolphus Peter Elkin, Fisher Rare Book Library, 5/2/17, University of Sydney. Adolphus Peter Elkin (1891–1979), Anglican clergyman; professor of anthropology, University of Sydney, 1927–56.

4   Elkin to P. Hasluck, 28 June 1951, Papers of Professor Adolphus Peter Elkin,

Fisher Rare Book Library, 5/2/17, University of Sydney; T. Wise, *The Self-Made Anthropologist: a life of A. P. Elkin*, George Allen & Unwin, Sydney, 1985, p. 228.

5   'The future of the Australian Aborigines: the second part of the presidential address to Section F of the 29th meeting of the Australia and New Zealand Association for the Advancement of Science, Sydney, August 22, 1952', in 'Australian Aborigines, articles and speeches, 1925–1965', Hasluck collection.

6   P. Hasluck to Elkin, 6 September 1951, Papers of Professor Adolphus Peter Elkin, Fisher Rare Book Library, 5/2/17, University of Sydney.

7   Elkin to H. E. Thoremann, Papers of Professor Adolphus Peter Elkin, Fisher Rare Book Library, 4/2/429, University of Sydney; see also Elkin to F. Moy, 21 January 1953: 'I have very little contact with the present permanent head, and of course the Minister shoots off to Perth' (Papers of Professor Adolphus Peter Elkin, Fisher Rare Book Library, 4/2/455, University of Sydney).

8   Report, 12 June 1959, 'Minister's instructions', NAA: M1776, 15.

9   Ibid.

10   P. Hasluck to R. S. Leydin, 2 January 1952, NAA: M1776, 5.

11   *CPD*, H of R, 18 October 1951, vol. 214, p. 874.

12   Ibid.

13   P. Hasluck to R. S. Leydin, 2 January 1952, NAA: M1776, 5.

14   Hasluck to Lambert, 12 November 1051, NAA: M1776, 5.

15   Wise to Lambert, 28 February 1952, NAA: A452, 53/9.

16   This policy was applied not only to Aboriginal mothers but to all mothers. Hasluck was influenced not only by his understanding of orphanages but also by an example among the older generation of his own family.

17   M. Fraser, *Common Ground: issues that should bind and not divide us*, Viking, Melbourne 2002, pp. 197–201.

18   *Bringing Them Home: report of the National Inquiry into the Separation of Aboriginal and Torres Strait Islander Children from Their Families*, Human Rights and Equal Opportunity Commission, Canberra, April 1997.

19   Historians who have treated this issue sensibly and sensitively include H. Reynolds, *An Indelible Stain: the question of genocide in Australia's history*, Viking, Melbourne, 2001; R. Neill, *White Out: how politics is killing Black Australia*, Allen & Unwin, Sydney, 2002, especially Chapter 4, 'The stolen generation: holocaust or fiction?', pp. 116–71; and A. Haebich, *Broken Circles: fragmenting Indigenous families*, Fremantle Arts Centre Press, Fremantle, 2000. See also the essays in *Aboriginal History*, vol. 25, 2001.

20   *CPD*, H of R, 6 August 1952, vol. 218, p. 45.

21   Wise to Lambert, 22 December 1952, NAA: A452, 53/9.

22   P. Hasluck to Wise, 17 April 1953, NAA: A452, 53/9.

23   Elkin to Moy, 21 January 1953, Papers of Professor Adolphus Peter Elkin, Fisher Rare Book Library, 4/2/455, University of Sydney.

24   Porter, *Paul Hasluck*, p. 202. See also the criticisms in G. Cowlishaw, *Rednecks, Eggheads and Blackfellas: a study of racial power and intimacy in Australia*,

Allen & Unwin, Sydney, 1999, pp. 179–83.

25   Moy to Elkin, 27 January 1953, Papers of Professor Adolphus Peter Elkin, Fisher Rare Book Library, 4/2/455, University of Sydney; A. Heatley, *The Government of the Northern Territory*, 4th edn, UQP, Brisbane, 2000, p. 140. Since that time, wrote Heatley, the part-Aboriginal people had come to form 'an important, respected and distinctive strand in the multi-racial society of the Territory'.

26   P. Hasluck to Lambert, 16 April 1953, NAA: A452, 57/761.

27   P. Hasluck to Wise, 12 May 1954, NAA: A452, 54/281.

28   C. Tatz, 'Aboriginal administration of the Northern Territory of Australia', PhD thesis, ANU, 1964, p. 206.

29   P. Hasluck, *Shades of Darkness*, p. 86.

30   Author's interview with Ted Egan, 12 July 2005.

31   Archer to P. Hasluck, Hasluck collection.

32   P. Hasluck to Archer, Hasluck collection.

33   P. Hasluck to Lambert, 6 June 1952, NAA: M1776, 5.

34   Memorandum, 7 July 1954, NAA: M1776, 6.

35   P. Hasluck to Lambert, 28 April 1952, NAA: M1776, 5.

36   Moy to acting director of Lands, 20 March 1952, NAA: F1, 1966/909/1, quoted in J. Dargavel, 'Persistence and transition on the Wangites-Wagait reserves, 1892–1976', *Journal of Northern Territory History*, vol. 15, 2004, pp. 5–19.

37   Dargavel, 'Persistence and transition', p. 11.

38   Lambert to Nott, 3 August 1962, NAA: F1, 1966/909/64 (a); Dargavel, 'Persistence and transition', p. 5; P. Hasluck, *Shades of Darkness*, pp. 106–11; see also D. B. Rose et al., *Country of the Heart: an Indigenous Australian homeland*, Aboriginal Studies Press, Canberra, 2003.

39   Memorandum in response to Melbourne, 8 October [1955], Sir Paul Hasluck papers, NLA, MS 5274, box 32.

40   Albert Namatjira (1902–59), an Arrernte man, came to national prominence in the late 1930s and 1940s as a landscape painter.

41   *CPD*, H of R, 17 March 1959, vol. 22, pp. 644–5.

42   'Minister's instructions July–December 1961', 7 December 1961, NAA: M1776, 20.

43   Australia and New Zealand Association for the Advancement of Science.

44   Wise, *The Self-Made Anthropologist*, pp. 229–32.

45   Elkin to R. G. Hill, 21 September 1959; see also Elkin to Judy Inglis, 21 September 1959, both in Papers of Professor Adolphus Peter Elkin, Fisher Rare Book Library, 5/2/210, University of Sydney.

46   *CPD*, H of R, 20 April 1961, vol. 30, p. 1051.

47   Ibid., p. 1056.

48   Ibid., p. 1061.

49   Ibid., pp. 1092–3.

50   A. de Tocqueville, *Journeys to England and Ireland*, translated by George

Lawrence & K. P. Mayer, edited by J. P. Mayer, Faber, London, 1958.

51   P. Hasluck to N. Hasluck, 12 February 1965, Hasluck collection.

52   Memorandum, 'Northern Territory patrol officers – attendance at seminar at Grafton on 22–24 September 1961', 'Minister's instructions January–June 1962', NAA: M1776, 21, 33–35.

53   *CPD*, H of R, 1 May 1962, vol. 35, pp. 1767–71.

54   K. E. Beazley, *Father of the House: the memoirs of Kim E. Beazley*, Fremantle Press, Fremantle, 2009, pp. 155–6.

55   *CPD*, H of R, 28 August 1963 and 12 September 1963, vol. 39, pp. 561 and 927–37.

56   Beazley, *Father of the House*, p. 157.

57   *CPD*, H of R, 9 September 1963, vol. 39, pp. 1176–8.

58   R. Baker, *Land Is Life: from bush to town, the story of the Yanyuwa people*, Allen & Unwin, Sydney, 1990, pp. 99–100.

59   B. Bunbury, *It's Not the Money, it's the Land: Aboriginal stockmen and the equal wages case*, Fremantle Arts Centre Press, Fremantle, 2002.

60   R. McGregor, *Indifferent Inclusion: Aboriginal people and the Australian Nation* (Aboriginal Studies Press, Canberra, 2011) provides a valuable analysis of the different meanings attributed to the concept of assimilation.

CHAPTER 14: THE NORTHERN TERRITORY

1   Hugh Barclay, oral history interview, NTAS, NTRS226/P0001, T306.

2   John Norman Nelson (1908–91), son of Harold Nelson (first MP for the Northern Territory 1922–34); AIF 1942–45; MP for the Northern Territory 1949–66; subsequently Mayor of Alice Springs and administrator of the Northern Territory 1973–75.

3   P. Hasluck, 'Pioneers of post war recovery', p. 5.

4   P. Hasluck to Lambert, 19 January 1953, 'Minister's instructions', 1 January – 30 June 1953, NAA: M1776, 3.

5   'Darwin town plan', 13 September 1960, 'Minister's instructions', July–December 1960, NAA: M1776, 18.

6   P. Hasluck to Fadden, 17 March 1953, 'Cultural development of the Northern Territory', NAA: M331, 164.

7   Hugh Barclay (1905–97), surveyor and director of lands, Northern Territory, 1948–68. Hugh Barclay, oral history interview, NTAS, NTRS226/P0001/ TS306; P. Hasluck, 'Pioneers of post war recovery', p. 5.

8   James Clarence Archer (1900–80), public servant; lieutenant New Guinea Volunteer Rifles 1940–45; deputy secretary Department of Territories; OBE 1956; administrator of the Northern Territory 1956–61.

9   Reg Marsh, interview by Nicholas Hasluck, 23 August 1988, Hasluck collection.

10   Roger Bede Nott (1908–2000), shearer and farmer; MLA for Liverpool Plains (NSW) 1941–61; Minister for Lands and Mines 1956–57; Minister

for Agriculture 1957–61; administrator of the Northern Territory 1961–64; administrator of Norfolk Island 1964–66.

11 Author's interview with Nan Giese, 9 July 2005.

12 Connellan to P. Hasluck (personal), n.d., NAA: M331, 163, quoted in E. J. Ling, 'Blame and martyrs: the Commonwealth Government's administration of the Northern Territory pastoral industry, 1911–1978', PhD thesis, Charles Darwin University, 2010.

13 Ling, 'Blame and martyrs', p. 148.

14 Hugh Barclay, oral history interview, NTAS, NTRS226/P0001/TS306.

15 'Minister's instructions', 1 July – 31 December 1955, NAA: M1776, 8.

16 Ibid., January–June 1960, NAA: M1776, 17, folios 431–3.

17 'Northern Territory forestry program: report from the House of Representatives Standing Committee on Expenditure', May 1978, AGPS, Canberra, 1978; C. D. Haynes, 'Land, trees and man (Gunret, Gundulk, Dja Bining)', *Commonwealth Forestry Review*, vol. 57, no. 2, 1978, pp. 99–106.

18 W. Stern, memorandum, given to author 26 May 2011. Stern adds: 'In 1979 the CSIRO Division of Tropical Crops and Pastures held a big symposium in Darwin…[At Katherine] I was invited…to a Townsville Stylo field day, organised by the local pastoralists' association'.

19 P. Hasluck to Fadden, 28 September 1954, NAA: M1774, 8.

20 P. Hasluck to Nott, 21 July 1961, 'Minister's instructions', July–December 1961, NAA: M1776, 20.

21 'Northern Territory: Scientific Liaison Committee, 2–8 February 1961', Hasluck collection.

22 P. Hasluck to Duguid, 10 July 1953, Sir Paul Hasluck papers, NLA, MS 5274, box 34.

23 'Minister's instructions', July–December 1962, NAA: M1776, 22.

24 Interview of Nicholas Hasluck, 23 August 1988, Hasluck collection; author's interview of Reg Marsh, 15 May 2002; J. Marcus, 'Pink, Olive Muriel (1884–1975)', *ADB*, vol. 16, pp. 4–5.

25 Olive Pink to P. Hasluck, 19 April 1965, Sir Paul Hasluck papers, NLA, MS 5274, box 34, folio 18. Emphasis in original.

26 Harry Giese, oral history interview, NTAS, NTRS226/P0001/T755.

27 'Introduction', P. Hasluck, 'Pioneers of post war recovery', p. v.

28 Hilda Tuxworth, oral history interview, NTAS, NTRS226/0001/TS561.

29 Author's interview with Reginald Marsh, 15 May 2002.

30 Ronald Withnall, oral history interview by Phyllipa Wyatt, 24 August 1976, NLA, TRC 462.

31 Harold 'Tiger' Brennan (1905–79), prospector; served in Second World War; MLC for Northern Territory 1955–71; Mayor of Darwin 1972–75.

32 Richard Ward (1916–77), partner in Darwin legal firm from 1938; MLC for Northern Territory 1947–49 and 1956–74; stood as Labor candidate for federal seat of Northern Territory 1966; judge in Northern Territory Supreme Court 1974–77.

33 Author's interviews with Nan Giese, 9 July 2005, and Ted Egan, 12 July 2005.

34 P. Hasluck, 'Pioneers of post war recovery', p. 4.

35 *CPD*, H of R, 6 September 1952, vol. 218, p. 1009.

36 Porter, *Paul Hasluck*, pp. 175, 190.

37 *CPD*, H of R, vol. 8, pp. 1355–7.

38 Porter, *Paul Hasluck*, pp. 176–7.

39 Ibid., p. 177.

40 Ibid., p. 178.

41 *Sydney Morning Herald*, 21 April 1958.

42 'Minister's instructions', January–June 1958, NAA: M1776, 13, folios 335, 353, 378–79.

43 Ibid., January–June 1959, NAA: M1776, 14, folio 32.

44 *CPD*, H of R, 19 March 1959 and 9 April 1959, vol. 22, pp. 857–66 and 1091.

45 P. Hasluck, Minute, 28 September 1961, 'Minister's instructions', July–December 1961, NAA: M1776, 20.

46 Porter, *Paul Hasluck*, p. 185.

47 Legislative Council of the Northern Territory, 'The remonstrance', 23 August 1962.

48 Porter, *Paul Hasluck*, p. 188.

49 A. Powell, *Far Country: a short history of the Northern Territory*, 4th edn, MUP, Melbourne, 2000, p. 227.

CHAPTER 15: PAPUA NEW GUINEA

1   P. Hasluck, *A Time for Building*, p. 3.

2   Ibid., pp. 13–14; H. Nelson, 'Papua and New Guinea', in Stannage, Saunders & Nile (eds), *Paul Hasluck in Australian History*, p. 152.

3   P. Hasluck to A. Hasluck, 29 July 1951, Hasluck collection.

4   Nelson, 'Papua and New Guinea', pp. 164, 169.

5   Porter, *Paul Hasluck*, p. 94, quoting 'Present tasks and policies', in Australian Institute of Political Science, *New Guinea and Australia*, A&R, Sydney, 1958, p. 115, and 'The legend of remote control', ibid., p. 12.

6   Downs, *The Australian Trusteeship*, p. 74.

7   Roy Kendall (1899–1972), British merchant seaman; intelligence agent during Second World War; newsagent in Brisbane; federal senator 1950–65.

8   P. Hasluck to A. Hasluck, 5 March 1952, Hasluck collection.

9   Ibid.

10 Sir J. K. Murray collection, Fryer Library, UQFL91, box 3, University of Queensland.

11 Gunther to Murray, 14 May 1952; Ivan Champion to Murray, 14 May 1952; J. M. Zimmerman to Murray, 14 May 1952; J. H. Ahearn to Murray, 20 May 1952, all in Sir J. K. Murray collection, Fryer Library, UQFL91, box 3, University of Queensland.

12 *Papuan Times*, 16 May 1952 and 6 June 1952, Sir J. K. Murray collection, Fryer Library, UQFL91, box 3, University of Queensland,.

13 Coombs to P. Hasluck, 23 May 1952, Sir J. K. Murray collection, Fryer Library, UQFL91, box 3, University of Queensland.

14 Porter, *Paul Hasluck*, p. 97.

15 D. Denoon, *A Trial Separation: Australia and the decolonisation of Papua New Guinea*, ANU E Press, Canberra, 2003, p. 17.

16 P. Hasluck to Casey, 1 February 1954, NAA: M1774, 3.

17 G. Whitlam, 'Paul Hasluck in Australian history', in Stannage, Saunders & Nile (eds), *Paul Hasluck in Australian History*, p. 8.

18 Downs, *The Australian Trusteeship*, pp. 134–5.

19 (Sir) Michael Somare (1936–), founder of Pangu Party 1970; first Prime Minister of Papua New Guinea 1975–80, 1982–85 and 2002–11.

20 Ian Smith (1919–2007), MLA Southern Rhodesia 1948–53 and Rhodesian Federation 1953–62; a founder of Rhodesian Front 1962; Deputy Prime Minister 1962–64 and Prime Minister [Southern] Rhodesia 1964–79; proclaimed unilateral declaration of independence 1965; yielded power 1979; retired 1987.

21 P. Hasluck, *A Time for Building*, p. 127: 'Somare told me this himself when he called on me in Canberra'.

22 P. Hasluck, *Australia's task in Papua and New Guinea*, Roy Milne Memorial Lecture, Perth, 10 September 1956, Australian Institute of International Affairs, Melbourne, 1956.

23 Memorandum, 'Minister's instructions', 1 July – 31 December 1955, NAA: M1776, 8, folio 317.

24 William Charles Groves named his son 'Murray'.

25 L. Megarrity, 'Indigenous education in colonial Papua New Guinea: Australian government policy (1945–1975)', *History of Education Review*, vol. 34, no. 2, 2005, p. 45; see also M. Duncan, 'W. C. Groves: his work and influence on education in Papua and New Guinea (1946–1958)', in Australian College of Education (ed.), *Educational Perspectives in Papua New Guinea*, Australian College of Education, Melbourne, 1974, pp. 181–8; D. J. Dickson, 'Groves, William Charles (1898–1967)', *ADB*, vol. 14, p. 340.

26 P. Hasluck, *A Time for Building*, p. 86; R. Cleland, 'Comments on *A Time for Building*', p. 31.

27 P. Hasluck, *A Time for Building*, p. 87.

28 Ibid., pp. 87–95.

29 P. Hasluck to Lambert, 29 January 1960, quoted in Megarrity, 'Indigenous education in colonial Papua New Guinea', note 39.

30 *CPD*, H of R, 10 October 1957, vol. 16, p. 1227.

31 (Sir) John Thomson Gunther (1910–84), director of health, Papua New Guinea, 1946–57; assistant administrator 1957–66; Vice-Chancellor, University of Papua New Guinea, 1966–72; knighted 1975.

32 H. N. Nelson, 'Gunther, Sir John Thomson (1910–1984)', *ADB*, vol. 17,

p. 457–9; see also D. Denoon, *Public Health in Papua New Guinea: medical possibility and social constraint, 1884–1984*, CUP, New York, 1989.

33 P. Hasluck, 13 June 1957, Diary, 13 June – 4 July, Hasluck collection.

34 Ibid., 18 June 1957.

35 Ibid., 21 June 1957.

36 Ibid., 25 June 1957.

37 P. Hasluck to D. Cleland, 2 August 1957, NAA: M331, 6, also quoted in Porter, *Paul Hasluck*, p. 161.

38 P. Hasluck, 19 June 1957, Diary, 13 June – 4 July, Hasluck collection. This was (Sir) William Yeo (1896–1972), from 1949 the notably opinionated president of the New South Wales branch of the Returned Servicemen's League.

39 P. Hasluck, 'Present tasks and policies', in J. Wilkes (ed.), *New Guinea and Australia: papers read at the 24th summer school of the Australian Institute of Political Science*, Australian Institute of Political Science, Canberra, 1958.

40 Downs, *The Australian Trusteeship*, p. 189.

41 P. Hasluck, *A Time for Building*, p. 260 and Chapter 23 generally. For a different point of view, see Downs, *The Australian Trusteeship*, pp. 186–95.

42 Ibid.

43 Downs, *The Australian Trusteeship*, p. 191.

44 H. Henderson (ed.), *Letters to My Daughter: Robert Menzies, letters, 1955–1975*, Murdoch Books, Sydney, 2012, p. 67.

45 *CPD*, H of R, 26 August 1959, vol. 24, pp. 565–9.

46 *Sydney Morning Herald*, 25 August 1959; *CPD*, H of R, 26 August 1959, vol. 24, pp. 602–604.

47 P. Hasluck to A. Hasluck, 'Sunday', Hasluck collection.

48 *CPD*, H of R, 30 September 1959, vol. 24, p. 1574–5.

49 Ibid., pp. 1577.

50 Ibid., p. 1604; see also Cleaver at p. 1581 and Turner at pp. 1598–9.

51 Ibid., p. 1584.

52 Downs, *The Australian Trusteeship*, p. 192.

53 P. Hasluck, *A Time for Building* (p. 360) shows that Hasluck considered that although the inland people of West New Guinea were 'much the same as those across the border under Australian administration', the coastal areas were peopled by several races.

54 This argument did not apply to the Indonesian claim to Portuguese Timor.

55 Woodard, *Asian Alternatives: Australia's Vietnam decision and lessons on going to war*, MUP, Melbourne, p. 34; N. Tarling, '"Cold storage": British policy and the beginnings of the Irian Barat/West New Guinea dispute', *AJPH*, vol. 46, no. 2, 2000, p. 186.

56 Woodard, *Asian Alternatives: Australia's Vietnam decision and lessons on going to war*, MUP, Melbourne, p. 34.

57 Casey to P. Hasluck, 1 July 1953, NAA: M333, 2.

58 R. Cleland, 'Comments on *A Time for Building*', p. 62.

59 P. Hasluck, *A Time for Building*, p. 361.

60 Ibid., p. 362.

61 Sir John Kerr (1915–91), a Sydney QC; later Chief Justice of New South Wales 1971–74; Governor-General 1974–77; knighted 1974. John Andrews was secretary of the Australian Institute of Political Science.

62 P. Hasluck, *A Time for Building*, p. 363. More light may be shed on this issue by current research from Dr Chris Waters, Deakin University.

63 Woodard, *Asian Alternatives*, p. 36.

64 P. Hasluck, *A Time for Building*, p. 365.

65 Ibid., pp. 366–7.

66 I have been unable to locate this story in the online archives of the *New York Times*.

67 *Sydney Morning Herald*, 21 June 1960, quoted in Watt, *The Evolution of Australian Foreign Policy, 1938–1965*, p. 261.

68 *Sydney Morning Herald*, 21 June 1960.

69 Ibid., 28 June 1960.

70 P. Hasluck, *A Time for Building*, p. 257.

71 *CPD*, H of R, 5 October 1960, vol. 28, pp. 1655–90.

72 P. Hasluck, Address, 10 July 1960, sent to DEA 14 July 1960, NAA: A452, 61/3897.

73 P. Hasluck, *A Time for Building*, p. 256.

74 Julian Amery to P. Hasluck, 8 November 1960; see also Brian Harrison to P. Hasluck, 18 October 1960, both in Hasluck collection. Before Harrison went to Papua New Guinea, Hasluck wrote: 'I hope it opens his eyes. He seems to have a very cheerful[?] African view of independence tomorrow and wicked colonialism' (P. Hasluck to A. Hasluck, 4 October 1960, Hasluck collection).

75 Downs, *The Australian Trusteeship*, p. 217.

Chapter 16: Time of transition

1 Athol Townley (1905–63), pharmacist; Royal Australian Navy 1940–45; MP for Denison (Tas.) 1949–63; Minister for Social Services 1951–54; Minister for Air 1954–56; Minister for Immigration 1956–58; Minister for Defence 1958–63.

2 P. Hasluck, *A Time for Building*, p. 6.

3 William Douglass Forsyth papers, NLA, MS 5700, series 15, folder 105.

4 P. Hasluck to A. Hasluck, 'Friday' [1959], Hasluck collection.

5 P. Hasluck to A. Hasluck, n.d. [probably 1960], Hasluck collection.

6 (Sir) David Brand (1912–79), MLA (WA) 1945–74; Minister for Works 1947–53; Premier and Treasurer 1959–71; knighted 1971.

7 (Sir) Charles Walter Michael Court (1911–2007), MLA (WA) 1953–82; Minister for Industrial Development and for the North-West 1959–71; Premier and Treasurer 1975–82; knighted 1972.

8 P. Hasluck to Holt and J. R. Willoughby, 8 December 1966, Hasluck collection.

9   Author's interview with Sir Charles Court, 11 August 2004.

10 Woodard, *Asian Alternatives*, p. 21.

11 See Chapter 9.

12 P. Hasluck, *The Chance of Politics*, p. 133.

13 Sir Garfield Barwick (1903–97), Sydney barrister; came to eminence appearing before the Privy Council in appeal against the Chifley government's nationalisation of banking; knighted 1954; MP for Parramatta (NSW) 1958–64; Attorney-General 1958–64; Minister for External Affairs 1961–64; Chief Justice of the High Court 1964–80.

14 D. Marr, *Barwick*, George Allen & Unwin, Sydney, 1980, p. 169.

15 Jeremy Buxton, 'History of the federal seat of Curtin', unpublished paper in the author's possession.

16 Hasluck's constituency files will not be accessible until 2020, but examples of his intercessions on behalf of constituents may be found in Sir William McMahon's papers (NLA, MS 3926). At that time both were busy senior ministers.

17 (Sir) Shane Paltridge (1910–66) was a bank officer before becoming a publican, and as a young man acted in minor roles in plays reviewed by Hasluck; federal senator 1949–66; cabinet minister 1961–66; Minister of Defence 1964–66; knighted January 1966 and died a few days later.

18 In *The Chance of Politics*, (p. 102) Hasluck places this incident in 1963, but P. Hasluck to A. Hasluck, 13 November 1960 (Hasluck collection), establishes the date.

19 Former senator Reg Withers. He said that Menzies came to this view after Sir Earle Page, a retired rural surgeon, trumpeted his expertise when Minister for Health (1949–55).

20 A. Hasluck to Henrietta Drake-Brockman, 28 January 1962, Henrietta Drake-Brockman papers, NLA, MS 1634.

21 Henderson (ed.), *Letters to My Daughter*, p. 85.

22 *CPD*, H of R, 28 September 1960, vol. 28, p. 1451.

23 *CPD*, H of R, 31 August 1960, vol. 28, pp. 648–52.

24 *Sydney Morning Herald*, 1 September 1960.

25 Quoted in *The Bulletin*, 28 September 1960.

26 *The Age*, 6 September 1960; see also the editorial of this date.

27 *Canberra Times*, 14 September 1960. Earlier Gluckman was quoted as saying: 'I know both Mr Hasluck and Brigadier Cleland to be humane, fair and liberal men' (*The Age*, 5 September 1960).

28 P. Hasluck to D. Cleland, 1 August 1961, NAA: M333/1, 11.

29 P. Hasluck, *A Time for Building*, p. 406.

30 P. Hasluck to D. Cleland, 24 February 1961, NAA: M333, 10.

31 P. Hasluck, *A Time for Building*, p. 370.

32 Henderson (ed.), *Letters to My Daughter*, p. 84.

33 P. Hasluck to Lambert, 5 February 1962, 'Minister's instructions', January–June 1962, NAA: M1776, 21.

34 Sir Hugh Foot's father, Isaac Foot, was a radical Liberal MP for many years, and his brother Michael Foot, a Labor MP, held various cabinet offices 1974–79 before becoming leader of the opposition 1980–83. Another brother, Dingle Foot, was Solicitor-General 1964–67.

35 R. Cleland, 'Comments on *A Time for Building*', p. 66.

36 H. Foot, *A Start in Freedom*, Hodder & Stoughton, London, 1964, p. 212.

37 Ibid.

38 Downs, *The Australian Trusteeship*, p. 240; P. Hasluck, *A Time for Building*, p. 398.

39 Porter, *Paul Hasluck*, p. 149.

40 R. Cleland, 'Comments on *A Time for Building*', p. 66.

41 P. Hasluck, 'Address to the Economic Society of Australia and New Zealand, New South Wales branch, 20 October 1961', Hasluck collection.

42 P. Hasluck, *A Time for Building*, p. 401.

43 Now James Cook University.

44 P. Hasluck, *A Time for Building*, p. 388.

45 Personal communication from Dr John Nethercote.

46 Edwards, *Arthur Tange*, p. 139.

47 Sir James Plimsoll (1917–87), an army major with Conlon's intelligence organisation during the Second World War, entered the DEA in 1947 and so had not overlapped with Hasluck. After able service in Korea 1950–52, he served in Canberra 1953–59 before appointment to the delegation to the United Nations 1959–63. Knighted 1962, Ambassador to New Delhi 1964–65; secretary DEA 1965–70; Ambassador to Washington 1970–74; Ambassador to Moscow 1974–77; Ambassador to the European Economic Community 1978–80; High Commissioner in London 1980–81; Governor of Tasmania 1982–87.

48 (Sir) Frederick Wheeler (1914–94), served at Treasury 1942–52; treasurer of the International Labour Organisation 1952–60; chairman of the Public Service Board 1960–71; secretary Treasury 1971–79; knighted 1967.

49 This paragraph is drawn from J. R. Nethercote, 'Territories – appointment of Eskie Lambert's successor – some notes', unpublished paper, 5 October 2011, based on the Sir Frederick Wheeler papers, NLA, MS 8096, box 10.

50 P. Hasluck, *A Time for Building*, pp. 418–19. In a rare lapse of memory Hasluck names Sir William Dunk as the chairman of the Public Service Board, but Dunk had retired three years previously. Booker returned to the DEA. His book *The Last Domino: aspects of Australia's foreign relations* (Collins, Sydney, 1976) is critical of Hasluck.

51 Wheeler to Menzies, 6 August 1963, Sir Frederick Wheeler papers, NLA, MS 8096, box 10.

52 Buxton, 'History of federal seat of Curtin'.

53 Shedden to P. Hasluck, 19 December 1963, Hasluck collection.

54 (Sir) Edwin Hicks (1910–84) entered the Commonwealth public service 1928; secretary Department of Air 1951–56; secretary Department of

Defence 1956–68; High Commissioner to New Zealand 1968–71; knighted 1965.

55 Woodard, *Asian Alternatives*, p. 260.

56 Formerly (until 1960) the Canberra University College.

57 *Woroni* (ANU newspaper), 20 March 1964, enclosed in C. G. Plowman to P. Hasluck, 20 March 1964, Hasluck collection.

58 *The Age*, 6 March 1964; *Sydney Morning Herald*, 6 March 1964.

59 C. P. Fitzgerald to P. Hasluck, 11 March 1964, Hasluck collection.

60 Hancock to P. Hasluck, 25 March 1964, Hasluck collection.

61 Sir Owen Dixon (1886–1972), judge of the High Court 1929–52; Chief Justice 1952–64; widely regarded as Australia's greatest jurist.

62 P. Howson, *The Life of Politics: the Howson diaries*, edited by D. Aitkin, Viking, Melbourne, 1984, p. 90.

CHAPTER 17: INDONESIA AND VIETNAM

1 *CPD*, H of R, 23 March 1965, vol. 45, p. 230.

2 See Chapter 9 in this book; Edwards, *Arthur Tange*, pp. 46–7.

3 Edwards, *Arthur Tange*, especially chapters 5–7.

4 Ibid., pp 138–39; see also Chapter 16 in this book.

5 Woodard, *Asian Alternatives*, p. 196.

6 Ibid., p. 148.

7 Author's interview with Don Kingsmill, 4 June 2004.

8 P. Hasluck to Tange (private and confidential), 2 November 1964, NAA: A1838, 1270/35/7; Tange to P. Hasluck, 11 November 1964, NAA: A1838, 1270/35/2.

9 A logistical issue has been pointed out to me in that a Commonwealth driver should have been in the car as well as Hasluck, Tange and Miss Dusting.

10 Edwards, *Paul Hasluck*, p. 151, quoting Hasluck's introduction to the Sir Paul Hasluck papers (NLA, MS 5274).

11 P. Hasluck to N. Hasluck, 13 September 1964, Hasluck collection.

12 Woodard, *Asian Alternatives*, pp. 269, 271.

13 Edwards, *Paul Hasluck*, p. 255.

14 Ibid., Chapter 8.

15 Plimsoll to P. Hasluck, 31 May 1970, Hasluck collection.

16 Crocker to P. Hasluck, 10 February 1969, Hasluck collection.

17 Peter Edwards, 'Notes on a conversation with Sir Paul Hasluck in his office, in Perth, Tuesday 7 August 1984', typescript in the author's possession, reproduced courtesy of P. Edwards.

18 P. Hasluck to A. Hasluck, 'Sunday' [1966], Hasluck collection.

19 P. Edwards with G. Pemberton, *Crises and Commitments: the politics and diplomacy of Australia's involvement in Southeast Asian conflicts 1948–1965*, Allen & Unwin in association with AWM, Sydney, 1992, p. 285ff.

20 *CPD*, H of R, 17 March 1964 and 16 April 1964, vol. 41, p. 523 and 1193.

21 Porter, *Paul Hasluck*, p. 228.

22 DEA, *Current Notes on International Affairs*, Canberra, June 1964, p. 45.

23 'Record of talks held at Soviet Foreign Ministry, Moscow, 28 October 1964', NAA: A1838.

24 This is the view that British historian A. J. P. Taylor controversially put forward.

25 W. J. Hudson, 'Problems in Australian foreign policy July–December 1966', *AJPH*, vol. 13, no. 1, 1967, p. 4.

26 DEA, *Current Notes on International Affairs*, October 1964, pp. 8–14.

27 G. Barwick, 'Australia's foreign relations', in J. Wilkes (ed.), *Australia's Defence and Foreign Policy*, A&R, Sydney, 1964, quoted in J. Cotton, 'The management of Australian foreign policy and Northeast Asia, 1962–1969', paper presented to Australian Institute of International Affairs forum on ministers for foreign affairs, 1961–1972, February 2013.

28 P. Hasluck to Geoffrey Burgoyne, 16 December 1964, Hasluck collection.

29 DEA, 'The future in South-East Asia', *Current Notes on International Affairs*, September 1965, p. 537.

30 DEA, *Current Notes on International Affairs*, June 1964, p. 45.

31 Beaumont, 'Paul Hasluck', in Beaumont, Waters, Lowe & Woodard (eds), *Ministers, Mandarins and Diplomats*, pp. 150–1.

32 The organisers included David Martin, Charmian Clift and George Johnston.

33 Copy enclosed with A. Hasluck to Henrietta Drake-Brockman, 30 May 1966, Henrietta Drake-Brockman papers, NLA, MS 1634.

34 Historians have largely agreed that the Japanese did not intend to invade Australia, but the sense of threat was widespread in 1942.

35 Minister to Plimsoll, 18 July 1966, Plimsoll papers, DFAT, quoted in G. Woodard & J. Beaumont, 'Paul Hasluck and the bureaucracy: the Department of External Affairs', in Stannage, Saunders & Nile (eds), *Paul Hasluck in Australian History*, p. 67.

36 P. Hasluck to A. Hasluck, 'Grand Hotel, Taipeh' [1966], Hasluck collection.

37 M. Sexton, *War for the Asking: Australia's Vietnam secrets*, Penguin, Melbourne, 1981, p. 49.

38 *The Times* (London), 3 November 1964.

39 P. Hasluck to McEwen, NAA: A1838/2, 69/1/3, part 6, quoted in Woodard & Beaumont, 'Paul Hasluck and the bureaucracy', p. 66.

40 P. Hasluck to A. Hasluck, 8 June [1964], Hasluck collection.

41 Ibid.

42 N. Hasluck, Diary, 6 September 1973, Hasluck collection.

43 K. Casey, *The Tigers' Tale: the origins and history of the Claremont Football Club*, Claremont Football Club, Perth, 1995, pp. 104–106.

44 N. Hasluck, Diary, 6 September 1973, Hasluck collection.

45 P. Hasluck to N. Hasluck, 13 October 1964, Hasluck collection.

46 P. Hasluck to N. Hasluck, 24 October 1964, Hasluck collection. The tiger remains an icon in the club room.

47   P. Hasluck to A. Hasluck, 8 June [1964], Hasluck collection.

48   Minister to Prime Minister (telegram 716), 16 June 1964, NAA: A4940, 1; Edwards with Pemberton, *Crises and Commitments*, p. 300.

49   G. Woodard & J. Beaumont, 'Paul Hasluck as Minister for External Affairs: towards a reappraisal', *Australian Journal of International Affairs*, vol. 52, no. 1, 1998, p. 66.

50   Eastman to Shaw, 22 July 1964, NAA: A1838.

51   Porter, *Paul Hasluck*, p. 233, quoting memorandum, Bundy to Michael Forrestal, 6 July 1964, 'Australian Country File', vol. 1, Lyndon Baines Johnson Library.

52   Edwards with Pemberton, *Crises and Commitments*, p. 318.

53   P. Hasluck to N. Hasluck, September 1964, Hasluck collection; Edwards with Pemberton, *Crises and Commitments*, pp. 315–21.

54   *CPD*, H of R, 11 August 1964, vol. 43, p. 21.

55   Ibid., pp. 179, 228.

56   P. Hasluck to N. Hasluck, 16 August 1964, Hasluck collection. He quoted the Labor frontbencher Fred Daly as saying: 'Doc Evatt has gone mad; Arthur Calwell is going mad; and anyone else would be mad already if he took the leadership'.

57   P. Edwards, *A Nation at War: Australian politics, society and diplomacy during the Vietnam War 1965–1975*, Allen & Unwin in association with AWM, Sydney, 1997, p. 25.

58   Personal communication from Jeremy Hearder, who for a time was the officer responsible.

59   H. S. Albinski, 'Vietnam', in Stannage, Saunders & Nile (eds), *Paul Hasluck in Australian History*, p. 176.

60   H. Kissinger, *A World Restored*, Weidenfeld & Nicolson, London, 1957.

61   He expounded these views in a meeting with the Italian Ministry for Foreign Affairs (Alfred Stirling, Diary, 23 October 1964). I owe this reference to Jeremy Hearder.

62   Woodard & Beaumont, 'Paul Hasluck and the bureaucracy', p. 70.

63   Ibid., p. 69, quoting NAA: A1838/2, 69/1/3, part 6.

Chapter 18: The year of living dangerously

1   P. Hasluck to N. Hasluck, 24 October 1964, Hasluck collection.

2   Giuseppe Saragat (1898–1988), founder of the Italian Democratic Socialist Party; Ambassador to Paris 1945–46; President of Constituent Assembly 1946–47; Foreign Minister 1963–64; President of Italy 1964–71.

3   P. Hasluck to N. Hasluck, 24 October 1964, Hasluck collection.

4   Ibid.

5   A. Hasluck to Henrietta Drake-Brockman, 16 November 1964, Henrietta Drake-Brockman papers, NLA, MS 1634.

6   Edwards, 'Notes on a conversation with Sir Paul Hasluck'.

7   Woodard & Beaumont, 'Paul Hasluck and the bureaucracy', p. 71.

8   G. Clark, *In Fear of China*, Lansdowne, Melbourne, 1967; 'Vietnam, China and the foreign affairs debate in Australia; a personal account', in P. King (ed.), *Australia's Vietnam: Australia in the Second Indo-China War*, George Allen & Unwin, Sydney, 1983; 'An alternative view of the hapless Hasluck', *The Australian*, 15 January 1993.

9   P. Hasluck to N. Hasluck, 1 November 1964, Hasluck collection.

10   *The Age*, 3 November 1964, p. 4.

11   [confidential 7580], 7 November 1964, NAA: A1838, 80/1/3/3/17, part 1.

12   Edwards, 'Notes on a conversation with Sir Paul Hasluck'.

13   A. Martin, quoted in Woodard, *Asian Alternatives* (p. 202). Woodard comments: 'Only twice in Australia's history have the two key external security portfolios been held by representatives from a single minor State'. No doubt the clever chaps from Sydney and Melbourne would have handled matters better, but this remark typifies the metropolitan condescension that confirmed Hasluck as a loner relying on his own judgement.

14   Woodard, *Asian Alternatives*, p. 284.

15   S. Ville & P. Simenski, 'A fair and equitable method of recruitment? Conscription by ballot into the Australian Army during the Vietnam War', *Australian Economic History Review*, vol. 51, 2011, pp. 277–96.

16   For this paragraph I rely on Porter, *Paul Hasluck* (pp. 239–40), drawing on the archives of the Lyndon Baines Johnson Library, Australian Country File, vol. 1, nos 126 and 126a. I have not had the opportunity of consulting this source myself. See also Edwards, *A Nation at War*, p. 26.

17   Woodard, *Asian Alternatives*, pp. 195–9; G. Freudenberg, *A Certain Grandeur: Gough Whitlam in politics*, Macmillan, Melbourne, 1977, pp. 44–6.

18   Tange, memorandum, NAA: A1838/379, TS3014/2/1, part 3.

19   Sir Frederick Scherger (1904–84), entered RAAF 1924; Australian Flying Cross 1940 for exceptional service as pilot and instructor; Air Commodore and DSO 1944, serving in South West Pacific; seconded to RAF during Malaysian emergency 1952–55; knighted 1958; chairman of Chiefs of Staff 1961–66; Air Chief Marshal 1965; chairman Australian National Airlines Commission 1966.

20   Woodard, *Asian Alternatives*, p. 206, quoting Tange to Woodard, 26 August 1995.

21   Ibid., p. 210.

22   Ibid., p. 211.

23   P. Hasluck to Waller, 22 January 1965, NAA: A1838/276, TS3014/2, part 4.

24   Ibid.

25   Woodard, *Asian Alternatives*, pp. 228, 240; NAA: A1838/276, TS3014/2/1, part 5.

26   Howson, *The Life of Politics*, p. 146.

27   P. Edwards, *Australia and the Vietnam War*, NewSouth Publishing, Sydney, 2014, pp. 112–14.

28   *CPD*, H of R, 23 March 1965, vol. 45, p. 233. Michael Sexton, in *War for the Asking* (p. 117), saw this comment as an attempt to exert pressure on the United States, but the Marxist scholar Rick Kuhn disagreed ('Laborism and foreign policy: the case of the Vietnam War', in D. Lee & C. Waters (eds), *Evatt to Evans: the Labor tradition in Australian foreign policy*, Allen & Unwin, Sydney, 1997, p. 81).

29   Greenwood & Harper (eds), *Australia in World Affairs 1961–1965*, p. 69.

30   *CPD*, H of R, 18 August 1965, vol. 47, p. 195. Of Calwell, Hasluck wrote: 'As the years went by I ignored what he said in his speeches and valued what he said in conversations' ('Sundry persons', Sir Paul Hasluck papers, NLA, MS 5274, box 39, p. 23).

31   Woodard, *Asian Alternatives*, p. 247, quoting Patrick Shaw, DEA representative on the Defence Committee.

32   Ibid., p. 248, quoting NAA: A4949/1, C4643, part 2.

33   P. Hasluck, *Mucking About*, p. 287.

34   This was a committee of service chiefs and public servants, not to be confused with the six-man committee of cabinet that on 7 April took the decision to send the battalion.

35   D. E. Horner, *Strategic Command: General Sir John Wilton and Australia's Asian wars*, OUP, Melbourne, 2005, p. 236.

36   Edwards, *A Nation at War*, pp. 47–51.

37   Howson, *The Life of Politics*, p. 146; P. Hasluck, *The Chance of Politics*, p. 131.

38   Peter Rupert, Sixth Baron Carrington (1919–), British High Commissioner to Australia 1958–61; cabinet minister 1961–64 and 1970–74; Foreign Minister 1979–82, resigning over the Falklands crisis.

39   A. Hasluck to Henrietta Drake-Brockman, 19 June 1965, Henrietta Drake-Brockman papers, NLA, MS 1634.

40   Edwards, *A Nation at War*, p. 51.

41   Ibid.

42   Denis Healey (1917–), member of the House of Commons 1952–87; Minister for Defence 1964–70; Chancellor of the Exchequer 1974–79; deputy leader of the Labour Party, United Kingdom, 1983–87; member of the House of Lords since 1987.

43   Edwards, *A Nation at War*, p. 65, quoting *The Age,* 30 June 1965.

44   Edwards, *A Nation at War*, p. 65.

45   Ibid.

46   Ibid., pp. 67–71.

47   L. Matheson, *Still Learning*, Macmillan, Melbourne, 1980, p. 65; G. Davison & K. Murphy, *University Unlimited: the Monash story*, Allen & Unwin, Sydney, 2012, p. 129.

48   *Canberra Times,* 30 July 1965.

49   Edwards, 'Notes on a conversation with Sir Paul Hasluck'; author's personal recollections of the debate. Edwards, *A Nation at War* (p. 395) states that Hasluck still recalled the unsettling effect of the heckling many years later.

50   *The Bulletin,* 7 August 1965.

51   *CPD,* H of R, 29–30 September 1965, vol. 40, p. 146.

52   N. Hasluck, 'Introduction', P. Hasluck, *The Chance of Politics,* p. 4.

53   Ibid.; *CPD,* H of R, 29–30 September 1965, 40, p. 146; Porter, *Paul Hasluck,* p 83; author's interview with Gough Whitlam, 31 May 2004.

54   N. Hasluck, 'Introduction', P. Hasluck, *The Chance of Politics,* pp. 4–5.

55   DEA, *Current Notes on International Affairs,* August 1965, p. 461.

56   B. D. Beddie, 'Problems of Australian foreign policy, July–December 1965', *AJPH,* vol. 12, no. 1, p. 3.

57   Edwards, 'Notes on a conversation with Sir Paul Hasluck'.

58   Denis Warner, reporting in *Sydney Morning Herald,* 2 September 1965.

59   *CPD,* H of R, 18 August 1965, vol. 47, p. 186.

60   *CPD,* H of R, 23 November 1965, vol. 49, p. 3040.

61   *CPD,* H of R, 20 October 1965, vol. 48, p. 1914.

62   *CPD,* H of R, 17 November 1965, vol. 49, p. 2852.

63   *CPD,* H of R, 10 March 1966, vol. 50, p. 177.

64   Marr, *Barwick,* p. 203.

65   *The Australian,* 23 December 1965.

66   *Sydney Morning Herald,* 18 January 1966. The comment was made after Hasluck's defeat in the contest for the deputy leadership of the Liberal Party.

67   But not entirely. At the time of Federation, Sir Samuel Griffith used his status as a privy councillor to communicate with the British Government behind the backs of Australian colleagues with whom he disagreed.

68   *The Times* (London), 2 January 1966.

69   A Hasluck to Henrietta Drake-Brockman, 18 January 1966: 'I know nothing but Paul has always been a dark horse' (Henrietta Drake-Brockman papers, NLA, MS 1634).

70   Fenbury to P. Hasluck, 25 January 1966, Hasluck collection.

71   Leslie Bury, interview by Mel Pratt, 10 November 1975, NLA, TRC 121/70.

72   Menzies to P. Hasluck, 21 November 1966, Sir Robert Menzies papers, NLA, MS 4936.

Chapter 19: Elder statesman

1   P. Hasluck, *The Chance of Politics,* pp. 125–54.

2   Alexandra Hasluck described Zara Holt as a 'figure of fun' at a viceregal dinner. 'She was wearing a full-length shift in fine wool, orange in colour, with buttons down the back. She seems to have gotten this awful middle-age fat, in the form of a belly, & while the shift concealed this, it really hinted at worse than if it had been revealed' (A. Hasluck to Henrietta Drake-Brockman, 'Friday' [March 1964], Henrietta Drake-Brockman papers, NLA, MS 1634).

3   P. Hasluck, *The Chance of Politics,* p. 134.

4   Woodard, *Asian Alternatives,* p. 259.

5   J. Hearder, 'Plimsoll, Sir James (1917–1987)', *ADB*, vol. 18, pp. 297–9; E. Hodge, *Radio Wars: Truth, Propaganda and the Struggle for Radio Australia*, CUP, Melbourne, 1995, pp. 80–127.

6   P. Hasluck, *The Chance of Politics*, p. 137.

7   Edwards, 'Notes on a conversation with Sir Paul Hasluck'.

8   D. Healey, *Time of My Life*, Michael Joseph, London, 1989, pp. 291–2; *Sydney Morning Herald*, 3 February 1966; Edwards, *A Nation at War*, pp. 87–9.

9   Edwards, *A Nation at War*, pp. 95–6.

10   *CPD*, H of R, 10 March 1966, vol. 50, pp. 172–82 (quote at p. 175).

11   *CPD*, H of R, 28 April 1966, vol. 51, p. 1293.

12   Memorandum of conversation, *Foreign Relations of the United States 1964–1968*, vol. 27, p. 28, quoted in D. Lee, 'The Liberals and Vietnam', *AJPH*, vol. 51, no. 3, 2005, p. 438.

13   Edwards, *A Nation at War*, pp. 107–12.

14   Ibid.; *The Australian*, 1 July 1966.

15   Edwards, 'Notes on a conversation with Sir Paul Hasluck'.

16   Memorandum, '1966 assessment', Hasluck collection.

17   South East Asia Treaty Organization.

18   Howson, diary entry, 1 July 1966, *The Life of Politics*, p. 228.

19   Edwards, 'Notes on a conversation with Sir Paul Hasluck'.

20   R. Clinton to P. Hasluck, 14 June 1967, Hasluck collection.

21   Howson, *The Life of Politics*, p. 263.

22   A. Hasluck, *Portrait*, pp. 261–2.

23   Howson, diary entry, 16 January 1967, *The Life of Politics*, p. 257.

24   C. Reich, 'Australia and the Middle East crisis of 1967', *Australian Journal of International Affairs*, vol. 52, no. 3, 1998, p. 339.

25   A. Hasluck to N. Hasluck, Hasluck collection.

26   A. Hasluck to Henrietta Drake-Brockman, 22 September 1966, Henrietta Drake-Brockman papers, NLA, MS 1634.

27   Ibid.

28   Economic Commission for Asia and the Far East.

29   A. Hasluck to Jill Hasluck, n.d. [probably March–April 1968], Hasluck papers.

30   After a lunch in 1966, Peter Howson, normally an admirer, wrote: 'I find Paul getting more and more inflexible in his views, which were always far to the right' (diary entry, 17 August 1966, Howson, *The Life of Politics*, p. 236).

31   Howson, diary entry, 6 September 1967, *The Life of Politics*, pp. 325–6.

32   H. C. Coombs, *Trial Balance*, Macmillan, Melbourne, 1981, p. 269; T. Frame, *The Life and Death of Harold Holt*, Allen & Unwin, Sydney, 2005, pp. 214–16.

33   P. Hasluck, *Shades of Darkness*, p. 123.

34   Coombs, *Trial Balance*, p. 214.

35   Ibid., p. 147.

CHAPTER 20: THE ROAD TO YARRALUMLA

1   P. Hasluck, *The Chance of Politics*, p. 148.

2   The only other guests were Bettina Gorton and Plimsoll.

3   Menzies to H. Henderson, 4 January 1968, in Henderson (ed.), *Letters to My Daughter*, p. 174.

4   Griff Richards, quoted in 'Sir Paul Hasluck', *Hindsight*, ABC Radio National, 9 July 2000.

5   Henderson (ed.), *Letters to My Daughter*, p. 175.

6   Bill Snedden (1926–87), a working-class Western Australian by origin, was MP for Bruce 1955–84; Attorney-General 1963–66; Minister for Immigration 1966–71, Treasurer 1971–72: leader of the Opposition 1973–75; and Speaker 1975–83.

7   Johnston to Commonwealth Relations Office, 4 January 1967 [mistake for 1968], FCO 24/177.

8   Sir John McEwen, oral history interview by Ray Aitchison, 20 October 1974, NLA, TRC 311.

9   *The Age*, 9 January 1968.

10   *Sydney Morning Herald*, 3 January 1968; J. Warhurst, 'Hasluck and the politics of the Liberal Party', in Stannage, Saunders & Nile (eds), *Paul Hasluck in Australian History*, p. 204.

11   Howson, diary entry, 3 January 1968, *The Life of Politics*, p. 376. On 6 January (p. 377) he recorded: 'I was surprised how many of [the younger members] would be supporting Paul Hasluck'.

12   Author's interview with Sir Frederick Chaney, 12 October 2001.

13   Edward St John, oral history interview by Vivienne Rae-Ellis, 5–7 July 1983, NLA, TRC 4900/70.

14   S. C. Shann, 'John Gorton's election to the prime ministership: a study of the nature of politicians', Honours thesis, Australian National University, 1969; see also A. Reid, *The Power Struggle, Shakespeare Head Press, Sydney, 1969.*

15   Malcolm Mackay, oral history interview by Bernadette Schedvin, 3 December 1984 – 12 November 1986, NLA, TRC 4900/78.

16   Sir John Gorton, oral history interview by Mel Pratt, 24 March 1976, NLA, TRC 121/78.

17   P. Hasluck, *The Chance of Politics*, p. 158.

18   P. Hasluck to Menzies, 11 January 1968, Hasluck collection.

19   P. Hasluck, *The Change of Politics*, p. 156.

20   P. Hasluck to Waller, 27 February 1968, Sir Keith Waller – papers from Washington, 22 Dec 1964 – 02 Mar 1970, NAA: M4323, 9.

21   Edwards, *A Nation at War*, p. 195; *Sydney Morning Herald* et al., 13 January 1968; CS file, NAA: A4940/1, C4279.

22   Edwards, *A Nation at War*, p. 193.

23   H. Bull, 'Problems in Australian foreign policy January–June 1968', *AJPH*, vol. 14, no. 3, 1968, p. 317.

24 M. Walsh, 'You ain't seen nothing yet', *Quadrant*, vol. 12, no. 6, 1968, p. 19.

25 Howson, diary entries, 2 May 1968 and 14 August 1968, *The Life of Politics*, pp. 420–3, 449.

26 *Financial Review*, 2 and 10 May 1968.

27 Walsh, 'You ain't seen nothing yet', p. 20; Edwards, *A Nation at War*, pp. 197–9. Gorton later said of Hasluck and Fairhall: 'they weren't working against me, but they weren't working for me' (Sir John Gorton, oral history interview by Mel Pratt, 24 March 1976, NLA, TRC 121/78).

28 Tom Critchley (1916–2009) entered the Commonwealth public service 1933; DEA 1946; soon respected as an authority on South-East Asia; successively High Commissioner to Malaysia, Ambassador to Thailand, High Commissioner to Papua New Guinea and Ambassador to Indonesia; retired 1981; AO 1976.

29 J. O. Moreton, memorandum, 13 November 1968, FCO 24/416.

30 *CPD*, H of R, 11 September 1968, vol. 60, pp. 930–1, 936–8; Killen, *Inside Australian Politics*, Methuen Hayes, Sydney, 1985; A. Hasluck to Henrietta Drake-Brockman, 22 September 1966, Henrietta Drake-Brockman papers, NLA, MS 1634.

31 Edward St John, Diary, 21 November 1968, ML, MLMSS 6660/9.

32 Moreton, memorandum, 13 November 1968, FCO 24/416.

33 Howson, diary entry, 14 August 1968, *The Life of Politics*, p. 450.

34 Sir John Hackett (1910–97) entered the British Army 1931, rising to become general commanding the Army of the Rhine 1965–68; principal, King's College, London, 1968–75; knighted 1962; author.

35 P. Hasluck to Menzies, 10 March 1969, Sir Robert Menzies papers, NLA, MS 4936, box 574, folder 24.

36 Menzies to P. Hasluck, 17 February 1969, *Letters to My Daughter*, p. 209; see also Menzies to H. Henderson, 21 February 1969, ibid., pp. 206–207.

37 A. Hasluck, *Portrait*, p. 268.

38 Alan Renouf, oral history interview by Michael Wilson, 23 November 1993, NLA, TRC 2981/6.

39 A. Hasluck, *Portrait*, p. 271.

40 P. Gregson, 'Record of the Minister's visit to the Prime Minister (Harold Wilson) at 6.30 pm on Thursday, 7 November', FCO 24/172.

41 P. Hasluck to Casey, 14 January 1969, Hasluck collection.

42 Ibid.

43 For instance, Alfred Stirling considered it 'a bad precedent. The next Labor government might use it disastrously' (Diary, 11 February 1969, DFAT).

44 Howson, diary entries, 10–12 February 1969 and 7 January 1970, *The Life of Politics*, pp. 486–8, 593.

45 'Happy the man who, like Ulysses, has voyaged well', from the 16th-century poet Joachim du Bellay.

46 William McMahon papers, NLA, MS 3926, box 269. In retirement, when an interviewer asked Hasluck about 'the heavy role that fear of mainland China

occupied in government thinking, he seemed rather to back away from this…He said that the point that he was concerned with was that the future of Asia depended more on what China did, than on any other single factor' (Edwards, 'Notes on a conversation with Sir Paul Hasluck').

47   Rusk to P. Hasluck, 4 February 1969, Hasluck collection.
48   The critics include M. Sexton, *War for the Asking*; G. Pemberton, *All the Way: Australia's Road to Vietnam*, Allen & Unwin, Sydney, 1987; and J. Murphy, *Harvest of Fear: a history of Australia's Vietnam War*, Allen & Unwin, Sydney, 1993.

Chapter 21: Governor-General, 1969–72

1   A. Hasluck, *Portrait*, p. 272.
2   *Daily News* (Perth), 29 April 1969.
3   Sir Murray Tyrrell (1913–89), official secretary 1947–73; knighted 1968; served on Queanbeyan Town Council 1976–80; joint Australian of the Year 1977.
4   Tyrrell to P. Hasluck, 6 August 1969, Hasluck collection.
5   A. Hasluck, *Portrait*, p. 281.
6   Sir Murray Tyrrell, oral history interview by Mel Pratt, 27 May 1974, NLA, TRC 121/54.
7   (Sir) David Smith (1933–), entered Commonwealth public service 1953; secretary to the Executive Council 1971–73; CVO 1977; AO 1986; knighted 1990.
8   Author's interview with Ellestan Dusting, 1 June 2004.
9   Personal communication from Ms Sue Boyd AO, who boarded with Miss Dusting in 1969–70.
10   Author's interview with Margaret Atkin, 8 June 2008.
11   A. Hasluck, *Portrait*, p. 277.
12   Cutting from the *West Australian*, Hasluck collection.
13   Menzies to H. Henderson, 4 June 1969, in Henderson (ed.), *Letters to My Daughter*, p. 219.
14   Alfred Stirling, Diary, 18 March 1972, DFAT.
15   P. Hasluck, *The Government and the People, 1942–1945*, p. x.
16   Ronald Withnall, interviewed by Phyllipa Wyatt, 24 April 1976, NLA, TRC 462.
17   P. Hasluck, *The Government and the People, 1942–1945*, pp. 125 and 125–48 generally.
18   Ibid., p. 306.
19   Ibid., p. 632. The 'Epilogue' is at pp. 623–35.
20   Ibid., p. 627.
21   Ibid., p. 628.
22   D. J. Mulvaney, review of *Black Australians*, *Australian Historical Studies*, vol. 14, no. 56, 1971, pp. 624–6.

23 Cutting from *The Australian*, Hasluck collection.

24 Bennett, 'Poet', p. 33.

25 P. Hasluck, *The Office of Governor-General*, 19th William Queale Memorial Lecture, Adelaide, 24 October 1972, MUP, Melbourne, 1979.

26 Malcolm Mackay, interviewed by Bernadette Schedvin, 3 December 1984 – 12 November 1986, NLA, TRC 4900/78.

27 Hasluck to Gorton, 29 November 1969, Hasluck collection.

28 'Mr Gorton reconstructs his ministry', NAA: M1767, 3.

29 P. Hasluck, 'John Gorton', *The Chance of Politics*, p. 175. This comment was written in June 1970.

30 See Chapter 15.

31 Downs, *The Australian Trusteeship*, pp. 463 and 462–69 generally.

32 Barnes to Fraser, 'Minute by the Defence Committee of a meeting held on Wednesday 15 July 1970', NAA: A7942, P134.

33 P. Hasluck, *The Office of Governor-General*.

34 A. Hasluck to N. Hasluck, 10 March 1971, Hasluck collection.

35 'Additional information', in P. Hasluck, *The Office of Governor-General*.

36 P. Hasluck to McMahon, Hasluck collection.

37 A. Hasluck's *Portrait* (pp. 272–92) is my main source for this paragraph.

38 Personal communication from Sir David Smith.

39 A. Hasluck, *Portrait*, p. 285.

40 Author's interview with Gough Whitlam, 24 May 2004.

41 A. Hasluck, *Portrait*, p. 291.

42 Ibid., p. 297.

43 Ibid., p. 299.

44 P. Hasluck, *The Office of Governor-General*.

45 Ibid.

Chapter 22: Governor-General, 1972–74

1 T. Bramston, 'Epilogue: Whitlam's true believers', in T. Bramston (ed.), *The Whitlam Legacy*, Federation Press, Sydney, 2013, p. 400.

2 P. Hasluck, 'Mr Whitlam's outlook in June 1973', 'Notes 1972–74', Hasluck collection.

3 Author's interview with Sir David Smith, 21 April 2004.

4 P. Hasluck, 'Mr Whitlam's outlook in June 1973', 'Notes 1972–74', Hasluck collection.

5 Ibid.

6 P. Hasluck, 'The Governor of Western Australia', 'Notes 1972–74', Hasluck collection.

7 Ibid.

8 Ibid.

9 P. Hasluck, 'Mr Whitlam's outlook in June 1973', 'Notes 1972–74', Hasluck collection.

10   A. Hasluck to Mollie Lukis, 1 May 1973, Mollie Lukis papers, Battye Library, Acc. 6135A/2–12, SLWA.

11   Same to same, 6 March 1972, Mollie Lukis papers, Battye Library, Acc. 6135A/2–12, SLWA.

12   Author's interview with Sir David Smith, 21 April 2004.

13   A. Hasluck to Maie Casey, 3 July 1973, Lady Maie Casey papers, NLA, MS 1840.

14   P. Hasluck, 'R', *Dark Cottage*, Freshwater Bay Press, Perth, 1984, p. 41.

15   P. Hasluck, 'Mr Whitlam's outlook in June 1973', 'Notes 1972–74', Hasluck collection.

16   P. Hasluck, 'Mr Whitlam's outlook in June 1973' and 'Discussion with Mr Whitlam, November 1973', 'Notes 1972–74', Hasluck collection.

17   A. Hasluck to Maie Casey, 19 December [1973], Lady Maie Casey papers, NLA, MS 1840.

18   A. Hasluck to Mollie Lukis, 11 November 1973, Mollie Lukis papers, Battye Library, Acc. 6135A/2–12, SLWA.

19   Ibid.

20   P. Hasluck, 'Discussions with Mr Whitlam, November 1973', 'Notes 1972–74', Hasluck collection.

21   A. Hasluck to Maie Casey, 21 April 1974, Lady Maie Casey papers, NLA, MS 1840.

22   Ibid. This was not the second Lady Kerr (guest list preserved in the Hasluck collection).

23   Ibid.

24   Vincent Clare Gair (1901–80), MLA for South Brisbane 1932–57; Queensland cabinet minister 1942–52, Premier 1952–57; after the Labor Party split of 1957, led Queensland Labor Party, merged with Democratic Labor Party 1963; senator 1965–74; Ambassador to Ireland and the Holy See 1974–76.

25   P. Hasluck, 'Mr Whitlam looks ahead, March 1974' and 'Proposed referendum, March 1974. The appointment of Senator Gair', 'Notes 1972–74', Hasluck collection.

26   P. Hasluck, 'The crisis of April 1974', 'Notes 1972–74', Hasluck collection.

27   N. Hasluck, memorandum, 12 May 1974, Hasluck collection. At the funeral he met the United States President, Richard Nixon, who looked 'terrible'. 'He has become rather stooped, and, generally, has begun to look rather furtive in all his movements.' Two months later Nixon, buffeted by the Watergate scandals, resigned.

28   P. Hasluck, 'Mr Whitlam looks ahead, March 1974' and 'Proposed referendum, March 1974. The appointment of Senator Gair', 'Notes 1972–74', Hasluck collection.

29   See Chapter 23.

30   The Country Party changed its name to the National Party in 1974.

31   N. Hasluck, memorandum, 7 July 1974, Hasluck collection.

32   Ibid., 9 July 1974.

33   Ibid.

34   *The Age*, 10 July 1974.

35   M. Harris, 'Man for all seasons at the helm of the good ship Australia',
      Weekend Australian, 10 September 1989.

CHAPTER 23: A VIGOROUS RETIREMENT

1   N. Hasluck, memorandum, 12 May 1974, Hasluck collection.

2   Patricia Daw had previously been a valued personal assistant to Alexandra
      Hasluck at Government House (A. Hasluck, *Portrait*, pp. 277–9). She later
      married Justice William Pidgeon of the Supreme Court of Western Australia.

3   Kerr to P. Hasluck, 2 August 1974, Hasluck collection.

4   'Memorandum by Sir Paul Hasluck', 10 August 1977, Hasluck collection.

5   Ibid.

6   Ibid.

7   A. Hasluck (ed.), *Audrey Tennyson's Vice-Regal Days: the Australian letters
      of Audrey, Lady Tennyson to her mother Zacyntha Boyle, 1899–1903*, NLA,
      Canberra, 1978. Hallam, 2nd Lord Tennyson (1852–1928), son of the
      poet, was Governor of South Australia 1898–1902 and Governor-General
      1902–04.

8   P. Hasluck, *A Time for Building*, p. 3.

9   C. D. Rowley, 'Hasluck and Papua New Guinea', *Australian Historical Studies*,
      vol. 18, no. 70, 1978, p. 118.

10   R. Porter, 'Meeting with Sir Paul Hasluck', 7 December 1990.

11   Edwards, 'Notes on a conversation with Sir Paul Hasluck'.

12   W. Sanders, 'Historian, reformer and critic', in Stannage, Saunders & Nile
      (eds), *Paul Hasluck in Australian History*, p. 117.

13   'An Inexact Comparison', in P. Hasluck, *Crude Impieties*, Rainy Creek Press,
      Melbourne, 1991, quoted in Bennett, 'Poet', p. 35.

14   P. Hasluck to Cameron, 16 November 1992, shown to the author by
      Cameron on 12 November 2002.

CHAPTER 24: AN INTELLECTUAL IN POLITICS

1   Luke 17: 8, King James version.

2   P. Hasluck, 'In my garden after reading Traherne', *Dark Cottage*, p. 55.

Bibliography

UNPUBLISHED MANUSCRIPTS

School of Pacific Studies, Australian National University, Canberra
Cleland, R., 'Comments on *A Time for Building*', Cleland papers

J. S. Battye Library, State Library of Western Australia, Perth
Halse, B., 'The Salvation Army in W.A. – its early years: "…Ours is a fast express train"', June 1990

Department of Foreign Affairs and Trade, Canberra
Stirling, Alfred, Diaries, 1947–74

Hasluck collection, Perth
Correspondence, books, photographs and memorabilia of Sir Paul and Dame Alexandra Hasluck preserved in the library, 14 Reserve Street, Claremont WA 6010, under the ownership of Nicholas and Sally Anne Hasluck

1   Family background
2   Boyhood, 1905–17
3   Modern School, 1918–22
4   Journalist, 1923–31
5   Marriage/travel, 1932
6   Private life, 1933–40
7   Journalist/Aboriginal affairs, 1933–40
8   War years/Canberra, 1941–44
9   External Affairs, 1945–47
10   War historian/suburban life, 1948
11   Parliamentarian, 1949–69
12   Minister for Territories, 1952–63
13   Aboriginal affairs, 1952–63
14   Minister for defence/External Affairs, 1964–68
15   Governor-General, 1969–74

16   Historian/writer, 1975–93
17   Retirement, 1975–93
18   Knight of the Garter, 1979–93
19   Aftermath
20   Generally

National Archives of Australia, Canberra
Department of External Affairs files, 1941–47, 1969–74
Department of Territories files, 1951–63

National Library of Australia, Canberra
MS 1009: Sir John Latham papers
MS 1535: Sir William Dunk papers, files 55–73
MS 1634: Henrietta Drake-Brockman papers, series 3, files 9–11
MS 1840: Lady Maie Casey papers
MS 3926: William McMahon papers
MS 4556: Sir Wilfrid Kent Hughes papers, series 3
MS 4936: Sir Robert Menzies papers, boxes 573/14 and 574/24
MS 5243: Finlay Crisp papers, folders 14 and 196
MS 5274: Sir Paul Hasluck papers
MS 5700: William Douglass Forsyth papers
MS 6149: Sir Hubert Opperman papers
MS 6453: Paul McGuire papers, series 4, box 18/2
MS 7886: Professor Oskar Spate papers
MS 8048: Sir James Plimsoll papers, series 1, folders 10–18
MS 8096: Sir Frederick Wheeler papers
MS 8255: George Briggs papers
MS 8328: Nicholas Hasluck papers, series 1 and 9

Northern Territory Archives Service, Darwin
NTRS226/P0001: typed transcripts of oral history interviews
T306: Hugh Barclay
T501: Hilda Tuxworth
T755: Harry Giese

Professor J. D. Legge AO, Melbourne
'Bits of autobiography: 2: My war'

Salvation Army Heritage Centre, Melbourne
Hasluck, E. M., 'Fifty years with the blood and fire in the land of the black swan'
—— 'Mrs Major E. M. Hasluck nee Patience E. Wooler promoted to glory March
    26th 1954'

State Records Office of Western Australia, Perth

SROWA 1184/1–3: transcripts of Paul Hasluck's interviews with pioneers, 1926–32

SROWA 3500A/1: correspondence concerned with whaling records in North America between Sir Paul Hasluck, Dr J. S. Battye and Mr M. M. Armstrong

SROWA 3499A/9/1–11: papers relating to Paul Hasluck's activities in drama, 1936–40

SROWA 4553A/1: Sir Paul Hasluck records, donated 19 January 1988

Fisher Rare Book Library, the University of Sydney, Sydney

Papers of Professor Adolphus Peter Elkin

The University of Western Australia Archives, Perth

File E01/136: 'P. M. C. Hasluck'

Australian War Memorial, Canberra

AWM67: Records of Gavin Long

AWM68: Records of Paul Hasluck

SECONDARY WORKS

Select publications by Sir Paul Hasluck

This is not a complete list of his publications; only those used as source material for this biography are included

Books

Black Australians: a survey of native policy in Western Australia, 1829–1897, Melbourne University Press, Melbourne: 1st edn, 1942; 2nd edn, 1970

Workshop of Security, Cheshire, Melbourne, 1948

The Government and the People, 1939–41, Australian War Memorial, Canberra, 1952

The Government and the People, 1942–45, Australian War Memorial, Canberra, 1970

Collected Verse, Hawthorn Press, Melbourne, 1969

The Poet in Australia: a discursive essay, Hawthorn Press, Melbourne, 1975

A Time for Building: Australian Administration in Papua and New Guinea 1951–1963, Melbourne University Press, Melbourne, 1976

Mucking About: an autobiography, Melbourne University Press, Melbourne, 1977

The Office of Governor-General, 19th William Queale Memorial Lecture, Adelaide, 24 October 1972, Melbourne University Press, Melbourne, 1979

Diplomatic Witness: Australian foreign affairs, 1941–1947, Melbourne University Press, Melbourne, 1980, reprinted 1988

Dark Cottage (poems), Freshwater Bay Press, Perth, 1988

Shades of Darkness: Aboriginal Affairs 1925–1965, Melbourne University Press, Melbourne, 1988

Crude Impieties (poems), Rainy Creek Press, Melbourne, 1991

The Light That Time Has Made, edited by Nicholas Hasluck, National Library of Australia, Canberra, 1995

The Chance of Politics, edited by Nicholas Hasluck, Text Publishing, Melbourne, 1997

Monographs and articles

'The founding of the society: some personal reminiscences', *Early Days: Journal of the Royal Western Australian Historical Society*, vol. 8, no. 1, 1977, pp. 7–22

'Promoting the better use of archives in Australia', Australian Society of Archivists, Canberra, 1981

'"Tangled in the harness": the constitutional debate', *Quadrant*, vol. 27, no. 11, November 1983, pp. 37–41

'Pioneers of post war recovery', published as Sixth Eric Johnston Lecture, NT Library Service Occasional Paper, no. 28, Darwin, 1991

Publications by others

Books

Alexander, F., *Campus at Crawley: a narrative and critical appreciation of the first fifty years of The University of Western Australia*, F. W. Cheshire for University of Western Australia Press, Perth, 1963

Arthur, P. L. & G. Bolton (eds), *Voices from the West End*, Western Australian Museum, Perth, 2012

Austin-Broos, D., *A Different Inequality: the politics of debate about remote Aboriginal Australia*, Allen & Unwin, Sydney, 2011

Baker, R., *Land is Life: from bush to town, the story of the Yanyuwa people*, Allen & Unwin, Sydney, 1999

Beaumont, J., C. Waters, D. Lowe & G. Woodard (eds), *Ministers, Mandarins and Diplomats: Australian foreign policy making, 1941–1969*, Melbourne University Press, Melbourne, 2003

Beazley, K. E., *Father of the House: the memoirs of Kim E. Beazley*, Fremantle Press, Fremantle, 2009

Bolton, G. C., *Dick Boyer: an Australian humanist*, ANU Press, Canberra, 1967

—— & J. Gregory, *Claremont: a history*, University of Western Australia Press, Perth, 1998

Booker, M., *The Last Domino: aspects of Australia's foreign relations*, Collins, Sydney, 1976

Bramston, T. (ed.), *The Whitlam Legacy*, Federation Press, Sydney, 2013

Bunbury, B., *It's Not the Money, it's the Land: Aboriginal stockmen and the equal wages case*, Fremantle Arts Centre Press, Fremantle, 2002

Cain, F. (ed.), *Menzies in War and Peace*, Allen & Unwin in association with the Australian Defence Studies Centre, Australian Defence Force Academy, Sydney, 1997

Casey, K., *The Tigers' Tale: the origins and history of the Claremont Football Club*, Claremont Football Club, Perth, 1995

Clark, G., *In Fear of China*, Lansdowne, Melbourne, 1967

Clark, M., *The Quest for Grace*, Viking, Melbourne, 1990

Coate, Y. & K., *More Lonely Graves of Western Australia*, Hesperian Press, Perth, 2000

Coombs, H. C., *Trial Balance: issues of my working life*, Sun Books, Melbourne, 1983 (first published 1981)

Coote, N. S., *Pioneers of the Collie District 1880–1930*, Literary Mouse Press, Perth, 1991

Cowlishaw, G., *Rednecks, Eggheads and Blackfellas: a study of racial power and intimacy in Australia*, Allen & Unwin, Sydney, 1999

Denoon, D., *A Trial Separation: Australia and the decolonisation of Papua New Guinea*, ANU E Press, Canberra, 2012 (first published 2005)

—— *Public Health in Papua New Guinea: medical possibility and social constraint, 1884–1984*, Cambridge University Press, Cambridge, 1989

Downs, I., *The Australian Trusteeship: Papua New Guinea 1945–75*, Australian Government Publishing Service, Canberra, 1980

Drabble, M. (ed.), *The Oxford Companion to English Literature*, 5th edn, Oxford University Press, Oxford, 1985

Dunk, W. E., *They Also Serve*, W. Dunk, Canberra, 1974

Edwards, P. G., *Arthur Tange: last of the mandarins*, Allen & Unwin, Sydney, 2006

—— *Australia and the Vietnam War*, NewSouth Publishing, Sydney, 2014

—— *A Nation at War: Australian politics, society and diplomacy during the Vietnam War 1965–1975*, Allen & Unwin in association with the Australian War Memorial, Sydney, 1997

—— *Prime Ministers and Diplomats: the making of Australian foreign policy, 1901–1949*, Oxford University Press in association with the Australian Institute of International Affairs, Melbourne, 1983

—— with G. Pemberton, *Crises and Commitments: the politics and diplomacy of Australia's involvement in Southeast Asian Conflicts 1948–1965*, Allen & Unwin in association with the Australian War Memorial, Sydney, 1992

Frame, T., *The Life and Death of Harold Holt*, Allen & Unwin, Sydney, 2005

Fraser, M., *Common Ground: issues that should bind and not divide us*, Viking, Melbourne, 2002

Greenwood, G. & N. Harper (eds), *Australia in World Affairs 1961–1965*, F. W. Cheshire for the Australian Institute of International Affairs, Melbourne, 1968

Griffin, J., H. Nelson, & S. Firth, *Papua New Guinea: a political history*, Heinemann, Richmond, 1979

Haebich, A., *For Their Own Good: Aborigines and government in the South West of*

Western Australia, 1900–1940, University of Western Australia Press, Perth, 1988

—— *Broken Circles: fragmenting Indigenous families*, Fremantle Arts Centre Press, Fremantle, 2000

Hall, R., *The Rhodes Scholar Spy*, Random House, Sydney, 1991

Ham, P., *Vietnam: the Australian war*, HarperCollins, Sydney, 2007

Hammond, J. E., *Winjan's People: the story of the South-West Australian Aborigines*, Imperial Printing Co., Perth, 1933; facsimile edition, Hesperian Press, Perth, 1980

Hancock, I., *John Gorton: he did it his way*, Hodder, Sydney, 2002

Hancock, W. K., *Country and Calling*, Faber, London, 1954

Harper, N. & D. Sissons, *Australia and the United Nations*, Manhattan Publishing, New York, 1959

Harry, R., *The Diplomat Who Laughed*, Hutchinson, Melbourne, 1983

Hasluck, A., *Portrait in a mirror: an autobiography*, Oxford University Press, Melbourne, 1981

Hasluck, N., *The Hasluck Banner*, Freshwater Bay Press, Perth, 2006

Healey, D., *Time of My Life*, Michael Joseph, London, 1989

Heatley, A., *The Government of the Northern Territory*, 4th edn, University of Queensland Press, Brisbane, 2000 (first published 1979)

Henderson, H. (ed.), *Letters to My Daughter: Robert Menzies, letters, 1955–1975*, Murdoch Books, Sydney, 2011

Hodge, E., *Radio Wars: truth, propaganda, and the struggle for Radio Australia*, Cambridge University Press, Melbourne, 1995

Horner, D. E., *Strategic Command: General Sir John Wilton and Australia's Asian wars*, Oxford University Press, Melbourne, 2005

Howson, P., *The Life of Politics: the Howson diaries*, edited by Don Aitkin, Viking, Melbourne, 1994

Kerin, R., *Doctor Do-Good: Charles Duguid and Aboriginal advancement, 1930s–1970s*, Australian Scholarly Publishing, Melbourne, 2011

Killen, J., *Inside Australian Politics*, Methuen Hayes, Sydney, 1985

King, P. (ed.), *Australia's Vietnam: Australia in the second Indo-China war*, George Allen & Unwin, Sydney, 1983

Lee, D. & C. Waters (eds), *Evatt to Evans: the Labor tradition in Australian foreign policy*, Allen & Unwin, Sydney, 1997

Lowe, D. (ed.), *Australia and the End of Empires: the impact of decolonisation in Australia's near north, 1945–65*, Deakin University Press, Geelong, 1996

Lynam, S., *Humanity Dick: a biography of Richard Martin, MP, 1754–1834*, Hamish Hamilton, London, 1975

McGregor, R., *Indifferent Inclusion: Aboriginal people and the Australian nation*, Aboriginal Studies Press, Canberra, 2011

Macintyre, S., *The Poor Relation: a history of social sciences in Australia*, Melbourne University Press, Melbourne, 2010

Marr, D., *Barwick*, George Allen & Unwin, Sydney, 1980

Matheson, L., *Still Learning*, Macmillan, Melbourne, 1980

Murphy, J., *Harvest of Fear: a history of Australia's Vietnam War*, Allen & Unwin, Sydney, 1993

Neill, R., *White Out: how politics is killing Black Australia*, Allen & Unwin, Sydney, 2002

Partington, G., *Hasluck versus Coombs: white politics and Australia's Aborigines*, Quakers Hill Press, Sydney, 1996

Pemberton, G., *All the Way: Australia's Road to Vietnam*, Allen & Unwin, Sydney, 1987

Porter, R., *Paul Hasluck: a political life*, University of Western Australia Press, Perth, 1993

Powell, A., *Far Country: a short history of the Northern Territory*, 4th edn, Melbourne University Press, Melbourne, 2000 (first published 1982)

Prasser, S., J. R. Nethercote & J. Warhurst (eds), *The Menzies Era: a reappraisal of government, politics and policy*, Hale & Iremonger, Sydney, 1995

Rayner, H., *Scherger: a biography of Air Chief Marshal Sir Frederick Scherger*, Australian War Memorial, Canberra, 1984

Reid, A., *The Power Struggle*, Shakespeare Head Press, Sydney, 1969

Renouf, A., *The Frightened Country*, Macmillan, Melbourne, 1979

—— *The Champagne Trail: experiences of a diplomat*, Sun Books, Melbourne, 1980

Reynolds, H., *An Indelible Stain? The question of genocide in Australia's history*, Viking, Melbourne, 2001

Rose, D. B. et al., *Country of the Heart: an Indigenous Australian homeland*, Aboriginal Studies Press, Canberra, 2002

Scott, E., *Official History of Australia in the War of 1914–18*, vol. XI, 'Australia during the war', edited by C. E. W. Bean, A&R, Sydney, 1936

Sexton, M., *War for the Asking: Australia's Vietnam secrets*, Penguin, Melbourne, 1981

Sphinx Foundation, *Perth Modern School: the history and the heritage*, B+G Resource Enterprises, Perth, 2005

Stannage, T., K. Saunders & R. Nile (eds), *Paul Hasluck in Australian Hist civic personality and public life*, University of Queensland Press, Brisbane, 98

Tennant, K., *Evatt: politics and justice*, Angus & Robertson, Sydney, 197(

Throssell, R., *My Father's Son*, William Heinemann, Melbourne, 198'

de Tocqueville, A., *Journeys to England and Ireland*, translated by Geo Lawrence & K. P. Mayer, edited by J. P. Mayer, Yale University Press, Haven, Connecticut, 1958

Trigg, S., *Shame and Honour: a vulgar history of the Order of the G* University of Pennsylvania Press, Philadelphia, 2012

Watt, A., *Australian Diplomat: memoirs of Sir Alan Watt*, Angus obertson in association with the Australian Institute of Internatio airs, Sydney, 1972

—— *The Evolution of Australian Foreign Policy, 1938–1965* ridge University Press, Cambridge, 1967

Whittington, V., *Sister Kate: a life dedicated to children in need of care*, University of Western Australia Press, Perth, 1999

Wilkes, J. (ed.), *New Guinea and Australia*, Angus & Robertson for the Australian Institute of Political Science, Sydney, 1958

—— *Australia's Defence and Foreign Policy*, Angus & Robertson for the Australian Institute of Political Science, Sydney, 1964

Wise, T., *The Self-Made Anthropologist: a life of A. P. Elkin*, George Allen & Unwin, Sydney, 1985

Woodard, G., *Asian Alternatives: Australia's Vietnam decision and lessons on going to war*, Melbourne University Press, Melbourne, 2004

Articles in journals

Beddie, B. D., 'Problems of Australian foreign policy, July–December 1965', *Australian Journal of Politics and History*, vol. 12, no. 1, 1966, pp. 1–11

Bell, K., 'The Midland Railway workshops 1920–1939', *Studies in Western Australian History*, vol. 11, 1990, pp. 29–42

Bull, H, 'Problems in Australian foreign policy, January–June 1968', *Australian Journal of Politics and History*, vol. 14, no 3, 1968, p. 317

Craig, T., 'Radical and conservative theatre in Perth in the 1930s', *Studies in Western Australian History*, vol. 11, 1990, pp. 106–18

Dargavel, J., 'Persistence and transition on the Wangites-Wagait reserves, 1892–1976', *Journal of Northern Territory History*, vol. 15, 2004, pp. 5–19

Edwards, P., 'Countdown to commitment: Australia's decision to enter the Vietnam War in April 1965', *Journal of the Australian War Memorial*, vol. 21, 1992, pp. 4–10

Gregory, J., 'Western Australia between the wars: the consensus myth', *Studies in Western Australian History*, vol. 11, 1990, pp. 1–16

—— 'Education and upward mobility in interwar Western Australia: the case of Perth Modern School', *Studies in Western Australian History*, vol. 11, 1990, pp. 83–95

Hasluck, E. M., 'Thirty-four years of full salvation', *War Cry*, 22 June 1929

Hasluck, N. 'The garter box goes back to England', *Quadrant*, vol. 38, no. 9, September 1994, pp. 39–43.

—— & F. wicky, 'Poetry', in B. Bennett (ed.), *The Literature of Western Australia*, University of Western Australia Press for the Education Committee of the 150th Anniversary Celebrations, Perth, 1979

Haynes, C. 'Land, trees and man (Gunret, Gundulk, Dja Bining), *Commonwealth Forestry Review*, vol. 57, no. 2, 1978, pp. 99–106

Hudson, W. J. 'Problems in Australian foreign policy, July–December 1966', *Journal of Politics and History*, vol. 13, no. 1, 1967, pp. 1–7

Hunt, S.-J. & G. Bolton, 'Cleansing the dunghill: water supply and sanitation in Perth 1878–1912', *Studies in Western Australian History*, vol. 2, 1978, pp. 1–17

Lee, D., 'The Liberals and Vietnam', *Australian Journal of Politics and History*, vol. 51, no. 3, 2005, pp. 429–39

McGregor, R., '"Breed out the colour", or the importance of being white', *Australian Historical Studies*, vol. 33, no. 120, 2002, pp. 286–302

Megarrity, L., 'Indigenous education in colonial Papua New Guinea: Australian government policy (1945–1975)', *History of Education Review*, vol. 34, no. 2, 2005, pp. 41–58

Murray, J. K., 'In retrospect – Papua-New Guinea 1945–1949 and the Territory of Papua and New Guinea 1949–1952', *Australian Journal of Politics and History*, vol. 14, no. 3, 1968, pp. 320–41

Reich, C., 'Australia and the Middle East crisis of 1967', *Australian Journal of International Affairs*, vol. 52, no. 3, 1998, pp. 329–40

Rowley, C. D., 'Hasluck and Papua New Guinea', *Historical Studies*, vol. 18, no. 70, 1978, pp. 118–26

Tarling, N., '"Cold storage": British policy and the beginnings of the Irian Barat/ West New Guinea dispute', *AJPH*, vol. 46, no. 2, 2000, pp. 175–93

Ville, S. & P. Siminski, 'A fair and equitable method of recruitment? Conscription by ballot into the Australian Army during the Vietnam War', *Australian Economic History Review*, vol. 51, no. 3, 2011, pp. 277–96

Walsh, M,. 'You ain't seen nothing yet', *Quadrant*, vol. 12, no. 6, 1968, pp. 16–23

Willis, I., 'P. M. C. Hasluck, *A Time for Building: Australian administration in Papua and New Guinea, 1951–1963*', *Labour History*, no. 32, May 1977, pp. 100–102

Woodard, G. & J. Beaumont, 'Paul Hasluck as Minister for External Affairs: towards a reappraisal', *Australian Journal of International Affairs*, vol. 52, no. 1, 1998, pp. 63–75

Wright, P., 'A liberal "respect for small property": Paul Hasluck and the "landless proletariat" in the Territory of Papua and New Guinea, 1951–63', *Australian Historical Studies*, vol. 33, no. 119, 2002, pp. 55–72

INTERVIEWS AND SOUND RECORDINGS

Conversations recorded in the author's diary

12 October 2001: Sir Frederick Chaney
15 May 2002: Reginald Marsh
10 June 2002: Sir Walter Crocker
12 November 2002: Clyde Cameron
20 April 2004: Peter Edgar
21 April 2004: Sir David Smith
5 May 2004: Jeremy Hearder
19 May 2004: Alan McKenzie
24 May 2004: Michael Berger
24 and 31 May 2004: Gough Whitlam
26 May 2004: Bob Swift

26 May 2004: John Burton

1 June 2004: Hugh Payne

1 June 2004: Ellestan Dusting

1 June 2004: Alfred Parsons

3 June 2004: Ian Grigg

4 June 2004: Don Kingsmill

11 August 2004: Sir Charles Court

19 October 2004: Sir James Killen

20 October 2004: Manfred Cross

1 February 2005: Lord Carrington

16 May 2005: Bill Hayden

9 July 2005: Nan Giese

12 July 2005: Ted Egan

14 November 2007: Sir Victor Garland

8 June 2008: Margaret Atkin

21 July 2008: Jill Munro

26 November 2009: Rosemary Carrodus

Oral histories, National Library of Australia

TRC 121/54: Sir Murray Tyrrell, interviewed by Mel Pratt, 27 May 1974

TRC 121/70: Leslie Bury, interviewed by Mel Pratt, 10 November 1975

TRC 121/78: Sir John Gorton, interviewed by Mel Pratt, 24 March 1976

TRC 243: Sir Keith Murray, interviewed by Suzanne Lunney, 14–18 January 1974

TRC 311/1–2: Sir John McEwen, interviewed by Ray Aitchison, 20 October 1974

TRC 462: Ronald Withnall, interviewed by Phyllipa Wyatt, 24 August 1976

TRC 477: Frederick Alexander, interviewed by Bruce Miller, 24 October 1976

TRC 541: Albert Kornweibel, interviewed by Joan Ambrose, 31 May 1977

TRC 1966: Reminiscential conversations between the Rt Hon. Sir Paul Hasluck
    and the Hon. Clyde Cameron, 15 April 1985 – 17 July 1986

TRC 2047/12: David Nickels, interviewed by Jan Adams, 18 July 1986

TRC 2194: Ric Throssell, interviewed by Don Baker, 30 January – 3 March 1992

TRC 2981/6: Alan Renouf, interviewed by Michael Wilson, 23 November 1993

TRC 4631: Peter Ryan, interviewed by John Farquharson, 10–11 October 2000

TRC 4900/55: H. B. Gullett, interviewed by Clarrie Hermes and Pat Shaw,
    5 March 1984 – 13 December 1988

TRC 4900/70: Edward St John, interviewed by Vivienne Rae-Ellis, 5–7 July
    1983

TRC 4900/78: Malcolm Mackay, interviewed by Bernadette Schedvin,
    3 December 1984 – 12 November 1986

Oral histories, J. S. Battye Library, State Library of Western Australia

OHA 402: Leslie Rees, 28 October 1980

OHA 494: Francis Joseph Scott Wise, 1978

OHA 2226: Kim Edward Beazley, 1983–85

Interviews by other historians

Peter Edwards, 'Notes on a conversation with Sir Paul Hasluck in his office, in Perth, Tuesday 7 August 1984'

Robert Porter, 'Meeting with Sir Paul Hasluck', 7 December 1990.

Radio broadcasts

'Sir Paul Hasluck', edited by Bill Bunbury, Hindsight, ABC Radio National, 9 July 2000

POSTGRADUATE THESES

Castleman, B. D., 'Changes in the Australian departmental machinery of government, 1928–82', PhD thesis, Deakin University, 1992

Ling, E. J., 'Blame and martyrs: the Commonwealth Government's administration of the Northern Territory pastoral industry, 1911–1978, PhD thesis, Charles Darwin University, 2010

Plant, J. D. E., 'The origins and development of Australia's policy and posture at the United Nations Conference on International Organization, San Francisco, 1945', PhD thesis, Australian National University, 1967

Shann, S. C., 'John Gorton's election to the prime ministership: a study of the nature of politicians', Honours thesis, Australian National University, 1969

Tatz, C. M., 'Aboriginal administration of the Northern Territory of Australia', PhD thesis, Australian National University, 1964

Acknowledgements

First and foremost, I thank Nicholas and Sally Anne Hasluck for their great generosity and patience. They have given me unrestricted access to the papers and books of Sir Paul and Lady Hasluck, and have been consistently helpful in finding and identifying useful source material in that extensive collection. They have not sought in any way to influence my interpretation of Sir Paul Hasluck's biography or my choice of material. They have borne with an elderly writer's tardiness when the completion of the project has taken more than twice as long as my original estimate. I acknowledge and value their support.

This biography has also enjoyed strong institutional support. Murdoch University has provided me with a place to work and all the necessary facilities, as well as the support of a collegiate environment. Research in Canberra was materially assisted by the grant of a Frederick Watson Fellowship at the National Archives of Australia. Their staff were all that a researcher could wish. I have also appreciated the support of a grant from the Australian Research Council. Sources consulted include the National Library of Australia, the J. S. Battye Library at the State Library of Western Australia, the State Records Office of Western Australia, the Australian War Memorial, the Mitchell Library at the State Library of New South Wales, and the Fisher

Library at the University of Sydney. In all these places I found a high level of support and service. A little anxiously, I hope that these institutions will continue to receive the level of public funding that enables them to meet the highest international standards in providing support for scholarship.

No historian works in isolation, and I have been particularly fortunate in the friends and colleagues who have helped me with comment and information about Paul Hasluck's career, as well as reading the manuscript in draft in part or in whole. John Nethercote has been a wise and knowledgeable guide to Canberra's political processes, and Jeremy Hearder has been a valuable source about Australian diplomatic history. Geraldine Byrne, Peter Edwards, Mike Fogarty, Jessica Hodder, Stuart Macintyre, Heather Radi and Tim Rowse have all helped me avoid errors and strengthen my interpretations. I have also gained from conversations and interviews with many of those who knew Sir Paul, and in the process have met some remarkably interesting Australians. They are listed in the Bibliography, but it is right that I should acknowledge them here.

In the production process I have appreciated the professionalism of Terri-ann White and her staff at University of Western Australia Publishing and Nicola Young as copy editor. Not for the first time, Andy Morant has been a loyal and reliable research assistant. I am grateful to the Hasluck family and the National Archives of Australia for permission to use the illustrations in this book, and to Brian Richards for his skill in preparing them for publication.

In conclusion, I thank my wife Carol for her consistent love and support. Amid the claims of her own professional life she finds time to read my drafts and cast an expert eye on my prose style. I think I can promise her that this is the last time she will have to live with a research project of this scale.

Geoffrey Bolton
30 June 2014

Index

574

This biography documents that as a journalist, historian, and politician, Paul Hasluck was early to the idea of the Aboriginal as an equal citizen. In the context of his times, Hasluck was outstanding in his early recognition of the full and equal humanity of Aboriginal Australians. This book is an overdue reminder that Hasluck was a leading agent of change in Aboriginal Affairs.

—Fred Chaney AO, Reconciliation advocate

Over Hasluck's long public life, from civil servant to member of Parliament to minister of state to governor-general, it was rare to hear him criticised for want of either energy or ability. He was, however, always under fire for 'remoteness', for being out of touch, and a 'martinet' for the rigid enforcement of petty procedures. Geoffrey Bolton most helpfully examines the measure of truth that this view might contain, and restores Hasluck to a figure far from dour and humourless, but a creative and, indeed, mischievous personality.

—Peter Ryan, former publisher Melbourne University Press

B QW K